Junkyard Kid

Junkyard Kid

Born in a Warehouse
Traveled the World

The Lucky Life Story of
Danny Langdon

Printed in the United States of America

ISBN Paperback: 979-8-9910020-0-4
ISBN eBook: 979-8-9910020-1-1

Cover and Interior Design: Creative Publishing Book Design

Contents

Acknowledgments

I could never fully thank all the people who have so influenced my life. Only a few are, out of necessity, credited in this book. Of course, the first is my family of origin, especially my dear mother and all my brothers and sisters, as is my wife, Kathleen, my children, and her children.

I thank all my high school classmates that made my early days so wonderful: especially Mac Soden, Venita Turner Philbrick, and Warren Wubker, who helped me recall the details of our days together. Special among my classmates is an old friend, Bobby Showalter, who initiated one of the early seminal moments leading to the person I became.

A special thanks to my surviving sister Lorraine, my nieces Jenny Peterson Banta, Michelle Hiskey, Kristen McKenna, and my nephew Mitch Townley for dusting off the webs of family memories. Mitch's binder, "Remembering Mother," was particularly useful in garnering quotes and recollections of people and events. Michelle's audio recording of her grandmother, as well as my own with mother, provided useful details and the opportunity to hear her voice again. Thanks to Scott and Jean Seaton for listening on a distant island to a very rough draft that was only then some preliminary feelings. Thanks to our good friends Kathleen Dowdey and Brenda Sample, who generously read the real first draft and made me rethink what I was trying to say. Thanks to Mac and Venita for the second reading.

Special loving thanks to my partner in life and business, Kathleen (aka Lee) Langdon, for her editing and patience in the countless hours I was writing at the dining room table or on vacation on our favorite island.

A special thanks to Bonnie Gregory for her excellent copy editing that turned my form of English into one that others more fully understand and use daily. Thanks to Larry Brown and Monica Hoene-Langdon for proofing in search of those errors that somehow are not always found through repeated readings. And a special thanks to my daughter Kim for accompanying me as we visited Twin Falls one last time to reorient me to my boyhood recollections. We had a great time roaming the surrounding area and the downtown where I so loved growing up. The opportunity to share with her my memories of that bygone time was very special for me.

Finally, many thanks to all the strangers I've ever met throughout the four corners of the world in my extensive travel. I've been blessed to experience and learned from each of you.

Danny, 2024

Life's Seminal Moments

The *Cambridge Dictionary* defines seminal as:
"containing important new ideas" that
"influence later developments"

Example:

Seminal moments are analogous to when one turns on a light bulb on a dark stairway, and it suddenly clearly lights the path before you. For example, when I made the decision to go into the Peace Corps that was a seminal moment. It provided an opportunity to safely transition from a young man graduating from college to a more mature adult who learned he could succeed in life in general, have a fulfilling professional career, extensively explore the world, educate others, and demonstrate compassion through actions that help the less fortunate or those in need of some assistance.

Throughout this autobiography I will identify certain events that significantly set the stage for what occurred thereafter. Some things just happened, as in the unselfish decision of my classmate Bobby Showalter to nominate me Sophomore Boys Club President, while other choices were well thought out, like my decision to join the Peace Corps.

The cumulative influence of seminal moments is what leads, in major ways, to a fulfilling life. In my autobiography I hope to demonstratively provide insights for others to find or create their own seminal moments.

Danny Langdon

CHAPTER 1

Danny in His Setting

It's true that I was born in an actual, functioning warehouse in Twin Falls, Idaho. Prior to my birth in 1938, my parents' business was without a set physical location brokering in the purchase and shipment of various kinds of hides, wool, furs, and pelts. These commodities were to be processed in those days for making such items as shoes, belts, coats, various leather goods, and other such items. This was prior to the innovation of synthetic materials that are now the mainstay for clothing and such. *L.L. Langdon* was the name of the business and its founding motto was, "Wool, Furs, Hides, and Pelts;" in later years to include other items in need of recycling.

In 1933 the business transitioned from our father driving to the physical location of farmers and ranchers to pick up hides to a rented warehouse where these items could be dropped off for processing and shipment. The business was gradually expanding and needed a permanent location. Having a physical location meant they could accept a "carload," as our parents referred to it—a quantity of hides from the local meat processing plant, as opposed to a single hide at a time. However in 1935 the rental of the warehouse they were using was taken out from underneath them by the owner, Mr. George Carrico. He had the opportunity to rent the lot on which the warehouse sat on a long-term lease to Sinclair Oil for use as a gas station. As fortune would have it, Mr. Carrico liked the Langdons and offered them the opportunity to buy the building

1

outright. He was also willing to relocate it a couple of blocks away onto a vacant double lot. Mr. Carrico would pay for the move since he would otherwise have had to tear down the warehouse for the new gas station. So all worked out for both parties, and my father and mother purchased the land and the relocated warehouse for $38.70 a month. It took several years to pay their loan off as the economy was still recovering from the Great Depression. Also, with a family of seven at that point in time (before my arrival), the times were hard, and living was often more about survival than convenience. The warehouse would remain at its location for four decades until the business was closed in the mid-1980s.

As a result of the establishment of The Warehouse (as we came to commonly refer to it, or also The Place or The Yard), the inventory of items to be purchased was expanded beyond wool, hides, furs, and pelts to include

Our Dad standing with his car in front of the Warehouse (circa 1937)

different kinds of scrap metal. Metals of various kinds like iron, copper, aluminum, brass, and lead, were needed for the technological advances of a growing nation and for impending World War II needs. The establishment of the warehouse would also cement the location where a permanent family house could be found nearby. Up to this point in time the Langdons and their brood had only rented various kinds of housing in town combined with camping out for the entire summer between rentals. The desire to ultimately have a close proximity of both business and permanent, fixed living quarters was very much valued and sought after by our parents. This resulted in a rather unusual combination of living arrangements for our family that will be detailed.

Obviously, packed in the company motto (as it appeared on the face of The Warehouse, calendars, trucks, and various venues) is a different kind of business and life for the family that depended upon it. Although it might appear at first glance to be an odd, even an unsanitary existence, for this new kid about to come into the world it would be filled with constant adventure that would lead to meaningful, healthy character development and pure joy.

Our Parents

I didn't know my father for long since he passed away when I was 7, but I hear from my mother and older siblings that he was a pretty good guy. He loved fishing, smoking cigars, playing pool, interacting with his customers, and, of course, my mother. He was 29 years older than she, and while that is a bit of an unconventional age difference for a couple, it was that way for a very logical set of reasons and reflective of the time. The Great Depression was an era in which the practicality of mere survival sometimes weighed more than love when it came to being married. I'll detail their relationship later.

Father, Lambert (Bert) Lucius Langdon, born September 2, 1882, was certainly industrious, although in his early manhood he was described by a cousin as, "a rambler, a gambler, and had a way with the women." Apparently, those were the seeds of youth in his early twenties as he

3

moved from Oregon, where his father had homesteaded, to Idaho and established himself as a "hide broker." Today that profession doesn't have much meaning since clothing items are generally constructed of synthetics. But in his day certain clothing—shoes, belts, hats— were made from animal hides, furs, or pelts, such as cows and sheep, as well as other various furry animals. As a hide broker my father arranged with farmers, ranchers, and butchers, to buy their animal hides that he would then sell and forward in bulk to a tanning operation in Oregon. There they would be processed to make clothing and other items.

Our father was married twice. He and his first wife, Myrtle Munn (born January 1893), had four children (Louise, Lynn, Archie, and

Our father Bert as a young man
with nephew Langdon Claypool

4

Dorothy), who would later, when I was born, be my half-brothers and sisters. When Myrtle died of cancer in 1928, Bert married my mother, Marian Orena Smith. He was 46 and she was 17. They had five children: Lucille, Bertine, Buzz, Lorraine, and the youngest, me. My life came to be three years after they established, in the way of a warehouse, a permanent location for their business in 1935. It was the place in which I was born and initially lived. It was the environment—the hub, if you will—as a kid I centered my life and explored from there to all over town, and eventually around the world.

As I already noted, our father ran his business initially by wandering the nearby counties seeking out farmers and ranchers primarily to buy mostly cow hides on consignment. By measure of his success he was judged trustworthy in the deals he made and as such established and nurtured many a close friend/customer. Our mother was actively involved in the business, going with dad to engage in the buying arrangements, maintaining the books, and in general, learning the trade. This would be critical, as it turned out, because he died in 1946. She took over the business as a widowed mother with six children still in her care and ran it for the next 40 years. How the timing of my father's death shaped me, along with the unusual environment I grew up in, is the foundation of my story to be told. I begin, therefore, with the place I was born—The Warehouse.

The Warehouse, aka The Place or The Yard

The Warehouse, a two-story wooden structure, sat on two large lots that combined, were approximately two hundred by one hundred twenty feet on the corner of Truck Lane and 2nd Street West in Twin Falls, Idaho. On the face of the two-story wooden structure, high on its front wall above the entry door, was emblazoned the name of the business in large black letters:

L.L. Langdon

Wool Fur Hides Pelts

Scrap Iron & Metals – New & Used Blacksmith Iron

It was obvious from the signage that this was a business of unique offerings. It explicitly was buying what were considered the leftovers of animals, as well as used metals of various kinds. It could all be recycled! That was the essence of my parent's business and where, in large measure, I played and grew up. It's not the only place I played and learned, but it was the hub of much of my early childhood development. It was where I was born, and the family lived in different configurations over the course of 10 years. I'd like to tell you what that was like as it was quite an unusual living environment by any "normal" living standards.

The Warehouse—a 1500-square-foot wooden structure—bordered an alley. Across the street was a milk-processing plant, Young's Dairy. Cattycorner there was a row of small, single-story businesses. Across 2nd Street West was a tire dealership named Stu Morris, and across the alley behind it was the International Harvester dealership. I liked to frequent the International Harvester because they had a machine for testing vacuum tubes for radios, and later for TVs. My mother's Aunt Bessie (her father's sister), then retired, lived in our community with her husband, Tim. They lived at the edge of town on a small farm, and Aunt Bessie appreciated my fixing her TV when it had a problem, for which I was paid in ice cream or her favorite baked pastries.

A couple of doors down from The Warehouse was my other very favorite establishment, a smithy. The blacksmith had a great laugh and a willing personality. As a kid, I thought he could make anything.

Thus, most of our neighborhood, a sprinkling of one-story prewar housing, was composed of small businesses struggling to survive in the years between the depression and the start of World War II. Such economic and geopolitical times would play prominent roles in expanding my parents' business which gradually evolved from hides and such to buying and processing for resale scrap metal for the war effort.

Over its fifty years of operation, The Warehouse served as a combination residence and business: a multi-use structure in which my parents made a comfortable, but physically demanding living. At the front of The Warehouse facing Truck Lane, there was an office area approximately

Warehouse circa 1940

25 feet x 12 feet. To the left as one walked in, there was a counter with a cash register on top and underneath the books to record buying and selling. The office area had a couple of glass display cases where my dad showed his modest collection of stamps, coins, and bullet casings. On the large wall at the back of the office was a magnificent collection—60 to 70 in number—of antique guns and rifles that Father had amassed. There were flint, wheel, and fuse-lock rifles and pistols, some dating back to the Colonial War. There were three blunderbusses often deployed on stagecoaches for security. For bad guys along a stagecoach route, these ominous firearms could be loaded with nails, rocks, salt, or anything imagined. The wide-mouthed blunderbuss would scatter a frightful pattern of destruction when triggered. There were other types of long and short rifles, some from World War I. At one point, my dad bought a whole crate of 9mm rifles from that war period and gave one each to a select few friends and clients. I inherited—that's me holding it on the book cover—one myself and even hunted with that long rifle that could, but never did, accommodate a bayonet. There was a strapping pair of .45 caliber Colts with their leather bandolier of bullets right out of some Roy Rogers or Buck Jones movie. In later years someone stole that pair

right off the wall—the only guns ever taken. There were other handguns of all persuasion, including one that had a small flip-up bayonet. There was a petite derringer and an old flint-lock pistol. One handgun was an American version of a German Luger that would one day play into my own history. There were even some swords, one of which was from World War I, and others much older, with handguards for protection when used by the pirates in my imagination. There was one very ornate sword intricately carved along its silvery blade with a handguard and scabbard in a shiny metal sheath. It was part of the dress code for Prussian soldiers in the 1800s. There was an array of other things I won't detail. As a boy, my friends and I would play with certain of these items (always

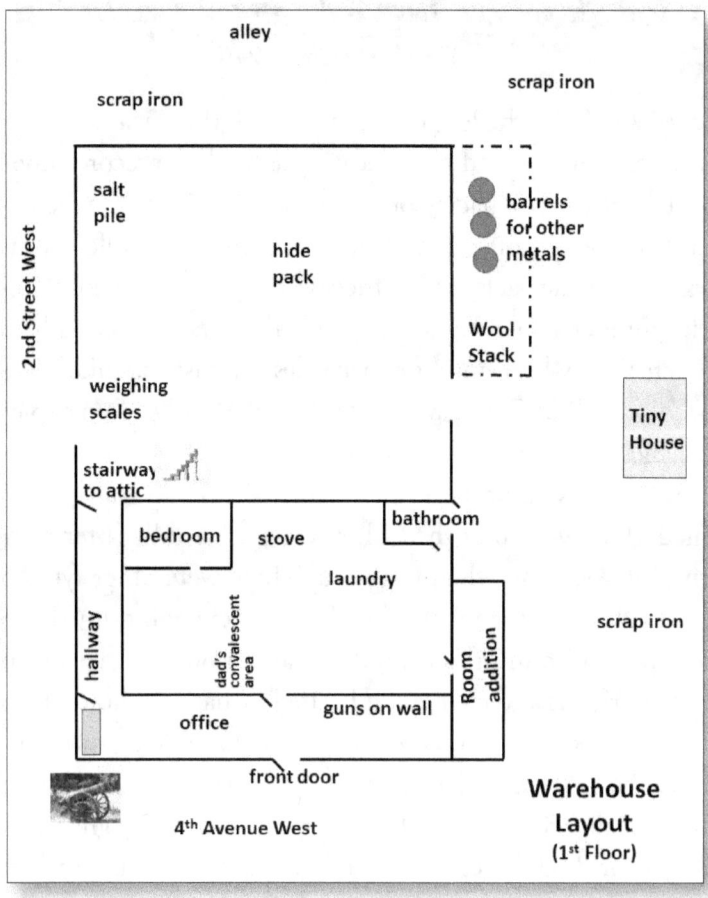

confined to the office area), knowing that all had been cleansed of harm they might cause. I was not so sure this was true of swords, but no harm came to any of us in our play as pirates and cowboys.

On the wall paralleling 2nd Street West, next to and behind the counter, the business displayed 9" x 17" cardboard and paper calendars for customers to choose from as they desired. I would drive nails in a row on the wall and hang 10 or so calendars at eye level. It was an activity I looked forward to every year in my youth. These changed every year and were generally western scenes typical of the Old West including cattle drives, wranglers roping a steer, anglers fishing in a stream, and wildlife of all kinds. Later my mother added calendars depicting kids playing baseball and other Americana scenes. My job was to organize this display and make sure it was well stocked. If not found there, a customer would ask if his favorite calendar was still available, and I would go in search of it in the storage area. For the really special customer, there were larger 2' x 4' calendars that came rolled in their own green tubes and my mother would designate who would get these. For the really, really special friends and customers, there was a mirror calendar, 11" x 16", with a wildlife scene etched on the mirror face, and a small paper calendar attached to the bottom. It also had a thermometer that told you the room temperature. Today I have a couple of those myself as well as both small and larger calendars samples in my own home. One of the largest is in my garage and so I am often reminded of those days when I park my car.

The front office area also had a potbellied wood-burning stove with comfortable leather chairs. There you could find my father and his customer/friends chatting over stories of their lives, tall fishing stories, business transactions, and other goings on. The office was, in some sense, a center for the exchange of information during an era when personal contact was how you learned what was really going on. Reminds me to this day of a gas station in Ethiopia when I was a Peace Corps volunteer. Everyone, it seems, stopped there and that was how communication happened on a personal level, without the internet or, indeed, without the simple convenience of a telephone in a Third World nation.

As you entered through a door below the guns on the wall, you came into a large room divided only by their assigned function into four parts. The largest section was dominated by a cast-iron stove with four lid-lifted holes to stoke the fire. A black stovepipe rose to and through the ceiling. During the few short years our family lived in The Warehouse the stove was used for cooking, but most years it served a secondary purpose, during years we kids were in our youth, teens, and college. It was the clothes-washing room. The coal-burning stove served the purpose of heating water in two large copper tubs. This would be used in washing the family clothes, sheets, towels, and such. A washing machine with a mechanical wringer sat in the room about six feet away from the stove. Mother would load the washing machine with whatever needed doing, move ladles of hot water from the copper tubs on the stovetop, add soap and cold water as required, and do load after load in this manner. Then she would manually wring out the clothes through the wringer on top of the washer and spread the wet clothing on wooden scissor-racks inside during the winter or outside on clotheslines when the weather was warm enough. For larger items like sheets, there were cords that had been laced back and forth across the room or typical clotheslines out in an open area of the warehouse. Washing was nearly a daily routine for a large family and one which I observed Mother doing on many occasions late into the evening. In the winter, the room was like a steam bath, with clothes hanging everywhere. Even when we moved to a more permanent residence, washing continued to be done in The Warehouse, mostly because it had the space the residence didn't. Washing clothes was a necessity of life that Mother did not outwardly seem to resent, but rather found a kind of relief from the other things she had to do, of which there were very many when she became a single mother by the time I was seven.

During these early times, my mother was a lover of flour sacks. During and before the war, flour was packed in white linen sacks. These were perfect and cheap material for dish towels, but also especially for use as diapers. I am sure all of us children donned those flour sacks in our infant years, and decades later she sent me a stack of sack diapers for my own kids. We used them as well as the disposable ones, but for a while we helped save the environment by using these flour sack diapers. I know for a fact that hundreds of these flour sacks found their way into her washing machine there in The Warehouse.

In the same back room close to the entry door, there was a smaller room, probably 8' x 10', with no door. It was here in his final year of life that my father spent his days confined to a hospital bed, as it could be adjusted for his aches and pains. At age 65 he was old for his time, and he had, as they used to say, a bad heart. I remember one of my sisters coming to fetch me from the local elementary school to say that he had passed. The last time I saw him he was lying in that very hospital bed in the back room.

There was a single toilet in a small room just at the back of the larger room where the laundry was done. It was accessible as well from the outside by a door that led to an area where scrap metal was piled. Outside and to the right of that door, sat an old antique ice chest, but I don't think we ever used it. Probably one of the many items our mother saved from the general scrap business and became part of her vast antique collection.

Finally, through a door near to where the stove sat, there was a single, and only, real bedroom. It was approximately 10' x 10' and other than actually being the bedroom for our parents for a short period of time, it mostly served as a storage room for family needs once we moved from The Warehouse to what would be our permanent residence. In this room I distinctly remember, in my later youth, finding and going through boxes of Hollywood magazines there above the only closet. They were most likely there from my sisters' education about a place that lay out in the outside world known as Hollywood. As a kid I'd pour through them myself to get some idea of what fame and fortune perhaps looked like. Given my environment those Hollywood scenes and people featured in the glossy vanity magazines looked very foreign, if not fake and unreal. I think this served as a lesson in what is real and what is not, yet claim to be, and one needs to learn the difference.

To one side of this large four-room area was another rather long room. It seemed separate by the design of its construction from the main warehouse, although it was physically attached. I learned late in life that it was an addition our mother's father had made at her request. It was a kind of living quarters for a while, but ultimately became a storage room for Mother's vast number of collectibles that she was gradually amassing and needing additional space. I distinctly remember numerous round wooden apple baskets full of antique salt and pepper shakers stacked one upon the other—she had at one time a collection of 3,000 shakers! When needed, Mother would pay my sisters a penny a piece to clean and polish these sets of ornate collectibles.

So much for the front half of The Warehouse. Let's move to those areas where the items of the business were bought, physically processed for shipment, or sold to customers looking for something they needed. You might think the remaining sections of The Warehouse was where the business "stock" (Hides, Wool, Furs, Pelts, and Scrap Metals of various kinds) was located for L. L. Langdon.

In the front office, next to the counter where the calendars hung, there was a door that led down a long, dark dimly lit hallway. This emptied into to a large, covered area that was "the back" of The Warehouse. This is the beginning of where the various items of the business were stored and would be processed for shipment or sale. First, at the end of the hallway, there was a door and as you swung it open you entered a large, dimly lit room that became much easier to see when the sliding door to the street was open to let the sunshine and products of the business in. There were no windows. To your immediate right was a set of narrow, creaky wooden stairs that went up to the second floor: we will get to that shortly.

To the left was a large sliding wooden door about 7' x 6'. When open, you could back your pickup in to unload the hides you had to sell. These were brought in by farmers or ranchers or their surrogates, such as from the local meat processing plant, The Independent Meat Company. L.L. Langdon was the single broker in the immediate area for buying hides, which were then sent to tanning businesses which needed and wanted to deal with a single entity rather than with each individual farmer, cattleman, or meat processor. So our dad, then our mother after his death, were brokers for various kinds and sizes of hides.

When cow or horse hides were brought in the back of a rancher's pickup or trailer, they were visually inspected for type, quality, counted, weighed on a scale, and noted in a register (accounting book) and on a payment receipt. Transactions were generally cash, but you could request a check. If a check was requested, a large check registry with three checks per sheet was unfolded and a check written. My mother had great handwriting and I always marveled at the smooth, bold artistic strokes in her signature.

Immediately after purchase, the hides were dragged over to the "pack" area, laid out flat with the hair down, and salted on the bare skin side with a thin layer of rock salt tossed from a big flat shovel. The broad metal shovel would be used to dig into a mountain of rock salt, carried to the hide, then broadcast evenly onto the entire skin side of the hide. The "packing" process, as it was referred to, was repeated again and again as each person brough their load to sell. Sometimes, when times were busy with multiple customers, laying hides wasn't done at the time the hide was bought as there were other transactions going on. Rather they were placed in a pile like some mountain of meat until a more convenient time when they could be laid out and salted. I remember attempting this packing of hides myself and it was arduous to say the least. An average hide could weigh 60 lbs.! Eventually, the pack—roughly 30' x 50'—stood four feet high. Over the course of two months they formed a rectangular mass as if layering a chocolate cake.

I'd like to mention a little about the smell that a pack of hides creates, and what it's like to be amongst them before they are finally ready for shipment. There is certainly no more single other gross activity in my parents' business than packing hides. Once I tell you of the other business activities, you may question my judgment on this point as to what the grossest business activity of L. L. Langdon was. But hides, as a commodity of the business, were gross to say the least. When friends came over, they were always aghast at the smell. Their repulsion at the sight of hides would be only further heightened by the constant presence of flies. It made one long for the cold of winter when, at least, the flies were gone. Yet the cold seemed to actually sharpen, with a pungent effect on your nostrils, the smell that was always present from the hides. So no matter what the season was, the smell would not fail to let you know that this was not a business environment for the timid. There is no adequate way to completely capture the smell, but I'll give you some ideas. It's a bit like the smell of vomit, but you don't gag. It has a highly pungent effect on your nostrils! I think that was the result of all that salt as it permeated and kept the skin of the hides wet so that they would not dry out. The resulting odor created a stinging sensation on the lining of your nostrils. Yet, at the same moment it had a harsh sweetness to it. Having lived with it for years, we accepted it for what it was, and for the family it represented the sweet smell of success in that it was part of our family's way of making a livelihood. It was business, and business needed to be done, no matter the smell or the difficulty of getting it done.

After the pack had risen as high as it could stand—before the layers of the cake could collapse—my parents would then negotiate with the tanning company in Oregon when to gather up and ship the entire pack.

Packing the hides, of course, was only the first stage of the overall hide business. You next had to process them for shipment. This was known obviously as "unpacking." As arduous as packing was, unpacking was more labor intensive. Unpacking required several workers working 12-hour days spread over two days usually into the late evening. Our parents would hire a crew of four stout men. Not that a woman couldn't do the work (such as my mother did) but for whatever reason in those days I never saw a woman unpacking hides other than her. It might be one of the only times a woman would be thankful that hide handling was man's work! You'd never convince our mother of that, as she was right in there doing the work with the men she hired. Temporary workers were usually solicited from the local unemployment office, and very few returned in subsequent days for well-paid work. Those who came for the first time had no idea what they were signing up for. You could assume that among an initial set of men, two would typically quit in the first hour or day. It was not only back breaking work, but seemingly constant, sweaty, and foul smelling. They more than earned their wage.

Typical invoice of various kinds of hides for shipment on Ironsides, December 4, 1950

The process of unpacking the hides from the pack was pretty tedious, and routine, but you'd get a sweat up from the constant effort it required. A two-person team would go to the back corner of the pack, find the ears of one hide in order to locate the two sides of the hide, lift and slide the hide between them with the skin side up laden with salt, drag the hide to the far end near the sliding door, pull the hide slightly over the edge of the pack, and dump and shake off the excess salt. Then, removing the ears (if still present) with a very sharp knife, they would cut and toss them into a barrel. The two-man team then neatly folded the hide into a square, as if gift-wrapping something for Christmas, with the hair side up until it was about 2 ½' x 2 ½'. It was lifted by hand to a scale where it was typed (horse, cow, or deer), weighed and recorded, then tossed up on the bed of a flatbed truck. Two workers on the truck would lift the hide and stack hide on hide until a new, yet neater, pack sorted by hide type was formed up to the very top of the 4' high flatbed truck with metal sides. All this activity took a minimum of 2 days to complete: sometimes carrying on into a cold winter evening, or a smelly summer night when the heat with the packing was unbearable. Covered with a canvas tarp, the truck was then driven to the tanning operation. So much for the hide business at L.L. Langdon. There was always plenty more work to do with the other animal commodities that were part of the business.

Processing hides was only one of the five major functions of L.L. Langdon. Aside from the emerging scrap metals that would ultimately dominate the business, three other animal commodities were also the focus of the business. These were, as titled on the company calendars, Wool, Furs, and Pelts. I'll describe each, then turn your attention to the metals part of the Langdon business.

Wool has always been a highly sought after commodity and is still so today. Wool comes from sheep, of course, and it doesn't get from them to you without a great deal of work to shear it from the sheep and get it to the mill. L.L. Langdon was one of the links in the overall process that ends in clothing being made. Years later I owned a small farm and had a few sheep, so I know what it takes to shear sheep. I always hired someone to shear the sheep as I do not have any skill with this task, nor did I desire it once I saw what was involved! I therefore know what it took for a broker, such as my parents, to receive either

*Sister Lucille (standing) and Dorothy (seated) on bails of wool
located on railway siding awaiting shipment on rail car*

wool as a fleece, or when the wool is sheared from the animal, and get both to the mill. Sheep are annually sheared for their wool, whereas once a sheep dies or is slaughtered for its meat, the hide becomes a pelt. That is how L. L. Langdon dealt in both loose wool and the pelt itself. First, the sheared wool.

If you have, as I have thus far described, visualized the blueprint—see illustration—of The Warehouse in terms of the office area, the backrooms with laundry, a toilet, the "bedroom" for dad's convalescent need in his last year, the other attached rooms for various uses, and the space for packing hides, you have left a loft area on the second story level attic that is pretty much the same footprint (front and back) as the entire first floor. This second floor of the warehouse was an entire open area with only two windows at opposite ends, a sliding door above the other sliding door on the first floor where the hides were unloaded and loaded, and an equally sized opening across the way for processing the loose wool for shipment. I'll describe the several functions this area of The Warehouse served over the years, beginning with the loose wool.

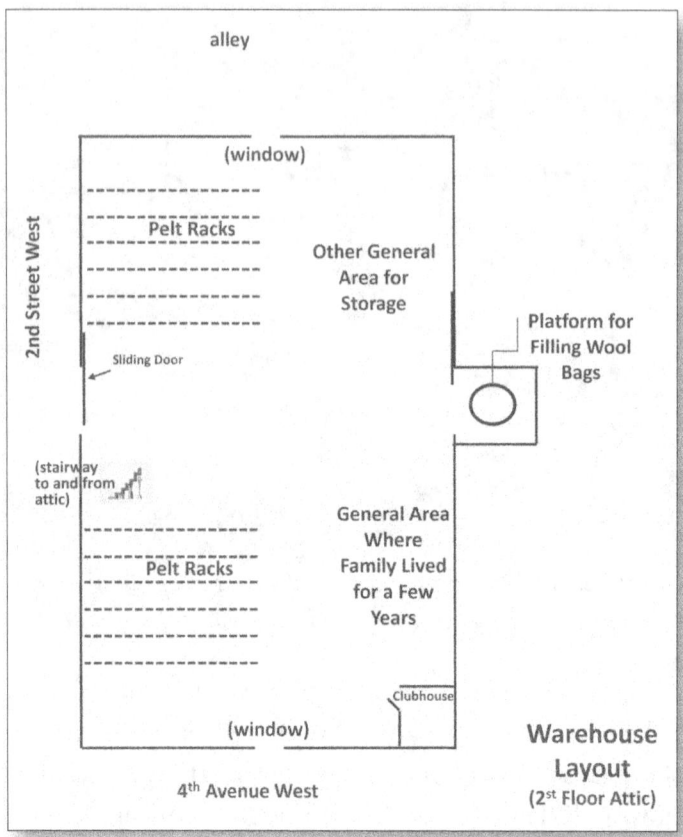

The predominance of the attic space was reserved to hang pelts and furs. There was a small area, protruding out from the building through a sliding door used for bagging wool. Otherwise the rest of the second floor housed a general collection of miscellaneous other items of the business and general storage. When the warehouse was rented initially in 1933, the whole of the upstairs was used as the family residence, but rather than distract from the description of the warehouse as a business, I'll hold off until later describing its use as an unconventional place to live.

The entire upstairs was one big open room from end to end, except for a small 6' x 8' enclosed room in the front with a door in a far corner nearest to Truck Lane. I am not certain what use it ever served originally, perhaps as an office, but this single small room was later used by me and my friends as our clubhouse. We once decorated the walls entirely with paper Pepsi bottle labels we found one day over near the Twin Falls Feed & Ice Company. I think Andy Warhol would have been so impressed with how we decorated our clubhouse! But it was the specific use of the second floor for the storage and processing of wool, furs, and pelts prior to their shipment that was most important.

As one went up to the second floor, accessible by the stairway previously noted, directly ahead on the other side of the attic as you reached the top level there was a platform around 7' x 7'. It stuck out from the existing flooring through an opening and was supported on one corner by a 4" x 4" beam to the ground below with two sides of the platform anchored to the building itself. Therefore, you could stand on the platform. In the very middle was a round hole 3' in diameter. A large 10' burlap bag would be placed down the opening of the hole to nearly the ground and secured in place at the top with a metal ring. With the bag thus secured, one would place loose wool time after time into the open end of the bag and tamp it down by jumping down into the bag and stomping the wool with your feet into every nook and cranny. I used to do it myself on occasion, and each time I was soon "Lanolin Kid," as the oily residue oozed from the wool onto my arms, hands, and clothing. Along the way I'd occasionally look for any ticks I might have picked up from the loose wool. You learned how to remove a tick from your all-knowing parents or siblings who themselves had to remove a tick or two. A lit match applied ever so gently near the tick's small body without killing it or burning your own skin was the most preferred method for removal of a tick in those days. The principle was that the tick didn't like the heat and would back itself away from having bored into your skin. It generally worked, but not always. If not, you pulled it out and hoped for the best.

Loose wool from several sheep had to be squeezed in until the bag was full—as the nursery rhyme goes. Then you remove the ring, stitch the end of the bag closed with twine, and tie the corners into pig-ears for the final touch. The full bag, weighing perhaps two hundred pounds, would be lowered to the floor below, rolled to one end of a covered area and stacked until there were as many as 50 bags of wool ready for shipment and sale. These, as was done with the hides, were loaded on the company truck, "Ironsides," covered with a canvas tarp, and driven to a designated mill in Oregon which had prearranged to purchase the wool. I am sure some of the famous, "Pendleton" shirts of the day were made of wool from L.L. Langdon. So much for the loose wool part of the business. We now come to the final two animal commodities: furs and pelts.

Over the years, furs of various types came through the doors of L. L. Langdon. The most common were fox, coyote, beaver, mink, and a small assortment of others like rabbit. Furs, unlike loose wool, were strung on metal "stretchers." This was necessary so that the fur was left in good and usable condition and not stuck to itself or to other furs when drying. On one of the upstairs walls, four or five stretchers, each with its type of fur, were hung on nails to dry, and when ready, were removed from the stretchers and shipped in gunny sack bags along with pelts. I used to trap muskrats on the stream along Rock Creek Canyon as my contribution to the pelt business and a small money source. One learned where muskrats burrowed just below the stream bank, and you set your iron trap just where they would enter and exit. Furs were purchased by the business for good money. This was true for hobbyists or full-time trappers—and yes, trappers still existed in the 40s and 50s.

Pelts were more common and in greater numbers than furs. The most common pelts were sheep or deer from the annual hunt. These, as with hides, were "wet" from the skinning process, so they had to be hung to dry, hair/wool side up. For drying, a series of 3" x 3" poles, 14 feet long were strung on two-by-fours that were mounted from the floor to the attic ceiling. The drying poles were stacked two high and a typical pole could accommodate six to eight pelts. As with the loose wool bagging, in performing the pelt hanging operation you could not help but get plenty of lanolin from the wool pelt on to your arms, hands, and face. When the pelts had dried and now stiff as a board, they would be removed from the wooden poles, tossed out a second story sliding door, onto Ironsides, covered with a tarp, and driven to a tanning operation—L. Bloom & Sons—in Brigham City, Utah.

There was a period of time in the business when an unusual type of fur was bought and sold by L.L. Langdon. It only lasted a couple of years, and always seemed to me, at least, a bit odd as a commodity. In retrospect, given our area of Idaho, it wasn't surprising as the proliferation of this particular animal by the thousands was wreaking havoc on the crops of local farming. This involved the famous Idaho, "Jack Rabbit" that so abundantly roamed the local sagebrush areas of southern Idaho that for a brief time, were killed and bought as a commodity. I can remember so many being bought that at one time a small mountain, 6' to 8' high stood just outside the warehouse. Mother recalled in a newspaper article how she bought as many as 15,000 rabbits a week for 10 cents each. They were loaded onto Ironsides and trucked to a mink-farming operation located in Sheridan, Wyoming. Sent whole, they were to be skinned and the meat fed to mink, while the fur was processed by others to line gloves, hats, stoles, and coat liners. The diversity of goods in my parents' business was something to behold and would expand or diminish with time as consumer needs and demands changed.

Now while hides, wool, furs, and pelts were the original commodities of the business, the need for these items was gradually waning in the late 50s. This was due largely to the development of synthetic materials as a substitute. Even societal views of wearing fur were changing. But it was primarily the looming dawn of World War II that had the greatest impact on business and the commodities it specialized in—one that would dominate its activity and very existence for the next 40 years. Scrap iron and other discarded metals would become our parents' primary business interest. Thus, while the original signage read, "Hides, Wool, Furs, and Pelts," a subtitle was added: "Scrap Metal -- New and Used Blacksmith Iron." It was interesting to note that the wording on various signage and such that denoted the business would always remain, even though certain commodities were no longer bought. It was as if all were never to be forgotten!

As part of The Warehouse at ground level, just behind the hide packing area, a large area shaped like a reversed L, bordering two walls of the building itself and two open areas, constituted where scrap metal would initially be stacked as part of the business. These became iron mountains, often reaching a height of 6 feet or so.

When the business first started, scrap metal was piled and processed only at The Warehouse location, but the quantity was soon getting too much that other locations in town for metal storage were needed. There were several of these other locations in our side of town and I'll enumerate each shortly as each played a role in my personal adventures as a kid, but let's understand first what constitutes scrap metal.

Metals of different kinds were typically brought in by those looking for some extra cash. There was every kind of metal you can imagine, but mostly iron from used agricultural or industrial machinery, as well as cars that had been junked. Other metals were wires from the utility company, parts of old refrigerators, water tanks, batteries for their lead, stoves, etc. You name it, you bring it in, and it was there to be bought, sorted, and further cut as needed to then be sent to a steel mill or other metal reprocessing enterprise. L.L. Langdon's was, as is more commonly known today, the original version of recycling, but on a much grander scale with regards to the breadth of products. Note: In 2021 the Jewish Museum of Maryland displayed an account of recycling in America and our mother's contribution was noted. It can be accessed online: see Reference section at end of this book.

As a physical part of the structure of The Warehouse there was a covered, open on one side, extension much like a covered parking area you'd see today as part of a condo complex. This area housed numerous 55-gallon metal drums that stored a variety of metals other than iron— lead, copper, brass, pewter, etc. Often when customers brought in their "pile of iron" there were other metals mixed with it. These needed to be sorted out, as steel mills did not want mixed metals interfering with their steel processing which utilizes iron as one of its key components. Thus, it took knowing your metals to separate each and you would be aided by use of a small magnet in your pocket since only iron attracts to a magnet, otherwise it took knowing the physical characteristics of each metal to sort them correctly. Of course, our mother knew metals by sight and rarely had to rely on the small magnet she kept in the side pocket of her Levi's. These other metals brought a higher price than iron and thus were worth the effort to sort out and sell separately.

There was also a smaller covered area in the same part of the yard for storing spent batteries from cars or trucks that had had their day. Batteries had to be taken apart—not by the Langdon business, but rather by other enterprises—for reprocessing the precious lead content found in their cells. As kids we were cautioned about the liquid acid contained therein. Frankly, for me, the sheer weight of the average battery was enough to keep me away from trying to tinker with one, let alone the fear of acid that stings and eats into your skin.

There was one particular metal source that I was especially fascinated with. That was the linotype and photo plates that were occasionally brought in from the one newspaper in town, *The Times News*. Looking at the photo plates (reverse images of pictures) simply sparked my imagination, images of things and places I'd never seen, but wondered trying to discern what they showed. Later, when I was a newsboy selling newspapers on the streets of Twin Falls, I got to go inside the *The Times News* and watch the giant presses that threaded paper to print the daily news that I was then selling on the street. It was a noisy operation of an almost deafening nature; still you had to wonder at the machinery as it fed, printed, folded, and stacked into a neat package of newsprint to be unfolded and consumed by the reader. Various parts of machinery that produced the printed pages would likely also one day find their way into Langdon's scrapyard. In an indirect way, my parents' business was part of the newsprint business, as it was part of other businesses and the lives of people in general.

As the pelt market gradually faded in the 1970s due to lack of demand, the upper area of The Warehouse became storage for a variety of other things. The family had long before vacated its residency in The

Warehouse, and the entire structure was exclusively devoted to business interests. Among other commodities that were bought then sent for reprocessing or resold to customers were items purchased at auction from the military base at Mountain Home. This included items like wool-lined boots and flight gear previously used in World War II. I used to wonder if the wool in those very boots originated from my parents' business and was perhaps even that which I had personally stuffed in the burlap sacks. I loved going through these unusual items bought by the business and saved a few such as a radio headset worn by air force pilots and an old pair of snow skis, long and sleek for cross-country skiing by special units in military service. Eventually I painted the tops of a set of those skis, and they were so ugly I never skied on them again. Still there were other oddities that came my way through the business and I was one to see the curiosity of how I might use such.

At some point my mother purchased a couple of old slot and pinball machines as scrap metal. Gambling was, and is still, legal in Nevada and thus where the slots had likely originated. We managed to get two of them working and had loads of fun playing the slots for free. Not winning a jackpot was easy since we never lost our money, nor did we gain anything other than the thrill of a "win"! A more fascinating non mechanical, all-wooden version of a pinball machine turned up as well. I have always regretted not saving it. Of course, if I had saved all that I then desired from the junkyard, I'd have my own scrap metal business to this day. The Warehouse was never at a loss for treasure to spark the imagination, but mostly to provide some fun. When you count the treasures, my mother personally accumulated from the business, as well as purchased here and there, it's an enormous listing! As she often said, "One person's scrap is another person's treasure!" Oh, my mother was so smart!

I think that's pretty much gives you a concise picture of the various business aspects and uses of The Warehouse. A business for sure, but also a playground for me and my friends who coveted the opportunity to explore what was found there. But there were two other parts of

The Warehouse that need to be described as they round out what The Warehouse, the place where I was born, was about.

As part of the two lots on which The Warehouse sat, there was a detached, one-room house, not much bigger than what we think of today as a "tiny house," like those sometimes used for the homeless. It was built by our mother's itinerant father, Hazel Jenner Smith, at her request. It sat there in the open yard out of place in the middle of other business operations. Like The Warehouse itself, this separate tiny home served multiple uses over time. I never felt it well integrated into the business, but rather there as a catch-all for general family use and storage. For example, for a year our sister Dorothy lived there during her transition out of our family life to then marry and live permanently elsewhere. Mother stored items there from the scrapyard she considered interesting or might be of added value. She definitely had an eye for such things. This tiny house was a small, symbolic example of our parents' skill at meeting life and business needs just as they had camped with the family for the entire summer on the Little Wood River to save money.

To round out the description of The Warehouse, it was not merely a place to house things and prepare them for sale to other businesses that would reprocess these commodities. It was a business, on a much lesser scale, which frequently sold certain things from scrap to meet select needs of individuals in the community. I'll highlight just a couple of examples, although there were many others such as the many needs of farmers, ranchers, local businessmen, kids, students, and others who came into The Warehouse. As a kid, it was wonderful to see and interact with these assorted members of our community. I can't recall any other kid who had the opportunity to interact with such a variety of people in the community he lived in like I did.

While the business was mainly that of buying iron and other used commodities, one of the other daily activities both inside and outside The Warehouse was that of people who would drop in to buy this or that: a piece of metal, missing nuts and bolts they needed for their machinery, or some piece of flat iron to build perhaps a wagon for general utility purposes. The business was a little like an old-fashioned hardware store, but in this instance for the used, rather than the new. For example, Mr. Toffelmier, the local editor of *The Times News*, dropped in at least once or twice a week. He was, in addition to his managing, writing, and editorial functions, an amateur inventor. He would tinker with building things made or repurposed from the scrap metal he found at The Warehouse. He sought out wires, bolts, and pieces of machinery he would use in new ways. He was a dapper man, always dressed in slacks, a white shirt, and tie. He would usually stop and shop at The Warehouse either on his way home from work or for a few minutes during his lunch break. The newspaper he managed was just a couple of blocks away and an easy walk to The Warehouse. He would patiently sift through the piles and drums filled with this and that looking for any item that caught his eye. He would say, "How much?" for a handful of this, as he held them in his outstretched hand, and Mother would give him a price, or just say, "Oh, just take that!" There was a special understanding between them as they talked about business or other matters of the community. That went on for at least two decades.

Another regular was the founder and owner of Herrett's Jewelry. He was a former shop teacher who, along with his wife, set up a jewelry business on Kimberly Road. You may not imagine a jeweler needing scrap metal, but Mr. Herrett, as we kids called him, was a man of many interests. For one, he had a lapidary for artfully shaping stone, minerals, or gemstones into decorative items. I recall going to his jewelry store to see those glittering items displayed under special lighting. In later years he also had an impressive tropical fish aquarium and a bird sanctuary.

However, it was Mr. Herrett's passion for the stars that really fascinated me and others in our community. He constructed a large, working planetarium with two permanent telescopes. Some of the moving parts, framework, and other items needed to build and operate the planetarium and the telescopes came from items he collected from Langdon's scrap metal or were made with blacksmith iron that our mother also sold. Combined with a high school friend of mine, who himself had a telescope and later became an astronomer, I was privy to night shows that fueled my imagination then and now. As a result to this very day I have been interested in seeing stars in countries that have dim enough light to see the multitude of heavenly bodies. Go see these for yourself in foreign lands like Iceland, Ethiopia, Fiji, and many others and you'll discover what I mean. It's an entirely different experience for the eyes, the effect on your psyche, and an acknowledgement that we are so small in the universe, yet so grand.

Through the years, Mother formed relationships with many others who came to the business. Kids who participated in the Future Farmers of America program through high school, could come and get free metal for their projects. A couple of mother's farmer friends would now and then offer me a dime to get something like ice cream, but I always turned them down. It didn't seem appropriate for me to accept money. They were just being nice, of course. I did eventually learn how to talk to adults in these exchanges. A shy boy at heart, I found such practice in conversations much more important than any dime could buy. I trusted these men because they were friends with my mother. I would not talk to a stranger for several years more, but in time I got over that shyness with strangers as well! I think my generation growing up in that day and age as part of what I call the lucky generation (say, 1935 to 1946). It was a time when you could trust strangers more than today, play safely as a child on the streets well into the night, find summer work as a kid, afford college, and buy a house as a young adult. It was a time when you opened doors for the elderly. Kind of miss some of that time of my generation. The Warehouse, and all the people who wandered in, provided this boy loads of safe experiences in learning to be social. It was more than just a business exchanging tangibles, it was also a safe haven for social exchanges.

By now you might have concluded in your reading that The Warehouse was large enough for L. L. Langdon. However space was at a premium for the numerous items found therein, and iron was constantly coming through the doors of the business. Over the succeeding years, lots of additional space was needed to receive and house iron before it was cut and processed. The Warehouse would remain the central hub around which other venues were acquired or rented to meet business needs. A brief description of each will paint the more complete picture of the business, as well as the environment we thrived in as children (not without lots of explanation to friends who didn't quite understand what we had or how we lived or for that matter survived in such surroundings). I'll mention one final thing about The Warehouse, then get to the other venues that were each, in their own right, as unique as The Warehouse.

Of all the various kinds of metal purchased by the business, there was one especially unique piece that sat on the corner where The Warehouse was situated at Truck Lane and 2nd Street West. It was, in its very nature, a symbol of an unusual business enterprise. That was a cannon from the First World War era. It had perhaps been in a local community park as a memorial, but the memory it served had worn off. I always thought it fitting that the cannon should find its way to our business. It kind of stood guard against anything or anyone who might destroy us. It was present for the entire 40-plus years of the business and only gave up its post when the business was sold. Today it is undoubtably part of other objects made from it, as has all the other scrap metals processed by L. L. Langdon. I always like the idea that the products from my parents' business are still to be found in so many objects and places to this very day and into the future. Our mother recalled in a newspaper article at the time when she saw some new steel piping sitting on the corner of a vacant lot near her business. The pipe was there as part of a building being constructed by the city of Twin Falls. The new pipe lay in close proximity to one of her scrap iron locations. She noted from its markings written on the side that it had been forged from iron processed by the very mill, Geneva Steel for the Pacific Pipe Company in Utah, where she had sent railway cars of scrap metal. To think that her metal had been processed and probably scattered to other parts of the world is a legacy! I've gone around the world and perhaps have seen many of the places where that very iron might be!

"The Hole"

Acquiring The Warehouse was a seminal moment for our parents in that it created, for the first time, a space they owned and would operate thereafter as their business. In real terms, it was a physical location where customers could come to sell, as well as acquire, the things to meet their needs. However, it wasn't nearly enough space for the mountain of scrap iron that was continuously coming in. These acquisitions were being driven in large part by the need for metals for the war effort. It seems L. L. Langdon was in the right place at the right time to meet a critical need, and this need would continue for years. The Warehouse, for its part simply did not have enough space for the storage of metals, so other locations in the immediate area were sought and utilized one after the other. The first was to become known simply as The Hole. On reflection these many years later, we could have perhaps better labeled this physical location in town "The Canyon," as it was certainly bigger than a hole, so I'll explain.

A block south of The Warehouse, up 2nd Street West, and between there and the main thoroughfare of Shoshone Street, there was a large vacant lot nearly the size of an entire city block. It had apparently housed a business or businesses at some time, but I never learned what that was. It was vacant, but not flat, meaning that it was mostly dug out about a story deep. From the vantage point of driving along Shoshone Street you would not know that it was there. Tucked down, as it was, it was an ideal place for my mother's business to receive and store iron without generally being seen by the public. She rented "The Hole" for about 10-years, as I recall.

All four corners of The Hole were steep, such that you could not try to climb down into The Hole from anyone of them. Nor could you go down any of the sides with the exception of a twenty-foot-wide dirt ramp that faced 2nd Street West. Trucks could be driven down and up this ramp and that is how iron was brought into and out of The Hole. Usually the transactional arrangement, including weighing, took place over at The Warehouse and you were instructed to drive to The Hole and drop it off in a designated place, "where you see an old plow on its side in the far-right corner." The seller was not supervised in doing this, merely trusted to go and drop it there. As the piles of iron grew at this overfill location, Mother would go for a few days and process the iron by cutting it into shorter pieces for shipment. She generally only had one full-time person for four decades, but mostly short time workers. When the need came, she would hire up to six part-timers for special work, like loading hides or iron for shipment. The work was usually part-time due to ebb and flow of processing the variety of items for shipment. The only full-timer, named Coy, was with her for 30 years or so and became sort of part of the family. Though an odd duck, he was very safe and loyal to her children and always kind. He was neither a father figure nor a friend, but perhaps a grateful guardian in appreciation to the woman who provided work to support his simple lifestyle. Together she would cut and sort the iron into piles of a length that the recyclers would accept for their mill operations. As he got older, Coy became more withdrawn and set in his ways, but my mother overlooked his peccadillos due to his loyalty. In reality, he was such a simple human that he needed his own guardian and that was to be our mother, and by proxy as well to her children.

Cutting iron—picture a long flat bar or car frame—was an art, if you can imagine it being that! This meant cutting pieces to usually no longer than 5 feet. Cutting was done with an acetylene torch. When the time came to ship the iron in a long railroad gondola car (imagine a humongous empty sardine can on wheels), the various pieces of iron would be loaded on the businesses' truck, Ironsides. The truck would be driven to a railway siding a few blocks away and driven up onto the wooden platform found there and the iron then tossed into the awaiting rail car. This required truck load after load in repetitive motion. Weighed at the railway scales prior to loading, the difference between the empty railway car and the one now loaded was several tons. That railcar was then attached to others going to designated destinations, and her railcar sent to the Geneva Steel works in Vineyard, Utah. I remember often sitting on the wooden platform and watching my mother toss piece after piece of iron into the railcar until perhaps 40 tons was stacked and ready to go. What a woman! What a mother! Hell, what an image of a man and a woman rolled into one!

My friends and I loved The Hole. It was a wonderful place to go biking because some of the corners sloped a little and you could ride your bike partly up as far as your strength would take you, then roll back as needed to recover. When we had worn ourselves out, Mother would give us 10 cents and we would go to the dairy a block away to buy a quart of our favorite flavor of ice cream, usually a combination of vanilla, chocolate, and strawberry (Neapolitan) in three layers. Our favorite location for eating the ice cream was on the metal roof of an old onion cellar across Sixth Street. After eating the ice cream with our fingers, we would then unfold the cardboard container and set it on the roof, waxed side down, sit on it and slide down the metal roof to the ground below. You would soon go faster and faster as the wax from the ice cream carton on the metal roof had less and less resistance between it and roof. There was a four-foot drop at the end, so you had to be ready to fly and land on your feet at the right angle without tumbling to the ground. Snagging your pants on the way down was a real possibility, but worth the fun and laughter. What entertainment for a group of boys not yet 10-years of age! What a playground we had in The Hole and other venues open to friends of the family.

"The Depot"

The depository of iron that came to be known as "The Depot" came a little later and was unique in that it sat catty-corner to an eatery that would become pretty much a second home to the Langdons. I'll get to the Depot Grill later as now you will learn what The Depot was and why it was important. Aside from The Warehouse, The Depot was perhaps the most visible locale for storing iron, thus in sight of the general public. For that reason alone, it had to present itself with some form of organization, and not look so "junky," which was by its very nature impossible. That's a little paradoxical, but the importance can't be lost due to the fact that it sat squarely on one of the main thoroughfares of the town, across the tracks and far away from the best areas of Twin Falls, but still visible.

One of several junkyard locations—The Depot—of L.L. Langdon in Twin Falls

This lot was 100 feet long from the corner of Shoshone Street, along 6th Avenue West and Wall Street, and it shaped to make a trapezoid. The backside was 125 feet and it ran parallel to an intersecting street where no longer used railroad tracks were still visible. The remaining two adjoining sides were of different lengths, probably 50 and 70 feet, respectively. These joined on the west and east sides. The lot had a one-story wooden storage shed where Mother would, as she did at The Warehouse, store special things that she thought had particular value. For example, there were a couple of metal buckets into which she would occasionally throw "grease caps" (think antique auto hubcaps). These occasionally surfaced in the scrap she had purchased and, being as old as they were, had added value to antique car enthusiasts. Later in life, when

I was restoring an antique car that she had given me, she gave me those two buckets of grease caps representing different models of car made in the USA and other countries up until 1975. Years later I remember selling one of the grease caps to a Rolls-Royce to a mate in Australia and gave others to fellow antique car enthusiasts. I eventually gave the rest, number around 65, to a museum along with the antique car I had restored and kept for nearly 60 years. That is just one example of what was stored at The Depot and how such treasures, once considered junk, had found their way to new customers or venues. Stored there were also old wagon wheels, antique metal hand water-pumps, an antique corn shucker for removing kernels, branding irons from numerous ranches, a blacksmith forge (that I have), and so forth. What fun it was just to go through this stuff and sometimes incorporate it into my life, especially when I had a small farm in Idaho. And as if all this wasn't enough, The Depot was directly across the street from the famed Depot Grill—the inspirational source of the name of this storage location.

On the side of The Depot that faced Shoshone Street there was a corrugated metal fence and, on its face in white and green letters, was painted the name of the business as proudly as you would advertise any on-going business. It read in bold, large cursive letters: L.L. Langdon. Besides the obvious that it was a sign naming a business, it was a statement to the community and to the strangers that came that way through Twin Falls and wondered what that pile of junk was on that corner. Over the course of the 25 years that this site existed the signage faded from the weather and there was eventually a missing piece of corrugated siding. This location, and the business lasted, until our mother retired in 1986 at the age of 75. Funny how the sign stayed another 10 years after she left town to live near our sister Bertine, a kind of legacy that she had been part of the community that truly embraced the lady who ran such an unusual business. I think her universal acceptance by the community was a testament to all she had done for the community, let alone that she was something rare: a woman in business and a business that was one that was supposedly a man's only business. Besides, The

Depot was just across the street from the best place to eat in town, The Depot Grill, and everyone knew the lady who came there, often with her family, to eat.

"The Backyard"

I am sure your backyard, if you have or grew up with one, is normally a space in the back of your house: most likely a nice grassy area with something like a swing or even a pool or barbeque, bordered with flowers and a nice tree and, of course, the manicured lawn. The backyard for the Langdon kids was so much different.

After initially living in The Warehouse for just a year after I was born, our family rented a house in another location in town for a period of time, until we moved in 1946, to what would be our first—and only—permanent residence, 313 4th Avenue West. It was just a block away from The Warehouse, across Truck Lane, and within easy access to our parents work when we needed them. Though being on the rougher side of town, safety from home to The Warehouse never seemed an issue, and it never was in that day and age. The house, a small single-story modest wood-framed three-bedroom—really two and a half bedrooms—with a tile roof, had one bath, a living room/dining room combo, small porches front and back, and a ridiculously small kitchen. It housed, due to its smallness, the remaining six children still living at home, including a near 7-year-old me. The house sat on one of two adjoining lots—the other was vacant for only a few months. The rest of the neighborhood, other than directly behind our house, was a mixed residential block with small, pre-World War II houses for the most part. I guess you could say that most residents were slightly above or at the poverty level. However they kept their residences clean and tidy for the most part. Most were long-term owners, but on the corner next to our house was a kind of cinderblock house that seemed to have a different family every other year, some of whom had their problems, as you could occasionally hear arguments going on. Mostly it was a quiet neighborhood, if trucks and cars constantly traversing on Truck Lane is your idea of quiet.

Langdon Family House located at 313 4th Avenue West

Behind and across the alley of the adjoining lot there was another vacant lot and, at some point, my mother began stacking iron on it as she had at other locations in town. This lot became known, even if it wasn't literally, as The Backyard—just another location for storing scrap metal. I have since wondered if she rented, owned, or just used that lot, but I never asked. It was just another location for her business. On it were the usual assorted piles of iron, but there were occasionally extraordinary items that certainly caught the eye and use of kids. One was an old combine. For those not familiar with one of those, it's a large machine (mostly made of iron in those days) on wheels that farmers used to pull with a tractor to cut and separate grain such as wheat or oats, in their fields. Imagine having a huge combine to play on—but that wasn't half of it! There was also an assortment of other iron, mostly mountains of miscellaneous things that could catch your imagination—or your pant leg—as to what they had been. But even better was an old P-51 Second World War airplane. The cockpit was intact with a seat and basic controls including a joystick and foot pedals that moved the flaps and aspects of the tail. The wings were intact, but there was no motor or propeller. Surely now you can see the implications of having that in your backyard as a kid. Add to that a small caliber anti-aircraft cannon from the Second World War and you have the makings of attracting any kid you so choose. Of course there were other things we found there as well. It was simply a beautiful iron jungle for all my dreams. Despite its primary intended purpose to store junk metal, I considered it my very own backyard for play as it was just across the alley from our house.

"The Other Pile"

We never gave this other location of stacked iron a formal name. It was just "The Other Pile!" Maybe we were trying to avoid any admission that it existed and was part of our residence at 313 4th Avenue West. For several years, until converted when I was 14 into a lovely side yard with grass, 2 willow trees, and an abundance of rose bushes our mother so loved, iron was piled on the lot adjacent to and part of our residence. It might seem odd to pile old rusty scrap iron in your own yard, but it was a practical business decision. It supported my mother's livelihood and that of her family. It was, in that sense, a necessity. Why pay rent for another lot when you have one right next to you that you own? Who were we to complain about junk in our play yard? For that matter, we thought, given its presence, live and play with it! We had enough space directly at the back of the house, although it was smallish, with real grass. That's as much that can be said about The Other Pile, other than what the average passerby must have wondered about our neighborhood with two scrap metal heaps piled with assorted iron amidst the modest houses.

Now beyond the various locales where iron was temporally stored as the satellites to The Warehouse, there were on occasion other temporary locations that were rented and used for the needs that arose as the business ebbed and flowed. These others were blocks away and not as accessible to me as a kid, but sometimes I'd visit Mother when she was working at one of these other lots. Other locations were needed since junk metal, after all, is a commodity that responds to supply and demand like other businesses. You had to know the market: when to sell to get the best price possible or hold on until economic conditions improved. Don't sell when the market is low. The iron wasn't going any place until you and the market decided, so don't panic. Fortunately, our mother was a skilled marketer of metals, hides, wool, furs, pelts, and whatever would bring her a living. I've illuminated those spaces that were often visited and became a playground and where to find our mother when she was needed. I used this menagerie of business locations as a boy with a flair for exploration and an imagination to go with it. Now, onto an introduction to the family known in town as The Langdons.

CHAPTER 2

The Langdons: Heritage and Family

I didn't, unlike most people I guess, pay attention to whether or not I was part of an ethnic group. I had no idea if I was English, French, Irish, German, Italian, Polish, or some combination. Frankly, it wasn't until I was 84 and my wife found a resource that I specifically learned I am Anglo-American, a fact that still doesn't mean much to me. I was just a kid and part of a very loving family that valued one another. We did things together, the older ones set examples for the younger ones, and they could be depended upon if you needed them. Given this, I want to describe our general genealogy as I came to realize it —the facts of which I first learned as a man in his thirties. I have, over the years, explored the broader implications of family from my own genealogical research by utilizing resources such as 23 and Me and Ancestry.com. Most of this work was done while in my 60s.

The Langdons have been, as it turns out, in America for a long, long time, from as far back as the 1600s. No wonder we feel welcome here! While living in Pennsylvania in the early 1960s, I went to visit a sister living in the Washington, D.C. area. I stopped in the Library of Congress knowing they have a fantastic genealogical section. Wanting to see what I might learn of our family I started by perusing the general card catalogue (no computers in the 60s). A card catalogue was the search engine in those days—an extensive, row upon row of file cabinets. Each cabinet had multiple long file drawers that held 3" x 5" cards on which were typed the topic, author(s), basic content summary of the source, resource type, and location in the library. Other print resources such as encyclopedias and resources indexes, were also available and could be physically accessed for related content which you would find at different physical locations in the extensive library system. Being a little brazen, even at age 27, I figured the name Langdon would surely be there in the card catalogue! To my surprise, it was. As it turned out, a distant relative had researched the general Langdon genealogy and posted in a binder a typed document of his discoveries/findings that the library had as part of its genealogical section. I poured over the binder of documents, took notes, and made contact by mail with the individual who had prepared it, Harry W. Harcourt. He forwarded to me my own copy of his binder about the Langdons and I was able to easily find a link to my great-grandfather. I won't bore you with the details, but subsequent additions to the genealogy by myself and others has shown a long line to the first immigrants from England (specifically Cornwall to America) in the mid-1600s. Beyond that, Mr. Harcourt cites some early evidence of lineage to 1039, but I haven't gone that far to validate its accuracy. Most were farmers but there were small businesspeople as well. Upon arrival they first settled primarily in Massachusetts, Connecticut, and Virginia. They then spread west, first to the Midwest (i.e., Indiana), and then, as the country grew, to the far west coast (i.e., Oregon and Washington). Mr. Harcourt noted, in general about the Langdons:

> *"The descendants of those—early settlers beginning in the 1600s— and probably of later branches of the family in America have spread to practically every State in the Union and have aided as much in the growth of the country, as their ancestors aided in the founding of the nation. They have been noted for their energy, industry, integrity, piety, perseverance, patience, fortitude, resourcefulness, initiative, courage, and leadership."*

Some in the family line distinguished themselves in the Revolutionary War, as well as fought for the North in the Civil War. One distant relative,

John Langdon, was a friend of George Washington when he was the governor of New Hampshire and was a signatory to the Constitution. So I am from a line that I am proud to be part of, but mostly curious about. I subsequently found a family crest supposedly ours. But when I saw that it included three hedgehogs as part of its coat-of-arms, I was far less impressed, but have accepted it at face value. Hedgehogs are, after all, unbelievably cute, furry creatures that roll themselves into a ball. More important is, of course, my immediate family that I am most proud of, and I'd like to spend a fair amount of time on them as the familial foundation and constant and consistent support to my own development. They all played significant roles in my life, if for no other reason than that I am the youngest, their baby brother.

My immediate family and I were kind of lucky to exist given a couple of interesting circumstances. Let's start with my grandfather since that is a fascinating story I have extensively researched and have often told. It tells of how my father nearly wasn't meant to be but given a few months. My father was born in 1882 (do the math), and I'm at the time of this writing in 2024, 86. He was the progeny of a man born in the Civil War period. Not sure I can even get my mind around that fact, but it speaks of a country that really isn't that old and a father who was an old man when I briefly knew him.

My father's father, Lucius Lambert Langdon (note the three letter LLL iteration as in the business and names of most of my brothers and sisters), was born 1852 in Massachusetts, and was a homesteader. That means he came out west to settle on land given to him by the US government. The land, called a homestead or land grant, of 160 acres would be given outright to him and his descendants if he would develop it and live for a designated period of years. That is how he came to Prineville, Oregon, sometime in 1880. He "proved up" the land as they say, building a home and started raising cattle and sheep. He and his wife, Emma Louise LaFrancis, had two children, Mary and Daisy. My grandmother was pregnant with a soon-to-be son, my father, when an incident occurred that would forever change my grandfather's very existence and provided a story to be passed down from generation to generation.

Grandfather Lucius Lambert
Langdon 1852 - 1882

Lucius, a hard-working diligent soul had a neighbor, A.H. Crooks, whom he seemed to have gotten along with in that Emma and Crook's wife were friends in what could be a lonely land, given the distances between neighbors living out in the wilderness. The Crooks had a daughter who had just married a young man, Stephen J. Jory. The Crooks desired to carve off 80 acres of their own homestead and set the newly married couple up. So Crooks and Jory set about to, as they say, "blaze" a fence line separating off said 80-acres. The issue that developed in doing this is that Crooks was taking 40-acres of his land and likely unknowingly taking 40-acres of the land belonging to Lucius—a court case later proving that was the case. It was probably initially a simple mistake on Crooks' part, but he apparently wasn't to be dissuaded of such by my grandfather's repeated efforts at verbal warnings. Grandfather, for his part, had apparently warned Crooks and Jory of the fact that they were impinging on his property and in a final act of desperation, told them not to come any further than a tree stump that marked his boundary. Well, as fate would have it, Crooks and Jory ignored this warning more than once, and one of them, or perhaps my grandfather, drew a gun one day and the feud was on. Rifle and pistol shots were exchanged and Lucius, apparently the better shot, fell both of them dead. He then went home and told Emma what had happened.

Word quickly got around and the next day a local man (who later would be the local sheriff) named James M. Blakely, rode out to my grandfather's cabin to see what was going on. Blakely described all this in a two-part series he wrote years later in the leading local newspaper, *The Oregonian*. In the distance, he accounts, Langdon got on a white horse and begin to gallop away. He called out to him, identifying himself, and Langdon stopped, returned and they talked briefly about the incident before going into the house for dinner. Blakely further remarked, as an aside, that, "Mrs. Langdon is quite the cook!" The casual nature, given the circumstance, is to be noted. They talked over dinner regarding what had happened and what was to be done. There being two sides to any story, my grandfather was apparently thinking that he had repeatedly warned them, and they drew first, so his side of the story was, the others were not in a position to give theirs. The soon-to-be sheriff and Granddad agreed that Lucius would accompany Blakely to Prineville and be held there the night before being transferred the following day to the county seat known as The Dalles. The Dalles had the only real jail in the area, Prineville having no such facility to incarcerate Langdon until a trial could be had. When they arrived in Prineville, Lucius was shackled to a bed in the local hotel. All might have proceeded through the wheels of justice, except that very night a group of 10 local men broke into the room Lucius was lying in, over-powered (supposedly) the local sheriff, and shot Lucius dead. The next day they found Lucius' hired hand, who had nothing to do with the incident, dragged him down Main Street and hung him from a bridge. It's apparent this group of citizen vigilantes had other motives in mind when it came to this incident, some saying it had to do with the movement of sheep and cattle in the valley. Thus began what would be a 10-year vigilante period in the region where others met their own fate at the hands of those who wanted things their way, including ideas regarding who could ranch, move what where, and be influential in local matters. Incidentally, when Grandma Emma learned what had happened to her husband, she came to town to get some answers. She purchased a pistol at a local store and confronted one of the vigilantes. No answer came forth and she retreated to claim her husband's body. A couple of months later my father was born on September 2, 1882. After a year or so, Grandmother moved elsewhere to Oregon, remarried, and had other children. It's noteworthy, by the way, that the two wives apparently remained friends, most likely knowing between them that these were men with no better means than guns to settle things so foolishly. A subsequent trial proved that the land in dispute was indeed Langdon's. Grandma died in 1937. I never met her, unfortunately.

With my father's origin laced with such high drama, you'd hope that my mother's story would have been a more normal one, but it too was certainly equally fascinating as my dad's. Born March 3, 1911, in Jamestown, New York, mother was the first child of Hazel Jenner Smith and Apollina Boehler. She was 4 when she and her only sister, Helen, were uprooted from Jamestown and sent west—really west! The triggering event that initiated this abrupt relocation to what must have seemed like a foreign land began with the discovery by Hazel that his wife, Appie, as she was known by her nickname, had had an illicit affair. Hazel, obviously incensed to say the least, rather than pursue a normal course of divorce or reconciliation, took their two children, boarded them on a train with his mother (their grandmother) and sent them to live with his sister Bessie. The thing is, Bessie lived in a small town far out west in Hailey, Idaho, where she was a nurse for the only local hospital.

Imagine getting off on the lonely small wooden train siding with the name Hailey on it after days of journey, plucked from the very loving arms of your mother? Neither would see their mother again, or for that matter even know where she lived or when she died until notified by relatives. Fortunately, the girls' grandmother was the most loving soul one could ask for. Though they were extremely poor, the grandmother knitted beautiful dresses, fed, and nurtured them, making each girl proud of what they had to wear; though otherwise poor. My mother continued to live with her grandma and aunt into her mid-teens, excelled at her education, completed the 10th grade, and loved sports. She often recounted going by horse-drawn sled in the snow, to another local village to play her favorite sport, basketball. I have a team photo of her and her teammates in quite stylish outfits! Oh, and she was a County Spelling Champion! At one such tournament, she recounted how she failed on the word, "acquaintance." She used to tell us she never knew why she didn't correctly spell that word she knew so very well.

With the death and without the support of Grandma Lyla, life took another major jolt on par with having to get on the train 9 years prior. Mother was thirteen when her Grandma died, and she and her sister continued to live another three years with their Aunt Bessie in Bellevue. However when she was 16, and considered an adult, she sought and found a job in another town, Twin Falls, Idaho some 70 miles south of Hailey. She learned of the job through a friend that lived in the nearby town of Gooding, Idaho. The job involved tending to a woman in her last year of life. That woman's name was Myrtle Munn Langdon and she had 3 children, two boys and a girl. The older boy, Lynn, was only two years younger than our mother. Their father, as the story goes, set a clear boundary that this 16-year-old girl was there to attend to his dying wife due to his sometimes being away for work. Apparently, he wasn't averse to taking his sons behind the barn for any lesson unheeded. The children, as Mother often said, did mind themselves.

Marian attended Myrtle Munn and they apparently became very close, but the friendship and the hospice would last barely a year before

Myrtle's passing. Now what was to be done with our mother's life, again solely on her own without a place to stay or food to eat? She could not stay as a single young woman with the family she was caring for. This was the period of time leading up to the Great Depression, and economic times were hard. Thus the circumstances she found herself became for her really a question of survival, especially as a young single woman without other means of support. In those days, what you did and why was more driven by the reality of life's mere existence than any question like love. In today's world, a concept like, "love" may prevail, but in those days not so much. Most living was driven by survival as necessitated by economic conditions. So this man with three children turned to that youngster (now all of 17-years old) and proposed that she marry him, continue with supervision of his children, and they would make a life together. After ever-so-brief discussion, she said, "yes." Can you imagine what that took? The condensed version of what happened is that it worked! I'll explain how.

Mother & Father with Dorothy seated on their car shortly after marriage

46

Marian Orena (Jenner) Smith, my mother, born March 3, 1911, had just married a man 29 years her senior. He had three children, the oldest close to her age, and she was now co-head of a household. Do you wonder what it was like for those children to take directions from their fellow teenage mother? As I only learned decades later from her and my oldest siblings, they all recognized that they depended on one another and therefore needed to make their existing age differences (or lack thereof) work. In the process of doing so, they came to love one another deeply and with profound respect that lasted all the decades of their existence. How wonderful for the first three children, especially when you consider that the five children that followed were seamlessly mixed into a family of nine. (Note: Bert and Myrle's first baby, Louise Lezel, lived only a few months and died in 1912. How I personally found this out is an interesting tale that I shall divulge later.)

At the time of their marriage, my father was still working as a hide broker, roaming around the nearby counties making deals with ranchers and farmers. This included buying sheep pelts from the herds tended by the Basques out in the desert areas of Idaho. He apparently got to know many a Basque in their solitary existence, tending to their flocks while living in their uniquely fitted horse drawn sheep wagons. Bert, as he was known to most others, was a self-starter and diligent man, but in those days, he was away from home a lot and that surely took its toll on his new bride.

As the family was expanding, Mother was taking a more active role in the business, first tending to the books, and then meeting various customer needs of their fledging business, L.L. Langdon. Initially dealing only in wool, furs, hides, and pelts, they would soon add other commodities. The Depression was barely in the review mirror, and the Second World War was looming. This clearly related to how they expanded the business. Used-up metals became an industrial need since things lying rusting and no longer used could be made into, if not a gold mine, then certainly a living. Metal was to be found all over the countryside in the form of worn-out farm machinery, in the cities because of small businesses like auto repair and light manufacturing, and down virtually any alley or vacant lot in small towns in the form of things like worn out stoves, refrigerators, lawn mowers, and the like. Much of this had literally rusted from lack of use during the Depression era. Businesses of all kinds began to gather up their discarded metal items and earn needed cash for recovery. Even kids could pick the scrap discarded there in many an alley and make nickels and dimes. Farmers could get something for what was rusting in the field or in the barn. Small businesses like auto repair, manufacturing, or even the local newspaper which needed to dispose of the type used for printing, could cash in on their old unused and outdated equipment. These "scrap" items needed a new home and to be out of the way, not piled in vacant lots and fields. That home would be the new recycling efforts like my parents' business. In those days, however, it didn't sound so pretty or environmentally beneficial. It was called "scrap metal"—a name that didn't exactly sound like something you'd like to be involved with, but to my parents it made sense. They started to accumulate lesser amounts first that became mountains of scrap in various locations in our town as the business grew. A little more detail on this unusual business is to follow, as it speaks so clearly of the man and woman who were our parents and running such an enterprise.

By 1946, L. L. Langdon, named after our father, had evolved from a married couple mainly running and doing the business without a physical office to a fledgling, but surviving business with a permanent warehouse in Twin Falls, Idaho. While the wool, hides, furs, and pelts part of the business was still steady, the business would not last too much longer with only those commodities to buy and sell. The aftermath of the war had brought forth the development of plastics and other synthetic materials. Thus, the need for natural, animal byproducts such as furs and pelts were fading, although gradually. My father died February 1, 1946, when I was 7, and our mother, with six children still at home (two others out on their own), literally got up the morning after he passed and for the next 40-years ran and expanded the business offerings. The reality of this was best expressed many years later when she was selected as Mother of Year (1952) and when asked to speak on the topic of "courage" as it related to her life, she noted to others:

I believe that it takes courage on mothers parts more and more as we face life today. In my personal life the greatest of courage I believe came when I faced the fact nearly seven years ago (when her husband had died and she was only 35) that I was left alone with six children to support. I had a very strange feeling and a very strong sense of courage that (next) day when I went to the office and unlocked the door and knew that from then on, I must run my business and look after my family alone.

When I say, ran the business, I mean ran it in the total sense of her direct involvement as both sole owner and management, as well as lead worker in what was generally a "man's business": knowing the value of everything bought, including its resale value, dealing with all kinds of recyclers (tanners, steel mills, etc.), using an acetylene torch to cut iron of varying sizes and shapes, arranging for and loading railroad cars to fill with scrap metal, driving a big truck, managing a work crew of men, and not being squeamish at handling a dirty, smelly horse hide, in addition to changing diapers and dealing with several teenagers. It was to her, and of course for us, a question of survival. Our mother stepped up to the plate in ways that I shall illuminate and make you wonder how she did it. Here's a picture of her typical day.

Mother would rise around 6 to 6:30 a.m., put on a long-sleeved flannel shirt, Levi's, and a bandana that tied back her brownish, medium-length hair. She slipped into a set of cowboy boots and strapped a Striker (scratch-lighter) to her side with a huge (six inch) safety-pin, along with a pair of shade-type rounded googles around her neck. Leather gloves and other paraphernalia for the job were at "The Yard" and would be picked up there always before 8:00 a.m., earlier if needed. No need to drive her family car to The Yard or elsewhere, as most often work was just a block or two away. There she had a pickup or the larger truck, known affectionately as "Old Ironsides," or simply, "Ironsides," to drive. Later in life as things got better, she was fond of driving her pink Buick that she loved, but only for pleasure, not work. She could easily walk to work.

As part of The Warehouse there was a hoist mounted to a truck for lifting really heavy items, a large weighing scales on four casters, knives for cutting ears off hides, and other tools of the trade like wire snippers. As she walked to her "office," I wonder what she thought as she had a few moments of peace before what was going to be yet another surely back-breaking day. Oh yes, she wore false teeth, by the way, and had one set for everyday use while the other was for work. Wonder why? Well, when you are cutting iron with a torch the sparks fly and your uncovered mouth is subject to flying metal, as is any other part of your body. As her youngest child I was known to play jokes on her such as putting a slice of Wonder Bread between those teeth as they lay by her bedside. When she awoke in the morning to find them her laughter was profound as it expressed love she had for her prank prone, playful child.

She would open up The Warehouse office by the front door, throw down her green Twin Falls Bank and Trust money sack for change and payments to customers under the counter. She would generally dispense change directly from the money sack, although she had a small cash register on the counter there in the office area. Then she'd walk down the long hallway and pull back the sliding (unlocked) doors on either side of The Warehouse. Everything else was open and subject at any time to those who might steal some items to resell to her or the only other competitor in town. Scrap items were not often stolen, and if they had been she would likely recognize them when they returned to her for purchase a second time. She had a sharp memory for the layout and contents of The Yard and other locations; it was like knowing all the pieces of a puzzle. She could overlook certain things, but would not put-up with being taken advantage of, especially as a woman in a predominately, if not exclusively, man's business.

Local merchants, or the more curious sorts, looking for this or that to build or repair something, tended to come in the early morning before their day got busy. Farmers with their scrap tended to come after noon as their work in the early morning fields demanded their attention before the sun got too hot. She would first balance the scales used for judging how much items weighed; their accuracy would sometimes be affected by dust accumulation, bits and pieces of this or that, or simply the outside temperature shifts of the seasons. She was meticulous about the accuracy of those scales as she had a work ethic that did not allow for cheating anyone from what was due them. At the same time, she had an eye for those who might attempt to do so in pulling tricks such as adding a bit of water to a hide or pelt to make it heavier than it truly was.

Work was year-round; particularly the need to cut iron for shipment that was never ending as pile after pile stacked up in numerous locations. She would usually check the two tall bottles of gas, acetylene and oxygen, which fed her cutting torch. The heavy iron bottles were mounted to a hand-truck and secured by chains that keep them in place. The steel mill required that iron be cut into acceptable lengths (5 feet or less) for shipment by rail and then for placement in furnaces to forge steel. If a gas bottle—a sizable 6', 14" diameter metal cylinder—was empty, she disconnected it with a wrench, set that one aside, then tipped and rolled a full 90-pound bottle on its bottom edge and eased it over to the hand truck where she secured it with the chain. She'd turn on the valves at the top of each bottle and you could hear the gas whiz through the 20 feet of hose to the brass torch itself. The shiny, twenty-inch length brass torch had two swivel knobs on the lower end where the gas hoses connected. These were used to adjust the amount of gas and intensity of the flame that shot out the end with a tip to it. She had the "striker" pinned to her right side and grasped it to be ready as she turned one of the knobs and it released acetylene gas, that she lit with a loud spark. A bright orange and slightly bluish flame would zoom with flashing intensity, much faster and louder than, say, a gas burner on your stovetop. She then magnified the flame to increase its temperature for cutting by releasing enough oxygen to create a smooth blue tapered flame about three to four inches long. The increasing sound of the flame demanded your attention, and she was adept at knowing when the flame was right.

Applying the torch tip close to, but not touching, a piece of iron, and moving the flame along, she would gradually slice the metal in half and the way it looked was as if butter were melting to the ground (thus the importance of the cowboy boots). It caused a bit of a Fourth of July effect, with sparks shooting off in all directions. Bits of iron dripped mostly down, but occasionally flared in multiple directions. If not careful and attentive to your work, sparks might ignite (and occasionally did) a pant leg, paper or oil laying nearby, or sear up toward your eyes (hence the goggles) or catch you on the cheek or burn your gloves or pit your false teeth. You never, never cut near a leftover gas tank that had been extracted from a car or old farm machinery. She would cut iron this way, ever so slightly bent over, for hours, going through iron pile, after pile, of various lengths and forms. She could devour a whole car frame, a piece of farm machinery, or cut an old water tank in half. As a kid I would sometimes come to The Yard to ask her a question but end up first sitting there on a rusted water tank watching her doing this work. She seemed to experience some kind of meditation like a Buddhist monk, and I'd observe her bobbing her head now and then as if at church saying the rosary. She was not Catholic, except in the small "c" sense, and her spiritual side was strong. I didn't like to startle her, and eventually she would notice me, turn off the torch, and ask, "What's up?" I might say that I was just bored, and she'd ask what I'd like to do (as if I had the answer)? Always patient, I think she liked the break and talking to her son until the work must, inevitably, continue, one piece of iron after another. I'd depart and she would strike up the torch again.

When her long workday was done, she'd typically come home around 6:00 p.m. You always knew she was home even if you didn't hear the front door. She always went first to her bedroom and threw the money sack under her dresser with a thud and clink of the silver dollars and other loose change it contained. She was grimy with dirt and grease from head to foot. Her skin was always a fine tan, as she had spent much of the day in the sun. She had worn goggles while torching and when

*Mother using Acetylene Cutting Torch to
separate an old water tank in half*

removed, there were two large circles of clean skin with deep blue eyes in the center. It kind of reminded me of a raccoon, not just because of the eyes, but how they stare piercingly at you and you alone. After the usual greetings and questions about how the day was for her children, she'd go to the bathroom and run a bath. She would soon emerge ever so much a woman, having left in the tub the manly ghost of her workday. She looked as if she were going to an evening event in a bright colorful flowery dress. She was an attractive woman but presented by her work and attire a male image for the workday, yet clearly a woman all other times. What a lesson for a young boy to know the difference, the really fine line between male and female. I am, to this day, simply in awe of her presence in all the years she was with us. Others were as well, as she was recognized in her community for her civic volunteer efforts, in addition to her unusual profession. She was named "Mother of the Year" in our county, then in the State, and eventually was selected nationally as first runner-up for "Mother of Year" in 1952. How about that!

Marian Orena Smith Langdon as
a young widowed mother of 8

Now on to the rest of the Langdon tribe.

Our mother, quoted in an article in the local *Twin Falls Times News* on August 9, 1952, said of her children:

"A child reminds me of a flower."

The reporter noted: "She hesitated for a moment to find words to express her thoughts."

"I guess it's the way they seem to unfold from birth."

She went on to also say in that same article:

"It's hard to tell anyone how I raised my kids. Each one seemed to help the next one. I can honestly say that not one of them ever gave me any trouble. I never could have made it if they had."

As was previously noted, my father was married before and had four children:

The first, Louise, died as a baby.

Lynn, the second, was 25 years older than me.

Archie, who was 21years older.

Dorothy, who was 14 years older.

Then there are five children of my mother and father:

Lucille, 8 years older than me

Bertine, 5 years older

Buzz, 3 years older

Lorraine, 2 years older

and of course me, Danny, born in 1938.

I loved, looked up to and adored each and every one of my siblings for a wide variety of reasons. Mainly, we had a way of honoring one another and not tearing each other down with jealousy or feelings of superiority, or just plain meanness. Psychologists have noted that warmth and structure are the two most important qualities in raising children. We had both in great quantity! The older ages of the first group of children naturally distinguished them from the second group that followed. This was largely because the first family had its own dynamics prior to the arrival of the second group, if in no other way than having different mothers, the absence of the father due to his work, and other factors. For example, the older group seem to be influenced in their view of life towards work immediately upon maturing. I largely attributed this to our father's view of the need for work just to survive. That was something of his generation, placing priority on the need to make a living because of hard times. He was very much influenced by the Great Depression of the 1930s. Thus, the first group of three did not think or perhaps aspire necessarily to further education beyond high school. I don't think our mutual father was a big advocate for education beyond getting a job. Our mother, in contrast, highly valued education and encouraged us all to pursue it, she herself having only been able to attend the 10th grade due to economic circumstances and the death of her grandmother. Still, even with this difference, there were no judgments about whether being more educated or not made a relationship different, but rather the relationship was to be cherished for what it was. Good work was valued as much as a good education. Circumstance is often an opportunity realized.

Now, a little needs to be said about each sibling as they individually influenced my life, as if in no other way, than being their "baby brother."

Quite understandably, Lynn (1913-1998) was the one brother and sibling that I knew the least about and I spent months and years trying to know and understand him. He was out of the house, married and had his first child (thus I have a niece older than me) before I came to be. He and his wife, Lois, had two children, JoAnne and Lauren. He was an industrious soul, following in our father's footsteps by setting up essentially the same kind of business in a town not far away. He eventually expanded his business to metal fabrication to support local farming needs and made lots of money doing so. We would get together for family Christmases and so he seemed perhaps more like an uncle than a brother. Gradually over the years I would stop by his business and we would chat about his life and mine. He was quite the collector of coins, stamps, Mayan artifacts, carnival glass, and whatever else he felt had value and interest to him, in that order. I think he had the drive for wealth perhaps more than any of us and he didn't mind talking about it. He was kind of a miser in his own way. We did virtually nothing together like I did with my other brothers, but I valued his obvious affection and support of me as a sibling. I was, when you think about it, probably a curiosity to him being so many years younger in age.

Archie (1917-1993), the next oldest, was a bit more like the father I needed, and a great brother. I loved the man and the person. He too, like Lynn, was out on his own by the time I was born so we never lived together. However when I was in the fifth grade, my mother had me go to Archie and his wife, Mary Sue's house, close to my elementary school, for lunch. Along with their three children (Lana Fern, David, and Robert) and Mary Sue's father, we would have a meal together. I'm

Mother with seven of her children (Buzz had passed) at a family reunion

not sure to this date what that was about—probably I wasn't eating enough of my lunch provided at school, or Mother felt I needed to get to know their family more since he and I had not lived together. It didn't matter; going there to eat was fine with me, and it soon stopped as quickly as it started.

When I was a teen, Archie and I used to get up at 5:00 a.m. He'd make buttermilk pancakes and drive us several miles to one of his favorite hunting spots on the Snake River near Thousand Springs. He always invited me along, sometimes with a hunting buddy of his named Buck. Archie was an avid outdoor guy and fisherman, as were our dad and mother. Most of all he had a winning personality, exhibited to everyone by his wide smile and laughter all contained in a tall, lanky frame. He was a service guy to his community who worked in a shipyard during the war welding Liberty Ships, who made friends easily, and who always had an ear for a young boy trying to find his way. He worked for our older brother in the metal fabricating business and made the business click with his personable ability to meet and service customer needs. I often stopped by his office in their satellite location, in Twin Falls just beyond the Singing Bridge, just to hang and hear him laugh and this went on well into my 40s. He always, always said he was proud of his youngest brother and my accomplishments. I certainly loved him in return for the man he was, and especially for being my big brother.

As a closing note while describing Archie, it was at his funeral that I learned I had another sister, Louise. After his funeral service I was reading Archie's obituary at the family gathering and noted that it said Archie was one of nine children. I immediately announced to the gathered family that this was some kind of printing error as I was only aware that we were eight in number. Half of the group of brothers and sisters present there in the room confirmed that it was eight and the other half said nine. It seems that after her death, Louise's name did come up on occasion in family conversation, but after some years when recollections faded, the name was not brought up as often, so the other half of us kids born much later did not know of her. Yes, there were nine children as I learned on that very day! I had another sister and I was glad to learn so. Still to this day, I have to catch myself when asked how many siblings I have, was it eight or is it nine?

Sister Dorothy (1924-2008), the oldest sister, was the family outlier, and I mean that in the most affectionate way. She was simply different. "A cowgirl through and through" I said in my eulogy at her passing, in that she was the embodiment of a spaghetti western movie at its very best. In her teenage years she had a horse on which she could out-ride any cowpoke. She did barrel-racing and was selected later in life for the Idaho Cowboy Hall of Fame. She and her husband, Carl, have had three different ranches during my life span, and I often went to each for a few weeks during the summer. There I could experience a different way of life and interact with their two children, Mary and Jenny. I would additionally have the opportunities to meet their rancher friends and learn about their rather conservative attitude towards life. They were always so welcoming to a young kid, especially since that kid was Dorothy's little baby brother, as she was so prone and proud to announce. These rancher friends allowed me sole access to their land where I would fish for hours, the only person on the stream. If someone else showed up (very rarely), I'd likely stop fishing as their presence had probably ruined for the day any spot I might turn to fish. Of course that made no sense, but even to this day I find it very hard to fish in the presence of others, a fact that keeps me from fishing almost altogether. Dorothy was very conservative, and I told her at one point that one of my daughters was gay and she had better get used to it. She did and I was ever so grateful to her for being truly my sister on that day and every other day. I told her how proud I was of her. I spoke of her love in the eulogy I gave at her passing. I'll never forget those 24 cowboys in their black Stenson hats seated in the last row of the church pews. Several came up after and thanked me for my words, and I got the distinct feeling they related to my words about my gay daughter and Dorothy's acceptance of that fact! Now that is a sister!

Now we come to the other five children of Marian Orena Smith Langdon. If there is anything in life my mother cherished it was her children. She apparently wanted plenty of them and had them. This was interesting since our father felt he had plenty already, but he wasn't the one to prevail, as it turned out. Makes you wonder what the dynamics were between them when it came to the subject of children. The results speak for themselves. I sure am glad it did, as I was the last of their offspring.

The oldest, Lucille (1931-2023), set the standard for the four others who followed. She often ended up being a surrogate mother, but yet still knew where generally to draw the boundary between that role and the one as a fellow sibling. Still, you knew you could turn to her when and if needed. Most of us are very independent, perhaps learned through necessity, so mothering by her was rarely needed. I think we final five, including Lucille, knew we had the backup of the real mom at any time, and we freely used it as needed.

Lucille was talented, popular in high school, and loved drama (and being dramatic). When she graduated from high school, she went immediately to live in the Los Angeles area while attending ballet school and furthering her interest in tap and modern dance. She lived with her former dance instructor from Twin Falls in Burbank. With encouragement from a new friend she met at USC, she heard that one could major in dance at UCLA, so she walked into the registrar's office one day and announced that she wanted to attend that coming semester. They must have thought her very brash, yet driven, as they were willing to work with her, and she was admitted that Fall. She called Mother by phone, explained her plan, and Mother approved. She choreographed numerous productions for the university and graduated with honors in both choreography and dance, for which she received a life-time achievement award from the university. She met and married her Navy commander husband, John Townley, as a fellow student at UCLA and they had three children, Mark, Mitch, and Kristen. Over 40 years she taught hundreds of dance students and lived, and taught, in various parts of the world. I was fortunate enough to be part of helping her, as a teenager in building sets and managing the lights for her yearly dance recital performed for the community, highlighting the many talents of their children. Besides, it was a terrific way for me to meet girls of my own age. She did a nice job of setting the stage of life as well for her immediate siblings, and we forever appreciated what she did for us.

Sister Bertine (1933-2014), or Tina to most, was for her immediate siblings our version of Dorothy with a different twist. She studied one year at UCLA, then another at what was then Colorado Women's College, but then decided that the academic thing was not for her. She was so much like our mother and indeed, years later, was selected herself as the Idaho State Mother of The Year. She married a well-educated dairy farmer, Kent Paynter, and they settled in rural New Plymouth, Idaho. They had a remarkably successful dairy operation of prized Black Angus stock. Kent was also a part-time dairy inspector. It was in this capacity that he was killed in a train accident when he and his coworker not able to see due to the tall weeds at a rural railroad crossing, there was a train that was headed their way as they crossed over the tracks. Like her mother had, Bertine rose to the occasion and went on to raise and educate four fine children (Lisa, Jeff, Marian, and Charlie) all through college, have many grandchildren, and be a community leader, organizing the county fair for many years. Her laugh, like Archie's, was special and her love for her brothers was unceasing. We had great times together. When I needed solid advice, she was the one I would turn to, as she had all the insight of our mother. She was also the leader who organized our mother's retirement. Our mother went to live on Tina's farm in her later years, in her own house, that provided independent living she was so prone to enjoy. She so loved to be in the daily presence of her grandchildren, as much as they loved being in hers. We took care of our mother in her retirement as she had so dutifully, and lovingly, taken care of us as her children. I know this all happened because of the love Bertine had for her family of origin and her baby brother was so honored to be loved by her.

Buzz (1935-1988) was my big brother. Another Lambert Lucius Langdon (Jr.), he chose to go by his nickname as he wasn't enamored with his legal name. Buzz was short in stature, but big in setting an example. If Mother said to take me with him while he was out with his friends, he did so without complaint. His friends knew Mrs. Langdon, whom they all respected, meant business, and they would include me in. He was quite a thespian, athlete, and immensely popular one in high school. He loved baseball, basketball, and swimming, all of which he excelled at. He married his high school sweetheart, Sue, and they had three children, Holly, Barry, and Tim. With a degree from the University of Utah, he had a successful career in broadcasting and in the newspaper business. He helped me get a job at our newly formed local TV station as a cameraman, an incredibly fun job to have as a teen. He was head of the local Chamber of Commerce when he died at an early age due to pancreatic cancer. The visitor center on the outside of town, on the rim of the Snake River Canyon, was named in honor of Buzz. At a celebration of his life as a character actor in many a local little theatre production (i.e. think Rumpelstiltskin), 800 people showed up to show their love for him. I am so proud to say that Buzz was my (sort of) big brother. He was, like me, a smart aleck; something I surely must have learned from him.

Brother Buzz (Lambert Lucius Langdon Jr.)

The sibling closest to me in age is my sister Lorraine Lyla (1936-Present). (Note another name involving the use of "Ls.") Even though she was the closest to me in age, I don't know that we had a lot of interaction growing up, other than our ever-present family activities of course. What I mean is that we didn't generally play with one another. That was okay, as we had a relationship in which we could support one another as the time and activity required. We worked together at the baseball park where she managed the concession stand under the stadium. That was my very first job and she helped mentor the new employee that I was. But she had the most significance to me in a personal way, and that was in my spiritual growth. I have always said to others that I learned of Jesus in the backseat of an old Ford. That is to say, I was in the back seat while she held me captive from the front seat one evening as we returned from a high school event. In what must have been one of her early attempts at evangelizing, she tried to convert me from my elementary Christian belief to a more profound one. She was successful to a degree, although I have built on that rock my own version of what it means to believe and serve—not surprisingly a remarkably close version of our mother's spiritual practices. It's interesting that Lorraine went forth in her life, with her husband, Jim Hiskey, to be a spiritual advisor to many young college level students, politicians, and other adults through their Christian ministry. They have three children, Peter, Paul, and Michelle. She is still around trying to outlive me! She was very helpful in my college days. We both attended the same university, so I had her to turn to during my emotional adjustments getting used to collegiate life and ways.

So, that's my aggregate blended family unit, a brief introduction to the business where I grew up, and next we come to the extraordinary combination of living environments where this all took place. I'll describe this in concentric circles of expanding experiences, gradually getting to the greater outside world through comfort with each experience, lessons learned, and mistakes I made, not to be repeated. I'll describe how this unfolded and the wealth of knowledge it taught me as it shaped what has turned out to be a full and productive life. Mine has been the product of a great family, combined with being part of the lucky (not silent) generation that made me very aware and comfortable with myself, my surroundings, and the world at large.

CHAPTER 3

The Langdon Family at Home
or Living Outdoors

As I began the account of my life story on the very first page, I noted I was born in The Warehouse in 1938. I resided and endured there for only about 14 months. I deliberately say "endured" as The Warehouse was clearly not conducive for continued family living, particularly as the kids got older and wanted friends over. However, we were there due to economic necessity and that was okay for us kids who saw it more as an adventure. Certainly the array of business commodities scattered about The Warehouse was a constant reminder of the unusual business and living arrangement that it was. As noted about each of us, we survived and thrived in spite of the unusual nature of that living environment. The Warehouse became both a business and a home for a while until the better improved accommodation of a real home was economically possible.

The history and use of The Warehouse as a business has already been described, but its use as a temporary family residence is to be especially noted for its uniqueness, if not its very oddity that others might find beyond the pale. I was too young to remember much, but I can assure you that my brothers and sisters cherished the days and activities spent there in that odd living arrangement.

It's important to note that our parents, with a family of five in 1933, were struggling to survive. They moved between assorted temporary rental housing and paired this with regularly camping the entire summer out of doors over the course of ten years. This was done to save money and they lived this way after the Great Depression from about 1935 until 1945. As mother noted in a recorded conversation I had with her, money was tight and they had to do some unusual things to survive. For example, when the warehouse was acquired in 1933 mother, somewhat over the objection of father, proposed that the family live for a while in the newly rented warehouse to save money, which meant living physically with all the commodities that were then part of the business, namely at that period of time hides, wool, furs, and pelts. Obviously, the challenge was to keep family and commodities apart as much as that might be possible, and it could only be done if everyone could allow for dealing with the smell, the physical presence of items that caused the odor, and customers coming in and out. The question became a matter of physical layout, keeping the family apart from the business as much as possible. It was, then decided that "home" would be upstairs in the open attic area and the business would occupy the entire downstairs. That seemed to make the most sense and so, given it was to be a temporary arrangement—if two years is considered temporary for anything—the upstairs was prepared for family living with what little extra money they had, which was very, very little. In doing so, they did something quite unusual, odd by any living standard.

Being used to camping in the great outdoors for extended periods of time and basic survival, they decided to hang a series of sheets from the rafters upstairs to create some semblance of private quarters for the children while the parents slept downstairs in an area just off the office. Although it wasn't pretty, it was practical, and you can understand how it might work if camping has ever been your thing, which it had often been and continued for this "Swiss Family Robinson" of their day. Aside from some heating challenges of the upstairs in the winter, it just had one other challenge and that would take some ingenuity and out of the box thinking on the part of our parents to figure it out.

From the attic there were two ways to get to the one and only bathroom in the entire Warehouse, both of which first required descending a set of creaky stairs, dimly lit by a single lightbulb dangling overhead. Once downstairs, the options were to either walk through a long hallway, pass through the office area, into the room where laundry was done, and then enter the bathroom, or turn right and walk through the hide storage area, step outside, and access the bathroom through its outside door entrance. Given these options in the dead of night, what would you have done as a kid who had to pee in the middle of the night? Can't imagine that many would think of the solution our parents hatched. Perhaps it was their junkyard mentality or the result of camping out so much. They decided, of all things, to put a drainpipe (think the downspout for rainwater from the roof of your house) through the second floor directly into the toilet below. I would love to have a picture of what that looked like and how it worked, but cellphones were not available in those days for posting to YouTube. It was practical for all its craziness and worked for "number 1", but not for "number 2." No one could ever say that our parents weren't practical, if not ingenious—and a bit crazy. That "only" lasted less than a couple of years and bathroom access became much more civil in all the years that followed—if you consider one small bathroom for everyone in our eventual permanent residence.

When The Warehouse/residence building was purchased and moved in 1935 to its permanent location, all living arrangements in the upper part of the warehouse came to an end. Although economic conditions for the family were slowly improving with a permanent warehouse location, the family could still only afford to rent housing; so that is what they did up until 1945. Of these, the one most memorable to me is the one they rented on Washington Street. That house still stands to this day and is a reminder of a family in a house where they could be neighbors with others—although a distance of about a mile and a half from The Warehouse. Lots of memories were built on Washington Street with other kids our ages, but as Mother noted in later years, "the kids did not like me being so far away (on some days) working at the warehouse location." Because of this, our parents made up their minds to find a permanent location they would own within easy walking distance of The Warehouse and where the kids could also walk to school on their own.

In 1945, just over a year before our father died, they found and purchased a house only a block away from the warehouse that was located at 160 4th Avenue West—the first ever and only ever permanent house we would have at 313 4th Avenue West. It became the permanent residence for what was, at the time, the remaining 6 children still young enough to be in residence (and we were soon to number 5, as Dorothy would soon marry). Because of his illness and due to lack of space at the new house, Father, and Mother, continued living in the warehouse while the kids, supervised by older sister Dorothy, lived the first year on their own in the new residence, Mother going back and forth to attend to general family needs. Our Father was pretty much bed-ridden and in need of hospice attention from mother and there was no room really in the new residence for him. I also think Father would not have wanted so many kids running around as he agonized in discomfort when he lay dying.

The house at 313 4th Avenue West (which has since been relocated on farmland south of town) wasn't a big house by any stretch and trying to house 6 children was going to be a challenge. It met all the other requirements they desired in terms of convenience to the business, a residential area of neighborhood houses, a small corner grocer just a block away, and easy walking to both the elementary and junior and senior high school we would attend. As was always the case with our parents and their brood, we made do with what was available to meet the circumstances. A little background will help understand why the new living arrangements could work.

Times were different in those days. People didn't generally, in small towns like Twin Falls, even lock their doors! Even in our less desirable side of town it was safe to walk around and talk to others. Crime rarely existed and if it did it was pretty much petty theft, including junk metals. Murders were unheard of. Break-ins just didn't happen. Kids were safe in their own neighborhood and other parents kept an eye out for one another. People were outside in the evenings, sitting on their porches as the neighborhood kids often played till dark and sometimes under the streetlights. As it turned out, our kind of living arrangement worked because these circumstances existed, let alone the cooperative attitudes of every child concerned. The house was what our parents could afford to assure general family welfare as they were climbing steadily over the years to greater economic security. They now had their own warehouse for a permanent business and now a permanent home ideally located nearby. This was stability like they had never known and the end to the days of renting and sometimes living out in the open, although camping for several more years would continue on the Little Wood River because everyone so enjoyed being there and together.

Our house was certainly not more than 1500 square feet. It had two and a half bedrooms, one bath, a front porch, a large living/dining room combination, a smallish kitchen, and a small back porch with lots of windows where the sun shone brightly. I have a bathroom in my current house that is bigger than the bedroom my brother and I slept in, and about the same size as the bedroom my three sisters shared. There was, in addition, an unfinished dirt cellar about 10' x 10', where canned fruit and jam in jars could be safely stored, and it housed the heating system that was initially run with coal, then later oil.

After the death of our father, our oldest sister, Dorothy, moved out and Mother moved in for good. Dorothy lived for a short year in the small house located at The Warehouse, the one Mother's father had built soon after the warehouse was purchased. Dorothy married and started her own family. Lynn and Archie were already out on their own, married and with their new families. That left Lucille, Bertine, Buzz, Lorraine, and yours truly living together with Mother at 313 4th Avenue West. It was finally, after all those years, a family truly under one permanent roof. The calming effect must have been almost tangible, but I am not certain anyone besides Mother felt the difference as such. Rather, our living outdoors, upstairs in the Warehouse, in rentals, and in varying numbers arriving and departing had been an adventure and I think taught us not only how to meet challenges but appreciate one another ever so much more. Even all those summers camping out brought us together since we were all that was present as both company and playmates. Our loving parents did the best they could over much of our formative years given the economic conditions, and we loved them for their efforts, resiliency, and the fun they created (and can now tell interesting stories about).

As I previously noted, the house had three bedrooms that could at most accommodate only two or three children. One room was, naturally, allocated to Mother. Another slept the three girls. My brother Buzz and I shared what could be best described as a half-bedroom: a kind of enclosed and heated porch area with large, multi-pane glass windows on two sides that would open to the warmth or chill of the outdoors. The boys' room would accommodate only a bunk bed, modest chest-of-drawers, and a small standalone closet. I slept on the bottom bunk where one morning I knocked a metal toy bank off the bottom slat of the upper bed on which it sat, and it smacked me squarely in the forehead. That scar is barely visible today. My three sisters all slept in one queen-sized bed, had a large chest of drawers with a mirror they shared, and a modest closet. There were two entry doors to their room: one for the single bathroom (also connected by another door on the other side to mother's room), and another door to and from the living room. They had to share minimal space for all the things that girls need. Only when a sister graduated from high school or went to college was there any additional temporary space available. The one bathroom in the house was shared by all, and it was tiny with a single sink, toilet, a bathtub, and barely enough space to accommodate each. My brother and I had to go through Mother's room to get to the bathroom—a fact that required, I am certain, Mother's patience for busy boys going in and out. To say that we were a close family is to put it mildly.

When the house was purchased in 1945 our Father was showing signs of his age—he was 63. He would die some months later in 1946. Because his heart was gradually failing, he was bedridden in his final year in a room of The Warehouse that he so dearly loved. He could never have been taken care of at a nursing home, which he would have hated, being the outdoor type that he was. He insisted on being at his version of home in the warehouse, so a room just off the office area was fitted with an adjustable hospital bed and Mother attended to him (just as she had his first wife) there during his final days, going back and forth from the business to the house a block away. He never did repose in the house he worked so long to have, but I think he preferred The Warehouse for his own reasons. Our mother stayed at The Warehouse in the evenings and attended to his needs while also transitioning the business to her sole care now that Dad could not work. This transitional period proved of critical importance to our overall family welfare when the day came that she would run the business on her own for the next 40 years.

Our home (feels wonderful to say such as I write), for all its smallness, was a warm place to live, have friends over, and promote shared, family values. We all sat together for meals in the dining room, or when just a few of us were around, we sat around the small kitchen table with its chrome metal legs and vinyl-backed red padded chairs. My sisters would be the ones to mainly prepare food as our mother, now widowed, was off working. Dorothy was shortly out on her own having married a couple of months after father's passing, and we, now numbering 5, all lived together with Mother at 313. What was important is that we were now physically in one place, eating together. There were no televisions, cellphones, computers, or other distractions back then. Everyone shared what went on at school, at play, at business, and what others needed. When we played card games, and we often did, sister Lucille would get mad when the cards didn't go her way and she would throw all her cards into the air. We had our friends over for dinner, or perhaps the night; we slept with them on the floor. We often joked that there were often so many kids in the house you didn't know which were brothers or sisters. In a way these other kids were kind of our brothers and sisters: we simply didn't have room in the house for all of us. We listened to music on a record player or the radio. We were together and it felt warm and loving, and our mother was always there. We put puzzles together and played Monopoly or other board games, and lots and lots of pinochle (the

71

card game). I got so good at pinochle that I used to, as a teen, go with my mother to her garden club games when they were short of players. I'd sit at a card table with three women, most of whom I didn't know. While they paid no attention to their cards, preferring to talk instead, this young boy did, and I often won one of the door prizes, usually an ashtray or crocheted doily. I think for me it wasn't about winning, nor the prize, but strangely about the company of women gathered. Among these, my mother was the exception given that she was a professional woman in an unusual profession. I sensed that the other women kind of envied her in a way that I did not necessarily understand. They certainly admired her and spoke glowingly of her to her young son sitting there with them at the table being serious about the cards he had been dealt.

Danny age 10 sitting in playing Pinochle
with the Ladies when one was absent

One of the most fascinating and incredibly important features of our family dynamics was how we constantly used our own brand of humor with one another. It persists even to this day and our mutual spouses, and their progeny know and use it. Perhaps we needed humor given the limited space we were all living in? Whatever the reason, it helps us live life with a certain amount of freedom; we learned not to take everything so seriously.

Our brand of humor was not that which seeks to tear down a person or make fun for the sake of fun of their thoughts, actions, and feelings. Nor did it have a storyline, as when a comedian tells a joke! Nor was it designed just to be funny; certainly not at another's expense. Rather, it's the kind that makes light of the ridiculous or the obvious. We all became quick-witted with one another and friends, and that proved of significant use when things got tense or tight. It's very useful as well in a marriage, if done right—my wife will attest to that, I am sure! Our lives together were far more valuable than the petty things that we could all worry about or use to maliciously cause another harm. This was particularly important in getting along in a physically limited living space, let alone dealing with each other as teenagers and later into the world at large as adults. I am not certain I can capture the brand of humor we use, no matter how many words or examples I give. You'll have to meet one of us in person, or perhaps glean it from some of the pages I've written here. Those married to one of us, like my wife, over time learned what that is, and when I hear my wife using that same kind of loving humor, it makes me smile in gratitude to my sisters and brothers. With respect to our mother, her remark upon hearing this type of humor was most often, "Oh, you kids!" She was definitely part of laughter together, and never the brunt of such. She was far too good a human being to ever be the subject of any kind of negative humor, thought, or action.

Eventually when the business in general was doing better and the iron pile next to the house could be moved elsewhere, Mother had a picket fence put in around the entire front and back of our house, including the lot next door. One year as a teen, I tried staining the fence using an attachment to our house vacuum cleaner; I burnt out the motor and went back to using a standard brush. I ended up throwing the vacuum in the junk pile across the alley with the P-51—it was our junk pile after all!

Grass was now growing on that barren adjacent lot where a metal jungle had once flourished next to the house, and two huge willows trees thrived, providing a bit of shade on hot days when we ate outside. As a teen I built a small patio of flagstone from the local hills and desert of Idaho and constructed a table in the center from an old wooden pioneer wagon wheel that came into The Warehouse junk. My mother amassed hundreds of such wagon wheels, some really old, from the Oregon Trail, which had literally run in front of our house. Later in life, my sister Bertine constructed a 150' fence entirely made of them on her farm. I have a couple wagon wheels still in my garden. I dug a hole behind our mother's house, not far from the patio, and installed a small pond made from a large scrap iron tank of an odd shape found in the junk. I put an old, previously used hand-water pump on top to deliver and circulate the water. It all began to look like just an ordinary house instead of the junkyard next to the house it had been. Still, across the alley remained "The Backyard" iron pile, a constant reminder of our parents' business.

Given the nature of Twin Falls as primarily a farming community, it wasn't unusual for strangers to show up at our house after business hours or even on a Sunday to proclaim that they had something to sell. My mother would accommodate what she could, and they were paid and told where to drop their "load" off in one of the scrap iron locations. As a product of this sometimes lack of division between work life and family life, we were often introduced to strangers. If our mother was not present at the knock on the door, we learned individually how to manage their needs, but often deferred their request to when she might return or could be found at one of the scrap iron piles in town. Dealing with others was for us an aspect of life quite different to the usual sheltered child. We seemed to take on the experience as a necessary part of the on-going business, though she never asked us to cut or load any part of it. It all seemed to work without an issue that I am aware of. This was noted by our brother, Archie, once when he was quoted in an article when she was selected Mother of the Year. He said, "If she used a system, no one knows what it is. She just sorts of works things in, business and social life, together. And she's a hard worker, you can say that." We certainly learned how to deal with people. I saw directly what our mother was doing out of necessity for us, and we sensed the need to do our part in living without complaint, and with much love and gratitude.

Our house was the center for all major holidays for the extended family like Christmas, Easter, Thanksgiving, and the like. A Christmas banquet necessitated a big, long dining table with leaves that could be added. With multiple chairs pulled up, it crowded nearly all the room in the dining/living area from side wall to wall. You had to suck your stomach in to get around chairs at the main table dominated by adults. It necessitated two or three card tables where the kids would sit, with the growing numbers of nieces and nephews. We always had a huge tree which seemed at odds given the size of the living/dining room combination, trying to accommodate the tree and everyone else. As we milled in anticipation and the smell of dinner permeated the rooms, some had to stand in the already crowded kitchen or back porch before being called to order. The smell of turkey or ham and all the fixings was wonderful, all prepared in that tiny kitchen. It was a dance to see how my mother and sisters could manage cooking in such small quarters. Fortunately, the refrigerator was recessed into the wall over the stairs that led down to the dirt basement. Thank goodness it was where it was in that it saved 9 square feet of precious space in the kitchen. The smell was a delight to your senses, and Mother, Lynn or Archie would carve the turkey and you could heap onto your plate plenty of white or dark meat, along with homemade dressing, sweet potatoes with marshmallows, cranberry sauce, fruit compote, peas, and pumpkin or banana cream pie for dessert.

The opening of presents at Christmas was a thrill. A bicycle for someone could be easily hidden at The Warehouse to be kept out of sight until the great reveal. The twenty or so kids (counting nieces and nephews during my teenage years) meant plenty of gifts were around the tree, even if some were pairs of socks. For a while I believed in Santa and wrote him a letter that I still have to this day saved from my mother's collection of memorabilia. He never wrote back, but I wasn't apparently disappointed! Old 8mm movie reels and 35mm slides in black and white, and later color, easily remind me of that time. Smiles abound on the film when I watch. Sweet recollection is such a warming feeling to the heart of days gone by.

In summary, before moving on to mostly to the description of me and my own life, let me summarize what it was and is like to be our version of a Langdon:

To be a Langdon you are confident in yourself. You diligently go to school (perhaps with near perfect attendance), do well, or at least think you have done well. You have a few close friends and are friendly to everyone else. You are not fooled by bad behavior or prone to treating others badly. In essence, you don't tolerate fools, or be a fool yourself. You use few words (in speech, not in writing), but those you do use have meaning and often with lots of humor to keep things light. You work hard and know what work is: I am, by the way, an internationally recognized expert on that very topic, work, that I'll explain in the chapter on my professional career. You realize everyone who's white or any other color is an immigrant just as Jesus was an immigrant (although likely not white). You value other people of other colors and foreigners because your ancestors were foreigners. You love your family and hope each will be another Langdon with the same fun and great times you have had and continue to have. Life truly can be a box of chocolates if you are lucky and can work to make it that way. According to McGill and Pearce (2005) in their book, "American Families with English Ancestors from the Colonial Era," such families, like the Langdons:

- Believe in freedom of the individual and in psychological individualism as one of the core values of Anglo Americans, particularly in middle-class families.
- Would rather not complain.
- Do not waste words.
- Gets on with the future.
- Experiences success that is evidenced by virtue.

- Believes that worried parental involvement is considered neurotic, and
- Ensures children are encouraged to go off to school alone, take the initiative, and achieve.

Having been introduced to the above referenced book by my learned wife when I was 84, apparently, I could have saved a lot of time analyzing who I was and just gotten with the program memorizing the bullet points listed above. I have so enjoyed the living of my life more than the writing and reading about it from others, but it's good to hear what others have said. Let's go on to a mostly chronological (although I skip around now and then when it seems needed) story of my life, and how that life is emblematic of what I think of as being part of a lucky family; let alone part of a lucky generation. I'll include a description of what I proactively did to make my life what it was.

CHAPTER 4

Danny Boy: Age 0 to 13

As noted, I am the baby of the family, Danny Boy.

I must say, first, that I have always liked my name and gone by Danny all my life. As my wife tells others, "That's not just a cute name I call my husband by; it's his real given name!" If you call me Dan or Daniel, it feels uncomfortable, and I might not even turn my head in recognition of your attempt to address me. To my way of thinking, Danny exudes youth and vitality. Now as an old man the name makes me feel more like a kid and I am prone on occasion to act so. Just ask my wife! So call me Danny!

I also confess that being the baby of the family—Mother's favorite as my sisters like to make note—has always been worn as a badge of honor. All her children were, of course, her favorite, but being the last I guess had a special distinction. I was certainly the beneficiary of all that loving experience and support from my siblings, and I am well aware that I sincerely appreciate it. It was a huge part of building the solid foundation of the person I am today.

Having described the setting of the Langdon living and business environment and who we are, I'll examine mostly myself and life experiences from here on. Our mother once noted, in an article written years later, that at the birth of her last child (me), she, "Prayed to God that I remain alive until he was 15 years of age." She felt, as further quoted, "After that I figure he could take care of himself." Because she had had

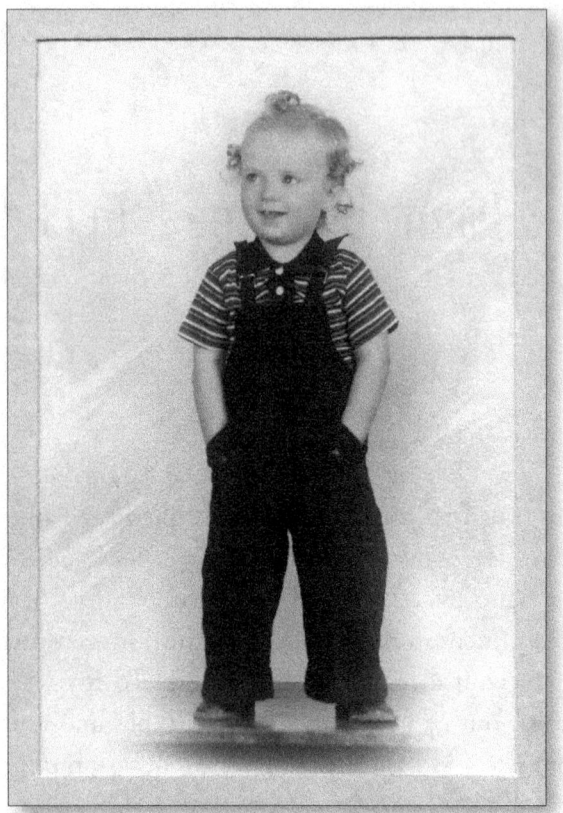

*Danny – Age 3 with locks curled
by his adoring sisters*

to go out on her own at age 16, it is not surprising why she chose that particular age. She not only lived to see her son turn15, but 58. She was later quoted to have changed her prayer to God after I had reached that tender age of 15, to "getting all my children through college." She lived to see that as well.

I want to start by especially noting that my brothers and sisters always, always set a good example for me—except perhaps for my brother, Buzz, when he smoked awful cigars for a while in his teens. Sitting with him and his friends in the back of a canvas covered pickup was not always a delight. Then again, they were taking me along for the ride and what a ride in life it was.

My siblings were all achievers, as I am. They had friends and I was by association, their friends' friend. They set a good example in school, and so my teachers knew them well; so I think expected something similar from me. Most of all, we had a family way of building one another up and not criticizing the others. The apple, as the saying goes, doesn't fall far from the tree! While that usually applies to parents and their children, it's also very useful to one's growth and development when you know you can count on the behavior of your siblings as a model for yourself. I sure did! Thanks to each in their own individual way.

I can say that my childhood, from 0 to 13 years of age, was great. I don't remember much prior to the first grade, but in asking others they don't either. Up until that time I stayed pretty much either at home and in the immediate vicinity of our backyard or was taken up the street by one of my siblings to the business location. One memory never forgotten happened around age 5. I was standing by my dad's truck with a garden hose in my right hand filling up the gas tank with water. I'd seen something similar at the gas station between our house and The Warehouse, so it seemed appropriate to me. When my dad and mother discovered the manner in which I was obviously trying to help the business, they quickly took the hose away and advised me not to do that again. There was no yelling or screaming, no spanking or berating. Their approach to parenting was always mild mannered, supportive, and appropriately administered.

I also do distinctly remember my dad laying in his hospital type bed and now know that those would be the last months before his death in 1946. Most other lingering memories begin at age 6. By then, my sisters took great delight in sculpting my blond hair into a curl at the top; pictures of which persist today. I am proud to say I still have most of my hair, but the curls are mostly gone except on the right front of my scalp where they practiced their delight in sculping my hair.

We had a couple of dogs, but no cats for whatever reason. When I later had a ranch, I had 9 cats, two dogs, and lots of other animals, so I am at heart an animal lover. As a kid I did have two dogs, or should I say one in that the other was really a shared family dog, Queenie. My dog was Susie. She followed me everywhere and often chased the pickup that I'd be riding in the back of for several blocks. She slept, not on my bed, but under the sheet at the very bottom every single night when I slept as a kid. I don't know how she could breathe down there, but I certainly knew her presence if I stuck a foot down too far and touched her. She would growl, if not nip you a little to stake off her territory. The thing is, Susie had only three legs, given that in her youth she tangled with a passing truck—not surprisingly on Truck Lane—and completely lost her right front leg. She could run on the remaining three legs with great agility and speed chasing after a car or pickup that invaded her territory; it seems she had not learned her lesson, but she did not lose another leg, thank goodness. The funny thing was, as a bird dog with fine short hair of black and white, she was a natural hunter. When I took her pheasant hunting in my teens, she would, by instinct, try to raise her right leg and straighten her tail in perfect pose as hunting dogs of that breed do. The problem was her right leg wasn't there, but that tail was straight back and on point! I loved that dog until she passed when I went off to college. I imagined she missed her playmate, as I did her.

Beginning in the first grade, I did have some struggles academically and that continued through to the sixth grade. You would think that this would lead to problems within, but I obviously overcame that, considering I am the author of a baker's dozen books, chapters in a dozen by other authors, and have had published numerous articles, given speeches, workshops, and lectures around the world. With some tutoring help in the 6th grade, and dogged determination on my part, and additional help from my mother and siblings, I gradually advanced in my studies. I did slightly above average academic studies, well enough that through the years—all 17 of them to the time of graduate school—were filled with building blocks that set a solid foundation for my adulthood. Here's what the problem was that got me off to a hard start.

In the first grade the school district for our class at Lincoln Elementary had decided that rather than teaching reading using the traditional phonics method, they would teach us reading by sight. I am guessing some consultants got it into their ears (or what was left between their ears) as school administrators that learning by sight was better than phonics. In other words we would learn words by their use and specific letters. That would involve lots of memorization and learning words in context. For whatever reason that approach did not fit me, and I struggled in spelling and sentence structure, and the negative consequence it had on me psychologically (as a little person who was failing in some of his studies in school). It really had a negative impact, especially on my reading skill, in which to this day I have little interest. It was bad enough that I and (I think) some others were held back from advancing to second grade. In my case that wasn't all that bad since my birthday is in November and I was the youngest for my grade level anyhow. Another year would not hurt, my first-grade teacher Mrs. McClusky concluded and suggested I repeat the first grade with her—perhaps she really liked me a lot? My ego, in silence, was a bit frayed I think, but I trucked on. I found that I liked my new first grade classmates probably more than those in my first, first grade. Odd how that worked out, as if it were meant to be that way all along!

For all my difficulties, all in all I liked my elementary school years. I still remember each of my teacher's names. There was for first grade, Mrs. McClusky, as I already mentioned, whom I had experienced twice. Two other favorites, as we all have for varying reasons, were Mrs. Holyoak for sixth grade, and Mrs. Hughes for second grade. I liked Mrs. Hughes because on Valentine's Day, she had given us all a shoe box to make a post office-like atmosphere. We found in our cardboard "mailbox" all the paper cards that each of us had prepared with crayons for that day, along with cookies. My mother, similar to the way you liked any teacher the best, was very popular with my classmates as she always provided a case of soda that was requested for the school's annual picnic. She also regularly served as a Room Mother for all her children's elementary school classes. I have in my possession a thank you card from one of those classes that must have warmed, as she liked to put it, the cockles of her heart. There's nothing like a mother who bribes her children's teachers and classmates towards popularity! It's just that she loved kids so much, and this was one of the ways she showed it, along with offering Old Ironsides, the business truck, when transportation was needed for a class activity beyond the school grounds or for the annual Boy Scout camping trip up into the mountains of Idaho.

From the period of time when I repeated the first grade until completion of elementary school, I was a below average student, as evidenced in my report cards that I still have. My teachers really liked me, thought I had potential, and tried their level best to help overcome my lack of adequate reading and writing skills. But it wasn't until the middle of the sixth grade that I finally received special needed help in the way of a private tutor my mother hired. I spent numerous sessions with a woman whose name escapes me. It was hard and tedious work for a young boy who wanted to be outside playing with all the others. It apparently worked as school studies, thereafter, while not a breeze, did get gradually better. I came to love courses in civics, some math and sciences, and while I never felt comfortable in English classes, I did make steady progress. I even drafted an essay for a contest that was highly rated and made me think I had some potential in the direction of writing. I am sure my 12th grade English teacher, Mrs. North, would have been ever so surprised to learn that her struggling student is now the author of several books! I still can't diagram sentences very well, but my composition and creative side are kept in order by the use of great editors; one of whom is my loving wife, and the copy editor of this work, Bonnie. Years later, one of my bosses mused that I should have been born as one half of conjoined twins, with my other my personal editor. He was right, and so I have made generous use of outside help for editing. Many thanks to all of you over the years. So my elementary school days I judged to be okay but challenging. Other than the school bully who threatened me on the playground for whatever reason in the 6th grade, I did fine. I'd like to leave my education aside for a while and return to it later as I now describe what it was like to be a lucky boy growing up in my neighborhood.

Danny (center second row, second seat) at
Lincoln Elementary in the fourth grade

Twin Falls, Idaho, in the 40s when I was a boy, was a small, farming community of about 10-12,000. They were mostly white, hard-working people of various ethnic backgrounds. Most of the core downtown was laid out on a grid with four corners such that subsequent streets were added perpendicular to the not quite a matrix square—more the shape similar to the State of Nevada. The reason for the odd shape is that the lower section of the downtown, generally south, runs that way along Rock Creek and the canyon through which it flows. The canyon defines much of the south side of town where we Langdons lived. The matrix of streets with its boundary was appropriately labeled in one direction as Avenues and the other as Streets (although recently they changed the streets from numbers to specific names). At the corner intersections of two of this Nevada-shaped "downtown," five roads form a five-way intersection when you enter the outer boundary of downtown from the north and east. Don't try to visualize that because it's not particularly relevant, other than if you drive to Twin Falls just be aware of what will happen when you enter the area to try to find downtown. I point out this bit of detail only because for a kid or driver, it meant that it was pretty hard to get lost downtown once you got into it, and the Langdons lived and had their business on the south side of town. Go outside that grid, and it might be another matter finding your way around. That easy downtown layout was important to me as I could go anywhere within it because we lived within it. Combine the simple layout with my pretty well-honed internal compass (the Boy Scout in me), and I could always find my way back home or to my parents' business. Just be mindful when you go into those side streets of Twin Falls, like Taylor or any of the others named after the Presidents, they are alphabetical in order and that helps. Otherwise, I never understood as a kid why the rest of Twin Falls was the way it was other than the result of sprawling urban growth!

Naturally, like any town, there are the well-appointed parts with nice houses, then those of more moderate means, and finally, "the other side of the tracks," as people are prone to declare such. We lived most definitely on the other side of the tracks—indeed there were, and still are, actual, functioning railway tracks on our side of the tracks. The reason for living where we did, on 4th Avenue West (or Truck Lane as I previously noted), made sense. My parents' business was scrap metal, hides, pelts, wool, and furs, and town folk are not generally prone to tolerate either the smell of hides—let alone a view of mountains of metal anywhere near their pretty houses and nice yards—or for that matter certain other kinds of businesses like the flour mill, stockyard, or ice plant on our side of the city. And since my mother worked primarily at The Warehouse or one of her other locations, her home needed to be close to her children for her own sanity as a mother, and of course, the demands we might make of her at our requests.

I'll provide, for the purpose of orienting you to the explanation of my growing up, a further detailed description of the physical environment of town as if walking east, then west, south, and finally north. This geographic orientation is critical to the general way I expanded my horizons throughout my young life from the time I was a kid and into adulthood where my horizons have become nearly the whole planet. It has a lot to do with the way my confidence was incrementally built to be a human truly of the world, not just the comfort of my immediate neighborhood or however you define your own comfort with the world or not. Some people, for example, never get much beyond their own community, county, or state, let alone some borders and oceans to other countries. That wasn't going to be me.

By far the most fascinating (to me at least) part of my general neighborhood and where I spent a large part of my initial play and exploration, was south, and then north of home. But I need to begin east as it was the direction where I was living and spent much of my early days. Being in my home (at 313 4th Avenue West and having immediate access across the street and down the block to 160 4th Avenue West to my parents business where they were so often to be found) was paramount both for my very being and my safety as a very young child. Therefore I often traversed east from home towards their business—primarily The Warehouse—most of the time in my initial forays into a world I knew virtually nothing about.

East

When you calculate it, my boyhood at 313 4th Avenue West was just one block and a walk across a street to The Warehouse located at 160 4th Avenue West. I could easily traverse between them on my own by around age 5. This might seem young to many of you for a child to wander on his or her own, but believe me, in those days it was safe, safe, safe. One just had to know how to get across the street at two key points, one of them being the ever-busy Truck Lane. I did! Anyone who knows me at age 86 knows that at age 5 it would not have been an issue, so don't get judgmental of my parents on this issue of my getting around!

On the right-hand side of 4th Avenue West, as you crossed the side street from our house and walked towards The Warehouse, on the corner there was a Texaco gas station where you could then buy gas for 19 cents a gallon. You could also get your oil checked and changed, water for the radiator, rubber tire innertubes pressurized, flats fixed, minor repairs made, and roadmaps to destinations both inside and outside of Idaho. All of these services were in the hands of an attendant, as you did not self-serve your gas in those days at the gas station. There were no credit cards either, so everything was in cash, or a personal check, if you were deemed trustworthy. My mother knew the owner and in turn I knew him and sometimes stopped for a brief exchange, usually over roadmaps. I especially liked to ask for and look at maps of another state so that I could imagine what it was like to be in places years before I would actually do so. Sometimes I aligned them with one another just to see how the country fit together. The owner and his attendant were always friendly and not seemingly bothered by my presence and questions. They were typically not that busy anyhow, and when they were I knew to stay out of the way but would often linger awhile to see what was going on and who came in—especially if they were from out of town as noted by the various license plates. There were lots of out-of-towners on Truck Lane since it was the chief bypass for trucks and out-of-state cars. As kids we were known to sit on the curbside grassy area at times and record the car license plate numbers by state as they passed by on Truck Lane—why I am not sure to this date. Where were they from, where were they going, and why were they so far from home--like California, New York, or Nebraska? What was sparked in the boy's imagination about seeing those states, or even the broader world? You'll discover more about this in the chapter on my travel addiction.

A little further on, continuing in the direction of The Warehouse, I would walk by small businesses that I did not really understand or care about. One was a sheet metal fabrication enterprise, but it was hard to see through the frosted windows what exactly they were up to and without that I wasn't much interested. You could, however, hear the sounds of metal being cut and crimped to make whatever it was they made therein. Across the other side of the street were mainly a few houses that eventually disappeared, replaced by other small enterprises.

Before crossing Truck Lane, directly across from the front door of The Warehouse was Young's Dairy. It fascinated me. There you could see through their windows a stream of empty glass bottles as they were filled with fresh milk. They also made ice cream. The owners, naturally named Young, knew Mrs. Langdon and I was welcomed in their business as well. But I was most often on my way to The Warehouse to see my parents, so I did not dawdle generally at any of the neighborhood businesses, except as I have noted, the gas station.

Crossing Truck Lane at 2nd Street West, where The Warehouse stood and across the side street, is where the Stu Morris Tire Company stood. Mr. Morris and my mother knew one another well given that they were in a direct line of sight of what was going on in their individual business. If space needed to be shared between them on occasion or to temporarily park their vehicles, they would accommodate one another. When he would repair a tire for one of her vehicles, he would walk across the street and let her know firsthand that it was ready. I learned from watching Mr. Morris how to change a tire but had little interest in the smelly vulcanizing process he used for retreading tires.

Just beyond where The Warehouse sat on the corner, (another hundred feet, and within the boundary of Shoshone Street that I dared not cross), was a business that I loved in my boyhood, youth, and as a man. It was the blacksmith business of Mr. Richard (Dick) Diamond. (By the way, as kids, we always referred to adults as Mr., Mrs., or Miss—never by their first name only.) He was a strong man in both brawn and character. He had a big smile, deep laughter, could cut and weld, it seemed, anything, and was kind to the boy in his presence who so enjoyed watching what he was doing. Whereas my mother cut iron in half, he welded iron together to make all sorts of things for local farms and general business needs. Later in life, he made a wagon to haul grass and leaves and such for my riding lawn mower tractor and also a feed trough from an old water heater cut in half that I used for the years when I had a small farm upstate in Star, Idaho. He and my mother were good friends. They seemed forged of the same hardy stock of people found in the metal business. On occasion he bought pieces of iron he needed for welding from her, and he sold her the pieces of leftover iron he no longer had a use for. They were both eking out a living for their families:

he often used the product of her trade, and she needed him to make things that eased her trade. Mutual admiration in their skills abounded, he as a blacksmith and her as a woman of iron in a "man's business." As a small boy with the assurance that I could safely transverse East (on a limited basis of a block or two) from my home, I set out thereafter to "Go West' young boy."

West

Boyhood friends, as it turned out, lay west and on the same block we lived at 313 4th Avenue West. Three doors down lived Donny and Sammy Harr and their sister. They had a cousin by the name of LeRoy who would sometimes be around from another part of town, but it was mostly Donny and Sammy that I palled around with. I don't remember what the Harrs did for a living, but they were very welcoming to the kid from down the block. I went there often and we all sat around on the floor listening on the radio to The Green Hornet, and The Shadow. For today's kids who have the internet, YouTube, TikTok, and television, I fear you miss out when the then primary source of entertainment was in the form of only a radio. I speak not of some fantasy period of time, but rather how, seated with others, gasping at the story line and sound, it was developing our imagination from what we were only hearing, not seeing. It was great fun for a half-hour or two, then we went outside and played in their yard or the jungle of scrap iron heaps near my home.

Sammy, Donny, and Danny played inside, outside, and eventually at my house and in the backyard scrap iron heap for as many days as our parents would allow. Our favorite activity was a game called Anti-Anti-I-Over. The Harrs' house was one-story, with a smooth single pitch roof that went up equally on the front and down on the back. The three of us, with an equal number of other local kids, would stake out our territory at the front of the house with the other team at the backside. Then, yelling, "Anti-Anti-I-Over," a tennis ball would be rolled over the roof to the other team. If they caught the ball, one of them would sneak their way from the back around one of the two sides and try to capture one of the other team members located at the front by throwing the ball to hit them if they could. Thus, if hit by the ball the victim would be yours and, on your team, now until no one was left standing. Played into the night, it was a raucous game and full of kid laughter. Combined with playing other games played mostly outside, like Hide-and-Seek, Tag, and others, we were learning how to relate. Our friendship lasted until the beginning of junior high and then broadened into other friendships, and eventually there was no more, "Anti-Anti-I-Over." Even with all this happiness and friendship, there eventually occurred an event that ended our close relationship, one that was just one of those childhood things, not to be forgotten as a lesson of life. I'll get to what that was, but I first want to confess something we were all part of that was innocent, as children will sometimes do, but could have been potentially much more compelling, if not fatal. It's something I need to get off my chest and I'll do so for Donny and Sammy as well. Fortunately, it didn't cause any death or injury; just some physical damage that I am sure was covered by the company's insurance policy. It has sat on my conscience whoa these many years.

One day the four (Donny, Sammy, LeRoy, and I) of us were over on the east side of town because that was usually the place where we could find the most fun things to do: The Hole, a creamery, onion cellar, and other venues for play. Just over a block on the north side of town we were aware of dirt that would burn. You say, "Dirt that burned, as with a flame?" Well, kind of. There was a dry-cleaning establishment—the same one where later as Boy Scouts we sold wire clothes hangers to the cleaning establishment for a fundraiser to collect money for the children's hospital ward. Perhaps that was payback for what I am about to confess? The dirt in question was actually the by-product of the dry-cleaning process used to clean clothing and such. Even as an eventual chemistry teacher, I am not certain what that chemical was, or perhaps I really didn't want to look up its chemical composition and know. In any case, if you held a lit match to the grayish dirt, it would burn with a very slight visible flame that didn't get all that hot, but it could burn you if not careful. We never, ever lit the entire pile of dirt, if that makes any difference in the level of our mischievousness, but rather only a small sample now and then. That's when we got into trouble that no one, at least in our mutual family circles, ever learned the nature of to this day. It goes like this.

We neighborhood boys had a fort we built from wooden soda bottle crates that were stacked as part of the warehouse of a famous soda company. It was quite an architectural feat for boys of nine and ten as we climbed 15 feet of gradually stacked wooden crates. These crates were the kind that when full, carried 24-bottles of soda, and were being stored outside the building until needed. Once at the top of the stack, we then climbed down the inside to where the four of us had our hideout and secret meetings. One day, as we were huddled around in the fort, one of us had brought some of the burning dirt wrapped in newsprint—not much, but enough to give the illusion of a campfire, or perhaps a burnt offering to the gods. To this day, I distinctly remember, as we were exiting our fort, asking the assembled group, "Is the dirt out?" and we were assured by someone (whose name will go unmentioned), that, "Yes, the dirt is out!" Having exited, we left in the direction of the horse corrals where my sister, Dorothy, used to keep her horse. As we reached the corral and pressed up against the wooden fencing, I looked around and saw a puff of white smoke coming from the pile of soda crates. It wasn't a very big fire, but a fire nonetheless and white smoke billowed up from the bottom of the fort like a smokestack. At that moment, we hear fire engines and we took off. Picture in your mind four kids running in the opposite direction of the fire: What were we thinking? In any case, the fire was quickly extinguished, no one and nothing was hurt, except our egos. That building is now gone, but not the memory. Sorry again about that! Danny and his friends were bad boys on that day.

It was with the Harr boys that I began to go exploring beyond the immediate neighborhood where we all lived, especially going south. Before describing the south side, the story of our eventually parting ways as friends bears mentioning here, and you'll excuse me from digressing from the West-East-South-North orientation to my life as a boy for this important occurrence that ended our days of play together.

One way or another, we got into the habit of some petty theft—not surprising considering we almost burned down a building. It wasn't much, only three times as I best recall. There wasn't anything big: just taking a candy bar here or there seemed easy, and only a small sum of guilt weighed on your mind as you consumed that delicious bar, known as a Baby Ruth. Apparently, we had enough collective conscience and fear of our parents that the four of us (me, Donny, Sammy, and LeRoy) made a pact. We would never steal again. However one day when we were downtown, I believe it was LeRoy who stole a cap gun from the 5 and 10-cent store. That was a big upgrade from a candy bar to an object you could retain and use again. That, in my boyhood mind, broke the pact and from that day forward we never palled around again. I distinctly remember to this day walking up the front steps to my house on the evening of that sordid day and saying to my conscience, "The four of us will never play together again." And we didn't. I am pleased to say that neither they nor I thereafter ever got into any serious trouble. But it was a lesson of life to be remembered forever. Years later Donny, Sammy, and I talked as adults and laughed about our adventures and times together in that neighborhood that was only a block long. It was the initial territory I adventured into and had so many useful and delightful experiences, and lessons learned. They were all important aspects of life and so beneficial for our personal development. Where we then go from there would be up to us, and as it turned out for all friends on that block, I am pleased to report that we all made the best of it.

South

By this stage of my young life I had finally gotten up the nerve—about age 10—with friends to begin exploring the area south of our home, principally the area from home to the Rock Creek Canyon. From the point of our home on 4th Avenue West, most of the roads south—5th through 7th Avenue West and 2nd Street West and 7th Street West—were generally filled with modest homes and small businesses: an onion cellar, the infamous horse corrals, and the soda-bottling warehouse. There was also a six-unit wooden, somewhat rundown, one-story apartment complex that housed low-income families, then a few single dwelling rundown small houses, and a couple of vacant lots rounded out the area until you got to the railroad tracks at the end of 3rd Street West. The tracks I refer to run east west and as kids we had no idea where they went or ended up at the most eastern end. We did know where they terminated west, and I'll shortly get to that. The railroad tracks were there and required caution of, but they were also fair game for playing on or near; especially where they crossed the old wooden train trestle over Rock Creek Canyon. On occasion, we placed a penny on the tracks, and once squashed by the train, retrieved it as some token of achievement to show others in the form of a mostly indistinguishable squished Lincoln head coin. Below the trestle was Rock Creek Canyon for our exploration, at least as far as we cared to adventure up and down the creek at that age. I don't generally recall seeing other kids, or adults for that matter, in our section of Rock Creek Canyon. I surmised they had their own sections of the canyon staked out as their territory, but we never were confronted with such groups, if indeed they ever existed. I could spend page after page on the south neighborhood, but I will have to summarize.

Just before you reached the canyon edge you passed a vacant lot, and a building housing something we never figured out, until you finally came to the Jerome Co-op Creamery on the corner of 7th Avenue West and 3rd Street West. It was, for all practical purposes, the only established business that stayed around for the years of my youth and beyond. But what my friends I and were really interested in was just beyond the creamery: the railway tracks, a train bridge, and a stream in a canyon known as Rock Creek. It was a wonderland of adventures for kids like us, and I took full advantage of it for three years as a boy.

As I previously pointed out, the railway tracks traversed East-West from what little I knew at the time. I rode these rails only a couple of times in my life. One had to go north of Twin Falls to the town of Shoshone to catch the passenger train. The rails in Twin Falls, and in my neighborhood, were merely a commerce spur used to reach the market where our parents transported and sold iron and other metals. It didn't matter where they went in my youth, just that they were there and to be cautious of. They were a dividing line not to go beyond for most people, but not us adventurous boys in our youth. Sure, there was danger; but we thought we knew better and acted upon our fear in mostly responsible ways. Where the railway tracks lay was rocky and dusty and at the canyon's edge. It's where the local hobos and bums as they were known, would sometimes collect and sit together and apparently share what they were up to. When I worked at the creamery a few years later, I would sometimes bring transient citizens excess milk and cheese that they always appreciated. They would talk to me ever so briefly and I was very curious about how life had brought them to living out in the open. It was too intimate to ask for details.

At the road's end, about 7ᵗʰ Avenue West, there is a long train bridge headed west crossing Rock Creek Canyon. It was made of wood (now of steel) all linked in a crisscrossing pattern as if constructed by a Lincoln-Log set that you might have had as a child. A single set of shiny tracks sat on top of the bridge. They terminated in the distance at what was known as a roundabout. That's where the train could have maintenance work done, but mainly where the train engine and its coal tender were literally turned around to go back east. I estimate the bridge was about 90-feet above the water, probably 10' wide, and 200' long. When you walked over the bridge—which you were not supposed to do, but we did—you had to step ever so carefully from one rail tie (the wooden piece the track sits on) to the next as there was a gap between them. There was no other walkway. You were sure you were going to fall between these numerous gaps as you traversed from one side of the bridge to the other side, but really wouldn't. I think that fear was more about the river and vegetation you could see below between the ties. Dropping a rock between the wooden ties gave one a sense of the height, when after seconds, it splashed into the water below. As an occasional alternative to stepping on wooden ties to cross the bridge you could try walking on one of the two tracks with your arms out to balance yourself. Whichever method you chose, the question lingering in your mind was always: Could you do this balancing act without falling off either the track or the bridge itself? It should be understood that you also had to keep an ear out (since your eyes were busy on walking the track) for an oncoming train, either head-on or from behind. There simply was not enough space for you and the train both and scant time if you were in the middle of the bridge trying to get to the far side. Not one of us ever got killed, so rest assured that we were relatively safe. However, the more adventurous of my friends would not necessarily always walk on top of the bridge but they would instead move along under it, on the cross-pieces that made up its lattice-work foundation. They would crawl and step from one crosspiece to the other all the way under the bridge. I was too smart to attempt this daring feat that required such an elevated level of risk! However, there were other instances of some degree of danger in the canyon that I did participate in, so let's get to those.

From our side of the canyon, we created over time a couple of paths to make our way down to the creek below. These usually involved jumping from rock to rock, then a short path, and then another series of rocks, perhaps scaling a small area of a cliff that was manageable for boys. Soon you were at the bottom and the creek ran from there in one direction a mile or so to another bridge where the local hospital is. That's the direction we usually traversed for fishing and general exploration. We rarely went the other direction as there was only a single rundown dwelling of some sorts, we had no interest in exploring. Rather we would exclusively head in the direction towards, but not beyond, the hospital. There are limits, even for adventurous boys, to knowing when not to go beyond your self-imposed territory.

All along the creek you could fish or trap muskrats, walk over a big pipe that crossed the stream to the other side, and explore a cave where water came out of one side of the canyon wall. You had to walk over the pipe if you wanted to explore the cave. There was always the risk of falling off the pipe into the stream, but it was worth the try and we

*Danny's boyhood friends in the 4th
grade at Lincoln Elementary*

dared each other with success. If balancing on the pipe did not feel safe enough, you could sit and shimmy your way across, but that took more time, wear on the bottom of your pants, and wasn't done if you were one of the cool kids. The cave was a long tunnel-like area that had been worn that way by what was obviously another source of underground water. You could walk into this dark tunnel some distance, but I must admit it was a bit spooky with an occasional bat scaring you half to death. Twice was enough for me. Mostly we fished in the creek and that is where the night crawlers collected in City Park were put to good use. Rock Creek wasn't as good fishing as the family experienced on the Little Wood River, but we were boys out for adventure, there for the fishing, and bragging rights that went with it! The other chief activities in the canyon were hunting lizards as they lay sunning on the rocks and the trapping of muskrats to earn spending money. Of course, we still played kid games or explored the cliffs to see what they might reveal. Surely native peoples had walked these areas long before we found them. We were exploring and expanding the range of our environment.

Once you had crossed the railroad bridge and walked a couple of miles, you came to the one and only public golf course in the area. The course superintendent was the father of a boy, Jim, who would later meet and marry my sister, Lorraine. It was his brother, Babe, that I was interested in, who was born just a few days after me. We were friends until they moved to Pocatello, Idaho about the time just before high school. I used to like to go to his house on the golf course because it was so different since it stood alone in the midst of all that green. He and I would try to get the gophers that plagued the golf course out of their burrows, flooding them with water, but we had little success given the many tunnels they have in their underground domain. Later in life I would see Babe play in the U.S. Open on a course only six blocks from my home in Ardmore, Pennsylvania. I noted his seriousness on the links compared to our days as youths, then realized that he was in his office there on the 16th green where he hammered out a ball deep in the sand trap. You never know what childhood events will link eventually to another in life. I played a little golf myself and, once won the company tournament, then gave up the game forever.

The Rock Creek Canyon, and anything in between it and my home was, in my way of thinking, an initial venture into the broader world that would eventually take me to 90 countries, and half of those three or four times. Because of all this, my decision to explore the south of town was an important formative time, in many ways, that I shall expand upon.

Immediately south behind our house and one-lot over was the scrap metal lot identified earlier as, "The Backyard." It's the one with the P-51 airplane, a combine, and assorted other piles of iron. The Harr boys and I used this area—away from our individual homes—for kid meetings, staging forays from there into other parts of the block where we lived, as well as acting like Tarzan in our own iron jungle. Besides this area, there was a "house" down the alley that was one of those basement-only houses—a flat top roof only two-foot off ground level. No Anti-Anti-I-Over on this house for sure! It was abandoned in our day, the roof removed, and it became a rather dilapidated pit. It was, like so many places in our part of town, one of those fascinating places to play, but back to, "The Backyard."

One day we got the bright idea, as young boys are prone to conceive, of digging our way to China. China, we had heard, was on the other side of the world, so in our way of thinking, it was attainable! We hustled up shovels and made some progress in digging a hole around 4' in diameter and 2' deep. It was enough for us to stand in the hole, judge our progress, and it was going rather slowly. It eventually dawned on us that this digging by hand shovel was slower than our patience, so we devised another means for digging. Looking through the junk (another general term for scrap metal and all other things found there) of The Backyard, we found a motor with a blade on it. It had once been part of a fan used in an office to attain some coolness on a sweltering day. This should work, we thought. It can surely dig dirt faster and easier than we could with shovels—now for power to run it. Everything was available in the junk, so we found old electrical cords, borrowed two or three extension cords from our parents, and soon strung out what was probably two hundred feet of extension cord running from my house, across the alley, and to the edge of the hole we were digging. Even at that age we knew enough electrical principles as kids to know how to wire and plug something in and so we did. The propeller spun as planned, although a little slower, given the great distance the electricity had to flow. We hit the dirt with the fan blade, and it clunked to a thud and stopped. We soon smelled burning wire in the motor housing, and thus our powered version of digging was over. With that, we tired of the journey digging to China, threw the motor and miscellaneous wiring into the iron pile, and went to play war games on the P-51. With the vast resources of my parents' business we were never at a loss for things to play with, build, or take apart. This attracted numerous "friends," lured in by the treasure that was always available. It was also particularly useful later on when I was a youth and then a man, in need of something I wanted to build. The easy availability of resources to spark and fulfill your dreams, expectations, and imagination is a huge deal to a developing mind such as I had, let alone an adult seeking to meet various needs around the house or farm. I had it all there in my parents' business.

Leaving home and heading south, only across the alley or even into the canyon beyond a few blocks, is not exactly taking as big a risk as is going out into the greater world. But, going south along 3rd Street West to the edge of the canyon, or down into it, or over it on the bridge was, for a kid like me, a big deal. Let's see what that meant for exploration in the final direction—North—for the young boy, in terms of confidence building and fulfilling his curiosity. As it turned out, North, unbeknownst to me, had more things to offer than I, at the time, realized.

North

As a boy, really up until the age of 10, I thought that going much of any place north to be kind of forbidden territory. I had stayed mostly within my east, west, and south corridor. I had, as an exception, regularly gone to one part of the north, my elementary school. I was comfortable walking to and from it, but that was about it. Lincoln Elementary was only five blocks from home and by the third grade I was allowed to walk to and from on my own. The only stopping point was a Sears store about halfway between. My sister-in-law, Archie's wife, Mary Sue, worked there and I'd occasionally drop in to say hello. As I passed to and from school, there were a few really nice homes on the way—a few mansions in my way of thinking. I remember wondering what the people and their kids must be like who lived in those better houses. From the general sense of this area we chose to do much of our future Trick-or-Treating here. We figured that the nicer homes would have the better, and large number of candy treats. "And we were right!"

A major reason I didn't often go north was because that was the direction that led to downtown. It just seemed too complex to explore, especially on my own, until I was finally ready a few years later in my youth. There were a couple of exceptions, but even these were on a direct path from home to slightly shy of Main Street. One was the Park Hotel, two blocks short of downtown, so it didn't feel like part downtown, but

I guess in retrospect it truly was. It was a large, stately brick building and it had a beautiful spread of trees in an open area. People from other towns often came and stayed there and events like weddings were often held. Once, my mother's pet cockatiel, a bird named Billy (who could mimic and say, "Pretty Billy") flew out the front door I had opened of our house to apparent freedom. We searched around the neighborhood in vain and went all the way to the Park Hotel in what seemed a futile search. I have always said, on reflection, that I didn't know until that day we looked for Billy just how many birds there were in the world. Every tree, especially at the Park Hotel, seemed to be filled with chirping birds. As we called out his name there, a familiar chirp was heard. I looked up and there he was perched on the upper ledge of The Times News building, next to the hotel. The Times News was our local newspaper outlet. Inquiring in their front office, I was allowed to go to the roof. There I saw Billy on the ledge, walked over, called him by name and he jumped on my finger just as he had other times in the house when I petted and helped preen his feathers. Billy was soon back home! Danny had played a part in his release, capture, and return. Nothing like the feeling of guilt of being the one who accidentally let the bird out, and then relief to also be the one who found him.

One other adventure slightly north, but not far, was the Pepsi bottling plant. No, it is not the same location or company where we had set the clubhouse fire of wooden crates! I liked going past this plant to witness the winding movement of empty bottles, as they made a clinking sound, along a conveyor. They were then filled, capped, and sent through a small door where they were packed 24 per wooden crate. In my youth I had often wished that I could work there someday but could never get up my nerve to inquire about employment. Perhaps my desire was fed by the fact that our family, for whatever reason, seemed to drink a lot of Pepsi. It was in the house, not as six-packs, but cases. Apparently, our mother had a thing for Pepsi and so its constant presence was her doing. We used to say as kids that we probably had more Pepsi in our bloodstream than the actual red blood. I am no worse for wear for the experience, but don't consume it much today, other than for remembrance—the diet version these days, when the urge presents itself. I am now a root beer guy.

Now, it wasn't like the family never left our immediate neighborhood when I was a boy. There were the annual stays, for the most part, on the Little Wood River for the entire summer, but there were other trips to here and there. With more income coming their way in the early 1940s, our parents gave thought finally to some kind of vacation that they had never experienced before. For example, we did go to Yellowstone Park a couple of times and once to Knott's Berry Farm in California when sister Lucille went off to college. I especially remember Yellowstone and walking right up to the edge of Old Faithful and looking in—something completely forbidden now, and wisely so. Most often we frequented the local natural hot springs that dot the southern edge of town as well as up north towards Sun Valley, Idaho. The larger one in the Ketchum area was particularly nice in that the main springs were inside a two-story wooden building and would echo with our shrills of excitement. Our visits to the Ketchum springs were combined with our living on the Little Wood River as both are in the same general area. There was another such hot spring, Easley, and I do remember my sister Lorraine soaking up one year too many rays and had developed lots of blisters on her back and the pain to go with it. However, it was the hot springs area to the south and therefore closest to home that we most frequented as a family. It was all outdoors and called Nat Soo Pah and especially fun for kids making lots of noise and it had a park for picnicking. It had a very large Olympic-sized pool or maybe it just seemed so to little kids, like me. When it was drained for cleaning, we could see the long sliver of algae that grew where the underground hot spring water fed into the pool at one end and refilled the pool down to the deeper end. It was great fun to slide down the algae and dive into the deeper water. There was also a set of diving boards on which my brother Buzz demonstrated his competitive diving skills. Additionally, there was a diving platform tower about 17-feet high. In my later youth I almost paralyzed myself, if not nearly killed myself: A friend dared me to dive into only 4 feet of water and scraped my forehead and nose, making me realize just how dumb that was. I'd save my dumb stunts thereafter for other things to challenge myself in life.

Our parents were certainly people who liked the great outdoors. Considering what Idaho has to offer, they had a playground of opportunities and took full generous advantage. As I learned later in life from my Mother, the motivation for camping was initially to save money because of difficult economic times, although it can be equally said they simply enjoyed the outdoor life a great deal; plus it was good for their children, thus both reasons fed their actions. Camping was taken to another level by our parents, therefore also by us kids. It was an adventure for a young boy to discover what the outside world was while still being protected directly by my parents and siblings. This, I think, was very important to my development, especially fostering a sense of well-being and curiosity. My wife has often commented that I must have been so used to outdoor living as a youth that today I seek not always the shelter of a house, but the outdoors wherein I assume another state of bliss that I find only out in an exposed environment. Sleeping on our deck, under the stars, on a warm starry night is not out of the question for me, although in my old age less so. Frankly, I don't like the bats outside our house as they fly by my head. My wife saw this beauty of comfort with the outside world for the first time when we stood in a forest of giant redwoods in northern California. She noted that I was mesmerized by their very presence. Being in the woods and outdoors, as we were so often as a family, was the beginning of my comfort with the outside world and subsequently so much travel that I did throughout my entire life. Such camping by the Langdons was taken to its extreme. I'll explain.

We camped every summer up until the time my father grew ill during his last year. Such camping excursions occurred practically every summer from 1935 until 1945. I was only six months old when I was taken camping for the first of seven times for the entire summer. All of this was driven, in the early family years, as a way to save money for a struggling family. It continued on, even after things got better economically, all the way through the Second World War until our dad's passing in 1946.

As I noted before the business had a permanent location in 1935, the family struggled economically. While our parents rented various short-term housing each year in Twin Falls during the school year, we spent the period of time from late spring through early fall camping. Thus we would live off the land—returning to civilization only when the kids needed to continue their schooling. During the long stretches of summer, Dad would leave the camp for a couple of days every two weeks or so to carry on the business brokering hides, pelts, and furs. Furthermore, because this was during the war period, rationing was on, and living on the cheap was paramount to mere survival. Camping, for all its ruggedness, really afforded an opportunity to live cheaply off the land. Fish became a standard part of our diet and sustenance. Equally important, it was also a time wherein the family was together, needed to entertain itself, and make do together almost always alone, void of outsiders and friends our own age. What that did for us all was priceless by any measure. I think all of us kids became who we are, in large part, because of that camping period year after year after year. We were our play group and it fostered getting along and taking care of one another. We became, as it were, self-sustaining and it lingered for the rest of our lives as a Langdon trait and has continued to be passed down to our children.

Generally, camping consisted of finding our special spot near a small creek (near Carey, Idaho), with enough shade from the hot summer sun on the edge of the sagebrush that covered the hills of the surrounding semi-arid desert. The trees that dotted the stream and provided what little shade there was afforded some relief from sunny days, aided by a little summer breeze. Fortunately, there was very little rain in the dry season that might adversely affect camping. The location and its natural beauty were ideal for outdoor living. Dad and Mother brought everything needed in Old Ironsides—their trusty International truck. Dad had made beds for everyone from angle iron crossed with chain-linked support, which could be rolled up for transport. Along with large down-filled feather mattresses and wool blankets, and a canvas top arched over the top and open back of the truck, we had an early version of a camper. It worked fine for the kids to sleep and stay dry. A large canvas tent was erected to house our parents along with anything else that needed to be out of the weather. The tent had a strong smell of oil that covered the canvas to ward off the rain and in the heat of the day could be sweltering. In the cool of the nights it was comfortable. My mother told me that the tent was big enough to fit four double beds, although it never did—only the one for them and everything else needed for camping and cooking. Dad had made his own stove-like cooking setup. It was made from a set of former iron tractor wheels that he had straightened. He then attached iron legs so it could stand off the ground. Next, he placed pieces of flat iron to make a large frying surface. Along with a Dutch oven that he loved cooking with, he often prepared sourdough biscuits. Cast-iron pots augmented the cooking setup and he even constructed a chest for all the necessary utensils, plates, and such that could be attached to a tree and lifted off the ground, safe from any animal critters that might pass our way. Wood was regularly gathered and stacked to be kept dry. This would provide the heat needed for cooking on the stove top, iron griddle or rack, and large frypan with a long handle (that had been given to Dad by his sister, Daisy, and which resides in my care today). All of this, except the pots and utensils, was made from scrap metal gathered from their business. What needed welded was done by their neighborly blacksmith, Dick Diamond. A campfire always seemed to be aglow to round out the living environment. Even our dog, Blacky, was ever present for comfort and he would follow us kids to fish, sitting under the shade of a tree 'til we moved on to the next fishing hole or back to camp. It was so peaceful and quiet, except for the ever-present sound of running water of the nearby cold river, an occasional howl of a coyote in the hills, and us kids at play. In the blackness of the night, just before sunset or early dawn, you could hear an occasional owl. Imagine the bright and numerous stars in the sky way out where there are no lights to get in your way to see the stars in all their glory; only the glowing coals of a fire left to burn until the morning, when it would be stoked for making breakfast. My, it was so nice to be alone together, day after day, and night after night.

While Mother did most of the cooking, Dad contributed on occasion his specialty items like biscuits, cornbread, and hash browns. She had the usual chore of washing clothes. She brought along an old boiler from the iron heap as well as a washtub. She'd heat water from the river over the open fire, use a washboard to scrub clothes by hand, and produce what she often called the "whitest clothes she ever saw," which she attributed to the river water that cleansed it, and the unfiltered sun of the day.

Our mother and father were equally skilled fisherman/woman, although dad claimed he was the better since he had lived longer. Dad loved fly fishing in particular and could ace an artificial fly that he had made into any "hole" of the creek while dodging the willows and other vegetation that lined the creekbank. My mother, for her part, preferred a spinner and worm combination and could cast accurately into any hole she chose. That bait/spinner combination was one that I adopted and used to outdo others with whom I fished in life. There was always a bit of competition between the two of them to see who could be the first at achieving "a catch for the day"—meaning your limit of fish allowed by law—as if there were anyone who might drop in to check! My mother, I think, had more patience "sticking to a hole," as they refer to it, until a fish or two caught her hook before moving on. Dad could not wait out a hole and was constantly on the move, as I was to become years later. They taught all of us children to fish, although I distinctly remember when I was four finding a lifeless fish on the end of a pole that I had left dangling in a nearby hole. I wasn't fooled by this maneuver when they claimed I had caught a fish for the first time and went on to hone my own fishing skills well taught by them. A burlap "gunny sack" fashioned to fit over one's shoulder, filled with a little long bank-grass and sprinkled with creek water, served as the place to keep your fish fresh while you continued, longing to catch the limit allowed. The fish, mainly cutthroat or rainbow trout, had a distinct smell in our gunny sack as you finished out the day of fishing and prepared to cut and clean them. All us children were taught how to clean a fish with accuracy and completeness in preparation for pan frying; you didn't leave for others such tasks to do for you. Fish were most often fried up that day. First, they were dipped in a batter of egg and flour, then placed in a huge fry pan with leftover bacon lard, and toasted to a golden brown, head and all. With some baked potato, corn, or peas, along with homemade sourdough biscuits, you had breakfast, lunch, or dinner around a campfire all summer long.

Dad fishing on the Little Wood River

A non-fish adventure while fishing occurred one summer on the Little Wood River. Our dad lost his favorite signet ring, with an "L," naturally, emblazed on it . He was fishing in one of his favorite holes, a semi-deep one with surrounding bushes and slippery rocks that are the flooring to streams of cold water. His ring had somehow slipped off, most likely caught on something when he removed his hook from a rainbow that he just caught, or perhaps when he placed the fish into the wicker creel that he preferred for storing his fish until he got back to camp. Anyway, a glance at his hand and he noticed his ring was gone. What to do? He peered and squinted into the water but the reflection from the sun and the depth made it impossible to see much other than rocks and moss, let alone a ring. He hurried back to camp, announced his distress to the family, and marshalled the clan to come help look. As he departed, he grabbed a canvas in case that would be of any help. Mom and kids looked; me from the bank as I best recall. Not having much luck, a last-ditch effort was deployed in the form of using the canvas he had brough along to dam up part of the stream. This made the fishing hole not quite so deep. A further look when the water was lower, and there was the ring! A truly family effort!

My mother, as I noted, was a very competent fisherwoman. She recounts the time she caught her limit (25 fish in those days), and if you returned to camp, you could go again for another try. She was very successful that particular day and on her second round had caught 24 fish, but she was determined to catch just one more to achieve her goal. She fished to no avail into the darkness till light failed. She recounted to me years later her extreme disappointment in not meeting her goal on that day.

There was another particular fishing event concerning Mother that I only learned about decades later, when I audio recorded the one and only interview with her about her life experiences. She told me in some detail about an afternoon in October of 1938. She was fishing the Little Wood and caught onto a fish and as was her style, pulled swiftly back on her rod and flung the fish on the grassy bank behind her. (I am prone to do this myself when fishing, so I know exactly what that technique involves.) As she turned to see the fish flopping on the grass, she fell flat on her tummy on a sandy river bar. She was pregnant at the time, and that evening, after fixing dinner for everyone, she experienced, as she described it, some "awful chill and sweat." She hardly slept that night. She further recalled how she got up and sat by the coals of the still crackling campfire. Soon Dad noticed and came to talk and comfort her. He encouraged her to avoid the chill of the night and she returned to bed. The morning came, and she was fine. A month later she delivered her final child, a son to be named Danny. I wonder if it explains any of my risk-taking behavior, or any of the other personality traits I have? If you are going to feel lucky about anything, that night and morning were perhaps luckier for her and me than I ever could have imagined.

It was pretty rare that anyone would pass our way seeing this large family all set up by the river. George Van Tillberg (the Langdon boys' barber), Seth Jones and their wives, came by one week and spent a few days with us. It was refreshing to have them there as the only other visitors were occasional Basque sheep herders, tending to a flock, wandering the nearby hills covered with sagebrush. Dad and Mother would sit with their friends or others for a cup of coffee and exchange information about what was happening, if anything, there in the desert and at home in Twin Falls. Rarely did a total stranger happen upon the family camped there. Dad would go into Carey or Hailey at least once a month, or to Twin Falls, to do business and get supplies of eggs, bread, bacon, potatoes, and other staples. Eggs, bought by the crate, cost 10-cents a dozen, bread was 10-cents a loaf, very thick bacon was 10 cents a pound, which then also supplied the lard for frying fish, potatoes, and the like. Considering where we were and what wasn't available, we ate well. A woman by the name of Ma Hector lived upstream and she occasionally prepared dried apple pie, for which our folks paid in fish. After a month's stay at one location, the encampment would be packed up and moved upstream for better fishing perhaps, or more abundant needed materials like wood, or hunting for grouse in the sagebrush. We played games, made whistles out of willow trees along the stream bank, carved our initials on wood, and generally created our own entertainment. For instance, Sister Lorraine distinctly recalls the time we concocted a game to see who would get the most mosquito bites in a day, and she was the winner to her best recollection. Around the nightly campfire our father, known as a bit of a troubadour, would sing. We saw millions of stars in the cold darkness of night without any light to disturb the view. We were a family living virtually off the land. We were together! We were so lucky!

*(left to right) Lorraine, Buzz, Bertine, and
Lucille camped on Little Wood River*

If there are themes to our living as a family and how we explored the environment around us, I think the following were always present in the home and out camping in the world:

- *Everything is a lesson learned.*
- *Take risks.*
- *Enjoy others—especially your siblings—and their accomplishments.*
- *Be nice to everyone, especially strangers and in any way different.*
- *Reinforce others.*
- *Do things for others in your community.*
- *Smile.*
- *Use humor.*
- *Don't tolerate fools or fools' thinking and behavior (including your relatives).*
- *Don't worry about things.*
- *Be loved and give love.*
- *Pass it forward.*

CHAPTER 5

Danny in His Youth: Age 13 – 18

I consider my youth to have begun when I started junior high. In Idaho, the education system is a 6-3-3, meaning 6-years in elementary, 3 in junior high, and finally 3 in senior high.

Until junior high, most of my activity was centered in the immediate vicinity of our house with the outer perimeter bounded by The Warehouse, The Hole, The Backyard, the yard next to our home, and the immediate neighborhood. Most were full of scrap metal. I made homemade root beer, capping around three cases that I stored in the unfinished basement. During the winter some bottles exploded from the excessive pressure of one or more ingredients. I personally thought my root beer tasted less than desirable, but my mother loved it. She was definitely the kind of mother who would make sure her son felt successful.

When I started attending Leary Jr. High at age 13, I gradually started to migrate further north of my neighborhood comfort zone, including our parent's business. The school was located just north of Main Street, so I was starting to come into contact with the better parts of a typical town, and essentially right through the heart of its downtown. Three years later I would go even further north to attend senior high.

I was still a pretty quiet, reserved kid with the usual set of oddities that characterize boys before they learn social norms and teen ways. For instance, from the junkyard I had gathered 50 or so blank keys that had found their way as scrap metal from a local locksmith. I strung them on a wire loop about 7" in diameter, looped it to fit on my pants belt buckle and carried them around for a few weeks. My brother Buzz and his friends got into calling me, appropriately "Keys." I was okay with that nickname, but after a few weeks the sheer weight of the key ring became too much, and I returned them to their rightful place in the junkyard. Perhaps it was all just symbolic of the many things I would experiment with in life and helped stretch my curiosity, bring personal joy, and teach me things about myself. That kind of curiosity lingers to this day.

Attending junior high was kind of a blank to me. It wasn't that I didn't enjoy it, but it took some getting used to since we were required to go from being in one classroom with one teacher all day to then several classes with different teachers throughout the day. I did okay, gradually improving my academic skills from the reading problems I carried with me from elementary school. I was working on my confidence without knowing it I guess, and progress was slow. I compensated, perhaps, by becoming a pretty mechanically savvy kid, having learned from all my adventures in the junkyard. I was selected, of all things, to be the projectionist for the variety of 16-mm movies that were shown in class at our junior high. It was an old Bell and Howell projector with intricate threading, and one had to learn how to get the film back into perfect timing, lest it flutter the projected image beyond visual recognition, accompanied by laughter from the students. I wore the responsibility as proudly as I had when I had been a crosswalk safety monitor in my elementary school days.

Having new classmates now from the other, more upscale, elementary schools (Washington, Bickel, and the private Catholic school) I made new friends after the Harr boys and I left one another behind. I hadn't completely come out of my shell by this point, maturing only slightly from the quiet kid I was known to be. I am pretty sure I was a little nerdy, as they say: as an example I had assembled one of those electronics kits with all the numerous electronic bits and pieces that require you to solder them into a functioning, integrated unit. I thus build a radio that didn't work very well. But rather than give in, I went on to assemble a more advanced amplifier for a turntable and speaker combo that worked very well and served my musical taste into my college and early adulthood. My mother had a vinyl record recorder/player and I liked to record my brother Buzz singing, and I even listened to a little classical music like Mozart and Rachmaninoff—nothing too serious, but I came to appreciate a variety of music. Perhaps this was due to the influence of both my father and brother Buzz, as both were accomplished musicians. Our mother exhibited a little flair for music as she played a small electric organ she had purchased and loved playing hymns while seated in her living room. Everyone in the family played a musical instrument, and while we never played a concert with one another, we shared an appreciation for sounds that soothe the soul.

Commensurate with attending junior high was the opportunity to further explore downtown Twin Falls. The route between home and school took me through downtown, so I could hardly avoid it. This was before any mall had been established which eventually bled the charm from the downtown area. While it was a relatively small downtown, it offered an array of things to spark curiosity and develop maturity in a young boy. I loved my town! It exuded safety for a boy who liked to explore and a feeling of community where people smiled and said hello.

Twin Falls had grown only a little from the time of my birth. The population was now perhaps 17,000, and growth was predominately north of town. Twin Falls thankfully retained its small-town feel during all my growing up years. There were only eight blocks essentially to Main Street where most of the stores were found, including two movie theatres, the Idaho Power Company office, Clos Book Store, Fredrickson's Ice Cream, Knight's Barber Shop (where I got my hair cut), Krengel's, Price Hardware, The Paris, Mayfair, a Woolworth 5 and 10-cent store, Twin Falls Bank and Trust, Idaho Department Store, Roper's Men's Store, and an A&W root beer stand. Sandwiched between a couple of buildings in the center was a shoeshine hole-in-the-wall operated by Al, our only black citizen, as far as I knew. On the fringe before other houses appeared was a bowling alley, a Sears

113

store, and an assortment of other small enterprises. I liked the Idaho Power Company building in my youth because you could stand at one end of the long outside display windows that joined other windows and wave one leg and arm up and down. When you did your image would be mirrored as if your body rose off the ground in a scissoring effect. It was the kind of silly thing only a kid would take delight in, and I had grown out of that somewhat by junior high. So doing it at age 16 seemed a bit awkward if someone should see me. However, to this day, I can be known to keep my youthful ways when it delights me or others: just ask my wife!

4th of July Celebration in downtown Twin Falls 1950s

Main Street, as it is so often named in virtually any city, became the principal place of activity for all youth who, in that day, "dragged Main!" I suppose everyone knows what that means, but just in case you don't: it's the seemingly useless behavior of endlessly driving (without parents) with your friends one direction from a commonly understood point (i.e. the Dairy Queen) to the other commonly understood point, which was the end of Main, then turning around and going in the opposite direction, all while looking to see who else was doing the same in their cars. Nowadays it would be considered a waste of good gas, I suppose, but back in the day it was a necessary pastime if you were "cool." I got in big trouble once doing such "dragging;" I'll save that story of woe for a little later in my tale. For now, let's stick to describing the physical layout of downtown and my venture into it.

Perpendicular and intersecting Main Street, in the very center of downtown, was the other main thoroughfare labeled Shoshone Street. On this less interesting road, the buildings were a mix of various businesses with churches, a city park, larger commercial enterprises like Willis Motor, a feed store, the flour mill and one of my most favorite haunts, The Depot Grill. Thus, in general, they were stores where services were provided. Funny that the town should be so divided (commercial vs. retail), as if, for some grand purposes, it might be serving its citizens. Shoshone Street eventually terminated south of town after crossing what was commonly referred to in those days as "The Singing Bridge." It doesn't "sing" these days, as it is now made of concrete—a fact that I think is regrettable. This bridge crossed the lesser of the two canyons on either side of town known as Rock Creek Canyon. The other much larger canyon on the north side was Twin Falls' version of the Grand Canyon—the mighty Snake River Canyon. Incidentally, it is the location where the infamous Evel Knievel, the stunt performer and entertainer of his day, attempted and failed to leap the canyon —a quarter of a mile—on his motorcycle. On Shoshone Street there was a third movie venue, the Idaho Theatre. It was surprising for a small town to have three theaters (actually four: the other, an outdoor one on the outskirts of town, also showed movies). The Idaho Theater is no longer there, but I once participated in a spelling bee in my youth which I resoundingly lost in the first round since I was a lousy speller, fostered during the first grade when I tried to learn to read by sight. I never did win the bike that was the top prize, but frankly, it was gathering all the Pepsi cap lids I collected that got me tickets for the drawing to be in the spelling bee. What was I thinking knowing that I was going to lose anyhow? I think experiences such as these were developing in me an attitude that engaging in the activity was more important than always winning.

As kids, we definitely preferred the Roxy. The Roxy was where a serial viewing of Saturday cowboy movies was shown and you could get in for a dime. If you knew how, you could sneak in the back door from the alley and enter through blackened curtains on either side of the screen—embarrassing only if friends recognized you and knew what you had done. At the other theater on Main, the Orpheum, there was a stage with a fine velvet curtain. It also had soft seats, unlike the Roxy's wooden seats. The Orpheum had a much nicer gilded-stage atmosphere with a balcony where, in that day and age, you could smoke. The smoke from the adults' and occasional teen sneaking a smoke, gave an eerie look to the movie light projected onto the movie screen as it passed through the smoke. One afternoon my sister Lucille and I were in the packed theater audience. She sat with all the ladies in the seating on the main floor while I was relegated to the balcony. She appeared on a traveling episode of "Queen For A Day" with the famous Jack Bailey as its host. Lucille was selected as one of six young women to vie for the first-place prize as Queen for a Day, replete with a crown. She won the crown, the title, and other prizes after telling Mr. Baily that what she wanted most in life that day was a washing machine for her mother who ran a scrap metal business. After that mother no longer had to use a hand crank ringer to press out the excess water from the washed clothing prior to hanging to dry. The new washer had an electric wringer on top that spun around and around, and a better wash tub with an agitator. Lucille won other prizes as well and it was quite a thrill for me to watch from way up on the balcony. What I was doing there with all those young and middle-aged women is beyond me to this day. I figure I must have been assigned to Lucille on that particular occasion as our mother labored in the scrap iron, and Lucille must have told me to sit in the balcony.

I stated we had four theaters in Twin Falls. The fourth was the drive-in theatre out across from the cemetery. We sometimes went as family or with friends. It was one of our older sisters that would generally drive the business pickup with us in the back, although alternatively one's friends would do the honor in their own family car. Sitting there in the dark with the metal speaker hooked onto the rolled-up driver's side window, it wasn't exactly the Roxy, nor did it approach the splendor of the Orpheum or the Idaho Theatre in town. But it had one advantage the others didn't: you could get out of the car, grab some refreshments from the wooden shack that sold concessions below the projection booth, and peek around to see what couples were necking in the car rather than watching the movie. As with the Roxy, there were ways to get in for free, such as driving with your headlights off in through the exit, or you could squirrel a couple of kids in the trunk or climb a fence for entry. The latter included an associated problem in that you didn't have a car window to hang that metal speaker from. Still, perhaps you were there to actually just walk around in the dark to see who was and wasn't there. That's a kid thing to do, of course, not a family activity. High school boys, like me, were more apt to be up to such hijinks!

I really, really liked roaming on my own around our small downtown. I was gradually expanding my environment and engaging with strangers, even though I was still shy and prone to being quiet. After school I'd often drop by the shoe store owned and operated by Morey Roth. He was the only Jewish person I knew, and he was full of kindness. He was very fond of my mother, if not perhaps in love with her, probably because she was a woman in an extraordinary business. He made frequent comments to me, always beginning by saying, "your mother," and then launching into something she had done. He had a bit of an accent that I didn't always understand, but for a bashful kid he was easy to be with. Besides, he let me use the machine that would x-ray my feet to confirm if a pair of shoes I was trying on correctly fit, but I had no authority to buy. As I bent forward to look through the tall machine's viewer to see my shoes for the limited recommended time or more, an ominous green light would glow as if sourced from a horror movie. Below I saw an outline of the bones of my feet clearly distinct from the inside edge of the shoes. Were they too tight or just, right? You had to judge for yourself unless

Morey begged your pardon and peered into the machine himself to have a look-see. I wasn't going to buy them in any case because my mother made such decisions, but it was fascinating to look at my feet in a new way. It probably was a horror in a different sense though in that x-raying my feet as often as I did could not be good for me! Who knew that such new technology could be so harmful? Certainly, Mr. Roth didn't know any better. It wasn't much worse, as far as I knew, than when I used to capture mercury in a glass jar. I would extract the magical liquid metal from thermometers that would show up in certain scrap metal, like refrigerators. Pouring some of those 30 ounces of mercury from one hand to the other was spell binding. It flows so easily from side to side, and if a drop dropped off, it spattered on the floor in all directions, never to be recovered from the dirt in such tiny droplets. What was I to know about mercury or x-rays? To this day, both my feet and hands are intact—none the worse for wear, considering all the warnings I've read with my science background since those days about x-rays and mercury.

During the downtown wanders of my younger days, I got to know a couple of ethnic groups without really thinking about things like "ethnicity." For example, I knew Morey, a kind person, was a Jew, and Al, was also a nice person, who was the only Black I knew at his shoeshine store. Both were wonderful lessons in diversity, even if on a very small scale. Later in life there were subsequent situations where the lessons learned downtown came to be useful in knowing how to treat others who are discriminated against. The small town of Twin Falls was a great place to learn lessons. That's not to say it was always perfect. Consider, for example, the things that were done to Japanese Americans at the outset of the Second World War. These were fellow citizens being held against their will at the local internment camp, Minidoka, just 58 miles from where I grew up. It was out of sight to the people of Twin Falls, but I am not certain that was out of their knowledge. As an older adult I've visited the site and it's a sad chapter in our nation's history. Still, I think I learned tolerance in Twin Falls from the small variety of people I interacted with and the friendships they had with my extraordinary mother.

Elsewhere in town I was a frequent patron of the only bowling alley—the Magic Bowl, as it was known. Just four blocks away, it was an easy walk from home. In our family, sister Bertine was the champion bowler. Short of stature at maybe 5'2" at best, she had the most powerful backswing I have ever seen. She would step to the backline, take three steps to where you release the ball and her arm would thrust the ball back and arch over the top of her head, then bring it down with a whoosh towards the pins. She was a state champion more than once, went to a few national meets, and inspired her baby brother to take up the sport. In my high school days I was president of the youth bowling league for a while, won a couple of trophies, and even set pins one summer for 10 cents a line. I also played the pinball machines located in the Magic Bowl lobby. I mastered one machine enough to play for a couple of hours using only the initial 10 cents to play two games. Our mother enjoyed the occasional bowling session and in her retirement was an active league participant.

Main Street was certainly the hub of the city for activity. As one headed south on Shoshone from Main, there was a gas station, seed store, flour mill, and on a corner, a vacant lot, shaped much like a slice of pie. This lot served as another of the locations where mother parked scrap metal. Across the street, next to the flour mill, sits the Depot Grill to this very day. Hard to believe that a restaurant could play such an important part in one's life, but in my case it did. There was also an old icehouse, the Twin Falls Feed & Ice (owned by my classmate, Barbara Sandy's dad), on 5th Avenue South that made ice blocks when refrigeration wasn't possible as in the case of camping. You could ask to have an ice block chipped for an ice chest or glasses of soda, or to churn homemade ice cream. My brother Archie and I would store frozen ducks there from our hunting ventures. Of course, somehow, I always had free access to explore the inner workings of these businesses, again mainly because my mother seemed to know everyone in town! As with many businesses in town, I was fascinated by what and how such enterprises worked.

In the other direction, north on Shoshone from Main Street, next to the Idaho Theatre, was the military draft office. It would play a key role for me one day as a young man subject to the compulsory draft that then existed. And across the street was an Asian restaurant called the Oriental Café that my mother loved. It, along with a couple of other restaurants, became frequent eateries for our family given that our widowed mother was a busy working woman. It is also to be noted, however, that she was an excellent cook when it was needed, and when time permitted.

I want to mention one other location on Shoshone that was particularly noteworthy. It was right across the street from the junior high. It's City Park—yes that's it official name—occupies an entire block with the city library across the street on the far side. This park afforded a couple of key activities for me in my youth, and after a brief description of how, I'll then come back to Main Street and all that it had to offer.

City Park was—and still is—a wonderful tree, bush, and flower-laced garden. It has the usual picnic tables, but also a magnificent bandshell where folks could gather for an occasional evening or afternoon concert performed by an all-volunteer Twin Falls Municipal City Band. I played a trumpet there one summer when I was in high school. It was, however, a different activity initiated about the time of junior high that I found particularly enjoyable and useful to do in City Park: my fishing buddies and I collected worms, known as nightcrawlers, there on the grass during many a summer evening! Not anything like collecting stamps or coins, but it was a useful hobby for a kid that had learned to fish with his parents on the Little Wood River or in the other streams that were around the city. For the young boy who could now go fishing on his own or with other friends in places near town, like Rock Creek Canyon, the City Park was the primary resource for catching our all-important bait that in turn allowed us to catch fish.

Now finding and collecting nightcrawlers takes some skill, let alone nerve in that some people are squeamish when it comes to touching—or even looking at worms—or heaven forbid, attaching one to a hook! They are fast little buggers when they feel –and they do—your presence trying to catch one as it slithers back into their burrow/holes. Nightcrawlers, unlike their brethren, earthworms, are much larger—usually 4 to 6 inches, and a nearly quarter inch in diameter. They can actually stretch themselves out to a longer length or squish their body to a smaller size. They have a distinctive orange ring that circles their wet, slightly slimy body. They are called nightcrawlers because they generally come out only in the coolness of the night and like it best when the earth and grass are a bit damp. The City Park was a great source for nightcrawlers given that the grassy areas were watered regularly every two weeks or so. So on my own or with a friend, we would slip into the park when the sun had fully set, get down on our hands and knees, and with the aid of a flashlight go hunting.

The secret to finding and catching nightcrawlers was to crawl slowly and show only the edge of your flashlight where the light is the dimmest. With due diligence you could spy on two or three crawlers just lying there doing what nightcrawlers do. Too bright a light and they would go back into their holes before you could make a move to capture them; too noisy, and they knew of your presence. A quick movement with your hand and tips of the fingers to place gently over their body, you then reached—having set the flashlight down on the grass—with your free hand to pick it up before it could slip out of your grasp and back into its hole. Even with this, it usually kept part of its body in the hole and would hang on tight. Other than finding them in the first place, this is where the real skill of hunting comes to bear: you are left to gently pull and try to extract the entirety of its body without tearing off a portion. A dead worm with only part of its body in your tin can, was not going to last long enough for you to get it to the stream and thread it on a hook. Believe me, dead worms are really stinky, and I never felt any fish worth its very soul, if it has one, would eat a dead worm—but I could have been wrong. Pull some, but not too much, on your prey as you are trying to get them to release. Being patient and not in such a hurry was key. Know when to hold up, know when to fold up, know when to run as the Kenny Rogers song goes. I am bragging a little, but I was pretty good at catching nightcrawlers.

So much for the general orientation to my hometown. This is a perfect point to transition to exploring from my house going south to what proved to be an extraordinary and delightful playground for fun and development. After that I will return to downtown Twin Falls and explore my junior and senior high school days. All of this provides the experiential environment for the development of a well-rounded youth as he becomes more and more comfortable with himself and others getting ready for the world at large.

To my way of being and thinking in my days as a youth, most of the "unusual" and personally interesting businesses of Twin Falls were not really downtown, but rather on our side of the tracks. For example, the Twin Falls Livestock Commission stockyard was near the train station (off Minidoka Street), across the railway tracks, a little further east of The Depot Grill. This was the highly commercial area where the ice plant, flour mill, train station and other businesses were; so what's not to like and explore as a kid? All were within an easy walk or bike ride. The stockyard was particularly fascinating both in my youth and much later in life, when I had a small farm.

Stockyards, at least for me, are fascinating not so much for the corrals and shoots that house and move the beef or sheep on sale there, but the sale itself. If you have never before been to a livestock auction, please do so before you die. What goes on there seems like pandemonium, but it is a well-orchestrated part of doing business—in this case, primarily buying and selling cattle, but also sheep and sometimes pigs, and an occasional horse is exchanged. It's all run by a kind of ringmaster known as the auctioneer. He or she speaks a language much like any foreign language. You have to experience and participate in an auction to begin to understand, and even then, only a few become masters able to speak the language. I've tried, and while I sound good, I can't direct an audience to the successful completion of a deal. Later in life when I had my small farm, I used to go to the local auction in Caldwell and buy my own sheep and cattle. Many a time I mistakenly bought five head when I meant to buy only one. I looked sheepish for my mistake that was subsequently corrected, yes, by the auctioneer. If you can't get to a livestock auction, try an ordinary auction of any type at all and you'll learn what I am talking about. Just be careful how much you think you bought and at what price.

Having mastered and made the south of our town my domain as a boy, I started to explore in my youth places very much further north of downtown. Two in particular come to mind. The first place is the location of a couple of falls on the Snake River, one of which gives its name to the town, Twin Falls. The other, Shoshone Falls, gives part of its name to one of the major cross points of downtown. It's obviously an American Indian name of origin (known as the Shoshoni) for which the water falls in question are rightly named. Both are on the Snake River. I'll describe these falls before mentioning another playground with a creek. Streams and large bodies of water seem to be a major playground throughout my boyhood and days as a teen.

Twin Falls—the falls themselves—were and are a beautiful place. Unfortunately, the said "falls" doesn't look "twin" anymore as half was diverted as a power source. The town itself is surrounded by farms and a series of manmade canals. It was once in history the largest irrigated tract of land in the world. The Snake River, the town's most prominent and famous feature, flows along the north edge of town and then through other parts of Idaho, and eventually joins the Columbia River in Oregon to the Pacific Ocean. Those rivers, by the way, can be navigated right up to northern Idaho and played a part in the explorations of the Lewis and Clark Expedition. The Snake River had so many features to attract not only the tourist, but the boy in me. It served as our primary duck hunting venue when we hunted ducks or geese in our youth. I used to wade parts of those mighty waters in my hip boots and nearly drowned a time or two on slippery rocks. Our favorite hunting spots were on a series of small islands and the best way to get to these was making ones way, wearing rubber waders, walking through the upstream lower end of the rapids. Other times, I had a one-man rubber life raft and would float the rapids after hunting and nearly turned the raft over twice. Another time I was with a friend's father in his power boat as we went downstream from the Perrine Bridge to explore the river. Along the way we happened on a sandy beach and landed there for a brief walk and look at the mighty canyon walls that towered above us. On the beach I found a couple of black obsidian arrowheads long left, I surmised, by a local Indian tribe. I left the arrowheads there knowing they were not mine to have, but theirs. We can't always take what we want!

At both Twin Falls and Shoshone Falls (a little upriver) my friends and I would go to the top of these falls in the dry season, when the water had backed away, and the falls were much smaller in water flow. In that way we could walk on the rocks above the face of the cliff where the water normally tumbled over. The grandeur of such a place I think had a powerful influence on me as I usually studied it more than thought of the associated danger! Another time we were riding our bikes down the steep grade of the road that led to Shoshone Falls when the chain broke on my Schwinn bike. Bikes in those days did not have separate hand brakes, rather the chain drove both the back wheel and applied the brake to the same when you pushed back on the pedal. I've always been one to immediately think what I would do in an emergency (like when I had looked a snake in the eyes fourteen inches away from my head), so I dismounted the bike on my left side with one foot on the pedal and the other dragging the pavement for dear life. I lost most of my shoe sole that day, but not my life's soul!

At another place on the Snake River (that we often went to as a family in my youth) was a place called Dierkes Lake. It was situated on a kind of switch back road near Shoshone Falls. There was a wooden shack where you could change into your bathing suit, a small lake to swim in, and another less frequented area for fishing. In the latter you usually unsuccessfully tried to catch whitefish, a kind of carp. You could see them swimming, all sixteen inches of them, so lazily in the warm water, but catching them was impossible. I spent many hours trying to catch a fish there that wasn't really worth eating. I still wonder why I did that, but I did! Perhaps it's what you see that you can't get, but you really want to try? The challenge, as in so many instances (especially in your unknowing youth), is worth the effort as long as you don't let it consume you.

Also to the north, where the College of Southern Idaho now sits, ran a small stream that we discovered one day exploring the area on our bikes and, of course, had to see where it led. It was basically in a field and was probably a feeder for the irrigation that is so prominent in the Magic Valley, as the wider agricultural area is called. Soon we found an old abandoned 30-gallon barrel and decided we could make a raft of it. We lashed on some boards we found lying around and set sail downstream. Things went pretty well until we discovered an oil slick sticking on our collective bodies from the leaking oil barrel we had found. You live, you learn! Oh, and we called ourselves "The Bareass Divers," and indeed we were swimming naked in that stream. It's what boys do!

Twin Falls was well-organized for little league baseball. Baseball was a big thing in town since it had a professional baseball park that served as the home of our Class C team affiliated, as a farm team, with the Yankees and part of the Pioneer League. They were known as the Twin Falls Cowboys, later relabeled the Magic Valley Cowboys once then owned by the local citizenry of the area—I still have my ten shares, but of no value since the team is long gone. Little league baseball, or knothole baseball, as it was referred to in our part of the baseball world, was the most often sought out summer activity for kids of all ages. If you wanted to be on a team, no matter your skill level, you could play. And you would get the most important part of the deal: a printed shirt, and a baseball cap. I played for four years. Most times I got on the team because my mother sponsored the team of 10–14-year-olds, and she made sure each player got the necessary hat and shirt. Most times a team was named, naturally, after the sponsoring business. For example, there were the Coke Bottlers, the Shotwell Electrics, and in our case, "The Scrappers," named to honor L. L. Langdon, without the additional label of Wool, Hides, Furs, or Pelts. If you didn't like the name of your team, you didn't have to play, but you didn't get a shirt or cap either. I didn't play or hit all that well, but I sure enjoyed the game! Oh, and if you played baseball, you were automatically part of the Knothole Gang (and part of the radio station's "KLIX Clickers; I still have my clicker) and could sit with your parents in a select part of the baseball park where the real professional baseball players played.

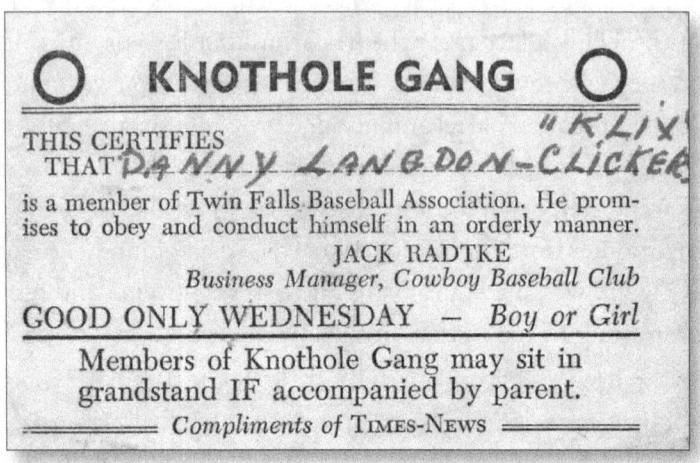

THIS CERTIFIES THAT *DANNY LANGDON-CLICKER* "KLIX"
is a member of Twin Falls Baseball Association. He promises to obey and conduct himself in an orderly manner.
JACK RADTKE
Business Manager, Cowboy Baseball Club
GOOD ONLY WEDNESDAY — *Boy or Girl*
Members of Knothole Gang may sit in grandstand IF accompanied by parent.
Compliments of TIMES-NEWS

This is Danny's Knothole Gang Card that got him in the special section with his parent to watch a game of the then Twin Falls Cowboys, a minor league team of the New York Yankees

It was around age ten, just after getting so used to traversing Rock Creek Canyon on my own, that I was given the opportunity to step well beyond the boundary of home. I went to another part of Idaho I'd never been to. It turned out to be the biggest part of my getting used to being away from home, especially without the comfort of family, as was the case camping on the Little Wood River. Even when camping with family I was known to try and take my personal mementos of home with me if at all possible. This new venture out of my security of home sweet home was made possible by my sister Dorothy. A few years out of the house by then and married to Carl Peterson, the man of her cowgirl dreams, Dorothy and Carl now lived on a ranch, and I was invited to come.

Dorothy's husband was a cattle rancher, and a cowboy if there was ever one. He was a man's man if there ever was such a real designation. He was tall, lean, and often had a toothpick on his lips, but was reserved and laid back. He wore, of course, the obligatory cowboy hat, or straw version of one when working, and was quite stately in a way that pretend cowboys are truly not. He could ride, pull a steer down, and ride with the wind. Considering how wild my sister was, he needed all the wind there was! They had three ranches over their lifetime, and I got to go to each one. My sister, probably with our mother's encouragement, asked me to come to their ranch, and I did many times. Initially it was for a week to get used to it, then longer periods as I got older, and for a break from my summer jobs before going back to college. The first time I packed several items from my room at home including plaster figures I had molded and other stuff I would not need but were reminders of home. Gradually I learned to just take myself, and of course, my fishing rod and waders (boots), and some of those nightcrawlers.

The Petersons' first ranch was way up in the Sawtooth mountains above Salmon, Idaho. Accessible only by four-wheel truck or jeep, you had to go in the Spring, Summer, or Fall as the narrow gravel Winter roads were often impassable. They raised cattle and often got socked-in during the winter. It was beautiful with a sloping grassland pasture for cattle grazing nestled in amongst the backdrop of the Sawtooth National Forest. The ranch horses wandered around in their corrals as if they owned the place, swatting off horse flies with their tail. There was a log cabin, split rail fences, a barn, and tack room. It was remote enough that my sister once shot and killed a black bear out the front door that was obviously after whatever was inside the cabin.

I learned how to ride a horse with little real success. It kept pumping my skinny little body up and down and I could not figure how to handle the coordination that riding requires in such continuous motion. Once, my brother Buzz and I were riding on the same horse and got bucked off when we met both a dog and cat at the same point of intersection on a path between the barn and the house. The horse first successfully bucked my brother off, then rode along the corral fence line, dragging my leg between his body and the pole fencing. Then, he reared, bucked me to the ground, and for good measure, stomped on my right rib. Nothing was broken fortunately, although my pride was a bit bruised.

I was, understandably, always a bit squeamish after that about riding horses, but I still managed a ride now and then again. Horses know better, I think, than to let me on them!

It was the second Peterson ranch where I really hit my stride and liked the most. It was 2000 acres that sat in the beautiful Pahsimeroi Valley, up from a postal stop called Ellis, and close to the tiny towns of May and Patterson, Idaho. The Pahsimeroi River, incidentally, empties into the powerful Salmon River that became my place of choice for my salmon fishing days, that I'll discuss shortly. First, the Pahsimeroi.

I've probably been to the Pahsimeroi ranch 20 times or more, but one of the earliest was certainly one of more memorable ones. One year, my brother Buzz and I took a bus all the way from Twin Falls to spend part of the summer at Dorothy's ranch in May, Idaho. It seems that the letter Mother had sent Dorothy containing the pertinent information about our arrival and the time we would need to be picked up from the bus stop had never reached Dorothy because when the bus dropped us off in Ellis, Dorothy was nowhere to be found. It was approaching evening, and the mailman who lived and tended to the one and only combination house and gas station that constituted the "town" of Ellis, called our sister on the party line, and told her what the situation was. It was then approaching the darkness of night, so together they decided it best to wait until the next morning and he would drop us off as he made his mail deliveries along the ten-miles route to their ranch. That night we slept on the softest feather mattress I have ever experienced; so soft that Buzz and I rolled together in the middle for the night's sleep, of which there was very little.

The next morning, we rode along in the mailman's jeep as he made numerous stops and deliveries to a great variety of mailboxes, mounted on poles or other devices, such as an old plow or milk can. And he chewed and spit tobacco all the way along the road, with his window rolled down, leaving a trail of foul tobacco chew behind us. Never ever will I forget that man and all his ways. But we made it ever so thankfully and had a great time, and a great story to tell again and again!

I simply loved the Pahsimeroi ranch, with all its varied activity and the man they called Fred, their long time hired hand. Fred was so kind to me and chuckled in a silent laugh whenever I did anything a greenhorn would do. He didn't say much, ever, but his communication was without words! Once, for example, I was riding the wood sled which was used to gather hay out in the pasture. I had got my rear cheek pinched between two of the tree poles that comprised the floor of the skid (without wheels) pulled by a horse. Rather than say anything, I toughed it out until my ass let loose. Fred observed all this, and he could only chuckle to himself as he saw the young quiet boy not let it be known that he wasn't enjoying the ride. We laughed about this many a time thereafter as he reenacted the story as often as he could to my sister and her family over the family dinner table. I was trapped, by the way, during such dinners, as the long booth dining table prevented my escape until the dishes were washed. Naturally, as a kid, I was one of the first, along with their two girls (Mary and Jenny), to have to enter the booth! Carl always sat at one of the two open ends with a toothpick in his mouth at the conclusion of dinner, while Dorothy sat across so she could tend cooking and bring the food to the table. That might include a chicken that she had shot in the yard that day and dressed right on the spot. They had all the rest of us kids and guests trapped till the evening meal and talk was truly done.

Besides family, the main thing I liked at the Pahsimeroi ranch was its setting. The area is a big valley scattered with numerous ranches. Running up the middle of the valley is the Pahsimeroi River. It's a perfect river: not too wide, not too rugged, and full of plenty of trout—at least at the time of my youth. I would be given permission by one of the ranchers, though a telephone party-line call from my sister, and I would go at daybreak by myself to fish. I used the traditional spinner-and-worm combination taught to me by my mother and I easily reached my limit, or perhaps a little bit more, within an hour and a half. The beauty and serenity of the sun coming up, the mosquitos wanting their breakfast of me, and walking through the middle of that stream with my hip boot waders on in the cold water was heavenly. I didn't mind the morning chill so much

129

as when the sun beat down relentlessly and it warmed both rubber waders and my back and arms. A couple of times I almost sank like an anchor as the water gushed into my boots when I waded into too deep a hole. The willow branches along the stream always saved me, and I simply drained my boots and trekked on to the next fishing hole. I'd go home to the ranch to exercise my bragging rights on the catch of the day. That evening Dorothy would fry the fish and they helped recollect for her and me our days as the Langdon family on the Little Wood River.

Later in my teens I ventured to the Salmon River, just above Ellis, still with its single store, and did days and days of salmon fishing. Most often I had that part of the river to myself, but over time others found my fishing hole. If you visit the area today there is literally a paved parking lot, and you find several fisherpersons jockeying for position—even using small dinghies. I had been the lucky one to have found and benefited from its abundance as a youth. I could catch onto a twenty-pound salmon and wrestle with it there on the line for 45 minutes and it was a battle of wills between me and the fish. As the great fish grew tired, I'd run up the bank and land it like some landing barge on D-Day. When I used to reflect on how that salmon made its way from the Pacific Ocean all the way to my point on the Salmon River, I was simply in awe of the nature of nature. It had lost half its original weight by the time I saw and caught it. These days I only rarely drive by that fishing hole on the river where I used to fish and dream of those days gone by.

Later towards their retirement, Dorothy and Carl settled on a third ranch. Downsizing to 320 acres (imagine that as a downsizing) their new ranch is in a pretty valley up near Lemhi and Tendoy, Idaho, near Hayden Creek. Dorothy's daughter, my niece Jenny, and her husband, Gary, keep alive the rugged looks of that ranch. I am a fortunate adult to be able to go and spend a few days remembering the good old days. And while the numerous antelope I used to see off the roadside while I drove to their various ranches have long backed away from the roads as civilization erodes the area, remembrances of those days are still strong. Later on in my 50s, I traveled that road again and saw a few antelope, and tears came to my eyes. Also, the fishing is not nearly as good as it used to be, yet perfectly adequate now for an old fisherman with high standards!

I think you have learned from your reading by this point that I had experienced a lot as a young boy, in a most extraordinary living environment. All those previous experiences and adventures were to pay off, it turns out, without my even being aware. I ventured out in young adulthood with so much more confidence than in my younger days, and generally on my own. What I have found is that life is one hell of a ride and I would come to relax and enjoy it so much for all that it has to offer!

Before I turn to describing my high school days, there was a kind of "priming" activity, as I like to think of it, that I participated in and it really helped me get over being so shy as I was in junior high, let alone initiated some leadership qualities I apparently possessed, but had no idea that I did. This social activity helped me to become much more out-going, especially in preparation (priming me as such) for high school where socialization is important to personal development. This activity was so seminal to my development that I would like to offer it up as a suggestion to other shy boys or girls. I became a Boy Scout.

My brother was a Boy Scout, so therefore I became, I suppose, a Boy Scout, although we were in different troops sponsored by different churches. His troop sponsor was the First Baptist Church, where my mother was a member for years and I was later baptized. I joined, however, the scout troop sponsored by the local Presbyterian Church across from the junior high. It was my new friends like Ellis Miller, Billy Durban, and others who got me involved in Troop 66. We were led by Mr. Warren Barry, the adult scoutmaster, who was so kind and instructive in so many ways as a male figure—perhaps important to me since I had lost my father at age seven. Under his guidance, I think we all became better boys on their way to being young teens and eventually adults.

I really liked scouting. You have to learn how to work at it as it's a struggle to earn certain merit badges among the 100 or so available. Scouting, as it turned out, fit perfectly into the outdoor adventurous life of our family. Much of scouting is lessons in learning fortitude, if not lots of patience trying to learn, for example, the Morse Code or how to tie different knots. Along with earning merit badges, going to summer camp in the forest and in the winter to the troops' winter lodge, scouting was much about fun and personally for me leadership, as it was about building friendships with others of my age. The winter lodge in the South Hills near Magic Mountain Ski Resort had its own modest rope ski tow, so we had our own kind of private mountain to enjoy. Other than the fact that I had to wear my sister's previously used ski pants (with the zipper on the side), I rather enjoyed skiing. Once I found a pair of skis in the scrapyard - used formerly by a Second World War ski patrol fighting unit - among various things in the attic of The Warehouse. I painted them white on top with a red strip down the middle and waxed the underside to a careful sheen. They were just ugly enough that I nearly abandoned winter sports altogether. Fortunately, it was the summer camping I liked the best, as it was warmer, more like camping on the Little Wood River, which I had much experienced and so enjoyed.

I was steadily earning merit badges and finally accumulated the twenty-one needed to be designated an Eagle Scout. I even attained the select Order of the Arrow designation, for those who know what that is. The principal skill for the latter was to camp on my own overnight on a mountainside with nothing but two matches, a drinking cup, a canteen of water, two uncooked eggs, a sleeping bag, and a bit of oatmeal. For a boy that had done all the camping I had, sleeping alone on the mountainside by myself was a piece of cake. I started a fire with only the two matches provided (that was the idea) and boiled the two eggs in the drinking cup I had but didn't prepare the oatmeal because I didn't particularly like oatmeal. I survived the wilderness without too much fright, stacking pine boughs over me to keep warm. The next summer I participated in a search and rescue simulation in which I was the lost person on the side of that same mountain. I found it an odd experience, because I had to tell those trying to find me as they were passing me by that I was the lost person. They were thrilled—as was I—to get off the mountain and have a donut to eat! Doing things like scouting and staying on the mountain alone did loads for developing my feeling of accomplishment, as well as helping me learn to take risks, and promoting my curiosity.

We did loads of other fun things in the Scouts that I think helped in my overall social development. In teams of four, we made our way down a small river on rafts we had made from logs we had lashed together. We went hiking to pristine lakes in the distant mountains and even found dynamite in an old, abandoned mine shack. I was smart enough (can't say that for one other scout) not to take any of it and we reported our finding to the scoutmaster. Another time we did a week's worth of camping at Alturas Lake. During an overnight hike, we stayed at another lake high in the Sawtooth Mountains. We returned the next day to find a tree had fallen, landing precisely along the middle of one of our fellow scout's pup tent. It was next to mine and had fallen slightly across the edge of my tent as well. A fellow scout was saved, if you think about it, the night before we returned!

As a part of Scouting, I was asked to be a Patrol Leader for a group of seven Scouts and we designated ourselves the Apache Patrol. In that role I once organized a fundraising effort for the children's ward of the community hospital. I was helping my mother visit polio patients when I became aware of the need for a new turntable to play records in the kid's area. I solicited my fellow Scouts to collect wire coat hangers from their friends, family, and even strangers, suggesting we go door-to-door. We collected hangers by the hundreds, tied them in neat bundles of 50 each, and sold them to a local dry-cleaning store, two hangers for a penny. We were able to buy not only the record player, but two dozen 78 rpm children's story records and presented it all to the hospital. That's scouting at its finest. And it taught me on a small scale that I could be a leader, and in subsequent years I built on the confidence of leading others.

Some of us ratcheted up the fun in another summer Boy Scouts event. This one really introduced me to many new kids like me, and some who were very different from me too. It was a tremendous learning opportunity that I was lucky enough to participate in: called the National Boy Scout Jamboree.

My brother Buzz (ever the good example, except for those cigars), during his scouting days, had gone to the National Jamboree in Valley Forge, Pennsylvania. So when the Jamboree came up as it did every four years, I attended the Jamboree at Irvine Ranch in southern California, near Los Angeles. It was ironic that many years later, in my professional career, I worked in an office building in the city of Irvine, built on the same Irvine Ranch where I pitched my tent, along with thousands of others. Who knows if my office and my pup tent were not on the same spot? The big benefit of attending the Jamboree was that I met and interacted with Scouts not only from all over the US, but also with some from other countries, so it was an eye-opening experience. We traded artifacts from our own states and countries, my contribution being chunks of lava from the lava fields of southern Idaho. Several movie stars like Bing Crosby, Bob Hope, Lucille Ball, Danny Kay, Red Skelton, Sammy Davis, and others came and entertained us. It became apparent to me that there was a big, wide world out there.

Seminal Moment: Scouting.
The influence that scouting had on me cannot be understated; a fact that I only really realized in writing this book. It was a transition point in my life from being very shy to recognizing that I had some leadership and management skills that were budding.

- *As a patrol leader I led my "team" to get things done like organizing the fund-raising effort for the children's ward at the hospital.*
- *I traveled near and far with others of my age outside my immediate family and I began to see the world and relationships in new ways.*
- *I achieved personal growth by becoming an Eagle Scout and Order of the Arrow; both of which required much diligence with loads of fun.*

Soon my scouting days and junior high were behind me. I entered high school and all that entails as a youth becoming a teen. The new high school had just been completed. Unlike the old high school that was within easy walking distance for most all my brothers and sisters, the new school was two miles on the other side of town. I was 16, and while I had learned to drive, my sister Lorraine and I generally got to school with sister Bertine who was at the time secretary to the principal. We had our own private chauffeur, you might say, for most of two years. However, in my senior year my mother gave me a car she had bought as scrap metal. She paid $50 for a 1930 Dodge DC-8 Business Coupe. It had been sitting in a local farmer's barn for ten years. As she was buying the scrap metal laying around his farm, he asked if she wanted to buy the Dodge as well. She towed it to our home, parked it in front, and let me know it was mine if I liked. It was the same way she had given my brother Buzz an old model-T Ford in his teen years. My Dodge had only 40,000 miles on it, and it ran after I put in a new battery and added fresh oil and gas. I kept that Dodge for 60 years, moving it all over the USA from one job location to another. Every time I began a new job, the Dodge was part of the relocation package. Over those 60 years, more miles were put on that Dodge sitting in a moving van than I ever drove it. I restored it to mint condition while living in California and in my retirement gave it to an auto museum in Tacoma, Washington, where it currently resides. I've been told it is the only surviving one of 126 originally made of that model. You can go see it if you like, sitting there among Bentleys, Cadillacs, Fords, and other fine antique cars. I consider its place in the museum as a legacy to the L. L. Langdon business and my mother's volunteer efforts.

Unlike junior high, I was pretty active in high school. That was all kickstarted on nearly the first day of the tenth grade when all the boys in my class of 300 were assembled in the gym to elect their Sophomore Boys' Club President. I had not thought of being the president, but seated next to me was a relatively new friend by the name of Bobby Showalter.

I was sitting in the gym on a bleacher minding my own business, quiet to myself, next to Bobby Showalter, one of the most popular kids in the sophomore class. Much to my surprise Bobby, spoke up out the

Danny's 1930 Dodge DC-8 Business Coupe Restored by him

blue and said, "Let's make Langdon President!" and they did. I have no idea what made him do that! There have been other such times in my life similar in nature that have led to the expansion of my world and what I have done, and therefore who I became. This was surely one of them; there were select others as I will note throughout the book as "Seminal Moments." These launched me into a whole new direction that I could not have seen or planned. And it wasn't the activity so much as it was what it taught me as possibilities of who and what I was becoming. Sadly, Bobby died just a few weeks ago as I was writing here and I so miss the times talking with my old classmate and friend. Thank you, Bobby Showalter!

From that very day in the bleachers I was launched into many a wonderful experience in high school. In junior high I had played in the band on my mother's suggestion, largely because all the other siblings had played an instrument. Lucille had played the accordion, Bertine the clarinet, Buzz the sax and ukulele, Lorraine the clarinet, and me the trumpet. I had originally started on a French horn but it didn't fit my style or look as cool as I wanted with my hand up the bell of the horn. As

136

anyone who has ever been a band member knows, the high school marching band practices early in the morning and marches at every football game. Being part of a group effort teaches you things about working together. I was also part of the smaller pep band that played at basketball games and occasional assemblies in hopes of motivating the student body. In college I sat in on occasion with a dance band, and it was fun. We played Glenn Miller, Tommy Dorsey, Benny Goodman, and other swing band hits of the 40s and 50s, also known as the "Big Band" era.

Danny – High School 1956

Being the Sophomore Boys' Club president did something to me that I can't quite explain other than letting me know I was liked and could lead. Later in high school I was senior class president for about two weeks (the results of election by raised hands vs. a formal ballot), then vice-president, and ran for student body president against my best friend, Mac Soden. Apparently, I lost the election by a thin margin, but it didn't make any difference to me as our friendship was much more solid than any office either of us might hold. Mac and I were loyal all throughout high school and beyond, and that surely meant a lot to both of us. We are still in occasional contact to this very day. His parents were solid members of the community and I so enjoyed visiting his mother on many an occasion, well to the end of my college years. They lived on the "good side" of town and seeing how they lived was an eye opener to this kid from the other side of the tracks. Mac and I weren't always goody two-shoes, but I guess you'd have to say we were 99% of the time. A couple of incidents might have made you think otherwise though, and it's time to squeal on what Mac and I did. We still talk about these incidents over fifty years later, so he won't mind if I do so one more time!

Danny (center) with two of his best high school friends, Mac Soden and Richard Crandall standing in front of his 1930 Dodge in 1957

I seem to have been well known by the cops in town, but not for any of the serious, nefarious reasons you might imagine. This was really because of my mother's community status, not necessarily any crime spree that I might have perpetuated. Anyhow, on with the other stories so you can fully know the magnitude of my criminal life.

Mac and I were out one evening over near City Park. Mac told me about this trick he'd seen other boys do that he wanted us to try and it would involve the two of us getting on either side of a street around dusk when we can't clearly be seen by a driver. As the driver approaches a given point on a quiet street, we would stand, visible on either side of the road, and pretend to pull as if a rope were strung between the two of us. The poor driver, not knowing otherwise, would come to a screeching halt, and we would laugh and run away. We tried, and it worked well on the first car, so we returned for a second attempt. Well, the second car that came along performed as expected, but this time it happened to be an unmarked police car. The officer on the passenger side, very unamused with our antics, stuck his head out and said, "Langdon, if you ever try that again, I am going to tell your mother!" Point made! Another time, on Cherry Lane where lovers went to make out, we were with a couple of other guys at dusk horsing around. One of us (name not to be revealed) took out a shotgun (the shell with powder only, no BB shot), aimed it in the air, and boom it went. Well, this guy comes running out of his pickup, enraged that we had interrupted his business with his date, and yelled and screamed in our direction. We never did that again either! After these two forays into the depths of criminality, we'd stick with playing pickup basketball at the local elementary school in Mac's neighborhood. Honestly, we didn't do anything wrong ever again, I think. Ask Mac if you see him.

On the more civil side of my high school days I went out for track for three years, but never earned a coveted cloth letter for my band jacket and won only one race on the low-hurdle relay team, for which I was awarded a blue ribbon. As I have commented many a time about my high school track days, I had great form going over the hurdles, just no speed between them. I guess that was because I was only about 5'5" all through high school. I also never seriously thought about playing football, basketball, or even baseball. I only made the junior high basketball team because when the coach lined us up to shoot free throws for tryouts, I made a couple of baskets. I wasn't that good on the floor with nine other players. I'd leave sports in general to my more talented brother Buzz who excelled at such endeavors. I'd enjoy being seated in the stands such as playing in the pep band that supported athletics in its own way.

I dated some, but not a lot—that shy thing—but certainly enough to get the experience and learn how marvelous it was, especially during the last year of high school. I dated a particularly wonderful young girl who, I think, set the bar for what I eventually wanted in a partner. Her name was Mary and she lived across the street from my best friend, Mac. Of course, I really enjoyed dating Mary. What was not to like in her pleasant smile, figure, and ability to carry on a conversation. Her parents were wonderful people as well: warm, gentle, and living the American Dream ,the same as Mac's parents. I often visited with both sets of parents during my college breaks to catch up on how their kids, my friends, were doing. I just had to walk across the street to visit both as they lived on the same street, Maple Street. Such knowledge of good parenting is highly impactful and useful, perhaps even more so for me, since I had a single parent. The knowledge gained from dating a nice girl and getting to know her parents and other good parents, made me aware of certain relationship behaviors I needed to pay attention to. Most of that came to practical use when I was to marry a year later after college. I think Mary taught me what it was like to be with a wonderful person of the opposite sex, who had wonderful parents, and was easy to converse with as a shy person. I like good people! Thanks to having Mac and Mary as friends, and also getting to know their parents, I experienced especially good role models beyond my immediate family.

There were several activities in high school I started participating in that helped me to grow up. I participated in a couple of high school play productions as a stagehand, joined and led the youth bowling league, helped decorate the gym for dances, was a member of the band, held some class offices, and did volunteer work outside of school as well. I remember enjoying "promenading" to '50s music at the beginning of dances in the gym after we had spent hours decorating it in some spring, harvest or winter theme. I don't imagine that's done anymore today. Promenading is when couples form two lines and march hand-in-hand with their partner as they join another line of couples till all were spread throughout the dance floor only then do you start dancing as a couple. It may seem kind of silly today, but it was part of being a teen, learning to socialize, and being with a girl. Since my sister was a dance teacher, I learned how to dance from her. She started me out with something easy: the Box Step. I remember it felt a little goofy dancing in a square on the floor, but it was a start. I soon advanced to the beat of Rock and Roll, and I think I am still pretty good at it—hips and all! My wife says I have a screwy look on my face when I dance, but you have to let yourself go to really experience the music, just as you have to sometimes in other aspects of life. Still love Rock and Roll! I do a fairly good rendition of Buddy Holly's, "Oh, Boy" on my guitar.

I suppose everyone going to high school knows there are times when you get a little silly. In my senior year, I persuaded four of my guy friends to join me, nearing our graduation, in performing a skit for the traditional "Senior Day Assembly." We dressed in borrowed girls' drill team outfits and did a little routine that got quite the applause, as well as loads of laughter. I think we looked pretty good dressed in short blue velvet outfits with white fur trim as we did a line dance shoulder to shoulder, arm clasping arm, kicking up our somewhat hairy legs as if our version of the Rockettes. In the annual "Stunt Assembly" for all class levels, we organized our class around an "Ali Baba and the Forty Thieves" number that went over big. Twenty of us seniors secretly hid in a small tent and emerged to much laughter as we began our production. We won that year's competition. Perhaps it was my sister Lucille's influence as a dance teacher that gave me the idea that things like this were possible. I felt blessed, I know, to have brothers and sisters, who in their own right, were so talented, and we could share together the applause that builds confidence and skill at whatever we wanted to try (while still being scared out of our pants). I still have a picture of the five of us boys in that chorus line, those outfits haphazardly held together at the back with safety pins. It all makes me laugh today and feel warm affection for those wonderful days—the '50s with rock and roll, innocents, and adventures.

During high school summer days I had plenty of guys to pal around with like Jimmy Alger, Bill Stowe, Herb Carlson, Ellis Miller, Billy Durban, Jerry Boyd, and, of course, Mac. Most of us had summer jobs that cut into our times together, but we did find time occasionally for pickup basketball at the local elementary school or when we would sneak into the Mormon LDS recreation (cultural) hall where none of us were members of the faith. In our senior year there was a German exchange student, Bernd Leusner, who was culturally different and interesting, if for no other reason than trying to communicate with him through our cultural and language differences. He has contacted me later on in life to tell me what a great time he had with me and how he appreciated that I had accepted him for being himself. That was my very first introduction to how to treat a foreigner, and I've subsequently since met thousands, then been the foreigner myself, during all my world travels.

In high school, I had a nice range of friends. I especially liked Ellis Miller. As a budding astronomer he had a telescope at his house, and I'd drop in for a look see or spend the night. Later in life he became an astrophysicist and professor. Others, like Bill Stowe, Herb Carlson, and I, went to college together and pledged to the same fraternity. We were known as "The Three Musketeers," as we were not only from the same town but hung together throughout our college days and stayed in contact in adult life. Bill started and ran a very successful winery, Indian Creek in Idaho, and I happily volunteered and drank a few bottles of his grapes. Herb, scarred mentally and physically due to a hunting accident that almost blew off some of his left hand, struggled a bit with life, but ended up owning a huge tract of land on what's known as Eagle Island. I imagined it worth a great deal of money, but mostly for him a haven of beauty and relaxation during his final years. We visited there a few times and reflected on our college days together and the way we laughed about so many things we had done together as The Three Musketeers. Isn't it great to have such memories?

I was occasionally, even during high school, still doing things around The Warehouse, but I could tell I was backing away from it and the other business locations of L. L. Langdon as primary sources of activity. Probably, in reality, I was transitioning boyish activities to youth or even young man interests. For example, at The Warehouse one day, I saw in a shed area what appeared to be a car without several of the necessary components to be a fully functional mode of transport. It was smaller than most cars with tires about ¾ the size of ordinary car tires. I learned that it was a very uncommon vehicle: a Crosley. Seeing that hunk of metal standing there in the yard, I got the idea of rebuilding the old Crosley into some weird transportation for personal use. It had the frame, steering wheel, four small tires, motor, and the basics needed to be a real car. However, it had no flooring, seats, tire rims, dashboard, basic wiring, or all that was required to start and monitor what's going on with the car, let alone a place to sit and drive. Oh yeah, and no covered body to protect passengers from the rain, wind, or rocks thrown up by any other vehicle. It fortunately did have a set of working brakes. With the help of one of mother's workers, we gathered and put all the missing pieces together, minus a body, from such things as a found speedometer from an old ambulance, and a set of taillights. Wiring was garnered from another car that had seen its day. We used two rusted iron tractor wheels cut in half to make four fenders to cover the tires. We found and added miscellaneous other essential parts, and finally two bucket seats from an old airplane that had been left to disuse at the local airport. This new, yet old, "car" eventually ran, though the valve-lifters were a little suspect.

As a teen with his first driver's license, I used it to drive this sort of a car on some of our local city streets but fearing my recently found friends the police (remember my incident with Mac), and without a required registration, I drove most times on dirt roads that were part of the canal system in the countryside. With no license plates, this was wise. I used this "car" mainly for the purpose of duck hunting along the canal. Making new things from the abundant supply at my personal disposal in the junkyard was an activity, I am certain, that was useful in developing my emerging curiosity by exploring possibilities: this translated later in life to fostering the creative side of my professional career. Professionally

This is the Crosley that Danny and Mother's hired hand restored to running order with various parts from the junkyard sitting in front of the family house in winter

I used my skills to develop business solutions, new formats for learning, and writing in general. Thus, in my formative years, there was a lot of trial and error before getting into the more serious side of life. To that end of maturing, I'll describe another summertime activity that was very helpful in developing a more outgoing nature for this shy boy.

During the summer between my junior and senior year, I was selected by the local chapter of the American Legion to be part of an eight-youth contingent who would attend what is called Boys State. It was held in the capital city, Boise. Boys State is a weeklong program where it is intended that young people learn about the workings of government—they had one for girls as well. It was an event that taught me several things I would have not otherwise likely experienced. Essentially you studied how the government is organized, assembled into mock political groups (whatever that meant to us young boys), ran and campaigned for various state or federal political offices and got elected, or not. We had to strategize our own campaigns. I ran for US Senator from Idaho. As part of my campaign, I prepared and handed out leaflets, and tried to be cordial to every other kid I met. I lost by three votes I was told—a trend of sorts since I had lost Student Body President in high school by about the same number. To my way of thinking, losing an election, though disappointing, was a lesson of life, not a defeat. Regardless, I ended up being appointed by the new student state of Idaho governor of Boys' State to be head of the Idaho State penitentiary, a job much more to my liking than being a senator. I was invited by existing prison officials to the actual old penitentiary, given a tour, awarded an honorary key to the place, and I pardoned more than one imaginary inmate. Since I liked political science in high school this was a practical experience for me to have had, and I learned a thing or two, not the least of which is how to lose an election honorably.

It was also during my high school years that I was fortunate to have a number of different summer jobs, so playing lots of pickup basketball or hanging at other teenage venues was somewhat curtailed. For our lucky generation that I was part of, jobs were plentiful for youth and I had my share of interesting, mostly paid summer work.

I was becoming an industrious kid, apparently, from all that activity in the junk piles, and much of that experience came to be useful in the eight different jobs I held during the summers of my high school and college days. Fortunately, the kind of jobs available in my small community were good for teens. These included farm jobs, but I was a city kid, and anyhow had no viable and reliable transportation, other than a bicycle, in my early working career as a teen.

The first job I ever had was selling newspapers on the streets of Twin Falls. Yes, in those days, kids were often hired to hawk daily newspapers walking up and down main street. Like something from a movie, I would shout, "Newspaper, newspaper, read all about it , get your newspaper right here! Only five cents!" As a teen, you also had the option to deliver papers though a routine bike route, but I wasn't interested in regular employment. I liked roaming downtown, and while I frankly didn't sell a lot after the initial investment of 5-cents for two papers that I then sold for 5 cents each, I was content with the effort and modest profit for the goodies I wanted to buy with my own money. You'll discover about me that money, even during my professional years, wasn't a big driving force, but I managed to do all right and I was having fun working. I found that I liked work of a select kind that was fulfilling and engaged me in being active of a different sort from ordinary play, a message honed by my mother; not so much about her own work, but about how to approach life, including the role that money plays. "You have to like your work if you are going to like life," or words to that effect she would say. Glad I listened!

I certainly didn't step up to a higher income bracket when I took on my next temporary work: setting pins at the local bowling alley. At that time there were no automatic pin setters. They were about to be introduced and would displace this particular summer job, but I was employed to gather pins that had fallen on a first throw and needed reset by human power and placed in the appropriate ten slots of a mechanically driven pin setting machine. Standing there in the pit where the fallen pins lay, you gathered the pins, lay them overhead in their appropriate slots in the setter, pulled on a release cord and the machine set the pins exactly in place. I was one of the young kids who learned to quickly gather the fallen pins so that by the time the ball traveled the distance of the return chute and emerged on the rack to be picked up, the bowler was ready to continue and throw their second ball. I quickly learned that the average bowler was not all that aware of young boys like me picking up pins and you had to keep an eye out for an errant six-pound bowling ball coming your way at great velocity. Never got hit, but it was close on occasion. When it was too close, you couldn't help expressing an inaudible set of select words directed at the bowler out of sheer caution, of course. For this I was paid fifteen cents a "line," which was good money for a kid whose main goals were to while away his free time on the alley's pinball machines and to save a dime or two for a root beer soda or chocolate ice cream cone.

I really stepped-up summer employment when I started selling concessions at the professional baseball games and annually when the rodeo was on at the county fairgrounds located in Filer, Idaho, just seven miles west of town. We went pretty much every day for the entire week the rodeo was on, not so much for the rodeo itself (except sister Dorothy who participated to show her horse-riding skills), but because our church, the First Baptist Church, had a food booth that served delicious homemade chili, burgers, and pie. My mother was usually the lead organizer for the booth, which was sponsored by her church group, the Amoma Class. I went along, as did my siblings not only for the food, but, of course, the fair rides and rodeo. I used to play bingo at a booth close to the church booth and won lots of prizes I really didn't need. Mother would take care of my winnings by redistributing the blankets, pottery, and stuffed animals I won to people she knew were in need. She also exhibited at the fair her vast collection of antiques, garnering quite a number of first prize blue ribbons. I have a horse story about a fair later in life I'll want to tell you about when I describe my family days, but back to selling concessions.

Surprising for its size, Twin Falls had a professional baseball team which was first affiliated with the New York Yankees, then the Chicago Cubs. They played in a magnificent baseball stadium constructed almost entirely of wood that was located on the other side of town from where we lived. Bleachers, 30-rows deep, were situated on the first and third base lines and behind home plate, and a ten-foot fence enclosed the outfield linking to the seating stands just after the area devoted to respective team pitchers' that warmed up on either side of the field. For those willing to pay an extra price or have season tickets there were three rows of select box seats along the first and third base lines, as well as behind home plate. A huge scoreboard in center field displayed game statistics and was updated to live game activity by a person who slipped wooden numbered cards into place each inning for strikes, balls, hits, runs, errors, and outs. There were painted billboards advertising local businesses all along the inside outfield fencing. You had to pay to get in or, if you knew how, get someone to hoist you up so you could climb over the ten-foot fence, letting yourself down without breaking an ankle. If you didn't care to see (or afford) the actual game inside the stadium you could wonder the outside area where cars parked and shag for the occasional foul ball that came over into the parking area, or a homerun over the outfield fencing. On three occasions I was the lucky one to run down a foul ball among the many teens that vied for this form of attending a ballgame.

One of the earliest memories of this well-supported and attended community event center that I can remember is the day the famous Yankee ball player and long-time homerun champion, Babe Ruth, died. They gave us the day off school and a minute of silence was called for at the evening game that was played that day. The team was called the Twin Falls Cowboys (later the Magic Valley Cowboys), a class-C ball club, just one step up from what was affectionately known as the "Lunch Bucket League," or class-D clubs. The ball players were all very young men with high hopes for the big leagues that were not likely to be achieved but they would give it their best try/shot.

For three or four years our sister Bertine (and Lorraine after her) had been managing and selling concessions in an area just inside the entrance to the ballpark. This staging area was used by young teens who would load up there, then wander in the stands with boxes of goodies strung by a strap around their neck selling popcorn, soda, and the like. That's what I wanted to do, just as my brother, Buzz, was doing. Now that I was of age, I am certain my sisters, being part of the management, held some sway in perhaps my being hired. Nothing goes further than a little nepotism when it comes to employment. I began my employment in the summer of 1954.

I had my job at the ballpark for one summer which continued for a subsequent summer stint. I began my employment initially selling bags of popcorn and peanuts, so appropriate for my small physical frame. Then, earning a slightly larger commission, I started selling candy and soda, and eventually, the second summer, sold cups of hot coffee from a heavy urn I carted around the stands. The peanuts and popcorn were easy products to sell, as well as the fact that the weight was easier to bear on your neck. Carting around and selling soda or coffee was another matter. Management kept telling me I couldn't sell these heavy items because of my size, but I was bound to prove them wrong. I eventually did. And the commission on sales was larger. Lugging a huge container of hot coffee was indeed a challenge and I wondered if my sales were sometimes based on sympathy for a 5' 1" kid carrying that much weight around? "Hot, hot, hot coffee," I would scream, similar to my previous job of selling newspapers on the street. It seemed the shyness that I was experiencing in my youth was itself screaming to go away and I started letting that happen in no small measure, I am sure, selling concessions as I interacted with various strangers (customers) at the ballpark.

I got pretty good at the sales process wandering around in the stands. By the sixth inning or so fans were pretty filled with their popcorn, hot dogs, soda, and sales started to ebb, and so I got clever to garner additional attention and sales. I had this phrase I devised, just to see if fans were paying attention as I stroll up and down the wooden steps: "Peacorn, Popnuts, Sodagum, Chewingwater, get em' while they're hot or cold!" Most people paid no mind as their attention was on the play on the field or the occasional foul ball that was up for grabs, but now and then someone would notice my ploy and, with a grin, buy a bag of peanuts to take home.

I had my sights on bigger things after two summers of hawking concessions. I wanted to be closer to the action on the field. No, not as a player, as I was too young and didn't have enough talent. How about being one of the batboys?

I became one of the local team's batboys between my sophomore and junior year of high school. Along with another boy, Earl, for two summers I learned a lot, but mostly had great fun. I shined the players' cleated shoes often without getting paid sometimes, went hunting or fishing with players, and learned new swear words. I was paid pretty well for a night's work retrieving bats, tracking down foul balls, and scuffing the new baseballs prior to the game: shiny new balls don't have the grip pitchers need to throw the ball the way they want. Plus, I got to have a free baseball now and then and any of the broken bats which I could then nail and tape together again for use in little league baseball. I got the job because I was nominated by the principal of our school, Mr. Flatt. Years later I would student teach chemistry under his supervision.

Danny (far right), batboy for the Magic Valley Cowboys when they were affiliated as a minor league team with the Chicago Cubs in 1956

For my next employment, I slid down the corporate ladder. It was a part time day job to my night work as a batboy. I signed up as an umpire for community baseball as part of the city summer program for youth. It was mostly little league baseball for kids, but occasionally I'd call games for the older high school boys who played in the American Legion level of baseball. It was the worst summer job I've ever had in my 60 years of work. It wasn't the umpiring that made it so difficult. It was the parents of the players. I would get behind the plate or out back of the pitcher and call game after game for kids ages 8 to 18. The young kids were easy, the older teens could be a challenge, but nothing like some parents. I especially remember this one time when I saw a pop-fly coming down along the third-base line. I ran over exactly where the ball was dropping and when it hit the ground, I put my foot on the exact spot where it landed. I looked along the hardly visible third base chalk line. It was clearly a foul ball and I yelled, "Foul!" Well, this father went kind of nuts on me, ran onto the field, argued with me for what seemed like an hour, but was only three minutes, and finally threatened to have my job. I remember thanking him for wanting my job in demonstration of the smartass that I was gradually becoming (and to this day)! A subsequent discussion between him, me, and the park recreational supervisor confirmed that I was neither going to have to change that call nor lose my job. However, I didn't sign up to be an umpire the following summer. I think I consistently followed my own advice for the rest of my entire professional career thereafter: I was learning what I did not like—and still don't to this day—conflict! I also learned that I didn't have to put up with egregiously bad behavior of fellow workers or managers, certainly not a parent out of control!

Things got a little more serious when I got my next job, essentially as an apprentice electrician. I wasn't technically an apprentice due to my age, but more the assistant to a real electrician. I learned from a classmate that her dad, the owner of a local electrical outfit (Shotwell's), wanted to hire a high school kid for the summer. They were going to be replacing all the light fixtures in our old junior high and the lead electrician doing the work needed a helper to carry metal conduit pipe, wire, string electrical cable, remove and replace old outlets and switches, and anything else he directed to be done. I got up the nerve (it really turned out to be my first job interview) and I went to see Mr. Shotwell. I told him all my knowledge (and no experience) about electricity, none of which was useful for the job. You may recall I had strung wire across the alley when we kids tried to dig our way to China using a discarded fan. Well he was apparently impressed enough to hire me! I got real hourly pay and worked essentially a 40-hour week with tax deductions—my first W-4 tax form—and a biweekly paycheck.

During my days with Shotwell's Utility, I am pleased to report only one hammer fell off a ladder and landed on my head, I got pinned against a transformer that was fortunately disconnected, and I was shocked a half dozen times connecting or disconnecting fixtures or replacing outlets. The real electrician who supervised and guided me was a gentle soul who patiently taught me how to cut wire, crimp conduit, and let me suggest how the work materials could be positioned to improve workflow. He even showed me how to stick my finger in a light socket and feel the flutter of the current rather than the jolting shock which, it turns out, is mostly in our mind from not knowing that it is coming—hard to believe, I know, but it's true! Just don't stand in a puddle of water should you care to try this!

I was by this time developing a knack for organization, and during the next summer when they invited me back to the electrical shop, I rearranged the storage room at their downtown office. I also went out on various jobs at homes and businesses with that same electrician who had taught me so much. I earned enough money to open my very first savings account and began to learn what real money could do for a boy, let alone where it might get him. I was learning, especially from this job forward, skills in organizing and improving things that went on to become one of the more important capabilities throughout my life. Years later, I eventually became a recognized expert about work in business and how it can be improved by everyone in the organization on their own initiative.

I don't know if my next summer job was necessarily a better job than being an electrician's assistant, but I found a job close to my neighborhood that allowed me to show some real initiative. I discovered this one pretty much on my own! Do you recall the Jerome Co-op Creamery building that I described earlier a few blocks south of our house on 4th Avenue West? It was near the railroad tracks and the wooden train trestle over Rock Creek Canyon. Well, I heard they were looking for someone, so again I got up the nerve, went into their office and inquired about summer work. I guess I hit them at the right time as they were hiring a temporary for the summer to work in their ice cream making operation. Imagine a young developing teen working in an ice cream making factory. And they made popsicles as well. Had I died and gone to job making heaven or what???

My new job was assisting the lead ice cream maker, a very nice but rather simple man who could have learned a lesson or two in how to manage and run things. This might be the very job that started my consulting skills that I eventually used so skillfully later in my professional career. You'll soon learn that I needed to hone my consulting skills (one of which is to speak up), and I am pleased to report that I did make that happen thanks to much of my varying summer employment.

I can report that the art of speaking up actually began one particular workday after I had been on the job for a month. In this case study I had observed, at the beginning of my shift, a glass bottle with some crossbones. Apparently, someone in maintenance had taken the liberty to reuse an empty bottle of flavored syrup normally used for preparing mint flavored ice cream and filled it with a cleaning fluid they used on the array of equipment that made the ice cream. I pointed out to my supervisor that he had just added the cleaning fluid—skull and crossbones clearly marking on the bottle—that he thought was mint extract into a 300-gallon mixture preparing mint flavored ice cream. He took a careful look, thanked me for noticing and speaking up, and we proceeded to dump the whole batch down the drain—all three hundred gallons.

Another time my supervisor delayed getting help to me as I will filling pint-sized containers of ice cream (with one hand, while folding them shut with the other hand) in rapid succession. The stacking table was completely full of ever-emerging containers. Having asked him repeatedly to clear the table and get the pints into their metal racks and into the freezer, my final way of getting his attention was to sling each container as it was filled over my left shoulder in his general direction. A dozen of these missiles finally got his attention. Thereafter he seemed to learn that I had good ideas. I am pleased to note that I have never again used the technique of throwing containers of ice cream in my consulting practice in corporate America or overseas. I have figured out what work is, and especially how workers can figure out how to improve their work practices themselves. In this way I don't have to tell (or throw things at) them, rather they do it themselves on their own initiative.

I really liked this summer job, if for no other reason than I got to eat all the ice cream and popsicles I could stomach. We also made this wonderful mint flavored chocolate covered ice cream nuggets of which I could not get enough. We also made cottage cheese in our unit of production, but I am only mildly attracted to its taste. Others in the plant made cheddar cheese, so I helped myself to an aged slice here or there or to fresh cheese curds right out of the tank. The second summer I came back and drove a refrigerated truck, making deliveries to local retail stores. I liked this work enough to think for fleeting moments that I could get used to the good pay that delivery driving provided. I was dissuaded from such thoughts however, knowing that I was to continue college, and that dream was merely that, a dream. Such misguided dreaming happened more than once in my summer working career and the next and final summer job proved the hardest to relinquish in favor the career path, I finally choose for me.

I came to have a summer job that I really, really liked. In the summer of my final year in college, I floated the notion by my mother that I might want to take a year off college to continue this particular employment. She, as before, dissuaded me of any such notion, and she was ever so wise for having done so. What was this summer job that I found so attractive?

My brother Buzz landed me a job at the local TV station where he was the assistant manager—again I sometimes had to take advantage of nepotism. The station, KMTV, had only been in operation for three years when an opening came up for a summer TV camera operator. Brother Buzz asked, with the general manager's permission, if I could fill in. What a job! I quickly learned how to wheel a very heavy studio camera on a tripod from one end of the studio to the other, dodging heavy cables that connected two cameras on the floor to the control room. Everything was broadcast live, including the commercials. We did the news, sports, and the weather with a man who often had a little wine before going on the air. Commercials were on poster cards held there on tripods, and the cards were moved in and out based on a printed script and the directions from the control booth. It was a loose, but professional operation.

We two camera operators, I, and an older guy, tried occasionally to crack up the news guy by giving him the finger. Other times we got rushed and the commercial didn't go quite the way it was intended. The work was dynamic and fun, one thing most especially. We ran a version of our own local "American Bandstand," like the ever so popular Dick Clark show in the '50s. To the tunes of rock and roll music, with girls from the high school in skirts and bobby socks and boys with sharp crew cuts, we swung those cameras in and out of the action. What a time! And I got paid for it! It would have been great if such times could have lasted forever, but they can't of course. That job was the end of my summer career of various kinds of temporary employment in my youth, but I want to close off my illustrious climb up on the non-existent corporate ladder as a youth by taking the opportunity to describe a job that I had witnessed only once and wished I had had.

You recall the professional baseball team for which I was the batboy for a couple of summers. The games, in or out of town, were always broadcast on one of our three local radio stations, there was no TV yet for this era of my youth! KVMV was the radio station that broadcast each game live, in other words in real time. Joe Clements, a baseball announcing legend in our community, did the play-by-play and was really good at his craft. He had a way of communicating realism over the radio to what otherwise you could only imagine since you didn't "see" the actual action. Every hit, foul ball, line drive, homerun, strike, or ball was called, along with his color commentary. You could literally hear the striking of the bat on the ball! At the home ball games you could see Joe high up in the booth behind home plate calling the action directly in line of sight with the batter and the field below him. Games were even broadcast when the team was out of town. One assumed Joe traveled with the team and called the games from that particular location, for example in Boise or Salt Lake City where one of the league teams was located. The truth of the matter was otherwise, as the saying goes, and I discovered such by pure chance.

One day, with my brother Buzz, we went to KVMV to pick up something he needed, and as it happened, it was game time and the team was out of town. Thinking Joe was out of town calling the game as usual, we entered the station through the front door, then through

155

another, till we entered a hall and passed a window through which we spied Joe seated behind a mic. Instead of announcing from out of town, there he was calling out strikes and balls right in front of us through a window. In the hallway we heard Joe on a loudspeaker as we saw his lips moving in sync in the booth. In a side room was a teletype (look it up) from which a ream of steady paper flowed with loud clicking sounds as it typed; then stopped until some new information was being sent. Joe would occasionally, between innings, go into this room and rip off a sheet of teletype paper, look at it, go back into the announcing booth, and continue calling the game. Yes, he was not at the actual game, but rather in the studio calling it from his home base, there in Twin Falls in the studio. It was all sort of fake (but real), down to the prerecorded crowd noise playing in the background on the playback audio tape machine, while the sound of a ball striking a bat he recreated with a pencil as he tapped onto a piece of hollow wood. That was the job to have, I thought, though I never had a chance in hell of ever having it. Still, it was amazing and so real, but unreal at the same time! Later in life I met and worked under many corporate executives whose jobs seemed to have similar methods of faking it. It was, by the way, the same network station where, when they added TV, I became a cameraman for the summer job I so loved the most. Imagine, one company with two jobs I would have perhaps loved forever, but I had other things in store for my future after those fun summer days of my youth. I ended my summer employment with college graduation in 1961.

It was by this time becoming clear that there was something about my personality that was appealing to others, and it certainly was a benefit to be the son of an extraordinary woman and baby brother to wonderful siblings. I was only about 5' 5" at the end of high school and would have to wait until college to grow another four inches. At class reunions I have attended since graduating from high school (my latest the 65th) nearly every classmate has a story to relate to me of an interaction with my mother. I find it interesting that a woman who was so much a part of a man's world at the time, often working under such dirty and stinky conditions, could be seen as a model for girls and women, and seemingly all my male classmates as well. I was growing physically as well as in other ways, and the girls of my high school class in their sixties (and now eighties!), wondered why I looked taller? I knew that I had grown in ways we all do; in my case I had a great time doing so.

As I leave my boyhood and youth behind here, I want to mention a special place where I often ate lunch or dinner. It might not seem like an exciting topic in the description of one's life, but the venue in question was next in importance to the very house we lived in and to The Warehouse. Its significance is anchored in personal communion with others, a feeling of being at home, and experiencing special memories. And it probably doesn't hurt that, it served great food—especially coconut cream pie!

Our mother, especially during my and Lorraine's high school days, was now parenting her last two children, still living at home. The others popped in and out for summer breaks from college; the oldest ones had married. It was now just mostly the three of us. While Mother was a great cook, with only one or two children now around she could not only afford, but better spend precious hours eating out during or after a long day's work. There was one place that would become like home to us with its own version of home cooking. To this day, it still sits on the same corner it did back then: The Depot Grill on Shoshone Street. It's located just shy of the so-called Singing Bridge that crosses at that point the Rock Creek Canyon. As a typical teen seemingly able to devour any food placed in front of me, I ate at the Depot Grill a lot. I loved the fried chicken, battered deep-fried shrimp, meatloaf, and especially that coconut cream pie I still long for.

The Depot Grill is a Twin Falls institution in every respect. It was owned, in my days there, by the Huller then after the Soran families, and they were like extended members of the Langdon family. The place was usually full of the farm crowd, local businesspersons, and the occasional traveler, as it was suggested as the best place to eat in town. When Mrs. Langdon came in from her work just across the street, and the place was packed, a place to sit was always found for her and her children. That sometimes was the butcher block in the kitchen—a location you can't sit today due to stringent health codes. We'd sit on pulled-up chairs, order our food without looking at the menu we knew by heart, eat, and be on our way. I'd say I went to that place of delight for sure once a week, but it's probably more accurate to say twice a week, spread over seven years of my youth. That was right up through my high school years, plus another three summers upon my return from college. I suppose going to the Peace Corps was what finally cut the cord for eating there so often—and that pie.

The Depot Grill was a practical eatery designed for the everyday needs of the average small-town clientele that included farmers, small business owners, laborers of an assorted kind, families, and kids. It had large booths that accommodated four to eight patrons. Or you could sit at a counter on swivel stools, use of a sink provided out in the open to wash your hands (these were farmers and laborers), and food that was (and still is, I surmise) home cooking—and that pie, oh me oh my! The owners and the patrons were mostly adults that I came to know as they stopped to say hello. They were the farmers who brought in their junk or needed something for fixing their machinery and knew Mrs. Langdon—or Marian, as she preferred to be addressed—who likely had what they wanted. They might even stop and ask her about something they needed from the junkyard or to drop off while she sat at the lunch counter. They were also the businesspeople who knew her trade and she frequented theirs as well. The Grill was convenient in that it was part of our neighborhood. One of our scrapyards was located just catacorner across the street, another one block away at The Hole, and The Warehouse just three blocks. It was a kind of community communication center for all that was or had gone on.

You can sense, I hope, that the Depot Grill was another home to us, not just a restaurant. You can still ask anybody in Twin Falls and they will give you directions to where it is! They will likely tell you, "It's just this side of the railroad tracks, down Shoshone Street, and just shy of the Singing Bridge," although I understand the bridge, unfortunately doesn't sing any longer since it was replaced. Do look for the railway tracks and don't cross over the canyon bridge. Imagine being a lucky boy and youth who ate well with other families; many of which you knew, but often others of whom were strangers, and you would wonder about them and the lives they lived. By the way, I took my prom date, Mary, as did other high schoolers, to the Depot Grill. That's how homey the Grill was. And I always go for a bite anytime I return to Twin Falls for whatever reason.

CHAPTER 6

Danny as a Young Man: Age 19 – 26

Even though we males are not yet men at age 18 or 19, it feels that way when you are on the precipice of manhood. There is a transition going on. You know you can smoke, drink, drive, vote, and be on your own if you choose. It's certainly a time when you feel yourself being more alone, within yourself, worrying about what you will eventually do in life, and generally spending more hours out of the house with more friends and strangers. You have to truly come to terms with yourself, no matter how many other people are around. Sure, you can get lost in drink at college for example, but is that what's important? Just having so called good times? If you want, you can get a job immediately and perhaps that will work for you? Some of my classmates went right into farming as their parents had, and that's good. Others got jobs in construction or went to work for others or started their own business. I respected all those decisions and indeed, later in life when I attended class reunions, I was sorry that I didn't know many of them like I knew others as close friends in high school. I guess you can only really know a limited number of people.

I felt really blessed that I was in a graduating class filled with so many very interesting, talented, and nice people. Our reunions were marvelous, and my wife always spoke highly of the people she met and their relationships with me, and my mother. Asked by others why that was so, I always joked it was the chlorinated water we drank in Twin Falls. Truth is, we were part of what I think of as a lucky generation. We didn't generally have many issues growing up like those in prior or subsequent generations to ours. The Great Depression, unnecessary wars, inflation, political polarization, false conspiracies, mass shootings, gang violence, rampant homelessness, huge personal debt, and the internet have all had their negative impact. I think, in general, the lack of such external pressures in life helped my generation cope more easily with our overall being and with others throughout our life experiences into old age. That why I have often claimed to others that we were the lucky generation.

The summer just before college I ran headfirst into a situation that really (excuse the language) *pissed me off,* perhaps like no other in my life up until that time. It might seem small, but to this youth of 19 it was just so unfair and indicative of the small-mindedness of some people. I'd like to recount the event here because it was particularly important to me at this time of my life.

My mother was very, very active in her community. She was on the church board and participated in other various efforts such as feeding the hungry, attending to the needy, visiting tuberculosis patients at the hospital, actively participating, and leading the Business and Professional Woman's Association. In addition to her work through the church, she also volunteered with polio patients as the chairperson of the March of Dimes. These were profound examples of her devotion to the needs of others. I think her efforts were rooted in both her spiritual side and her own experience of growing up on the side of poverty, as well as in the examples set by a loving grandmother. In another book I wrote about her life, "My Mother Can Beat Up Your Father," I recounted her volunteer side in much detail. It's important, as well, in telling the following to recall here that she had already been honored as Mother of The Year in Idaho by 1953.

There came a time when she wanted to become a member of a particular group for reasons that weren't known to me, but they were

Cover of book Danny wrote about his mother, titled My Mother Can Beat Up Your Father, *published in 2006*

to her. I had been in a kind of similar group, DeMolay, as a youth, for reasons I can't even recall—probably because I had friends who were. These organizations typically have meetings rich with ceremony. One was a group for women that my mother had an interest in, so she applied. Perhaps indicative of its true nature, you were only selected by the unanimous vote of the other members and could be "black-balled," as it is known, meaning any one single vote against you meant you were out, or, in this case, not in. The organization, called Eastern Star, did fine work, but they had a problem; there is a kind of exclusiveness that can be detrimental to their very existence. It's not itself the organization per se, but certain members among its flock, sisterhood, brotherhood, or just because kids are trying to be kids. That's my issue. She was rejected for membership because the son she needed to qualify her membership from a related fraternal organization known as the Masons, was not her child by birth. That hurt in a way that must have gone deep into her heart for a mother who insisted all her children were "her children" and that included stepchildren. It certainly aggravated me and the entire family. Even though Archie, the son in question and a highly active Mason, was her son for all practical purposes (and not thought of as anything but that for reasons I've already explained), he should have counted. Someone in the Eastern Star didn't think so and she was rejected for membership. So I took it upon myself to become a Mason in tedious agony, because not only do I not generally like joining groups and their meetings, but I hated all the memorization I had to do to become a member. But I did. She thereafter was voted in as a member of Eastern Star, and I thereafter didn't go to any Masonic meetings, and all ended well as it should have originally. Incidentally, I pass no judgment on the Masons (my brother, Archie, was one, after all one and rose to its highest ranks as a 32nd degree Mason), but rather my disappointment was with the Eastern Star, or more specifically that one single member who blackballed Mother so unfairly over that dumb-ass rule. My mother always did say, never tolerate fools; as you probably can tell, she passed on that rule to me, and I am proud to report that I seem to have taken her advice to heart. It should also be noted that Mother went on to lead that particular chapter of Eastern Star in Twin Falls, but also became the grand poohbah of a couple of other regional chapters in the state of Idaho. They just didn't know what they were dealing with when it came to crossing her—or her son!

Now that I was emerging from adolescence and finally able to drive, I could explore on my own the greater world around Idaho and beyond. I could, for example, drive to my sister's ranch in central Idaho, do some fishing there, and stay for a few days. Along the way I remember one time I saw an eye-catching mountain, stopped the car, and decided to walk up its steep side to get a better view of the valley below. I think, in retrospect, it was indicative of my developing curiosity about things at that age: and would be true throughout my life. As I ascended the mountain I was almost on my hands and knees climbing due to the steepness of the slope, when I stopped dead in my tracks and saw a coiled rattlesnake looking at me squarely in the eyes, not more than 16 inches away. I can say I learned how to back away instantly. And there were similar adventures when I decided to run without stopping around Red Fish Lake where I was camping. At one point I swam across an inlet in the freezing water with no one around to help should I cramp up. I was testing myself it seems, for reasons I did not even know, but the testing always felt worthwhile and I learned what to do and not do.

I don't know if I ever actually decided to go to college. It was kind of expected of me by example since all of my immediate brothers and sisters did. Of course there was my mother's encouragement. She always said that you can have a good life without an education, just look at her own, but she had this thing for education, knowing full well that it increases the likelihood of a better life if you make it so. She always said how much she enjoyed her school days, even though they ended in the 10th grade. I believe that certain things such as education(and others I shall note), are" tickets," as I call them: things you can earn that make other things possible in life. Education is one of the more important ones. I found others (i.e., an advanced degree, the Peace Corps, writing and publishing, etc.) that were also great tickets to enhance the quality of my life. I am so thankful to have been part of a time when opportunities were plentiful, so long as you kept an eye out for them and chose to make of what they do in the way of character development.

I had no idea what I wanted to study in college. I had trouble getting into an out-of-state institution because of my grade average (somewhere around a B minus), but I could go to either of the two state colleges—in fact, they had to take me. I chose the University of Idaho, probably because it was the farthest away, but also because I liked the campus atmosphere. Atmosphere, ambience, quality, exceptions to the rule, and other attributes like being real have always been a part of what I strive for in life. You'll see it again and again in the way I lived, worked, and traveled. Speaking of being part of a lucky generation, can you imagine going to college for only a $75 tuition fee, and about $300 for room and board *per semester*? Compare that to today and the debt one has to endure in order to begin working and living life on one's own without, as we were able to do as a generation, the added financial pressure. I was lucky yes, but also truly blessed to have grown up in such a time of opportunity.

I initially settled on studying electrical engineering. My best friend, Mac, from high school and the two summer jobs as an apprentice electrician and TV cameraman, were the factors that most likely influenced my decision. Neither of these had much direct relationship to each other besides electrical. This choice turned out to be a big mistake as I hated the program. Also I was so initially nervous of the whole higher education thing where you are really on your own. I failed the introductory engineering drawing course (managed to pull a D) and capped the first semester with just under a 2.0 grade point average, which was not good enough to be initiated that semester by the fraternity I was living in.

At the beginning of my second year, the university administered one of those vocational interest inventories that was designed to help students like me decide what major they were suited to. I already knew it wasn't engineering. I was, from the interest inventory results, apparently suited to be a forest ranger. That made sense given my extensive camping days as a boy who had spent entire summers out communing with nature. I also had, as well, been a Boy Scout, fished many a stream, and even got lost and found in a forest. The fact that the University of Idaho had a leading forestry program might make one wonder if the interest inventory was perhaps a bit slanted to the university's needs, rather than mine. Thus, I didn't opt to go into the forestry program. Rather than select an alternative immediately, I really needed to settle in, improve my grades, and explore other academic options. It would take me every one of those four years at university to learn how to study and pass tests. Gradually I got better at it.

Before describing the major I finally decided upon, I'll address, strange at may seem, the living environment I chose, as it was very consequential in getting myself comfortable with the university experience. It was only after settling into my lodging of choice that I could work on my grade point average and hopefully graduate in something, rather than nothing. I knew that (not so surprising once you know me), I needed some structure, which is itself surprising since I don't like to be told what to do. Living as I did in a fraternity is largely about just that. Through it all, I could be a bit of a rebel and do things my way as it turned out in life. To live where I did was perhaps one of the best decisions, but that's not to say it is right for everyone.

Fraternities get a bad rap, and they deserve it when they do things that are simply stupid such as hazing students or engaging in far too much drinking and partying. I experienced some of this, but I knew boundaries enough to make sure it never hurt me or made me do things I didn't want to do, i.e., drink too much! The atmosphere in our fraternity was good. We were the only fraternity on campus with a housemother and while that might seem a bit childish to some, it afforded learning gracefulness and manners you need as an adult. For example, the senior brotherhood insisted as freshmen we eat the evening meal together in a formal setting with a napkin, knife, fork, and spoon each placed on their proper respective sides. We were to use eating utensils as they were intended, to promote a form of civility (etiquette) if you will, while not stooping over or eating with our mouth open or while talking. There were senior members at the head of the table who would advise you on any inappropriate behavior, including eating habits, at the table to be corrected. We also escorted the housemother to dinner each evening as we were required to meet with her (in her tiny living quarters in the frat house) for half an hour before dinner. She was a confidante, could sew buttons on, and also a lady you could talk to about interesting things, as well as about problems we might have in relationships or with our studies or others in the close quarters of dormitory living. Even more so, perhaps, it was that she was teaching us how to properly interact with the other half—females—of campus and the world, in how to treat them as equals—a lesson well needed for developing young men in all aspects of living with others. I give special thanks to Mrs. Cummings for helping me get started in college and into the greater world on the right track. I was in a secure environment where I could concentrate on my studies, figure out a major, and further develop as a young man. I did.

College, for our generation, was a safe environment, unlike today. The only serious incident I had was early in my freshman year when

I contracted blood poisoning from a minor scratch during my first semester. One day I saw this red line running up my right arm, about four inches long and I had a terrific headache. I tried to tough it out, but little things can end up being more dangerous than looking a snake in the eyes or climbing a canyon cliff or riding your bike down a steep road with faulty brakes. I spent a week in the university infirmary and thanked the doctors for all their work on me. I had survived this and the second year of college, so what was I now going to choose as a major?

I came to like chemistry through a couple of organic chemistry courses I had taken when I switched from engineering to education. I eventually decided on becoming a teacher, mainly because of two high school teachers I admired. Mr. Arnold DePaul taught political science, and I loved his course so much I requested to be allowed in his second course on the advanced topic of political science, a second try at his teaching, that he usually denied as a personal practice to students. I persuaded him to let me enroll nonetheless, and he did. I learned a lot about the world out there and our own government as it was intended to be by our country's founders. The other class that influenced me toward teaching was a chemistry class taught by the former principal of the high school, Mr. John Flatt. I didn't do that well in his class, low Bs as I remember, but I found the subject suited to my evolving "systems" way of thinking. That, as it turned out, matched my inherent aptitude and I would make a career out of being a person who could organize and solve things for others in a variety of corporate arenas where I innovated new approaches to work, managed and taught in the ensuing years.

Speaking of organizing and solving skills, one of the most useful outputs of collegiate undergraduate studies was what I learned about doing research. You have to write lots of papers and give presentations in college. You are struggling to find ways to just get through. You like certain courses and can't stand others (and the professors who teach them), but sometimes the course is required, so you make your peace with it and the professor. For example, I took a Russian history course one time where the professor had the audacity to tell me I earned an A, but he had chosen to give me a B+ instead, thinking I would try harder the next time. What kind of logic is that! Still, I came upon a resource available to everyone which, as it turned out, was seminal in my general success not only in college, but future work in the business world: I learned how to do research and the primary source I used was the library.

Seminal Moment: The Library: Discovering How to do Research. *You might think a library could not initiate a seminal moment, but it can open the world to you without having to step one foot into that world, except for the fact that it makes you want too ever so do that much more. Not just the physical world, but the world of ideas, knowledge, and what others have previously thought:*

- *It provided the means and ways for researching things and ideas.*
- *It showed a wealth of knowledge to build on my own ideas.*
- *It was a quiet place often to myself where I could get some needed study done without the interference of activities and others who would tempt me otherwise to join them (i.e., those constant parties).*

Not being much of a reader of books, I wasn't much of a library guy in high school, although I cherished and personally knew the school librarian (Mrs. Iverson), whose son was a friend of mine. Unlike today's world where you can get information without even physically being there, libraries in my day were hands-on use only. By this, I mean you had to physically go and look through the extensive card catalog, know the large book resources that summarized where articles and studies were to be found, and then needed to physically find those on the extensive library shelves, and it goes on and on. It also helped to personally get to know the librarian when you could not find what you wanted, no matter how many aisles you wandered in and out of, like some giant maze. I used to spend hours in the university library not only studying, but going through books, research papers, thesis studies, newspapers, and encyclopedias. I learned where virtually everything was in the university library. (In later days, I would contribute some of my own published works to those shelves.) I developed my own system of writing quotes and content I needed for course papers on 3" x 5" index cards, each annotated carefully with the original sources. These I would eventually spread on the floor of my fraternity room and put them in an order that fit the topic. I'd then figure out what was missing, go back to the library and prepare the missing cards, insert those in the order of what I was doing, pick the stack up and write my paper, complete with an annotated bibliography. When my papers read well and were complete with resources properly cited, that was half the battle to at least a B: now how to bump it up to an A. Having one of the first electric typewriters in that day and age helped make all my papers look professional, and probably got me an A- rather than a B+ or B rather than a C. In my subsequent career, I became a researcher of new instructional designs (and then later to define a formula for work as a behavioral paradigm for business), and those initial library skills I had learned in college really came to bear. What you do up front may just be useful later, I found, again and again. Even during my Christmas or spring breaks from college, I used my hometown library to find what resources were available to support my college course work. I was such a frequent patron of my hometown library, and came to know the librarian so well, that she gave me my own key to the door. I could come in on weekends, holidays, and closed evenings to use the library at will. Now that's a small town at its finest.

I completed the required 30 credits of chemistry needed to qualify as a high school teacher and earn my Bachelor of Science degree. I was subsequently certified by the State of Idaho as a secondary school teacher, but I had the drive to do one other thing before I began down the teaching path full time: to pursue a graduate degree.

I fulfilled my student teacher practice requirement (nine weeks) in my old high school under the supervision of my sponsor, my high school teacher, Mr. Flat. He introduced me to all five periods' of students on the first day, told them I would teach the class for the next nine weeks, and then he promptly left the classroom, never to return for the entire nine weeks. I was on my own unless I called him in for advice—I only did this once. One of my nieces, poor girl, was in my third period class, and

I held her to the same standard as any student. However I kept her father, my brother Archie, informed of her progress on the side. She did well, considering her uncle was learning the ropes himself!

Before describing what, I studied in graduate school, I'd like to mention that I participated, at the University of Idaho, in a program that even puzzled me as to why I ever got involved. As it turned out, it was to be another building block, mostly on the leadership front, in my development. By law, I was enrolled in the ROTC (Reserved Officers' Training Corps) at the University of Idaho only because, as a land grant college in those days, males had to take mandatory courses in how to become a soldier. It was the

Danny with his Mother attending his college graduation from the University of Idaho in 1961

time of the Cold War, and ROTC enrollment was a requirement if you attended certain so called "land grant" colleges and universities. It was a two-year obligation, four semesters of military-oriented courses in your freshmen and sophomore years. These courses could be followed, if you volunteered, by two more years of courses to become a second lieutenant in the regular army with the obligation to serve two years on active duty following college graduation. It seemed to me at the time that I could hardly plan for one semester, let alone two more years of someone making me march to their orders. The captain of our ROTC unit was so mad at me for not signing up to become a soldier by taking advantage of the military courses offered in my junior and senior years, and I understand why. I had been in a leadership role during my sophomore year of ROTC and he thought I had qualities to become an officer in the regular army. I'll explain.

Our university army ROTC program at the University of Idaho had a fancy exhibition drill team that used the old Second World War, M-1 rifles to do competitive intricate marching routines. It is to be noted, a very heavy rifle for marching. The marching involved a group of 18 to 24 student soldiers in three columns responding to commands from the Drill Instructor. This was all done, with rifles twirling, in various patterns as the unit moved in unison of columns split in various directions, then returning to march together once again. Such a routine might have made today's America's Got Talent.

In the second semester of my freshman year, I signed up again for this special marching unit and rather enjoyed being part of the group. We practiced and participated in various competitive meets against other college ROTC programs, like the one close by at Washington State University. Well, I got pretty good at marching and in my sophomore year I was made the commander of the drill team—designated a First Sergeant since I was only a sophomore and not in the advanced program (that I would later reject). I showed initiative and developed new routines that involved throwing our rifles to one another in two intersecting circles and it was kind of unique and fun, but also nerve-racking to plan and compete as the leader of the unit. I remember one competition with other universities in which we were spot on, yet we placed third, for reasons I could not fathom. During the next competition at another university, I gave an order in the wrong direction and two of the three columns split in uneven numbers and went their respective wrong ways. While this was unfolding the column in the middle didn't know what to do next, and you might say, marched to its own drummer. Cognizant of the mistake I had made, I gave a loud command, never heard before or thereafter: "All hands, come back," followed by another never before heard command, "This.s.s.s way!" It worked perfectly, as if we had practiced it a hundred times before and we continued on and finished our routine. We won first place for that meet. I am sure it's because the judges, figuring that anyone who could rectify so well the mess he had caused, deserved to win. You just never know!

I had determined now nearing the end of four years of undergraduate study and ready for graduation with a Bachelor of Science degree, that having a master's degree was important to one's future opportunities as a teacher, especially if you were going to one day aspire to anything beyond like a principal or superintendent of education. A college education was relatively cheap in those days so the investment to reward ratio was on your side! It's one of those "tickets" I mentioned earlier to advance to a better life. I would, at a minimum, even if I remained just a teacher, get paid a better salary with an advanced degree. I asked the principal of the high school I was currently student-teaching at, Mr. V. L. Lefebvre, where he recommend, I go for a master's degree. As he had gone there himself, he suggested the University of Missouri as they had a well-regarded college of secondary school administration; he had personally studied under the tutelage of a prominent professor of that program of studies. The University of Missouri also happened, incidentally, to be where my brother Buzz had gone for the initial part of his journalism studies. The additional opinion of the high school chemistry teacher, Mr. Flatt, who I was doing my student-teaching under, confirmed my choice to attend that particular mid-west university. The stars seemed to be aligned.

I applied and was accepted as a provisional student who would have to prove himself in the first semester in order to be able to continue, and I did. I was assigned to the same elderly retiring professor that had provided guidance to Mr. Lefebvre. In his final year of professorship Dr. John Rufi, gathered me under his wing, insisted I take no more than one year to complete my studies and guided—almost more like fathered—me to the completion of a master's degree in Secondary School Administration. He was a wonderful and wise adviser, although I learned that many students were afraid of the high standards he set for student study and avoided taking his courses until he had retired. I thrived, however, in his presence. He did one rather unusual, if not odd, but charming thing; he wrote to my mother upon completion of the first semester to inform her of my progress. Unusual, I know, and unheard of in higher education, but it had a nice touch to it, and she really appreciated his character and his words. In a letter to me that I received shortly after graduation and after entry into Peace Corps training, his salutation to me began, "My good friend, Danny." That bond between senior educator and new, fresh young educator was never to be forgotten by me and greatly appreciated at the basic level of human-to-human mentorship. It's no wonder this fine man typically got a 99% response to every survey he sent, which he did annually, to the graduate students he mentored in excess of 900 over his professorship. This was such a strong and exemplary example of how teaching is an honorable profession.

Achieving my advanced degree proved more strategic than I had ever imagined and would soon realize. Before telling you how that was, I'll mention an incident that shook this youth from Idaho to his core and from and on which I became a solid advocate for human rights. We may have had, as far as I knew, only one black person, Al, in Twin Falls, Idaho or the single Jew, Morey Roth, both of whom I loved visiting on occasion. I knew the difference between right and wrong when it came to others who don't have the same color of skin (economic status or whatever), but the same red blood and bones.

Up until this point in my young life I had only encountered secondhand experiences that convey prejudice; not an actual in-person experience such as the one I am about to relate during the last half of my graduate schools days. Prior to that time, there was an encounter on a ship, the Arkadia, returning from my European studies that had given me an idea of the prejudice others hold of fellow human beings. A fellow student and I were assigned seating at dinner each night with twenty gals from Tennessee. It should have been rather a sweet experience for two guys to sit with that many pretty girls. However, as it turned out, they exhibited, more than once, outright prejudices during dinner conversation when it came to the ship staff that served them—yes, they were black! These young ladies, and I use the title loosely, had a problem and it wasn't us two guys at the table with them! Hearing prejudice and experiencing it (as I did in the following other instance to be described) has two different effects on you, but neither is to be tolerated. Our experience on the boat with those girls paled to the outright firsthand prejudice I experienced while away at graduate school in Missouri.

In the winter of my second semester, Dr. Rufi had taken six of us graduate students on a field trip to Kansas City to observe public school administration in action at a major school district as part of our studies. We stopped halfway along the drive at a local diner and went in to get a bite to eat. No sooner had we sat down when the waitress came over, handed each of us a menu, but not to one of our fellow classmates. He was black. She informed us that they don't serve black people. This was 1962, mind you and I had never experienced prejudice directed at a person I knew, let alone one who was with me—a fellow student and a fellow human being.

Hearing what the waitress said, without any discussion, we all stood en masse and informed her that if she could not serve one of us, she could not serve any of us. We left the diner! Point made, lesson experienced that prejudice was not to be tolerated and hopefully never experienced again, but even that would not be the case as I would learn about life. I certainly knew what to do if it ever did happen again. My mother, as I have already noted, did not tolerate fools and I wasn't going to either. When I went into the Peace Corps it unfortunately happened again, and the Peace Corps knew how to deal with it—in the press! I was pleased the Peace Corps supported efforts to not tolerate prejudice, at least none that I ever witnessed.

On a far less serious note, while at graduate school, I took a bus ride to Kansas City for what was known as a" Pre-Induction Physical" for the purpose of possibly being drafted into the army—the Vietnam War was looming. Sixty or so college students and other young men from the various towns along the way, many from the rural towns of Missouri, had our physicals conducted in a large warehouse in Kansas City. Six hundred naked bodies are not a pretty sight, especially while they are getting poked at and questioned. Even though I have bad eyesight, wearing glasses as I have since the third grade, I passed the physical and was declared eligible for the draft. As it turned out, I was soon to be drafted, but I ended up being saved by something I could never have foreseen.

Nearing the end of graduate school one day I happened to wonder into the University Placement Office designed to help would-be teachers find a job. They had open positions listed from all over the country. I was hoping to find a teaching position, since I figured I wouldn't be able to apply for any administrative position until I had some experience under my belt. I was particularly interested in the Denver area, being the westerner that I am, and specifically with a new community called Cherry Creek. However, on the wall was a poster that caught my attention. It was asking for volunteers, especially teachers, for a new program that would send them overseas to developing countries. This was 1962 and the program had been initiated by President John F. Kennedy, months before, in a then famous address in which he said, "Ask not what your country can do for you; ask what you can do for your country." It made me think of what that might be, and I wrote to the Peace Corps office in Washington, D.C. to see what they had for would be chemistry teachers. They wrote back immediately and told me that there were two opportunities in the immediate future after my graduation: these were in Ghana and Ethiopia. I had to look at a globe—we had such things in those days in the library—to see where both countries were and decided that this could be an opportunity to really stretch my boundaries—especially my interest in travel. I had already seen much of Europe, so what about some place really out there, like Africa? I chose Ethiopia for that very reason—it was in another part of the world. After graduation, I went home for a short period of time, then I went off to Peace Corps training in Washington, D.C.

Training for our Peace Corps group was at Georgetown University. It was a nine-week program. I would have to get my affairs in order before I could depart the country. The first step was to obtain an exemption from military draft. I wrote to my draft board in Twin Falls, headed by a Mrs. Pearl Aldrich. She was a hardnosed person who really wanted to draft my brother Buzz as she felt he had purposefully eluded the draft. In fact he had not but had married while in college and had a child by the time his name came up for the draft; thus he was exempt. I feared in my mind that his still single brother would be used to fill his spot. However, the real decision was up to the draft board which was composed of local citizens. They approved my exemption from 1A to 1H. It was only later I learned that I had been first on the draft list for that July of 1962, just a month after I graduated from the University of Missouri. I had no idea when I asked for the exemption but I was the lucky guy all the same. As a result, more than I was aware of at that time, I dodged (metaphorically speaking) a bullet that came to be the Vietnam war. I can honestly say that I would have gone if required, but I never was, so I never did. Apparently, I wouldn't need that ROTC experience after all. A couple of other subsequent sets of circumstances that lay ahead for me also precluded my going into the military, even though my exemption had extended my liability to be drafted until I was age 35. It seems my own version of manhood, not the pretend kind at college, was to begin as I literally stepped out right after college into the greater world at large. I was moving to a foreign country about which I knew absolutely nothing. As fate would have it, I could not have been any luckier than to have gone to a more fascinating place like Ethiopia; especially to experience and come to love its varied people. I'll tell you why later when I describe this portion of my professional career.

In closing the account of my fulltime academic studies, I wish to recount a couple of travel opportunities that established a profound impression of my view of the greater world as I saw it then, in the early '60s, and would experience from the vantage point of the two-year Peace Corps service that was imminent. These two experiences greatly influenced my decision to go to Ethiopia. After telling you what these were, I'll get to my manhood in the real world where things really started cooking for me.

The first experience I want to mention had the opposite effect on me than what it might have on most people. That's not meant as a judgment that having such an effect is somehow bad for others, as we all learn in our own ways. But for me, it was a sign of who I am and what I wanted in life, so from that standpoint the experience served me well.

Between my sophomore and junior years of college, my fraternity asked three of us to represent our chapter at the national meeting of Beta Theta Pi. The annual meeting was being held on Mackinac Island, Michigan. Now Mackinac is simply a charming place with no roads and old stately buildings amidst a well-appointed setting. The ambience was something that I had never seen before and one step, I imagined, from a Deep South plantation. It was opulent, had almost exclusively black people doing the work, and an unreal feeling to the world around it. But I was a mostly immature young man from Idaho from these ways of the world. I was not used to pretense, and I didn't feel comfortable when I was immersed in it. I came away from that setting realizing that I was a country kid who was developing sophistication and appreciation for the real things of life. I wanted to approach life with honest perceptions and appropriate action; not participate in fictitiousness, pretense, or dishonesty. That particular environment, on that island, felt either too fake or beyond me. I would rather seek out other venues for myself (and my family of the future) that were, to my of thinking, real and hopefully include people very different from me. This has presented itself numerous times in my travels, opting for living or directly interacting with people of a nation—what I consider real things of real value—rather than being a more prototypical tourist. My second experience, also during my collegiate years, really drove this home in even more personal and profound ways.

One of my fraternity brothers, Randy Lytton, mentioned in passing as summer break was approaching between our junior and senior year, that he was going on a study tour of Europe, sponsored for credit by the University of Idaho. He suggested I should look into it and maybe I might want to go too. A couple of other students I knew were going as well, including Barbara Sandy from my high school graduating class. I was intrigued! I'd never been out of the United States and had visited only six other states—four in the northwest, and California and Nevada.

What would it be like to visit a foreign land? And not only one, but as it turned out, thirteen countries! I talked to my mother about it, and she jumped on the enthusiasm train in supporting the idea and, next thing you know, I was signed up for a seven-week study tour of Europe. In retrospect I am sure our mother's support of such adventures as this was a way for her to live out what she herself longed to do but had not had the opportunities to realize. Blessings on her for such support of her children in developing their skills, view of the world, and how to live a productive life.

There were four of us from Idaho who were going on the tour. My fraternity brother, Randy, Barbara from my hometown, and another student by the name of Stan. To get to our departure on a ship out of New York City, my mother lent her car to drive the first leg of our journey to the east coast of the USA. Our ship, the Ascanta, was sailing out of New York City bound for London, then we would take a ferry across the channel to La Havre, France. There we would assemble with the rest of the group from various parts of the US. Her car was a pink and white 1959 Buick Roadmaster, loaded with chrome. We drove to Jamestown, New York, the birthplace of my mother and home of her relatives she had not herself remembered well of from her brief child-hood. The trip was mostly uneventful driving through several states I'd never seen before, but there was an incident as we approached the state of New York. The right front tire nearly came entirely off as one of two joints holding it broke and the tire hung up against the remaining joint. Once we jacked up the tire, the tire hung in a scary way parallel to the road. This happened while we were going 55 mph. We had it fixed, thanks to AAA. After a brief visit with relatives, leaving the car until our return in seven weeks, we boarded the ship in New York City for a five-day sail to England.

Our passage ship was hardly a luxury liner. It was rumored to have been a converted war transport that was once partially sunk and had been recommissioned for transporting tourists instead of troops. Whatever the truth there was little room for what should have been 900 people but was more like 1600 students. Most of us slept in hammocks, two high. It was so crowded that I preferred staying up all night over putting up with too many students and their antics during the day, so I slept during the daylight hours and prowled around all parts of the ship at night. In the dead of the night, I discovered access to the engine room where I could see all the going-ons. I was fascinated with all the machinery of the engine room, including a giant pendulum that indicated the sway of the ship. My curiosity, homed in the scrapyards of my youth, was finely tuned to experiencing so much metal in action as it drove the ship, with me, on its journey. It was all Jules Verne like!

With a slight touch of seasickness from our Atlantic journey, we arrived in Southampton, made our way to London, and spent three days mostly walking around experiencing unfamiliar, new sights. For example, we did one rather unusual activity. Three of us guys paid dues, at a rate of $3.00 (actually 1 British Pound) annually, for a year's membership to a revolving strip club—a little like the other time in East St. Louis when taken to a seedy nightclub by my hitch-hiking companion). Older female performers strutted and partially stripped to 45 RPM records. It was, to be crass about it, a striptease operation in several small bar rooms with little lighting, serving watered down drinks. The whole experience was truly gross as we laughed our way through a couple of shows. As a result we only took advantage of a two-time punch on our membership card—remember it was valid for an entire year! We quickly moved on to more cultured activities like seeing Big Ben, Buckingham Palace, and sitting in Trafalgar Square where pigeons landed on our heads. It was all so much different, I discovered, than Idaho or anywhere else I'd been and experienced in my youth up until that time. Was I in for so much more!

At the outset of our voyage, four of us guys made a collective agreement that whoever threw up first crossing the ocean had to buy a steak dinner for the others. While all of us managed to cross the Atlantic without incident, crossing the English Channel was a problem for one. As best as I recall, the steak dinner was served up in La Havre. It wasn't, technically I suppose, exactly throwing up in the Atlantic, but water is water before you get to the continent of Europe, where we were joining the rest of our tour group. We boarded a bus that would be our home for the next seven weeks, and off we went.

Our study tour group was composed of 10 boys and 10 girls—a rightful matching of the sexes we all thought. We paired up as such when it came to several social events including numerous bars and some very nice nightclubs. The group included, in addition to our University of Idaho professor as travel and instructional guide, two elderly spinsters. These ladies acted a bit like chaperones. We never did discover why they were on our tour—perhaps due to a booking error—but it was a blessing as they were simply good sports about so much silliness from college students. Their presence also probably reduced the amount of swearing and other antics seemingly out of control by young people out to have a good time, as well as learn some lessons about life and the world at large. This was going to be a fun trip, but more important, a fantastic learning experience about different cultures and their long history.

We traveled to thirteen countries in all. As we entered each border, major city, historic site, major industries, or government entity, we individually gave preassigned presentations on what lay ahead. These were augmented with short lectures and guided tours by our professor in residence on the bus. We visited the newly formed Common Market, met with Basque separatists (one of whom was assassinated a month later), watched the Running of the Bulls—the San Fermin Festival—at Pamplona and the bull fight itself. The bull fight was gross, but with laden tradition. We drove though Spain, from Madrid to Zaragoza to Barcelona. It was the time of the dictator, Franco, in Spain and along the road every mile it seemed was a solitary soldier at attention with his rifle. They were even stationed outside churches. It was both spooky and terrifying, all set within the boundary of a simply beautiful country and its people of rich heritage. And it was so old, unlike Idaho or the rest of the US. We met with various government and business leaders, did some great sightseeing, ate really fine food, and imbibed lots of really excellent wine and beer.

I initially kept a detailed journal that got shorter and shorter in length the further into our travel, perhaps because of much too much drinking or late-night antics? I think it was really because I was gradually enjoying the many experiences far more than the writing about them. We saw so many things that I had only read about in books, magazines, newspapers, or seen on the screen at the Orpheum Theatre in Twin Falls. The cities we saw like Paris, Zurich, Rome, Innsbruck, Barcelona, Copenhagen, Berlin, Venice, Bruges, Oslo, Stockholm, and the numerous small villages and lakes of Switzerland, Luxembourg, and Belgium, as well as the city-state of Monaco, were charming. Each had a different language or multiple ones, and I only spoke one. I learned to use hand signs and other gestures to get what I needed but didn't know the words for. There was something called the W.C., and if you needed to go to the bathroom, stop asking for the restroom. They also used something called a bidet! Most Americans think it's ridiculous to have, but later in life I learned the difference and believe me, it's a great device for later life comfort. I made sure one was installed in my home when I remodeled it in 2001. I saw an American woman in a fancy hotel emblematic of "The Ugly American," well described in the book of the same title written by Eugene Burdick and William Lederer. She was loud and nasty to the young woman cleaning her room. I took umbrage and admonished her behavior, telling her not to be such a jerk. Of course she continued to take her wrath out on me, but then again, I don't tolerate fools. It was a lesson on how not to be when traveling.

Stockholm, Copenhagen, and smaller villages were jaw-droppingly old and beautiful. Indeed, I learned what old was: not the American view of a hundred or two hundred years, but more like hundreds of years.

For me, this first-time journey into foreign lands was to be unlike the usual tour led by a tour guide or in the comfort of a cruise ship. Having to study everything before seeing it was far more impactful than cruises where you drop in for a few hours and leave with meaningless trinkets. My boundaries for experiencing the entire world were falling away. There was obviously much more to see if I thought about and acted upon it!

This was making me see what I had not realized was possible. I would dedicate myself to doing so for the rest of my life. Travel is a must for everyone if you really want to understand humanity: its needs, ancient sites, glamour, art and music, and its terrible side of poverty, lack of basic services, inequities in society, and disease.

Eventually, we had to go home and we went our separate ways from various points in Europe. Four of us boarded a boat—the Arkadia, of the Greek Line—out of Amsterdam, where I ran out of money and ate scrambled eggs with my remaining four dollars over the course of three days. The trip around Europe had been wonderful and I could not wait to go back, and elsewhere too. I dedicated myself to go again while I was young, then again at middle age, as a professional, a tourist, a student, an old man, or a volunteer. We were the lucky generation, and we were going places. How I managed to embark on that journey for a lifetime began with the study tour of Europe. The next step would no longer be as a student, but as a Peace Corps Volunteer to help others in the world. I would find the Peace Corps adventure, by the way, a very seminal experience as it prepared me for all of life to follow, including marriage, a career, extensive travel interests, a view of my place and meaning in a life well lived, virtually always with a smile on my face for having done so. It was as such a training ground provided by an agency of the U.S. Government that would take me there, assign meaningful work, commune with others of like motivation, and protect me while in a foreign place and then back at home when I was once again on my own turf. A meaningful, challenging work experience to start from as a precursor to entering the world of work and play.

Training for the Peace Corps contingent to Ethiopia (there were nearly 350 of us when we initially gathered) was held for six weeks at Georgetown University in Washington D.C. Most would complete the training, but not all. It was an ill-conceived training effort by a newly founded branch of the U.S. Government, and its startup faults were further compounded by the cancellation of a second training location at the University of Utah, where half of the trainees were supposed to be instead. Now there were twice as many trainees in Washington, D.C. without twice the staff or means. Still, they made it work and we received a good orientation to the mission at hand—teaching in a third world country.

The training included rudimentary skills in Ethiopia's national language, Amharic, (although there are numerous dialects), and an orientation to the different regional Ethiopian ethnic cultures. Then there was an extensive health check with lots of shots and pills, and dental work that would not be available to us for the next two years. Up until that moment in time I had never had a tooth filling and somehow, they found twelve teeth to do work on. As a teaching college in dentistry, I am certain only half of those fillings were needed, but then again, I was going somewhere for two years without any dental practice available. There were introductions of Ethiopian staff, including the man who would be my headmaster (principal). His name was Ato Adam Abdallah. Ato in Amharic is "Mr." and, as is the custom, he went by "Mr. Adam," and I was "Ato Danny."

The volunteers were from every state of the union and I met on a bus outing one who would eventually be my best man when I got married. Ray Capozzi was from New Jersey and had never met anyone from Idaho, nor was I familiar with anyone from New Jersey. We were seemingly of two different cultures ourselves, although not nearly as much a difference as the one in which we were going to serve. He was fascinated with me as I was with him, and we relished the differences in what they taught us about how to judge and treat others. He is a good friend to this day. We have shared many laughs and experiences from our separate travels, but certainly our bond began with our mutual work as volunteers in the Peace Corps.

Our training included talks from very prominent experts. State Department personnel who had served there, the U.S. Ambassador to Ethiopia, representatives from the Ethiopian Education Ministry, and cultural anthropologists like Margaret Meade who came to lecture on the societal differences we should expect between our way of living and that of the Ethiopians. I can tell you from my own subsequent experience that the differences were vast, made even more so in that Ethiopia is not simply one, but multiple cultures with multiple languages. Dr. Meade's assessments actually fell a bit short of the reality we came face to face with. The Ethiopian culture is rich and warm, measured in centuries of time, not the mere few hundred years of America.

There were a handful of Ethiopian government and educational representatives who tried to acquaint us with their ways and country, a task only really possible by going and experiencing it. All in all the training worked and built a certain level of camaraderie amongst disparate strangers, young and older, who would build a shared identity to their valuable mission of teaching the young of Ethiopia who might not otherwise get the opportunity to advance their nation, through education of their citizenry.

A week before we completed training and departed, we had a very special outing. It was an event at the White House. There we were joined by ten other smaller groups of volunteers who were going to other countries. There were 600 of us on the lawn of the White House on a very sunny day. By then our group had been whittled to 278. I believe, other than the Philippines, we may have been the largest group to ever go to a single country. We were all teachers and would double the number of secondary school teachers in Ethiopia. On this day, President John Kennedy stepped out of the White House to address in reality what had only been his dream a year earlier. He spoke, as he was known to so eloquently, of the mission of the Peace Corps as we stood in a semi-circle behind a single rope barrier. It was, as you might guess, an inspirational address to send his Corps out to help the world better understand America while learning useful skills, ways, and means of the volunteers' efforts in setting up water sources, nutrition, health, and, in our case, education. It was something special for this young man from Idaho to be in his presence, there with my fellow volunteers, eager to do something for our nation, but also for ourselves. When he finished speaking, he stepped forward onto the lawn, and began walking down the line to shake a dozen hands or so. When he got right in front of me, he turned to go back into the White House. I blurted out, for whatever reason, "What about Ethiopia?" He had a fondness for Ethiopia and its Emperor, Haile Selassie. The emperor would, only a year later, attend and march in President Kennedy's funeral procession down Pennsylvania Avenue. Hearing me, he turned back and walked towards me, reached out and shook my hand. "Ethiopia, huh?" he said. I don't remember what I said in reply, but the boy from Idaho was star struck. I didn't wash that hand for three days. Later, when we first arrived in Ethiopia, I was the first—dare from my new friend Ray Capozzi—volunteer to shake the hand of Emperor Haile Selassie when he invited our group to his imperial palace as a thanks us for being there. The second occasion to meet him was during my first year on assignment when he entered my classroom on the dedication of our newly built secondary school in Harar. And the third, when we were invited to a reception in Harar at his palace. What a time I was having on the way to a fantastic adventure!

Now, I can write an entire book about my Peace Corps experience; others have about theirs. I'll summarize as there is so much about my life there and what it did for me, and what I trust I did for my students. It's just that Ethiopia was so special, and I would be living for two years beyond the boundaries of what little I knew of my own town, state, and country. Now I am in a foreign land where I was the stranger, yet so welcomed to help. So here's a capsule full of what that was like.

Strangely, going to Ethiopia wasn't, in my way of thinking once I landed on its soil, much different than being in Idaho. That may seem an exaggeration, but it really isn't. Ethiopia is a semi-arid nation south of Sudan, bordered also by Somalia, Eritrea, Kenya, Djibouti, and now, the newly created, South Sudan. Southern Idaho is also a semi-arid area that was recovered from the surrounding desert. Southern Idaho's agriculture is only more productive now because of a series of canals that move water to make for a lush, growing environment. Today Ethiopia is doing the same, evidenced by the soon to be completed dam on the

Blue Nile that originates in their country. So where I came from and where my new residence was had many things in common, but other things that were so dissimilar, as I soon experience firsthand.

In early September 1962, two Trans World Airlines airplanes flew into the capital of Ethiopia, Addis Ababa. On the airplane approach and then drive into town, you could readily see the then third-world nature of the country. To put it mildly, it was surreal: like going back to a time you had only read about or seen in a documentary film that didn't present Africa very accurately, as it turned out. The drive into town was evidence enough to let you know you were in an environment that you'd never even known existed. Two-wheeled Gari carts with a padded seat pulled by horse were in common use as rudimentary public transportation (think a version of a taxi pulled by a horse). Thatched tukuls (round huts) were dotted here and there. If not that more common version of a home, it was a less exotic metal, corrugated roof on top of adobe walls with only perhaps a dirt floor. Everyday local villagers donned what appeared to be dirty rags but started out as a brown woolen garment. Such garments had become linked to dust and sweat when it's all you own. This everyday wear was worn alongside an occasional beautiful woman or man in their pristine national dress made of a white cheese cloth and lined with beautiful colors on the garments' boarder or worn around the neck. To round out the couture there stood a bearded priest, with his carved cane, dressed stately in colorful robes and protected from the sun by a multicolored parasol. The contrasts were stunning. The setting surreal. Your eyes could not help but look, but you had to try not to stare so that you didn't appear to be judging. I am certain I was rather admiring the beauty and the harshness of a culture so different than any that I had previously experienced. I must tell you it was wonderful!

Most of the city throughfares of Addis Ababa were, except in the heart of the city of thousands, mostly dirt roads and dust kicked up everywhere. Smaller meandering streets joined one another and were crowded by hundreds of people mostly walking, with others on donkey or horseback. The few cars and minibuses snaked through the crowded streets seemingly always filled with a horde of people. The more prevalent donkeys were laden with firewood or straw. Women carried huge loads of goods slung on their backs or supported with a headband from their multi-colored shawls that carried what they had to carry. Others balanced a gourd or two of water, gathered from a stream, precariously on the tops of their heads. None of this was in any way like Twin Falls, Idaho, or any of those countries I had visited in Europe, and not even slightly approximated family conditions camping on the Little Wood River. It was all simply fascinating and that was just the first afternoon of our arrival. What was it going to be like when I reached my assignment? We had not, in our earlier training, been prepared for what we were about to experience.

Following two weeks of introductory in-country orientation at the University College of Addis Ababa, our specific assignments were made official, and most dispersed into the countryside to smaller villages, but also, as my case, to a major urban area; not so much cities like we know them, but large villages that had been there for hundreds of years. My fellow volunteers and I, 30 in number, took an hour and a half flight from Addis to Dire Dawa near the Somalia border, then a bus ride for the final 40 minutes to our new home, Harar. During that brief journey we observed baboons scurrying the cliffs of a steep drive up from the valley floor to the high plain on which Harar sits in a semi-arid area. On our entrance into Harar I immediately liked our new environment and looked forward to exploring its defined oldness. I definitely thought we had landed better than my initial impressions of Addis Ababa. For one thing, it was smaller, though not that small, and it had a defined character that I would come to deeply appreciate and love.

I was assigned to the Harar Teacher Training School (HTTS) in Harar, Ethiopia, not far (50 kilometers) from the border town of Jijiga, along an ancient caravan route over the surrounding desert. Ethiopia is part of what is known as the Horn of Africa in that it, along with Somalia, Eritrea, and Djibouti, juts out in a horn shape as part of East Africa into the Red Sea.

Harar for its part, being on the western border of Somalia, was made up of Muslims and Coptic Christians, but the majority were Muslim. That is not true of the rest of Ethiopia which is predominately Coptic Christians. Ethiopia is comprised of several different tribes including what was then the ruling tribe, Amhara. Haile Selassie, the then emperor of Ethiopia, was its head. The predominant tribe of our region was then known as the Aderi—now known (since the revolution that overthrew Haile Selassie in 1974) as the Harari. Most of the population is Sufi or Salafi Muslims, but there is a mixture of Amhara, and Gala (now Oromo); the latter spoke their own language, Gala. The country's official national language is Amharic. It is interesting today to note that the Harari speak what is referred to as, "the language of the city."

All languages—perhaps it's more accurate to say, dialects—that are part of Ethiopia are difficult to learn and so further compounded the difficulty of learning to communicate in just one dialect. They are beautiful dialects with explosive, guttural sounds that make listening to them a bit harsh yet pleasing. I didn't learn any one of the languages enough to be highly conversant, but I did learn a sufficient amount of Amharic to impress locals in that I had at least tried. This was true for most of the volunteers, although there were exceptions who truly learned a local dialect, and I much admired their doing so. My friend Ray was one of those who made the sincere effort to speak and use Tigrinya. I guess being required as a volunteer to teach in English—the second official language of Ethiopia, introduced by Haile Selassie following his return from exile after the Second World War—merely exacerbated our not learning and using the official national language, Amharic. If you don't use it, you can't learn and retain much. As I noted, I did learn enough to sound as if I could speak a few words fluently, but I was pretty limited when it came to bartering for goods on the street or in the few stores there were. I could at least count and knew the local currency when buying goods, so I managed.

Today, I still say hello in Amharic to the many Ethiopians I see working in airports, Ethiopian restaurants that dot our American communities, and sometimes just walking into stores like IKEA. They are both stunned to witness a white guy saying, "hello" (in Amharic, "Tenistelin"), followed by, "How are you?" in the correct gender form of:

"Indemin adderah" for male,

"Indemin adderish" for female or

"Indemin adderu when in the presence of both sexes.

When I correctly address them, they light up with a broad smile, as they are apt to do about many things in life. They are people who smile and laugh a lot. At the same time they are reserved; not making eye contact with strangers they wanted to first study, but too shy to ask about—of course there is the language barrier that keeps potential conversation from happening. We are "forengees," as they call us in a whisper. It is to be noted their use of English is much better than our Amharic, given that they are taught in English exclusively (except for their native language courses) after the sixth grade. They are not only physically beautiful, but simply some of the nicest people you could be privileged to come to know in the entire world. They have a way of wholeheartedly loving their children with both mother and father so mutually involved. Their ways could serve as a model for us all in rearing children, promoting family ties, honoring the aged, gathering around the table, welcoming strangers, and treating friends well. I think my family days growing up had these same principles, thereby fostering a bond that links me to their way of being. That may explain, more than any other reason, why I so enjoyed the brief two-year stay I had with them. I was very lucky to have had the privilege to do so and I cherish the memories of my time spent there.

Quite understandably, as a third-world country at that time trying to gradually advance to something resembling the twentieth century, Ethiopia had its challenges. The place I was stationed felt more like the 9th Century, as if I knew what that was. While the city itself is an ancient enclave dating back to at least the tenth Century, it had advanced at one point in time to become a leading Muslim center, then declined. It is still considered one of the most holy sites of the Muslim world.

The city of Harar once had seven entrances or gates; only five have survived time and stand (though a bit crumbling) to this day. During my time there, except for the new imperial palace, a few modern government buildings, the military academy and our school, the city was wedged within winding narrow streets and sorely lacking adequate public lighting for the dingy passages. The buildings have a unique style in this region of the country. They are constructed of locally sourced, pounded stone and clay, as both are used to create mortar and plaster to cover the walls which are then whitewashed. Walled compounds are created for several dwellings that share mutual walls, a courtyard, a common entry, and possibly a kitchen as well. One gets the sense of an old, but close and comfortable living environment that links its inner residents together. I've always liked the ubiquitous whitewash of the city as it denotes that its inhabitants are a united people rather than the multiple colors and styles of our own dwellings in the western world that sets us apart from others in our communities. It further exudes a kind of equity, rather than the divisive opulence that westerners seem to want to boast about.

At that time there were almost no cars other than those that belonged to the governor's office as well as various ministries, a few minivans, small buses for travel to other villages, some military vehicles and our two jeeps that served Peace Corps needs. Most people traveled on foot, often leading donkeys carrying produce, straw, or wood. Women balanced colorful baskets of vegetables and other goods, carried chickens, or balanced gourds of water or oil on their head with a child cradled at their side. There are simply beautiful artistic woven baskets of all kinds and shapes for all kinds of uses. There are those that cover the food (Injera and Wat) or contain household items. Dust and dirt cannot be avoided and there are constant flies in your face. Even the paper money smelled of damp dirt and was gritty. It doesn't sound very charming, I know, but I found it ancient and fascinating just the same. It was wonderful to wander about and bargain for goods I wanted. There was no refrigerated meat market, by the way, so you bought what you needed off a quarter of beef hanging (with flies on it) by an overhead hook on a pole in a stall more crudely constructed than the houses. All vegetables came directly from the surrounding fields, and you had to wash these well in order to avoid amoeba or other things that might enter your body and make you deathly sick. For a while we actually washed our lettuce with Tide that we then rinsed with sanitized water. Meat was always cooked well done—there was no such thing as medium-rare—due to the presence of tuberculosis in virtually all cattle, who appeared so thin on their skeletal frame.

Unfortunately, famines plague the country rather predictably, every ten years or so. While I was there, we had a locust infestation by the millions and while dating my girlfriend (who was later to become my wife) I'd come to her house and there, on the concrete front steps, was a stack of shed termite wings that stood about two feet high. The next year there were moths in the millions. In their larval state they were short—an inch and a half in length; black creatures squirming along the ground no matter where you stepped. On my way to school over the course of a couple of weeks, I must have inadvertently killed 10,000 as, step after step, I'd squish another group and the sound it made was like walking on eggshells.

The constant presence of flies is something you just have to get used to. I noticed right away that adults and children would not always swat flies away from their skin or eyes, as we are prone to do out of habit. They generally tolerate them by allowing them to crawl on their skin as opposed to brushing them away, only to have them then swarm yet again around their face and eyes. It was common to see children breast feeding while the flies encircled their mouths and their eyes. Mothers covered their infants with the ragged edges of their own clothing to protect them as best they could. Twice, at least, while lecturing in class, I actually swallowed a fly and could do absolutely nothing about it. Perhaps all those flies in my youth at The Warehouse where the horse and cow hides were laid out prepared me for all the infestations I had to live amidst in Ethiopia. This, as with other things I might say about my host country, was a privilege to be present in and teach—not done with some kind of judgment of what's wrong and needs fixing or is just gross, but what you are helping do something about in your own small way! Rather, and this is important to understand, such prevailing conditions are what they are at that time and things either needed to be done to make it better or they would continue as they were. For instance people would die not on average at age 65 as in America, but 38 as was common in Ethiopia if something were not done to make it better. Our job was to help make things better and that was in the form of education. Fellow human beings were living in such conditions, not understanding that they might die because of it.

I contracted *amoebic dysentery* (a human protozoa disease) once while there and was in agony for a week. I got it while hiking with two other volunteers because we wanted to see a flat top mountain in the far distance—prominently visible miles away from our home in Harar. Local lore had it that Mt. Kundudo was the spot where Noah's Ark had landed. We walked three days, aided by three donkeys that carried our tents and other supplies. We were constantly greeted by villagers who were perhaps seeing white men for the first time. Often the children would gather around in a semi-circle and watch us as we pitched our tents or ate out of cans our food they may never have experienced. We had no idea how to tie anything on a donkey and it showed. Along the way I became very thirsty. I drank some water from a stream, knowing that I should first boil the water, but didn't. I paid the price. Other volunteers contracted roundworms or tapeworms, diarrhea, malaria, and other diseases. Nobody in our group died fortunately; a fact that cannot be said about other Peace Corps groups over the decades. I know for a fact that one poor unfortunate volunteer was killed by a crocodile.

As I previously noted, I had been told at that time that the life expectancy of an Ethiopian was about 38. Nowadays they have made many advancements and things are better, but there are still numerous villages where things are slow to come. There continue to be lingering issues with the availability of adequate and potable water supply and the threat of famine never seems to subside. I was one of the lucky ones who had a backup system through the support of my own country and fellow Peace Corps Volunteers. Ethiopians needed their own backup system, and we were there to help build one a little step at a time. I loved living in the midst of it all and doing what I could to help a little!

It might seem a bit ironic that I taught chemistry to young 16 to 18-year-old students who had been selected from throughout their nation to be prepared as elementary school teachers. They were to have at the direction of their education ministry, a full academic program, as would any western high school. While it seemed odd to be preparing high schoolers to be elementary school teachers (whereas in our country we prepare college graduates to be teachers at that level), it was quite necessary. I thought it must have been that way back home in early America. Children on the prairie were often taught by the slightly more educated on the wagon train or in their new community. Ethiopia was simply at the stage America had been at a hundred years ago. Our students would, upon graduation, serve at least two years teaching in an assigned remote village where otherwise any educational opportunity might not have been possible. Our Peace Corps effort would make a significant contribution to the education of a nation.

The teaching staff of HTTS was an ethnically mixed group from several countries. The Peace Corps contingent alone amounted to half the faculty, totaling fifteen of the thirty teachers. PCVs taught subjects in science, math, English, arts and crafts, library, education practices, home economics, and music. Foreign nationals were British, Indian, German, French, Israeli, and a delightful and fascinating woman from Madagascar. There were, of course, Ethiopian teachers in select teaching assignments such as their own language and history. At the time I was the only full-time high-school level chemistry teacher in the country. The ministry wanted a full level of science curricula that simply did not usually exist at the secondary level of education.

I was fortunate to have a chemistry laboratory for the use of teaching, located in an outbuilding across a playfield from the main school building. I am not sure how it had been previously used, as the school was relatively new, but it had lots of glassworks (i.e., test tubes, beakers, etc.). The fact that they were buried in a half inch of dirt told me that the facilities had not been used for some time. There were also blowtorches to use with for what should have been Bunsen burners. Just before Thanksgiving of that first year I learned there was an extension college, Alameya Agricultural College (renamed Haramaya University after the 1974 revolution), sponsored by Oklahoma State University, about 40 minutes away. It turned out to be a touch of Americana very much out of place. It was surreal to see the suburban style homes in the midst of what was otherwise a mostly ancient living environment. The college was midway between Harar and the nearby trade route city (think camel train) of Dire Dawa. I managed to talk a chemistry professor from the extension college into donating a half dozen Bunsen burners to our school. They worked so much better than the unruly blowtorches we had for lab work up until that time.

Among other challenges of the laboratory, there was also no constant uncontaminated water supply that we could rely on to do accurate lab work. In fact, the water was turned on only a couple of times during the week to let our school and houses fill our 55-gallon barrels with needed water. In the back room of the lab where chemicals were normally stored, if you can believe it, I found a water still that had never been hooked up. I wrote to the manufacturer located in the States, and they sent me a diagram of how to set it up and get it running. We put an additional 55-gallon drum on the roof as a more reliable source for running water, and it fed water around the cooling tower as the still slowly dripped distilled water into another barrel. I thereby was designated the supplier of distilled water for the school and whoever needed it in the community.

At the end of my first year, I compiled a list of needed chemicals that were missing for class experiments and sent my request to the central educational ministry office in Addis Ababa. As the new school year approached during my second year of teaching, several wooden crates containing a complete set of new lab glassware arrived duplicating what I already had, but the delivery contained none of the chemicals for experiments I had requested. As it turned out, apparently the education ministry had in storage a plethora of lab glassware that had been given to them by one of the United States USAID programs, so when I placed my request, the ministry sent me what they had, probably feeling at least they were doing something. Well, we were, after all, the Peace Corps, so we would make do for our second year by using what was available. To my mind, in this instance the lab was half full, not half empty. Or, you might even say, in this instance, that the lab was twice half full (of glass works)!

I loved teaching my Ethiopian students. The student body was about half boys and girls. They were orderly, raised their hand to speak, and always stood when they had a question. They were very polite, eager to learn, and especially to see how Americans were so different from them in ways that they would often then try to emulate. In addition to my regular teaching assignment of five periods of chemistry I was the teacher representative for their version of the Boy Scouts, and at the end of the school year of my time there they presented me with a beautiful hand-crafted, pure gold emblem of the Boy Scout Life Badge, symbolized as a heart. I still have it. Thus you see again how my days spent as a Boy Scout in America came in to play for the Boy Scouts at my new school.

Thirty-five years later when my second wife, Kathleen, and I went to see my old teaching grounds, one of those students presented himself to us quite unexpectedly. We had stopped at the local Ras Hotel on one of the main streets of Harar, near the gas station where locals often meet to chat over a special honey tea drink, they are fond of. Kathleen and I were having a cup of local coffee (coffee originated in Ethiopia), when a tall, distinguished man in his business suit walked up, and said, "Are you Danny Langdon?" I said, of course, "Yes!" "Well, I was one of your students!" Only then did I recognize the face of the young boy whom I had taught so many years ago on the stately man who stood before me that day, in his business suit and tie, thirty-five years later. He was now a Supreme Court Judge of Ethiopia and just happened to be in town for a meeting with the local provincial Governor. What a feeling that was as we sat and reminisced about our days together. You just never know who you are going to influence and meet again! How lucky I was on that day that could never have been foreseen but was surely destined!

Seminal Moment: That Student of Mine.

Meeting that Ethiopian student again as I did so many years later was seminal in that it affirmed not just that my time had been well spent in Ethiopia, but about how I should treat mankind in general.

- *I find that's true when delivering food for our local food bank and a client extends me a simple, "Thank you!" and I smile and say, "It's my pleasure."*
- *I find that true when I smile at a stranger in the grocery store and he or she smiles back.*
- *And while traveling the world meeting strangers who say, "Hello" in their language and I smile in acknowledgement of our commonality as human beings.*

Our group of 30 Peace Corps volunteers in Harar were split disproportional between my school and miscellaneous other small elementary schools of much lesser means. The six or so elementary schools in the city had mostly dirt floors, little if any lighting, few books, or resources, but plenty of kids with smiling faces. My first wife, Patricia, taught in one of these schools. My school, HTTS, was housed in a newly constructed modern building that stood in contrast to the adobe and tin roof structures of the elementary schools in town. Villagers in the surrounding area lived in what is known as a Tukul. It's a thatched, round hut made of branched walls, a thatched roof, and mud backed to close the spaces between the branches. This sort of living environment is where most of our students came from, small villages from throughout Ethiopia. They had been selected to leave their village and attend our school for three years because of the desire they each had to be educated and serve others.

By contrast, we Peace Corps Volunteers (PCVs) lived in scattered quarters throughout the community of Harar. I would summarize our dwellings in general as meager quarters that we made into our own

197

version of "home-sweet-home" using local furniture, a kerosene generated refrigerator, and a wood burning water heater for your bathtub. We could afford to fix our accommodations the way we liked, something most Ethiopians could not necessarily afford to do. May not seem so when I describe the first place I lived but believe me it had its own structural issues being as old as it was during the time six of us PCVs inhabited it. First however, a little description of where the emperor of Ethiopia lived when he visited Harar.

The emperor, Haile Selassie had several residential palaces scattered throughout the country. Since Harar was home to their version of West Point, there was a stately palace located not far from one of the seven gated entrances to Harar. The emperor—King of Kings, Lion of Judea, as he was stately referred to—would come annually to parade the troops. Oddly, the rocks that lined and marked the main road to the Academy were annually painted white in preparation for his ride from his palace through town to the military academy. On one occasion while in Harar, he invited our contingent of PCVs to a reception at his palace following the dedication ceremony of our new school. There were trays of fruit, injera and wat (their wonderful national dish), raw vegetables, and raw meat. We had been told in orientation that 90% of the cattle had tuberculosis, so we passed on the meat, as well as the vegetables that carried their own waterborne amoeba. However, the spicy injera and wat were deliciously prepared with lots of Burberry powder, which I loved once I got used to the heat of it on my insides. Wat is a marvelous kind of stew concoction that you eat with your fingers by tearing off a piece of unleavened rubbery bread, called injera. This is best done by scooping up a piece of the wat (I particularly like the Doro, chicken, version) and eating the entire morsel in a few bits. I can even get it today in my hometown of Bellingham, Washington. There is a very nice Ethiopian couple (Mulunesh Belay and Ato Takele Seda) here who prepare their national dishes the authentic way. They delight when I enter their café, Ambo, and greet them in their language. She knows exactly how Danny Boy likes his wat, served without placing the wat on the Injera, with an extra piece of chicken and a hard-boiled egg. It's best enjoyed with friends and lively Ethiopian music in the background. Two of you can even feed one another this food wrapped in its own sleeve—it's a manner of communing with others that is so much a part of their rich culture. Enjoy it along with their honey beer, and you have a culinary feast. Also try (if you can find one in a bigger city in the USA) going to a Coptic Christian Church. You'll glimpse a feel of this rich culture, and they will be so welcoming. If you are lucky, you will get to experience the music, colorful attire, and multicolored parasols used by the priests. I personally think their depiction of Jesus likely appears truer than any attempt I've seen in western cultures. When my first wife and I married in Ethiopia in a small chapel, on its wall was a giant mural depicting the Savior that was so realistic that it might make you wonder if it was from a photo, had the technology been available at that time. Given that Ethiopian Jews are one of the Semitic tribes of Israel, it therefore follows that He likely looked more like them than the more common Caucasian version, with blue eyes, we see in Western cultures.

During my first year in Harar I lived in an old rundown palace. Although it was referred to as a palace, it was far from that. In our terms it would probably be described as a once nice residence that had seen far better days by the time us six boys moved in. It formerly belonged to one of the emperor's nieces, and it had nice marble floors. It had a living room, five bedrooms, kitchen, two bathrooms, and a dining room. I lived with six other male volunteers. We got along well considering the disparate personalities, not to mention drinking habits. A delightful fellow Ethiopian teacher, Ato Sebsibe, lived with us as well and his presence provided ample opportunity to gain firsthand experience about their culture in more personal ways. Besides becoming a close friend, Sebsibe was a rich resource for developing our understanding of Ethiopia, which included enjoying the local honey beer. He and I stayed in contact over the years. I can't forget his sparkling eyes and warm fraternal humor. Many years later I returned for a visit to Ethiopia and he and I revisited old times. Unfortunately, it was also a sad day, as his eldest daughter had died just a few days before, in a highjacked airplane that crash landed off the Seychelles Islands. (She was a flight attendant.) They were a big family with big dreams, and tragedy had beset them. Their culture and their people are so rich in so many ways. He was a perfect example of these beautiful people.

Since the Peace Corps required that we live as our teaching counterpart did, whether Ethiopian, British, French, German, Indian, or Israeli, we hired a cook. Our cook had previously worked for the French Foreign Legion so our first initial meals were huge usually consisting of seven courses. We soon found it necessary to tone down his approach to meal-making. For example, he loved using a variety of colors in his dishes, so we had some weird looking purple cake and puddings that we had to counsel him on. He thought we were the strange ones! We also had someone who cleaned the house. That just seemed at odds, not quite right for us to have as Peace Corps Volunteers, but it was what it was. Certainly, food and clutter-wise, this household of males was better off for the help. Once, for a Thanksgiving after I had married, we bought a large bird that looked like but wasn't a turkey. I think it was something called a greater bustard. (I had seen one, along with other animals, on the Serengeti Plain while on my honeymoon.) Our cook, for his part, was sure we had asked him to roast up a vulture as he took us outside and pointed up at the birds circling in the sky above. Those Americans! It wasn't, by the way, a vulture, but as Peace Corps Volunteers we might have entertained the idea of roasting one had we been presented with it around Christmas time.

Lots of things had to be done to make our living quarters comfortably habitable. In my bedroom, which I shared with another volunteer, Eldon, we could see through a huge crack into the next room. Then there was all the work required in order to take a shower, or at a minimum, a bath. Just outside the kitchen was a 55-gallon barrel sitting sideways on a brick fireplace. There was plumbing in the house, but no way to get heated water from the outside brick fireplace inside other than to carry it in a bucket. So we secured a hand-pump and rigged it so that when you heated the water in the barrel on the fireplace, you could pump it up to a second 55-gallon barrel on the roof. Gravity would take the hot water to a shower in either of two bathrooms. Some of my knowledge gained while growing up in The Warehouse, as well as my electrical work as an apprentice, came in handy for making the house a bit more livable. Actually, my having grown up in Idaho (rather than New Jersey, New York, Kansas, Indiana, Texas, or Alameya, Ethiopia as my housemates had) paid off for me in my ability to adjust to such living conditions. Remember: I had lived outdoors for several summer on the Little Wood River and lived in a Warehouse (and with, of course, all those flies). I can't tell you the number of times that I wished for Mom and Dad to show up and rescue us in Ethiopia when I could have really used a choice few items from their numerous iron piles.

At the outset of my second year of service I met and married another volunteer. Patricia was from Vallejo, California. She taught in one of the local elementary schools. She lived with a half-dozen other women in a big house at the other end of town. I'd walk a mile and a half to see her along a partially paved, then a dirt road. I personally characterized the city to others as more of a large village of probably 60,000. Hyenas prowled the city at night and on my walk home after a date that usually constituted sitting around and talking in her living room (since there was little to do in the way of dating), I'd typically see two or three hyenas under one of the few streetlights. They seemed to hold no harm for me, nor me for them. That was true except during the fasting time of Ramadan—the holy month of fasting for Muslims. Since, like you and I, hyenas like to eat meat and during Ramadan there are less scrapes of food… you get the picture! I had had enough experiences (i.e., snakes) growing up in Idaho to be cautious. I must say, I loved looking firsthand and up closely—from a distance of often twelve feet or so—at the power of these animals. There was, in fact, a so called, "Hyenaman" on the outer wall of Harar and at night you could go see him feed the hyenas by hand. Yes, he would stick out a cattle bone in his hand for their fierce teeth to grab and devour. I would go back years later to again see this, and many other creatures in the wild of Africa! The adventure and caution of how to conduct myself was surely bred in me during my days growing up in Idaho, out in our own version of the wild outdoors.

Patricia and I dated for a relatively short time and decided to get married there while in Ethiopia. I don't think either of us was really thinking of what we were about to do in such a strange place, but we were, as they say, young and in love. In addition we were Peace Corps Volunteers and aren't we supposed to be able to do anything??? Common knowledge had it among PCVs that you know a Peace Corps Volunteer because he or she can take a shower with a glass of water!!

Our marriage ceremony was quite an unusual event as you can imagine, taking place in a third-world country. We invited the Emperor of Ethiopia, Haile Selassie, but he didn't come of course. To invite him was a sign of courtesy to my way of thinking. Every one of the volunteers pitched in to assist in their own way, utilizing their unique skills. Adriene made a lovely silk white wedding dress for the bride with numerous buttons down on the back, and a veil to go with it. Others prepared hors d'oeuvres for the reception, decorations for the tables, and served as bridesmaids. My friend Ray was the best man, and Pearl, the country head of USAID (located in Addis Ababa), made a layered cake and flew in with it the day before the wedding ceremony! The airline balked a little at giving a huge wedding cake its own passenger seat, but Pearl appealed to their love of Love, and they let her and the cake on the plane! Ethiopians do love Love. A locally stationed detachment of US military guys, part of a Military Advisory Group (MAG) assigned to the "West Point" of Ethiopia in Harar, contributed the champagne. Eighty guests of eleven different nationalities braved the drive out into the desert and over a stream to a small chapel run by three German Catholic priests at a place called Bisidimo. Oh, and by the way, the chapel was part of a leper colony hospital for those who had contracted that dreaded disease in a country that was one of the few to still harbor it. As we exited the reception and rode away in our Jeep, the 300 or so patients lined up on either side of the roadside and waved to us, and we waved back, complete strangers brought together by this auspicious occasion. It was something I have never forgotten. It's so much like the Ethiopian culture to be so nice and into so much LOVE! Both the bride's parents and my mother came for the wedding. They met, by utter chance, on their individual journeys at the airport in Athens waiting for their plane transfer. Can you imagine the exchange: "I am going to see my daughter get married in Ethiopia." "How about that, I am going to see my son get married." You just never know.

Seminal Moment: Marriage
Like being born or dying, marriage is seminal in all ways in that it:
- *Creates a direction of life that combines, if you are lucky, both a personal relationship with another person and, from that, a family.*
- *Creates so many wonderful moments with our children.*
- *As a couple we supported one another both professionally and in personally fulfilling ways.*

We honeymooned throughout Kenya, Tanzania, Zanzibar, and Uganda for a month. In Nairobi we witnessed Jomo Kenyatta, the anti-colonial activist and then long-term first indigenous president of Kenya, speak on the floor of their version of parliament with such eloquence as they fought for their freedom from colonial rule. It was yet another experience I shall never forget that forge your view of the world and how to live as a human being.

As part of our honeymoon we organized our own safari, as packaged tours were virtually nonexistent then, and if they did exist, they were certain to be out of a Peace Corps Volunteer's budget. By pure chance we met two pairs of other young people who were doing their own independent travel. They were separate sets of two guys and two women about our own age. The six of us teamed up in a shared Land Rover to trek the Ngorongoro Crater, Lake Manyara, and the Serengeti Plain. As a bit of a prank, one of the guys attempted to auction off one of the girls to a Maasai Warrior in a small village of mud huts. Turns out it only fell through when she lit up a cigarette—thank God! Wildlife seemed so plentiful and at that time it was. We seemingly saw every conceivable kind of wild animal from lions to wildebeests, cheetahs, giraffes, water buffalo, jackals, gazelles, zebras, elephants, boa snakes, pink cranes, kudu, more hyenas, and on and on. We saw the snow on Mt. Kilimanjaro and rode the source of the White Nile in Uganda with hippos and crocodiles. Patricia and I even experienced an elephant charging us while riding in a small Volkswagen bug in the jungles of Uganda. My world, first in Ethiopia, then throughout other parts of Africa was expanding in the best and most exciting ways. I was the lucky boy from Idaho experiencing so much about world politics, different cultures, and so many beautiful countries and their people. Surely, I would want to return for more, and I did years later.

To close out this chapter, I would like to relay a poignant experience I had in the Peace Corps that taught me something about mankind, and how it can go awry in the way of a belief that makes no sense—and needs fixing.

The Peace Corps, especially for volunteers in a teaching role occupied only for the academic year of nine months, did not want its volunteers lounging around within their host country doing nothing for the summer months when school was not in session. Each volunteer, therefore, had to find a community activity in which to participate for two months. Many volunteers continued their teaching in some capacity in their community, while I chose a role at the local hospital.

Now you can probably guess that the hospital was not a typical community hospital as we know them in the USA. There was nothing approaching a Cedars-Sinai or Mayo Clinic, nor even a small hospital in a farming community. Far from it, these are rudimentary facilities that lack basic medical technologies, sufficient diagnostic machines or the right kind, sufficient surgical supplies, and highly trained staff. Doctors, for the most part, were foreign nationals. Even I, with no medical training, had some basic knowledge due to my having earned a first aid scouting badge. I knew a few things about basic sanitation, and while I didn't do much technically in this particular hospital, I did anything requested by the head doctor as his designated assistant. He was a Czechoslovakian surgeon. He was a wonderful man in his 50s, and appreciative of the young man who tried his best to be of any help to him. I was, I surmised, a clear head and person of action he could rely on to do whatever he asked. Thus, I fetched instruments, occasionally applied a bandage, comforted a patient, and saw unbelievable diagnoses of illnesses that I had no idea existed. For example, I saw tropical ulcers protruding from people's bodies, all kinds of tropical diseases caused by flies and mosquitoes, trichinosis, hookworms, malaria, typhus, things that live in the lakes, streams, and drinking water the population drank, and fly larvae (maggots) like Myiasis. I even saw a young child that had been bitten on the head by a hyena. My medical exit-card issued to me when I left the Peace Corps had in excess of 20 things that I and others may have been exposed to. I have already related how I contracted amoebic dysentery and was treated for it. There were, most notably, a couple of additional things that I experienced that I have not forgotten, given the impact they had on me. They are not traumatic enough to have adversely affected me, but they were experiences that most humans on the planet will never experience. The first unusual circumstance, for me at least, was the birth of a baby which may not seem so uncommon until I tell you what it was. The second was a patient who had leprosy.

Obviously, there is nothing remotely funny about leprosy, but when this patient presented himself in the doctor's office, initially to me and the doctor's Ethiopian medical assistant, what happened next was a lesson in how fear can capture a moment where ignorance is at its root. As the patient entered the doctor's office for initial diagnosis, the assistant jumped up, ran out of the office, and returned a couple minutes later with a dispenser of fly spray. It was one of those long tube contraptions with a container of liquid fly spray at one end, that you pump with a handle similar to a bicycle pump; the bug spray comes out the other end in a mist that permeates the air and floats to the ground. The medical assistant frantically sprayed the entire office, as well as the patient in question, and stopped short of spraying me and the doctor. The assistant obviously didn't understand what leprosy was even though he knew the sight of it. His hysterical actions would do no good, of course, but he had to try something to quell his own superstition. What does that teach us about what we don't know and how that may affect us, not to mention that patient? A lesson learned. The second experience had a much greater impact on me.

One day the head doctor was hurriedly called to the maternity ward. Normally this would require only a midwife, as is the custom in Third World countries. In this case, however the woman in labor had a fetus not only in breech, but also additional complications brought on by a practice that is prevalent in certain parts of the world, one that the World Health Organization has long sought to eradicate, as have other numerous humanitarian relief organizations. Women, in certain cultures, are sometimes subjected to a form of circumcision, known commonly as female genital mutilation (FGM). The patient in question was one who had this performed on her in her youth and was now in labor. It's not important that I describe what this means, but only to let you know that it complicates both surviving the condition, let alone what it can mean for childbirth itself. The doctor asked that I assist him in what would be, on the surface, a simple way within my skill range—talk to her and hold her shoulders down to avoid movement that might interfere with his aiding in the birth. The doctor was successful in using tongs to deliver the child, the mother survived, and I was simply exhausted. To see firsthand what ignorance of some—men, in this case—means for others is something you don't forget. Somewhere there is a child that I helped, in a small way, to be! That child, that mother, and this man were all lucky on that day.

Seminal Moment: The Peace Corps

My decision to join the Peace Corps was a seminal event in that it:

- *Assured me that I could survive and thrive on my own outside of the protective environment in which I had been raised.*
- *It was there in Ethiopia I honed my skills as a teacher; knowing that I could make a living.*

- *Intensified my longing to see the world from the point of view of, first and foremost, personal contact with the indigenous population of which I was always a visitor, followed by seeing all the interesting things there are to be experienced.*

CHAPTER 7

Danny the Married and Family Man

I've been lucky to have been married twice. I don't recommend it to everyone, or even being married at all if that is what you desire. For me, being married worked, even with one divorce which is a little analogous, in my opinion, to the death of loved ones. I have experienced the loss of one child, most of my siblings, and a mother and father; thus I know what sorrow is. Marriage is to be cherished for all that it brings, even if it ends. I'll briefly trace my married life to explain why I feel this way, and the impact on my life in general.

You'll recall I married in Ethiopia while in the Peace Corps. That was 1963 and my first marriage lasted 27 years. The divorce happened well after our two girls were out of college and on their own. My first wife and I were young when we met, engaged after only three weeks of dating, and had no idea how to select one another or what marriage was supposed to be about. Nobody gave us a user manual on courting, and certainly not on the many facets of all that is marriage. Her parents were married all their adult lives and died together. I had a mostly single mom who ran a business and did a great job raising her children—Mother of the Year. But let's face it: we don't have any idea what we are looking for in a mate or how to be a family. It's mostly all made up on the fly. Generally, our version of marriage worked well, and we had a life together slightly in excess of two and a half decades.

A few years ago, at my second wife's encouragement, I wrote a book for husbands on how to be a good husband. Kathleen had often said to others I am a good husband, and so she encouraged me to write a book describing how that is achieved and what it entails. Titled, *The Good Husband: 50 Practices That Will Make You Nearly Perfect*, it attempts to capture not just how to be a good husband, but perhaps more importantly what to look for in a male or female that will make them a good partner; hopefully forever. I think both my first wife and certainly me, needed that guide 27 years before we divorced, but it wasn't available. I had not even had the experience to write, let alone realize most of the needed content. We had been married 23 years from the time of our Peace Corps service to when our children went out on their own. Of course, living is in the doing, so there are no guarantees. It surely would have helped to have some guidance rather than through various hard knock experiences!

My then wife, Patricia (Pat), and I had a good life. Among other things beyond parenting, she is a talented watercolor artist. We responded well to marriage and all its reality, having our first child, Lisa, then abandoning New York City and my studies at New York University as we went back home sort of. We settled in Pleasanton, California and bought our first home for $29,500. We had our second child, Kim, there and did family and neighborly things. We were good at it and happy, but, as they say, had our share of issues.

We moved two more times, first to Pennsylvania then, to Idaho, and settled into a life doing new family things in a combination of rural and city settings—she with her art, and I with my job and farming. We kind of had it all, as "The American Dream." We raised our two girls through some typical challenges that all kids provide but are proud to note that our children became very productive and nice adults that we were—and are—very proud of.

Our family life was spent mostly in three locations from coast to coast. After our brief stint in New Jersey following the Peace Corps, the first was four years in Pleasanton, California, then ten years each in Ardmore, Pennsylvania, and lastly near Boise, Idaho. Each move was necessitated by changes in my employment and ultimately worked out for the best, both for the family as well as for me professionally. I think we, as a family, enjoyed each location we landed in and made the most of each for their true uniqueness. I had, for example, clearly expressed a desire not to spend any more than ten years in Pennsylvania and that's how it worked out. I was, naturally, thankful at one of those periods to be back in Idaho the most, but that is no surprise given that I was born and raised there. I am confident that we all came to love Idaho for our own individual reasons.

Our time in Pleasanton, California was relatively short, as I was getting established professionally in a new kind of work beyond what I had been prepared for academically. Pleasanton was not chosen by us, but rather because of employment that I took on. As luck would have it, the location provided an excellent base to begin life as a family in several ways. The community was relatively small then, mostly farming in nature, during the time period we were there from 1965 to 1969. We acquired our first home in a lovely developing neighborhood with other families in similar circumstance to our own in terms of our age and economic demographic, and for my wife, Patricia, her parents were close at hand. Our girls made friends that lived across the street from us, and we had other parents of our own age to socialize with. While it was a short stay, it was an excellent beginning to foster family life, especially for the children in their first few years.

Our next move to live in Ardmore, Pennsylvania for my work in nearby Bryn Mawr was also good for our family, our two girls now approaching grade school age. We domestically upscaled to a charming two-story older colonial style stone house in a very pleasant neighborhood. We had good neighbors, and I had an easy commute to work, just two miles away, by bicycle, train, or car. Having easy access to Philadelphia and the "Main Line" area brought a sense of sophistication that we had not experienced before as a family. We made some new circles of "friends," which exposed us to the concepts of both "old money" and "new money." For a boy like me from Idaho, this was quite a change, but I was adequately prepared to handle both the unusualness, let alone how it felt pretentious. I am sure studying the ways of such people was more

211

interesting than participating with them in social interactions. I am sure each of my family members came away from living in Pennsylvania with what my current wife refers to as, "interesting sociological experiences." Isn't that the truth! I can truly say it was a worthwhile learning experience for me and my family. The contrast to then living in Idaho later was something to behold and learn from. I'll elaborate.

While in Pennsylvania our two girls attended an interesting variety of private, Christian based, and public schools as we searched for the right combination to meet their individual needs. The private school we found to be a little too snooty, the Christian school a little too dogmatic, and the public school good, yet inadequate, in ways that can't be solved with an influx of funds alone. I shall never forget the day Lisa came home during her days at the private school (Baldwin) and lamented that our house was so small! At 3,200 square feet with four bedrooms, a study, large living room with a marble fireplace, crown molding in all the rooms, full basement and attic, a beautiful chandelier in the dining room, and so on, how could our home be considered as anything but nice, if not a bit opulent with a nice yard and garden? I'd say the girls—and us as parents—were learning a thing or two about the inequities that exist in our society, as well as the attitudes of the rich. Aside from this disquiet, with gorgeous trees in a safe and interesting neighborhood, the new place we called home was a locale with charm, fireflies, and overall good schools for the kids.

Pat began to prepare herself as a watercolor artist. With a thriving art community (that had fostered the talents of well-known artists like Andrew Wyeth) here in the Brandywine region she was in the right place for tutoring, classes, and finding inspiration with and from other artists. I took a couple of opportunities to start on a doctorate degree again, but each seem to have roadblocks not worth the effort, so I turned my efforts to writing, getting published, and offering some workshops on the side for extra income to support our advancing lifestyle. Our times spent in Ardmore were good and met both our family-oriented and professional goals for the ten years we were there. We even bought a small cabin on Cranberry Lake in north Pennsylvania and spent a few weeks now and then fishing, catching frogs, using an old rowboat, and admiring beautiful scenery with water lilies. One more little story about our time in Pennsylvania before I move on to our next family location.

One summer morning in Bryn Mawr I had taken the day off and had to swing by our local bank to make a withdrawal of needed cash. ATMs had just come into general use and were found exclusively on site at your bank. Not thinking I would be meeting anyone I knew that day, I was dressed in old Levi's, a slightly soiled shirt donned for doing yard work, and had forgone shaving that morning. I pulled up to the bank to use the ATM. As I did so, I passed four or five people just standing there next to the ATM. I wondered what was going on, but I was focused on making my cash withdrawal, which I did. As I turned back towards my car (and thus the group), one of the men stuck out his hand and said, "Congratulations! You are our one millionth ATM transaction for a customer. We'd like you to come into the bank where we want to have a reception and give you some gifts." I apologized for my appearance, but they took some press photos with me and ushered me inside where we drank some champagne, munched on cookies and cake, and they presented me with a very nice large TV and other goodies. We conversed for another half hour or so, during which the branch manager discovered in conversation with me, as it so happened, that my wife was currently displaying her artwork on the bank walls. He admired them greatly and bought two of her paintings right there and then. Imagine going home, still dressed as I was, and announcing that I had a large TV in the trunk of the car, and here are some cookies they sent home with me. And oh, by the way, two of your paintings have sold and here is a check for you. You just never know when you are going to be the lucky one millionth transaction.

Certainly, in my way of thinking, our most consequential family relocation was the last when we moved west to Idaho. It was to be the place where all of us, up until the time of our divorce, would settle in permanently and where my ex-wife and daughter at present live. As with most any family, this period of time is significant in large part because it was where our children experienced their teen years and later went off to college. We lived on a farm and perhaps had our best years there, but also experienced most of our struggles as a family with teenagers and all that that brings. It was where our marriage ended.

My wife and I decided to settle on a small six-acre farm 18 miles out of town in a small berg called Star. I was about to become a "gentlemen farmer" or "rancher," depending on which title builds your ego the most. I decided on a farmer because that was closer to what it was. My sister Dorothy and her husband were the real ranchers with 2000 acres, so six acres barely qualified as a garden next to that! And if one was to factor into the equation the number of animals I had, well my sister Bertine and her husband, Kent, had a real farm with milk cows that they made a living off. So I was not a real farmer with respect to the number of livestock or what I planted and harvested, but I called myself such as my own personal inside joke. I was a part-time farmer with a full-time professional job. Got the picture?

If pressed to express the truth I am sure I loved both my job and the farming, but I really think the farming won out over the paid job as Corporate Director of Training for the Morrison Knudsen Corporation. Generally, we gentlemen farmers where we were located had restricted covenants that governed how many animals we could have on the farm. Therefore I generally had five cows (White Face or Angus, sometimes a beautiful, Swiss, with those huge Betty Davis eyes), 15 sheep (mostly Suffolk), a couple dozen chickens (Rhode Island Reds), a mean goose, and somewhere between 2 horses and a pony. Oh, and I had a 10,000 square foot vegetable garden, a beautiful rolling pasture, and a one-acre pond at the bottom of the rolling pasture between me and two other gentlemen farmers. The pond (in which I later put 100 small mouth bass) was a great place in which to climb into my one-person rowboat and sit out in the middle of the pond to just ponder the beauty of the place and find needed moments of serenity. How lucky I was to be there, I said again and again to myself and anyone who might listen. I was known to do exactly that, sit in the boat or lie in the pasture when anything seemed a bit much, which it rarely was in that kind of living environment.

Farmhouse in Star, Idaho with 1 acre pond at bottom of pasture that Danny created and put 100 small mouth bass

I realize I am dwelling on my fondness for the farm rather than the job I had, which itself was very rewarding, but I was learning so much on the farm and feeling so close to nature. I found myself, for obvious reasons of scale along, being fulfilled in this environment more so than when I was a kid and we raised only a couple sheep in a discarded wooden refrigerator box on the front porch of my mother's home. Some examples of the experiences reveal why.

For one I learned how to dock tails and castrate sheep. Now this may not sound like anything requiring great intellect or offering a large return on personal development, but to the sheep it was a much-needed necessary service. The need has mostly to do with the sanitary condition of the sheep's rear in the first instance and development of the meat in the second. Docking the tail was simple—a quick snip of a knife, followed by a powder, if needed—to cauterize the bleeding. You can, as an alternative, use a kind of rubber band to dock tails, but that, even to me, seemed cruel and unusual punishment (for the sheep, not me).

Now, compared to tail docking which just sounds nicer or pleasant (for me, not the lamb), learning how to deliver a lamb was a real eye-opener. Delivery requires you to do things you would otherwise never think of trying until you simply have to. Pregnant ewes sometimes need help delivering those cute lambs that we all love to pet. This "help" requires the farmer (Moi in French), even the gentlemen farmer, to reach with his hand and some arm, up into the uterus of that ewe to find where that cute lamb is breached, or perhaps sideways to how it should for normal delivery.

Nothing more needs be described about raising and tending to sheep, except one other needed practice of sheep farming that deserves special description. It turns out, the gentlemen farmer (or fulltime one) has two options for this sheep raising need, known as castration. Castration is performed on male animals, such as needed for dogs, sheep, cows, horses, and others. For sheep it can be administered in either of two ways. I am proud to say, I only did one way, and never did the second. The "acceptable way" is, similar to the docking process of the tail, the simple use of a sharp knife. Not necessary to describe specifically how that is done other than to say it involves the sheep's scrotum—wince, wince gentlemen—and the testicles. Use of a knife is the most often used method for a reason that will shortly become apparent even as a novice.

I was witness, on three occasions, to the alternative method of castration, which I came to summarize by the word ignominious, because my neighbor, a man I had become close with as a fellow gentlemen farmer, was a "show-off," I think in a kind of perverted way. By the way, he was, at the time, the assistant attorney general of the State of Idaho—neither profession nor action on his part being that directly related in practice. I imagined he was, however, a tough Assistant Attorney General based on his sheep tending skills.

It seems it is or at least was, the practice of Basque sheep herders, often alone, who devised a unique way to castrate sheep. Unlike me, they did not often have a friend who could help them hold the lamb securely since castration is not something a sheep looks forward to (of course they have no idea what is coming their way). So the lone sheep herder, or my friend in this case, uses their teeth to extract the testicles. I vividly remember with dismay the first time seeing my neighbor do this. I said afterwards, "How do you go home at night and kiss your wife after doing such a thing?" He didn't have an answer and I wasn't about to try that particular technique of castration. I strictly used the more modern technology of a good old sharp pocketknife. Before we leave this topic, I wish to point out that I never did try this technique neither on my sheep nor my male cows—soon to be steer—given that a typical cow's size speaks to why, let alone the way I have seen them kick a horse or the horse them, or tried to kick our mean old goose that was left on the farm when we bought it. By the way, that goose used to like to snip my dear wife by the buttocks for some reason but went too far one day with the horse and did not live to honk another day. I loved that farm, the goose, the other animals, and have often just driven by it on visits to Boise to rejuvenate the memories. I'll mention only one other farm animal, then move on to the full-time regular jobs I had for money rather than pleasure.

I personally can't imagine a farm is a farm without animals. I've mentioned the menagerie that we had which was limited only by covenants imposed by our neighborhood homeowners association that didn't really exist after everyone had bought their homes and established themselves. Thank God for that in this case, as I have been associated with two other homeowner associations. I have stories to fill another book if I don't decide to start a professional practice aimed at providing psychological help for people who get so involved in micromanaging HOAs that they contribute in no small way to their total disfunction.

One of the pets we had was a pet lamb—a large fluffy Merino with fine soft wool. A sheep usually becomes a pet most often because a new lamb never gets completely accepted by its mother for whatever reason. It thus is designated, unrightly by mankind, a "bummer," or "bum lamb."

In addition to the fact that little lambs are adorable (just ask Mary who had a little lamb), I'd been raising sheep on Mother's front porch since I was a kid, so I kind of have had a pre-existing affection for these critters. Ours is not to question why, because it is what it is. As a kid, my mother wanted (I surmise) us to have the experience and responsibility of raising animals (lambs and chickens as compared to pets like dogs or cats, which we also had) I guess as some practical lesson perhaps in child rearing, but probably mostly for the experience and responsibility of assuring their existence under our personal care, but also the lesson to be learned from the eventual final demise of the animal for needed sustenance. Mother would find a large wooden box that a refrigerator had been shipped in, place straw in the bottom, then three or four lambs and expect us to feed them using a big soda bottle with a rubber nipple attached to it. We learned to create and adhere to a schedule to warm the milk, make sure it wasn't too hot to drink (yes, you tested it yourself, nipple and all, or squirt some milk on your arm), and put it in the lamb's mouth often with some difficulty as they tended to get over excited. It would typically take about 10 minutes for them to finish a whole bottle. This feeding frenzy often happened, in our case, in the late night or early morning hours, so we children were prepared early in our lives to sacrifice a little sleep for the benefit of an animal that truly depended upon us. Maybe, now that I think about it, the lesson was in persistence and not letting that little lamb die because of your neglect. As I keep saying, I learned a lot. By the way, those lambs and their crate were sometimes located at The Warehouse, but they were just as likely to be found on the front porch of our mother's house. It was easier having them at home given that going down to The Warehouse in the middle of the night to do our assigned duty (including occasionally cleaning out the box of lamb droppings) was taxing, even for a kid. Oh, and we also raised on occasion a few chickens from chicks to full grown birds. The same kind of box with the addition of a heat lamp did the job of raising a small flock of fuzzy yellow chicks into full grown chickens of different varieties. Years later I realized all this was practice for my having a farm as it came to be with my own family. And on the farm was a very special pet. His name was Billy, our pet sheep. I would like to give high praise and honor to him, as he was a very special pet for my family. Billy had real personality.

You can't help but love a lamb. You love 'em all, but you can't keep 'em all. As a farmer, gentlemen or otherwise, that's a rule whether you like it or not. You can name them, and we often did: a couple of cows were named Pete and Repeat or Moo and Moozappa, for example. Billy became our pet by way of exception from slaughter, which is the fate of most farm animals. We gave him a name with all the amenities of a long life and other residuals such as occasional petting, talking with him as if he were one of the family, special feed as might please him, and one other special Bennie: if the front door had been inadvertently left open, his coming in, walking the various rooms before you discovered him, and leaving a trail of his little black droppings marking his path, territory, and his point of egress, you hoped. He truly would follow you, as the story line goes, "all the way home!" We loved that Billy until one day we had to bury him in the back pasture, on a hill where we once had watched him running around. A few other animals died for the usual reasons that go with farming, but none got the treatment Billy did. Farm animals, which die for whatever reason, are usually picked up by the guy who collected their carcasses in order to then deliver to those who make tallow (soap). Life on the farm is not like life in the city anywhere. I was blessed to experience both.

I realize I don't seem to be able to get off the subject of the farm but that's because I truly loved farming and I believe the family did in their individual ways. Maybe I should have been a real farmer? Na I am a technology sort of guy who likes to research and solve things—not that farming doesn't have loads of that in its own ways.

When we bought the farm, at the bottom of a sloping hill there was a small, usually muddy, pond. It was only ever partially full in the late spring due to the small amount of water runoff it collected from other real farms surrounding us. It could—and often did—dry out during the first couple of years we lived there. One year I figured we (the two neighbors across the way and I) needed to improve on the pond if for no other reason than it would provide a constant water source for our small fields of wild grass; we each had about 4 acres of pasture. So I got together with my fellow gentlemen farmers and suggested we raise the dam a couple of feet, install a new spillway, drill, and have a pump installed up near the road in order to stream fresh ground water which would build a pond about an acre in size. We put the plan into action and it worked beautifully. It created a lovely 1-acre water source. There was a guy in town who sold us water lilies and one day he and two of his associates showed up to plant the lilies in the pond. I directed them where to go in order for them to plant the lilies in the ideal part of the pond. I returned to the house, and half an hour later I look down towards the pond to see how the work was progressing. There I see three buck naked—two men and one woman—frolicking in the water, their bare asses sometimes bobbing up above the water as they dove under to secure the plants to the muddy pond floor. What could I possibly say? Those water lilies really multiplied in the shallow end of the pond and were gorgeous when they flowered, and soon frogs came and added a melodious sound to an otherwise quiet evening.

Once the pond fully developed, I decided to add some fish with the thought of fishing from my rowboat. Just something for the pleasure of it. I found a guy who was commercially fish farming just a few miles away along the Boise river. Armed with a 55-gallon barrel I had him fill it with 100 smallmouth bass. When I went over to buy the bass fingerlings, the owner shared a lesson he had learned about fish farming the hard way. Seems when it came time to harvest the fingerlings (a fish the size, yes, of your finger—about 10-15 centimeters), you used a giant vacuum like hose device and pumped them into a waiting tank mounted on a truck, much like milk is transported from the farm to the milk processing plant. The only problem, he said, is that he forgot to put the hose end where the fish were to be dumped in the truck's tank, and instead of releasing into the tank, the fish went directly into the Boise River! He recalled the number lost to be around 120,000 little fishes. Incidentally, those bass I placed in the pond grew like crazy but I moved away about a year after I placed them there. I've always wanted to go back and catch one.

Don't you wish you had a farm? I did and it created meaningful experiences for me I never imagined I would have in life. Sometimes I nearly forgot that I had a paid professional life which did not include farming. Selling free range chicken eggs or a quarter of beef or lamb to friends and work colleagues was hardly a way to make a living. Therefore, I will now return to the topics of family and my real job.

From my perspective, our marriage ended for reasons that were not very easy to resolve. Through all our years of marriage we didn't seem to learn enough or master the skill required to process what needed processing between us. This was especially true after our children were away and on their own. It became increasingly hard to get through some of our issues: specifically to have productive discussions that would resolve the issues and move forward, rather than cause us to repeatedly live in the past. Our days in the Peace Corps were easy, as was years living thereafter filled as it was with life's numerous activities that occur on-the-go while raising kids. The two of us alone together was nice, but we (or maybe it was just me) could not maintain the marriage relationship. It was my idea to split, but she knew that I loved her and as the years have passed since our final day together, we have come to understand that parting was good for both of us. We still connect when our daughter (which she doesn't) or grandchildren (sometimes) are ever in need, and we keep up with each other regarding our general wellbeing in life. It was, for lots of reasons, a good marriage. It just got broke.

As it just so happened, just after the time of our separation I was recruited to a job in California. It afforded, as it came to pass, an opportunity to get away and kind of start anew! Also as it came to be, the company I was working for, MK in Boise, folded a couple of years after I left. Strange that this has happened to three companies I worked for in my career. I've often joked to others that I caused their collapse or they just missed me and my skills. Of course neither of these reasons were the case, but it was ironic that I was one step ahead of employment catastrophe, just as I had been in not being drafted for the military. I wasn't avoiding any of those circumstances that befell my career, but I was sure lucky, lucky, lucky three times.

When I got to California and soon thereafter had my marital status reset to "Single," I met a woman who herself had just divorced. I knew her professionally as we used to see one another at the annual meeting of our professional association's conference which was held in various major cities. As with others we knew, we would typically exchange greetings along the lines of, "Hi! How are you? What have you been up to over the last year?" I'd say our yearly conversation was typically about a fifty-word exchange, given the brevity of conversation I was known for with strangers that I saw again only once a year.

One of the things I knew following my divorce is that you didn't want to rush out and make mistakes you were not aware of the first time in finding a mate—not that my overall first marriage was a mistake. Rather, it's just that when you decide to get back in the hunt, make sure you know what you're hunting for. Heaven hopes you have more experience the second time to take advantage of. Just don't ignore it! If I was to date again, I thought, I had one overriding criterion: to be with someone who could process their own stuff (to be honest, I used another four-letter word); then as long as I was able to process my own stuff, we could have a greater chance of successfully processing together! Kathleen Swanick Whiteside was the answer!

Kathleen and I spent days and hours going over how we would handle "peanut butter" as she likes to phrase it. Peanut butter is the natural stuff that comes up between couples as they make their way towards what they seek as a healthy and honest loving relationship—which we definitely have achieved. She had, as it turned out, her own challenges with her ex and had come to realize she had to find her own path to what good processing as a couple is. Some of that path she discovered from an Adult Children of Alcoholics (for women) program she came to attend. Through this 12-step program, she worked on herself and became better prepared than me, perhaps, with solid advice on what makes for a good marriage—a fact that I truly appreciated. Given our shared criterion for a new relationship that had the potential to become ever so much more workable, we discussed a lot on how to resolve differences of opinion given the different personalities (I'll address later specifically how) that we have. And further beyond that, what would be done concerning our children and this new relationship? She still had one of her two children living at home. When would we introduce each other to all parties and how during the dating process? Where would we live? The questions went on and on. Most importantly, and I keep coming back to this, it was how we successfully processed everything from business to personal issues, individually and collectively, that confronted us.

I confess I had never done so much preliminary talking regarding achieving clarity and consensus, but it was so necessary before making any more serious commitment. I even met her parents and siblings, but I won't say how that affected my decision to continue dating. We did so much talking things out that I wasn't sure we would ever get around to marrying (or even sex) but we did and postponed both until we married at the end of 1991. I don't mind confessing that I have only had sex with two women, and I married both before doing so—an old fashion idea, I know, but it was, for me, the right way to be. I am old fashioned (but prefer to be considered an old soul) in other ways as well, like still opening doors for the elderly, which now includes me hoping others will do the same for me (and they often do). Kathleen and I have been married 33 years and I am pleased beyond any words I might write or possibly express. Throughout all its pages, I can say that the book I wrote for husbands is, perhaps, really the story of the immense and powerful love I have for Kathleen. That's because much of what I became as a good husband, and the ways I have improved as well in a good marriage, is because of her. I am confident she feels the same about me.

As a father, I can't say enough about my wonderful children; like everything in this book they too need a book to do them justice. I'll describe my children, and then Kathleen's children who are now fully my children as well, just as my stepbrothers and sister are fully my brothers and sister.

Lisa, our first child, was a challenge from day one. She was a beautiful baby. The kind that others in a grocery store stop you and commented about. She was born with one of her feet turned up at the ankle and had to wear a cast for a few months as a baby, making those same people in the supermarket wonder what we had done to our child. A bit rebellious and demanding with her own say on doing virtually anything, she was quite the challenge to have as a first child, but just the kind of child you want to have and love. She had a great smile and a quick sense of humor and was so talented. We chose private schools initially for her, thinking they were better for our children, then switched to public schools when broader socialization was needed.

Lisa, unfortunately contracted MS when she was a young mother. Her battle with the disease was admirable given that she prevailed in mothering and being a working single mom. I was so very proud that she became the loving mother she was to her own four children: Brittney, Justin, Trevor, and Ryan (who has autism). She had that kind of strength like her grandmother raising children alone and working in her own jungle of challenges as a single mom.

Lisa sadly died of cancer of the appendix in 2013. The best thing I ever did in life as a human and a dad (along with Kathleen) was to go to live with her in Boise during the last five months of Lisa's life. We lived together in her house with her son Ryan while the two other boys transitioned out on their own: Brittney already living independently. At bedtime I read to Lisa just as we had together when she was a small child. Kathleen and I changed her dressings for cancer treatment like I had her diapers and swapped out her colostomy bag because of kidney failure. She and I talked into the wee hours about her pain and the struggles she sought to solve, and I was there when she needed her dad to give comfort and talks that console. Now 48 years old, at bedtime, I read her favorite book, "Where the Red Fern Grows," by Wilson Rawls. We read and talked late into the night as she gradually fell asleep. We ended on page 182 a couple days before her passing, and I have yet to read the remaining words by myself. I've requested of my wife that she read the final pages on my own deathbed or shortly after I am gone. In that way, both Lisa and I will get to hear the remaining pages together. Not every father gets the privilege to be with their child when they are born and when they die but let me recommend it if it should present itself, God forbid, to you. I recorded a StoryCorps account of our final days together that you can listen to if you are so inclined. It can be found at: https://archive.storycorps.org/interviews/mby010998/

Our second child, Kimberly (Kim), was the easy child we all hope for as parents to maintain our sanity. She is, I am proud to say, pretty much like her dad, although unlike her dad, she has paid off her mortgage. A bit quiet and reserved, you can tell she thinks her way through things, and enjoys her life, especially her marriage and children. She is very successful in her work as an app developer and enjoys the challenges that life brings. She's an avid cyclist, regularly going into the hills of Boise, Idaho or riding the 45 minutes to work in Eagle along the Boise River trail. She has started to travel a lot more, with her dad's encouragement. Kim laughed a lot as a child and did well academically as well as in sports as a distance and cross-country runner. I had to especially chuckle at one event when she informed me, after a race I had seen her run, that she ran for the color of ribbon she most desired on that day. She got a blue one. A unique approach to running, but rather healthy when you analyze it. I think she knows what is to be valued as well as done for the experience of something and be satisfied within oneself. I hope I exemplified that to her. She certainly makes me feel good in my old age as I approach finality. Talking to her by phone as she cycles home once a week is something I look forward to.

From the time we moved to Boise, Kim really liked horses. Initially she had a small Welsh pony named Sugar. It was a feisty animal that had an attitude of its own. It seemed to take delight in my chasing it around the pasture trying to get it in the barn for a needed shot or transport to a 4-H event. Kim went through a couple of other horses, one that was 16 hands, as they are measured in height, by the name of Rillito. It was a horse my sister Dorothy sold to us for Kim's advancing equestrian interests.

Kim got involved in 4-H for general riding interest and one day participated in a rodeo ceremony wherein the riders holding American flags typically, ride into the center of the rodeo arena and put on a brief show of horsemanship. After the rodeo was all over and dusk had descended upon us, I went to help her load Rillito in our homemade one-horse trailer attached to our small Chevy Luv pickup—every gentleman farmer needs a truck and trailer for transportation of horses, sheep, and cattle. I simply could not get that horse into that trailer as I had so many, many times before. Frustrated, with the black of night fast approaching I looked over from the dim parking lot to the brighter rodeo arena. I see a single cowboy collecting his gear. I walked over and asked for his assistance. He obliged me, as any cowboy would, and came over and tried his hand at getting the horse loaded. I was kind of pleased to see that he, too, had initial difficulty. But he knew more than me. He used an old cowboy trick: he put a long rope around the horse's ass, tied one end to the tailgate of the trailer and put the other end of rope through an air-vent like hole in the middle-front of the trailer. With the horse sort of harnessed up as such, the idea was to pull the horse into the open back of the trailer. This is supposed to help easily guide the horse in so you can then shut the gate behind it—its ass. The idea, if you can visualize it, is that you can pull that horse right into the trailer, but I think that assumes you're dealing with a horse without an attitude, which I knew this horse had. Sure enough, the horse started to go in but then balked, at which the cowboy tightened his pull on the rope. The horse, for his part, backed up and reared a bit, causing the trailer to tip to one side, about twenty degrees, I would estimate. This tilt slightly twisted the hitch of the trailer to the pickup, and I thought I'd never be able to put the two together again and make it home, but it held. And thanks to that cowboy's belief that no horse would ever get the better of him, that horse went into that trailer. We drove home, unloaded the horse with greater ease, and never loaded Rillito into that trailer again. We sold the horse after my daughter had grown up and gone off to college, and the person who purchased the horse had to come and get it in their trailer by themselves.

Kim married a wonderful partner in Monica Hoene. They have two of their own twins (Miles and Annika) that have excelled in academics and are on their way to excel in life. I also have a great-granddaughter, Zoey, (a blessing from Lisa's daughter Brittney) who is quite a gymnast and student. This is all to say that my family turned out very well and their dad and grandfather and great grandfather are so proud of all of them. I'd like to share just one more story about Kim and then I'll move on to Kathleen's children.

In case you haven't read between the lines, Kim is gay. I found out when she was 18. Before she came out a boy she was dating just after high school called one evening while our family was having dinner. I answered the phone there in the kitchen next to the dining table, and he says right out of the blue, "Mr. Langdon, do you know your daughter is gay?" I said bluntly in return, "Well if she is? That is none of your GD business!" and hung up the phone on the little, self-righteous smart-ass.

It took a week for her to confirm that she was gay, and from my upbringing I was all in for that truth. She was and is this fine human being and that's all that counts! That's the way Langdons are. A few years later, when I learned the Boy Scouts of America were no longer allowing gay men to be Scoutmasters, I sent to the national headquarters the hard-earned Eagle Badge I had been granted in my youth. A few years later they changed their mind again and allowed gay men to be leaders. I hope the change in their policy had something to do with me and that Eagle Badge! I've also been a contributing author to a book, "A Family & Friend's Guide to Sexual Orientation," authored by a treasured professional colleague of mine, Bob Powers. By the way I was told the book was a bestseller in Portugal, of all places. I've been to that country a few times and it doesn't surprise me in the least. I already told you the story of telling my sister I had a gay daughter and she had better get used to it. She did! Those Langdons: you always know what they will do when it comes to doing the right thing! I am so proud of my two girls, and I long for the days when I held both in my arms at the back of church service and my arms simply ached from the weight and the squirming, but I would not let them down.

I have two other children to be proud of as well. Kathleen's children gave me the opportunity for a second chance at fathering without any of the authority to do so. Kathleen's daughter, Jennifer, who now goes by Johnilee, wanted her mother to marry a movie star after she divorced. It had to be someone with a huge head of curly hair as I recall, so when she married me, I was kind of a disappointment to her: my hair barely went beyond my ears. I was neither a movie star nor did I have any longer those curly locks that had been so lovingly groomed by my sisters. The truth is, she wanted her mother to herself and didn't want to share her with this guy she was dating. I remember once walking down the street together in San Pedro. We were in the early days of dating. The two of them were walking in front and I was dragging myself behind as if on some kind of invisible leash. Jennifer was ignoring me completely and had her mother all to herself up ahead on the sidewalk which made me feel like I was just some guy seemingly stalking them. I'd obviously have to win Jenifer over! I was fortunate at that time in my professional career that I was a performance technologist (of some international repute) specializing in behavioral improvement. So what would I do to win Jennifer over? The answer was pretty simple. Never tell her what to do or judge what she does. Rather, sit back and when she needs help (kids always do eventually), be the man on the spot who gets it done. An example will suffice to make the point that perhaps will be of help to others meeting the need I was faced with.

My time came when Jennifer was graduating from a local private college in the Los Angeles area. At the last minute (which she is known for), she needed a van to move her stuff out of her apartment at the end of the term, which so happened to be that very day. Of course, all the vans in the greater Los Angeles area were out moving all the other students who had made reservations in advance. I managed to find one—for a premium price—large enough to move a family of six. I showed up at her apartment at the appointed time, we packed, and she was moved. After a couple more times I was helpful in responding to her needs, she learned that I was a man of action who loved her mother very much. Perhaps my revenge was years later when she had to study my business model—The Language of Work Model™—as part of her graduate studies in the field in which I am a recognized expert. In fact, in the oral defense phase of her graduate studies, she had to defend me against another colleague's model for learning. How about that? Now, as she informed me and likes to proudly note, "she is my "spare daughter," something that is so close to this boy's heart because of the biological daughter I so miss. I very much needed that and continue to. I am the lucky one! As if that wasn't enough of a contribution to my family, later she had her own child, Hazel (or Allie, Ethan, or Zellee as my own personal nick name for them). As an extension of logic, I now have a "spare granddaughter." What a fine addition she is with her great musical style on the guitar and intellectual prowess with adults that I have never experienced with any child who's becoming an adult so quickly. I am looking forward to what Hazel does with their life: do travel, child, I so recommend.

My wife's son, Nathaniel, (Nathan or Nate) is, of course, the son I didn't have. He was 16 when I moved into their house in West Lake Village, California. He is very methodical and organized but had, as teens are wont to have, some bad habits. One of them was leaving milk cartons, glasses, and other dishware in the family TV room on a regular basis. When I mentioned replacing the dry bar at the end of the room with a dishwasher, he got the point. We moved on from there to get to know one another. He helped me build a pond in the backyard that I think he had always wanted but had not been realized by his real dad. Again, you win them over, not tell them over. He joined the Peace Corps out of college like his "other father" had, and thus we share that common bond. He is an interesting vortex healer by trade; I'll let him explain to you one day what that is. I know, for my part, both of Kathleen's children are wonderful adults and I could not be any prouder if they were my very own, which they truly are. As I told you in the introduction, there is no such thing as stepchildren or stepbrothers and stepsisters in the Langdon frame of being.

I want to close off the family narrative with one additional member of what became our new family unit. While this is not a person, like many a household, it is a kind of person when you consider the way they are treated and coddled. That is, of course, in this case, the family dog who was part of the deal brought by Kathleen and her children into this marriage. Her name was Mitzi, a Miniature Poodle, with white curly hair and about the size of a medium-sized fire extinguisher, and she had a yap to go with her small frame.

Now I love animals. I've had four dogs, nine or more cats, a pet goose, a pet sheep, a pet mouse, some pet ducks, fish, numerous domestic cows, chickens, and other animals that, while not always made pets per se, seemed like they were until you had to slaughter certain of them for obvious reasons. Our pets were so personal to us that we used to even name them. For example you'll recall that the sheep and cows had names such as, Moo, MooZappa, Pete and RePete, and others. While Mitzi was not my type of preferred dog (I had, for example a large German Shorthair by the name of Buddy on the farm) Mitzi had one huge benefit that I shall briefly elucidate upon.

I was reasonable enough as a husband to occasionally take Mitzi for a walk to do you-know-what. We were living at that time in the sophisticated city of Santa Monica, California. When you walk a poodle in Santa Monica, it turns out, women seem to think you are an okay gentleman, and they want to both (in this order) pet the poodle and say hello to the man. I found that charming. However Mitzi was an older dog in her last days, and she would, on occasion, faint! Yes faint, such that at the end of the leash you had what appeared to be a dead dog! I got used to it as the dog would recover in about 45 long seconds and we'd be on our way again. I told my fairly new wife, based on my farming days during which I had worked with vets tending my animals, that her dear Mitzi had mitral valve prolapses, a heart condition. Kathleen had no reason to believe me, and she didn't. Subsequently, in consulting a local Santa Monica veterinarian who specialized in pets for an exorbitant fee, the vet informed us that, "Your Mitzi has a mitral valve prolapses, and that will require $800 to not fix, but let her live perhaps another year." Knowing that my vets on the farm charged no more than fifty bucks for such a call, we settled on the use of a diuretic that gave her another eight months of walks in the neighborhood. When you take the children, you take whatever else comes with the marriage. I kind of miss old Mitzi for all the benefits she accrued for me on those many walks, let alone the humor of it all.

I've saved the best for last, but really the first of my second marriage. My wife, Kathleen, is my soul mate for sure. Prior to our retirement, we were in business together as equals for 25 years as we are now in life for 33 years and counting. I learned how to process peanut butter with and because of her. I became a better man to her and others. My travels of the world, that currently total 90 countries, include at least half of those in her presence. Without her I don't think I could have been as successful as she has the skills that I lack. We are so different on the right/left brain scale or on an Enneagram that you'd have to wonder how we could be so successful together and so loving. It's to be noted, perhaps, that I made a shift in my perspective when I married her. She has honed me a little—at least as much as my malleability will allow.

With Kathleen, perhaps it's our differences that provide mutual strength and compatibility. You know the differences that make you appreciate one another when you know how to process good and bad shit? Perhaps it's just real Love manifested in the great respect you have for one another. Yeah, I think it's that RESPECT and a whole lot more. I'm the lucky one in the final analysis. I have this song I sing to her with my guitar that captures what I think of her. It's titled, "Lovin' Her Was Easier (Than Anything I'll Ever Do Again.)" That's the truth! Google it and listen and you'll feel what I mean when you hear Kris

Kristofferson sing it. Now I can die, but not until I am ready. Bye the bye, my dad was known as a bit of a troubadour, as was my Brother Buzz, who played a couple of instruments and had his own jug band replete with washboard, bass player, and banjo or ukulele. I think I come by my singing naturally and love playing my guitar in all various styles: hymns, country and western, folk, and a bit of rock and roll. Ask me to sing Buddy Holly sometime.

Seminal Moment: Kathleen.

I kind of feel I'd be in no place without my Kathleen, my love. She is what has made life so rich and so complete. It's all based mostly on the profound respect I have for her as a human being and how she works with me as her soul mate. For all the seminal moments in my life that I address in this book, this is the most important.

- *We created a wonderful, fulfilling life together sharing moments in the morning all the way through daily living and lots of travel.*
- *Our business was successful largely because of her.*
- *Our retirement together is filled with love and adventure.*
- *I love waking up with her and seeing her lying there in the dead of the night, and the mornings that usher us to live another day together.*

CHAPTER 8

Danny as a Professional: Age 26 – 65 or so

I am not sure how to confess it, but when all is said and done, I am not certain I like work! It may seem odd, as I am considered a leading international figure on work, and how to improve it in business through the Language of Work business model that I originated. I'll shortly get to the model I made a mid-life career of and its importance to society in general, but it's just that I'd rather be traveling or contemplating ideas than doing work; but who wouldn't? I don't want to give the impression that I don't work or won't work, or don't work efficiently. I do and I am very good at it, according to others. I get lots done at home, have worked successfully for numerous businesses, been very active in our consulting business, and had leadership roles with others whose job it is to improve work in business. This is evidenced by the numerous evaluations of my different employers and clients who have liked and rewarded me for my work!

Throughout most of my career, I estimate in a typical day you could say I spent four hours actively managing, producing outputs, or arranging things. Then I spent another three hours thinking about work as it related to all that activity, but not producing an output—unless you consider thinking an output, which in a way it is.

Most people engage in tangible activity as their version of work that results in outputs. I played a little, dreamed of possibilities, and took a twenty-minute nap nearly every workday. I did so throughout my career, but less so when I started to work for myself in our own consulting practice, and never in the presence of a client.

Napping occurred almost always after lunch, as eating has some debilitating effect on my capacity to keep my eyes open, let alone think with any degree of productivity. We can't all produce quality work working like a robot—which I fear business today doesn't buy into. However, science seems to support my position concerning work and napping. I have read that many of us—perhaps a third—need a nap, third don't, and the remaining third feel worse after napping. I know I am in the first third, and so a brief sleep was good for me throughout my career. After a nap I could continue writing productively and organizing with great efficiency, which allowed me to then think and plan for what else I would have to do or manage, usually for the next day or more long-term projects. Napping at work in the spare classroom, or even under my desk, was probably known to others and I freely confessed my doing so and was never fired or admonished for sleeping on the job. Perhaps it suggests something for the typical employer who punishes those who do need a nap by saying, no one will be allowed to nap. So I actually do like work, I just don't let it consume me and I get, as a result, lots accomplished. Just ask my partner in life and business and she will confirm my attitude and productivity when it comes to work. Let's see how my career unfolded within this framework.

As we ended our days in the Peace Corps, my wife (Patricia) and I had to begin thinking about the rest of our lives and where that would lead. I was now an experienced teacher (of two years) and solidly knew I could do that, and I really enjoyed teaching. I also had the additional academic credential of a master's degree that prepared and qualified me to someday be in school management, such as a principal. Thus, I wasn't concerned that I wouldn't make a living, nor advance in the field. However, being physically located in Ethiopia at that particular time of transition had its challenges given that it was hard to seek out a teaching job from so far away. Believe me, snail-mail (the only option in the 1960s) in that part of the world was pretty slow, magnified by being halfway around the world in what was then an essentially third-world country. You could not be assured the mail would go out, let alone be received. Packages had a way of disappearing or requiring an extra fee that didn't seem to actually exist. Even telephone transmission was not only hard to establish, but exceedingly expensive. I once called my mother to let her know I was engaged and would marry, and it cost $25 for three minutes and getting the connection through three operators (at a local post office) was daunting. I even had to send a letter in advance that I would be calling on a specific day and time.

My wife of one year and I had been living in the protected economic cocoon of the Peace Corps. It provided a temporary sense of security during the last year of service while we decided what would come next. Six months prior to departure from our service, we began talking about what to do next and where to locate, and we decided that I would attend college to get my doctorate—an ambition I had given lots of thought to as another "ticket." Thus, I applied from a distance to New York University, and as usual, was accepted on a provisional basis. I was getting used to that status, and although a little trying on my self-esteem, I was okay with it. I knew how to prove myself to others when needed—just ask the electrician I helped in my youth, or the supervisor in the ice cream factory when I saved him from potentially poisoning people who liked mint ice cream, or when I applied to the University of Washington upon graduation from high school and wasn't accepted. I even, with some audacity, applied to Harvard from afar in Ethiopia, but wasn't accepted. I think I always thought these were merely hurdles and opportunities put in place to prove other people wrong in their assessment of you or me. Not being accepted is not negative, but rather something better than not trying.

I am not certain how well we thought out the decision to go from Ethiopia to New York City. It was easy to transition from Idaho to Ethiopia (for reasons I've already explained), but the reverse order moving from a country pretty much in the ninth century to a megalopolis like New York City proved to be more daunting (you think?). It turned out to be exactly that. First, we had to get there, which turned out to be a magnificent and enriching adventure all on its own. We made our way to New York City by way of stops at my wife's hometown, Vallejo, California, and then mine in Idaho before traveling cross-country and settling in the New York City area for a year. I'll wait to tell you the details of our numerous adventures from Ethiopia to home sweet home America when I address my adventures as the travel addict I am.

When we finally departed the Peace Corps in July of 1964 and arrived in the NYC area, we stayed for a few days at the house of my best man's parents who lived in Teaneck, New Jersey. It was good to meet them and see our old friend, Ray. We shared lots of stories about the similar journeys we took coming home from Ethiopia on nearly the same path across India and Asia. As I would soon be attending NYU, Ray's parents were able to give us some helpful advice for finding affordable housing which meant that we would not be residing in New York City itself. Rather, we rented what we could afford: a two-room apartment without a private bathroom that was part of a residential house located in a town called Bogota (sounded like Thailand), New Jersey. I would commute three days a week to NYU, first by bus over the George Washington Bridge, then transferring to the "L" subway, riding from 186th Street all the way down to 4th Street, to where my classes were held at Washington Square. I soon got very used to sleeping on the "L," like any long time New Yorker. Patricia found a local job in the billing department of a hospital in Englewood, New Jersey. We were now resident citizens, like everyone else around us; just trying to get ahead—and we were expecting our first child.

Lisa was born May 2, 1965, at a hospital in Englewood. Needing to supplement our income for our expanded family, not only did I take twelve credits of graduate courses that first semester, but I also got a job teaching chemistry starting that November in a high school in Park Ridge, NJ. I liked teaching my American high school students, and they seemed to like me as well, even asking me to be the teacher sponsor for their high school play, "If a Man Answers." Turns out it was a little risqué for our period of history, but other than having to replace the lead because she kept showing up late, the play went well, enjoyed by proud parents and their proud sponsor. My teaching experience was so much different from the teaching days just months earlier as a Peace Corps Volunteer and teacher of chemistry in Harar. As our lives unfolded stateside, we found ourselves as adults now stepping onto our own without the carriage of support provided by our secure and well-defined jobs with the Peace Corps. Change was coming fast, as life in America always seems to, and it was so different from our prior life abroad and it took a toll in getting used to it. This rapid change showed on me, I think, in particular. I was quite surprised about this since I was a resilient kid, growing up as I had. I am pleased to report I faced the difficulty of the adjustment no worse for wear.

The transition to being back in civilization brought more change than I had expected. The sudden thrust from Ethiopia into New York and New Jersey, combined with a child and a small apartment, without a private bath or even a private toilet for my pregnant wife, came into sharp focus. Even in Ethiopia my wife had her own bathroom! Going from Idaho to Ethiopia was far easier than going from Ethiopia to New York. I should have thought about that! I did love the academic program at NYU, but not the school and the living circumstances. I acutely felt the impersonal nature of the university as compared to both my University of Idaho and University of Missouri experiences. (Of course being single in those days.) I felt as if, as I often said to others, I had to make an appointment with my advisor's secretary to then make an appointment to see him. Compared to the personal nature of assistance in both my previous university settings, it was just one more sign of the hurry-up, impersonal mentality of crowded New York City. We decided this wasn't for us and that we would go "home", so to speak, and begin anew—again. She wanted to go to California to be near her parents, so when the school year ended, we packed everything we owned into our green and chrome 1960 Chevy station wagon and set out across the country, once again, to Vallejo, California.

Before departing NYU, I had been receiving a very useful monthly newsletter from the National Peace Corps office. It was intended to keep returnees up to date on Peace Corps happenings and had a section on job prospects. A listing caught my eye and would prove to be the launching point for a new, yet related career for me, one that would make use of the skills the boy, the youth, and the new adult had honed and been educated towards all along. That opportunity, as luck would have it, was just 45 miles south of Vallejo, where we landed in July of 1965. We were out of the Peace Corps, had our first child in diapers, and needed some time and space to ponder what our new mission in life would be. We found it.

The Parks Job Corps Center was one of the first "great society" installations, under the President Johnson administration, as a joint venture between the U.S. Government and private industry. The program was just getting off the ground when I first discovered it and is still going strong today. It is an education/job skills program to train up the hardcore youth of America who have failed societies system of justice (or injustice depending on how you wanted to look at it). These are young men and women who get into either legal trouble or have simply dropped out of school and need a productive and encouraging alternative to jail time or meandering the streets. They generally need help both educationally as well as vocationally. I would hire on as a teacher once again, and from there wonderful things came to happen for me and my family.

Within a week of moving in with Pat's parents at their home, I made an appointment for an interview at the Parks Job Corps Center in Pleasanton, California. They were looking for teachers alright, but not necessarily your usual type with accreditation. Rather, they wanted men and women who could first relate to youth and model acceptable behavior, and second, teach. This might mean hiring a former bartender, parole officer, mechanic, or whatever special type of person who could communicate with teens—troubled ones at that. I figured they probably weren't interested in a former chemistry teacher, but I did have one thing most didn't: Peace Corps experience in another culture. That skill of being able to relate to another culture, even if it were my very own, was to be my ticket. I was hired on the spot to teach what they called Personal Development: a combination of math, English, and social development skills useful in getting and keeping a job. The academics of math and English were taught alongside a parallel program of learning a specific job skill, such as culinary arts, gas station mechanic/attendant, auto mechanic, electrician, etc. This combination would give the students something to build on provided they remained enrolled with us for what turned out to be, generally, six months to a year. These students really needed time to foster their "how to get along with others" skills which were perhaps even more important than job skills to job success! Of course both are important!

During my first year I taught 4th and 5th grade level 15 to 18-year-old dropouts, and they were quite the load of attitude at times. I even had one of them threaten me physically, but I was there to set an example, and I did. I was perhaps not streetwise, but I was a kid from Idaho that knew to not put up with any guff and to be firm, yet in a caring way. I even volunteered to sponsor the on-base radio station where young men got to act like deejays for the others in the so-called, "Camp." I listened to more Diana Ross, Fats Domino, Little Richard, and others of that era than you can imagine. But teaching was my main assignment, and as a result of how I approached it ushered in a new skill I didn't realize I had: writing.

Little did I know that having taken on the Job Corps experience I would never teach chemistry again. Part of that was driven by the credentialing requirements of the State of California. To get fully certified in my teaching specialty, they would require me to obtain six additional graduate chemistry credits beyond the 30 I already had with a master's degree. I'll never forget scouring for a graduate chemistry course to take in our area, and only finding one given at the nearby nuclear engineering lab located in Livermore, California! I'm not sure of the exact title of that course anymore, but it read something like, "The Thermal Dynamics of an Electron as it Passes Through a Semipermeable Membrane,"—hardly a course that I thought might eventually relate to high school chemistry teaching, so I was out for taking that course no matter what. Putting that aside, what really changed my professional trajectory was what came up while teaching Personal Development requirements as part of the job corps curricula.

The most important thing I did in my short teaching career with the Job Corps was to write my own teaching material. Using standard lesson plans and books was not going to work with this population that had already failed using such materials and methods. For example, I wrote what turned into a successful program: "How to get a Job," complete with a lesson plan, workbook, job forms, overhead visuals, and a dictionary of terms used by the labor unions. I wrote another program on, of all things, dining room behavior and supplemented the lesson with a film. I shot, edited, and produced the film myself on my 16mm hand camera, along with a teaching guide. These learning materials went over well and were adopted by other Job Corps centers. After a year of teaching and writing such materials, I was asked to join the center's Curriculum Development Department. Within six months I was the head of that fledgling department and on my way to a new career path, which did not leave teaching far behind, but rather provided me with a new career emphasis, corporate training. There would be no more teaching chemistry, which I dearly loved and was good at. My way of doing things for others was emerging, and I rolled with it. Rather than up front teaching, I was preparing what the teacher would teach, and later what the trainer would train about in various business settings. I was doing a lot of writing and managing others.

During my second year at the Job Corps Center as a Curriculum Development Manager, at the weekly meetings held by my boss, he began to pronounce at each meeting an ominous statement to close our meetings: "If a good job comes along, take it!" This seemed odd, and we began to wonder if he knew something we didn't. I began to take him at his word after the third time he said so. A friend in another department told me about a company in Palo Alto he knew that might be looking for people who could write business training materials. The head of that company was Dr. William A. Deterline, who would later become my mentor in a new, but related field, known as Educational/Instructional/ Performance Technology. Heeding the admonishment at the Job Corps staff meetings, I called for an appointment. Circumstances can really sometimes make all the difference.

During my interview with Dr. Deterline, President of General Programmed Teaching, he outlined how they wrote training materials for various companies like Hewlett Packard, Bank of America, Transworld Airlines, Pacific Gas and Electric, and so forth. He took note of me for my background in the Peace Corps and how I had written training programs using a certain kind of format—the Core Package—devised by a fellow professional, Dr. Robert Meran. At the Job Corps I had participated in and supervised writing the development of ten Core Packages (i.e. Culinary Arts, Auto Mechanics, etc.) related to various job skills. While Dr. Deterline took especial note of that, he wanted to hire me to write what was a newly developing approach to learning known as "Programmed Instruction." I knew virtually nothing but the basic elements of this methodology. He said he would train me and offered me a job on the spot at twice the salary I was making, which honestly wasn't very much. What happened the first day I showed up for work was startling, to put it mildly. As they say, sometimes you have to be in the right place at the right time.

My new employer, General Programmed Teaching, was located in Palo Alto, California just across the bay from where we were living in Pleasanton—in those days a 45-minute drive. I walk into Dr. Deterline's office on a Monday morning anxious to learn how to write programmed instruction. Over the weekend I had read a little about PI. I'd previously written some what are known as "measurable behavioral objectives" for one of the training programs I had developed at the Job Corps Center. I'd read of introducing small bits of written instruction followed by appropriate feedback as an important aspect of programmed instruction. This requires a learner to perform his newly acquired knowledge

241

or skill to show mastery before continuing their learning of subsequent content or skills. Just bits of mostly terminology not to look too stupid as I prepare to enter his office. He welcomes me and instructs me to sit across the desk. He says immediately, "By the way you are not going to be writing programmed instruction! Rather, you are going to be my administrative assistant in charge of developing training program. You will directly supervise our 26-member staff." Mind you, I had about six months' experience managing others (a staff of 5) in the job I was just leaving as a new manager.

It seems what happened over the weekend is that he had a meeting with the head office in Chicago. They informed him they weren't impressed with his administrative skills, but rather wanted to better utilize the research and development expertise he was noted for in the training industry, so he had a new full-time job (still president, but with a new emphasis), and it seemed I had mine.

My two years with General Programmed Teaching were fabulous in that I was given the opportunity to gain experience and use a wide range of skills in learning formats for the design and development of training. I managed the staff while keeping my hand in the development of select programs of interest to me and my developing skill set. WAD (as he was affectionately called by the staff) and I traveled throughout the U.S. giving his workshops in instructional technology. At the third such workshop, this one for Transworld Airlines, he opened the workshop, introduced me, and turned the instruction completely over to me (much to my surprise, if not shock) to teach for the remaining two weeks it ran. I was getting mentored at the hands of a man who was once a student of Dr. B.F. Skinner himself, the renowned behavioral psychologist. In turn, WAD introduced me to numerous researchers and leaders in the emerging field of Performance Technology. I worked with many of these experts (Mager, Horn, Morgan, Gilbert, Kaufman, et al) on important projects, like for the Bank of America where we saved the company a million and half dollars in the first six months using our new system of learner-controlled instruction. I went to national conferences with him and gave my first professional presentation in front of what were becoming my fellow professional colleagues. In four years I had come from a chemistry teacher/graduate student to a new field where I developed new skills and saw lots of potential. What happened next sprung the lid wide open for additional professional growth and possibilities.

At the Job Corps I had met a colleague with whom I became close friends. He was an instructor in auto mechanics with a bent to training design like me. Richard Mentzer left the Job Corps just before me and went to work doing training for a big insurance company in the New York City area. We stayed in contact while I was still at General Programmed Teaching managing the development staff. WAD had gone elsewhere after my first year to form his own consulting business and I didn't like his replacement, but I was still learning and doing. One day, Dick called and said he'd been asked to recommend an "instructional designer" by a college for life underwriters seeking certification for their new center that would be researching adult learning. He recommended me and let me know they would be contacting me soon.

The research center, which was just conceptually incubating, located in Bryn Mawr, Pennsylvania, was to be part of The American College of Life Underwriters. This is the college/institution for conferring the professional designation known as a Chartered Life Underwriters (CLU) on life and health insurance agents. While it didn't sound too sexy to me, I was willing to listen, and was quite surprised when they flew me out to see the place and interview. The new research center was to be located on a beautiful campus without students—sort of. There was only one class in each of the 10 technical subjects that were offered (i.e. like Estate Planning), run on a kind of "test the subject matter" basis before the course would go live nationally to the mass of students who actually gathered in their local town for continuing education. The content didn't interest me as much as the prospect of being part of a leading center in new ways to achieve adult learning did. I saw that I could be a founding part of it from the very outset and dreamed of doing things that I'd never done before.

*Danny working in his first office at The
American College a year before the new Adult
Learning Research Center was completed*

I don't think, in retrospect, they knew what an instructional designer was, but they had been told they needed one. With three years of experience under my belt, I was relatively new to the field, so my small amount of experience worked in my favor rather than to my detriment. Furthermore, I had taught workshops on the subject with WAD, so I came off pretty knowledgeable during the interview. I signed on with a personal commitment to be there for ten years since I didn't really see myself and family living out the rest of our days in Pennsylvania or any other place out east. We did, in fact, end up staying ten years. Actually, I ended up being laid off in a very strange way that I shall shortly elaborate on, but I stayed almost exactly 10 years from the date of hire.

The new job was absolutely fascinating and was located in a wonderful work environment where one simply loved to be and work. I initially worked in an old house on the campus while the new research center was being built within eyesight. I even got to have some input on the design and layout of the new video production, photography, audio, graphic arts, and classroom set-up. This included what would be my new corner office overlooking a beautiful pond. (Side note: One day I looked out the window of my office and down below was a couple in the act of making their version of explicit love just as my secretary walked over to see what I was looking at. I digress!)

During the ten years I was with the Adult Learning Research Center, I innovated three new learning designs for delivering learning and oversaw the development and testing of several courses, film, TV, and audiovisual programs. I wrote lots of articles, gave a dozen professional presentations, and published my first book. I attended numerous conferences to stay current on the latest thinking and practices concerning the developing field of Performance Technology. For instance, I attended a workshop in Chicago given by the leading figure in media theory, Marshall MuLuhan, author of "The Medium is the Message" who predicted the world wide web 30 years before its development. At another conference I presented at, a professor from the University of Gottingen, Germany who had read my work reached out to me and wanted to exchange thoughts on his research into educational methods. This meshed well with my emerging expertise in what became known as instructional designs—learning/training methods. I had been working with 65 authors on a project I had initiated on the side from my regular job: writing, editing, and ultimately having published a forty-volume series of then existing instructional designs being used in industry and academia . This work became the definitive resource of ways to structure training and educational programs.

This wonderful company that I was privileged to be a part of even allowed me to do work on the side to earn extra money for my family needs, as well as to promote my own professional growth. I organized and conducted my own marketing efforts for a workshop on the training/learning methods I had innovated or learned about from colleagues. These workshops were marketed to various training developers and managers in business. I also did a little consulting with various book publishers, such as McGraw Hill, helping authors finish the development of their books and texts. I assisted Sperry Univac in designing ten training modules for their new computer system that was coming online. It was a wonderful ten years of professional growth. I was elected secretary of an international professional training association, the National Society for Programmed Instruction (NSPI); in later years rebranded as the International Society for Performance Improvement (ISPI). At their annual conference I met and interacted with many leading professionals in my field and conducted several workshops at various local chapters of NSPI/ISPI. From 1989-90 I was the international president (as was my wife, Kathleen, years later). In 1990 we held our annual international conference in Toronto. It was the largest conference the association had ever held. I remember very well opening the five-day meeting at a sit-down breakfast attended by about 2,200 professional colleagues. When I stood up and said, "Welcome to Canada," the two giant two-story doors of the ballroom open and in marched the Royal Canadian Drum and Bugle Corps of the Canadian Mounted Police. They marched, swirled their drumsticks, drummed, and played their bagpipes in kilts around the entire room, came to a halt at the center of the room, and played, "Amazing Grace," and the Canadian and USA anthems. The ballroom full of attendees came alive like you would not believe. On the day of our closing banquet and awards ceremony, the theme and decorations

Danny addressing the International Society for Performance Improvement as its international president during their annual conference in Toronto, Canada 1989-90

were based upon the newly successful Phantom of the Opera staged by the renowned production troop in Toronto. The lead female singer came to my table and personally sang an aria, then, presented me with a gold lapel pin of the phantom mask. What a day, what a night! Not bad for a kid from Idaho. Talk about luck! Or do we create our own luck?

*Danny in discussions as part of a meeting
on business performance improvement
strategies at the White House - 1990*

It was while being associated with ISPI over the course of my initial 30 professional years of work, that I initiated the idea of forming a small "concept sharing group," which became known as "The Tucson Seven" (named after the location where we first met). It was a small think-tank of the leading figures in our profession, each of whom had their own models and templates for how best to meet performance needs. We met several times and freely collaborated together with the idea of sharing our professional experiences and techniques for the greater good. To have been part of and had the support and respect of my fellow colleagues is an honor that I cherished. I had come of age professionally.

Towards the end of my association with The American College, as I previously noted, there was a newly instituted sabbatical program. As with this type of program at any university, it was designed to reward long term service by faculty to promote individual research and teaching. I was soon the victim of sabbatical dread. I don't mean my sabbatical was bad. It was, in fact, fantastic! I mean that the sabbatical program at this hybrid kind of college had its issues when first launched. Rather than rewarding its professors, you might say it went a bit awry!

It seems the first person who was granted sabbatical was summarily let go while he was away. The consensus among the faculty left behind to watch from our home turf was that this did not bode well for the new sabbatical program. The second person granted sabbatical leave was also let go while he was away. That too didn't exactly inspire others on the faculty who were nearing the qualification for sabbatical leave to want to actually go on leave (or maybe it should have been labeled, "Leave and Gone!") As it turned out, I was third in line to earn the right to a sabbatical. Not only was I let go but I was told I would be before I even departed for the sabbatical yet was allowed to go on it anyhow. Confused? I was. I don't know if anyone ever asked to go on a sabbatical after that again; I think the program was abandoned (you think!). As it happened all worked out perfectly for me since my ten-year self-imposed contract had come due and I was ready to go. Here's how it works out for lucky me.

The beginning of my six-month sabbatical started, with family, in Göttingen, Germany. I had been invited to the University of Göttingen (think a noted institution where Oppenheimer and others studied) by Dr. Karl Heinz Fletsig, a professor in educational pedagogy. We collaborated on our mutual findings concerning various means for training and learning—mine on instructional designs and his on methods of education. After that, the family and I returned to the US and continued the sabbatical by driving around the USA for six weeks. During this phase of studies I had scheduled to see a dozen and half colleagues that I had met over the years, mostly at numerous ISPI and other professional conferences. Still others I came to know as contributing authors that were part of the forty-volume series I previously noted. While driving in a meandering way from Pennsylvania towards California, I decided to make a loop into Idaho to visit with some family members we hadn't seen in a while. One of them, Bertine, lived near Boise, Idaho, so since I was passing through, I stopped in Boise to inquire about potential employment with a company I had known of growing up in Idaho. It was one of three major companies headquartered in Boise. The name of the company was the Morrison Knudsen Corporation (MK for short). It was an international construction, design, and engineering company of about 50,000 employees who worked on projects all over the world. Some of their projects were building the Hoover Dam, The King Khalid Military City in Saudi Arabia, and lots of other things domestic and internationally. Can you believe it, they were looking for a Corporate Director of Training and there I was, only by pure chance, in the guy's office who was charged with hiring. I just went there originally to find out information and see if the company needed someone like me and it turned out they did! And I was born and raised in Idaho if that should make any difference. I listened to the guy (Julien Hansen), took the job, and finished my sabbatical and relocated late in that year, 1979. I loved this new job as much as my previous ones, with the bonus being the location—especially the location! I was back in Idaho, the seed of my roots! But it was the residence we would establish that proved so interesting to me and my family, in addition to leading a professional effort that would feed my travel addiction.

While at MK I did some interesting projects with an emphasis on performance improvement in both management and major project implementation—especially project management of big engineering, design, development, and major construction work. I was going to be in my groove improving other people's work performance, but this time for a major Fortune 300 company. Over the time there I interacted with lots of nutty people I reported to, but I kept my eye on my capabilities and proved myself again and again. Could I last more than 10 years, you ask? Let's see.

The work at Morrison Knudsen was a good job. It was, naturally, a bit of a winding-down from being a researcher of new learning methods but was perched much more on the practical side of helping a company be the best it can. I had a small staff, and we wrote and delivered several training programs concentrating on management development with an assortment of practices that improved the opportunities for the company to garner multimillion-dollar projects. I went to Colombia, South America on five different occasions to deliver training myself and also to China to evaluate the training of another major competitor of ours—Bechtel. I worked on some absolutely fascinating assignments with a General Motors plant developing simulation training for a new giant Komatsu automated stamping machine used in the manufacture of automobiles; GM was trying desperately to get America manufacturing of automobiles competitive with the rising Japanese auto industry. I was going out to see the world while working, and that theme of traveling for various work assignments would magnify through many other trips years later in another working role on my own.

One of the many training programs I developed and delivered working for MK had a profound impact on my becoming more outgoing. Thus, as the saying goes, it may be possible to teach an old dog a new trick or so. A particular project manager (of which there were many in construction, design, engineering, mining, and railroading in MK) asked me to improve the oral (team) speaking presentation skills of his technical people—mostly engineers, quality and safety personnel, and others. They are technical types who think and talk their own special engineering or technical language, sometimes in excruciating detail. That doesn't necessarily make them skilled when having to stand before a potential new client and pitch to them how they would construct this or manage that. A team presentation is, after all (especially to the potential client who is listening and evaluating), a team presentation and not a separate one, two, or three-person show. You have to sell yourself as a team, and the emphasis is on both team and selling. So, I designed a new approach, driven not by the marketing manager (who typically designed and assigned roles in the oral presentations), but rather by the engineers who through the leadership of their designated project manager, put the presentation together as a team, so they therefore would own and present as a team.

The mechanics of how I achieved this are not important here, only that my way of doing it started winning new work at a rate 300% more often than the previous ways. This made quite a difference, as you can imagine. One time, for example, one of these teams was giving an oral presentation to the Los Angeles County Board of Commissioners regarding a multi-million-dollar project in the LA area. I worked with the team to structure the presentation using my new approach. One of the LA commissioners, evaluating whether to award us the contract, said that it was the best presentation he had ever heard. That commissioner was none other than George Takei—you know him better as Sulu from Star Trek. Not bad since some of the credit went to the guy from Idaho named Danny. It's fair to say I was improving my own presentation skills while teaching others how to improve their own. Years later I found that giving presentations myself to a couple thousand people wasn't as nerve-racking as I thought it was going to be. You never stop learning, unless of course, if you don't try or you die. I wasn't planning on the latter for a few more decades, and yes, I'll get around to what those plans are for my finality at the end of the book. I am still alive, so let's get back to my working days.

During the last couple of years I was with MK I personally knew the then CEO and president of the company. We were fraternity brothers a year apart who had lived in the same frat house at the University of Idaho. He wasn't a particularly good CEO as he literally drove the company into the ground, and it sadly folded a year after I left. His reign (an appropriate label for it, along with his wife's involvement) had been previously written up by others so I won't go into their scandalous relations and its then effect on the Bendix Corporation. At MK one of his usual practices was to hold semi-annual, all-hands meeting with the employees—about 600—there in the home office and I, of course, attended. At some point after all the irrelevant questions had been asked (rather than what was really on employee's minds for fear of retribution) he would turn to me somewhere in the audience and say, "Where is Langdon? He always has the hard question you all are dying to ask" Given the cue, I would stand up, secure in the knowledge that we are true fraternity brothers (hopefully), and ask, for example, "Why are executives putting new carpeting on their floor of the home office while laying off necessary staff?" He would answer in generalities, as executives are prone to do, and somehow, I kept my job until I was recruited by another company in California. I'm glad I did, as I noted before, since MK was on a short leash and soon gone itself. I had escaped another failed company that I am assured was not of my doing. Rather, each had provided immense professional growth opportunities and I was blessed to have work for each.

By this time I was in my tenth year of employment at MK. You have learned by now that I don't seem to have known how to work in any one company for more than ten years. One day I was sitting with an MK vice-president of marketing I knew discussing his training needs, when at the end of our conversation he announced that he had passed my name onto a guy he knew in an environmental engineering company that was looking to hire someone like me. As it turned out what that company really wanted was someone who could envision and guide their desire to have a Total Quality Program, which was a new fad for business at the time. I knew very little about such an initiative (just as I had in previous interviews with other companies where I ended up being employed), but by now had extensive background in developing new programs and services. I could speak intelligently, if not necessarily always with much expertise. This particular company, based in California, asked me to fly over to Portland, Oregon for an interview at their regional office. As I was seated on the airplane, I began talking to the guy seated next to me. I quickly learned that he was the one who would be interviewing and potentially hiring me. All went well and a couple of months later, while my divorce was progressing, I was off to the last state of our union I ever thought I'd live in a second time. It turned out, for two great reasons, to be a timely and important move. One, I eventually found and married the woman of my dreams, and second, we eventually started our own consulting business. First, about that environmental engineering company and what happened there and the impact it had on the rest of my professional life. It turned out, in the most significant way, to be the most important concept I would ever originate, and upon which a business would be built.

I suppose one of the worst ways to begin a new job within the first three days is to almost get arrested at the airport because you are carrying a gun. This was a decade before security at airports tightened due to 9/11, but this airport did have a modest, electronic screening process all passengers had to go through. It was an innocent and understandable mistake, but it happened, and I came clean and explained it to my new company. They bought my admission of ignorance, and I continued employment with them for another two years. I shall explain.

I had just arrived in Torrance, California, to begin my new job with International Technology and I was asked to go to their home office in Pittsburgh. I was going to introduce myself to my new boss's boss and get the feel for the company at a higher level. I had driven to Torrance from Idaho in my new Mazda Miata. One of the issues in moving that arose was that the moving company, whose van contained all my worldly possessions (including my 1930 Dodge), would not allow firearms to be transported in their van. Because of this I was forced to transport my little arsenal of six rifles (most from my dad's collection) on my own and I had put Dad's Luger pistol in the corner pocket of my overnight travel suitcase. You can probably see where this is going. Yes, I grabbed the overnighter without remembering that the gun was temporarily in the corner pocket. When I got to the John Wayne Airport (seems ironic that it was an airport with his name), I decided to go directly through security rather than check my bag. The surprise looked on the screening agent when she saw the gun on the x-ray immediately triggered knowledge on my part remembering the pistol's location. I immediately apologized, as if that mattered, and they pulled me aside. Interestingly enough they questioned me for only about 40 minutes, kept the gun (with its magazine of 6 shells), and I was allowed to continue my journey.

Three months later I received a call to appear at a lawyer's office near the LA airport. He represented the FAA. He lectured me for about half an hour on why taking a gun on an airplane is not allowed (as if I didn't already know), the possible penalty of a year in jail, and/or a fine of $10,000. He said I would not likely qualify for the maximum of either considering this was my first offense. Rather, he offered up the question of how much I thought I should be fined. I said, "I don't know, what do you think?" He said, "How about $2,000?" I said, "How about $1,000?" He agreed and the deal was settled. On reflection later, I think it helped that I had a letter from my mother explaining that the gun in question was part of her husband's gun collection, and she was sure her son had no nefarious intentions in carrying said gun onto an airplane. I think it was the letter that really sealed the deal because how many times does a small-time operator have a letter from his mother explaining his crime?

All of this soon would have faded from memory or impact were it not for another time six months later when I was talking to this guy in the office I had been transferred to in Irvine, California. He starts telling me about being at John Wayne Airport with a gun and what happened following that. Like me, he went to the lawyer, got the lecture, sealed a deal, paid, and got his gun back, six months later just as I had. I say to him, "What kind of fine did you pay?" He says, "Five thousand dollars." As I told him I had paid only one thousand myself, I asked, "Did you have a letter from your mother?" "What?" he says, with a puzzled look on his face. In reality he was one of those kinds of argumentative guys and I suspect the lawyer just didn't like him! I've always known to be nice to anyone associated with the justice system (remember the car antics with Mac and the town policeman?), and I had the backing of my mother.

International Technology, IT for short in the trade, was a relatively small company with several regional offices, but it was at that time the leading company in the sector of environmental studies, testing, and remediation. During my two years there I developed (along with a colleague I stole back from MK who had become a really close friend) and implemented several programs aimed at improving management and team quality. But there was one project initiative that profoundly changed the remainder of my professional life; one that, incidentally, brought together all my previous years of performance improvement and design research, along with what I had learned from many of those leading experts in my field who I was lucky to have associated with and learned so many valuable lessons from. This would become my most single important contribution to mankind. It sounds monumental, I know, but it's the way I feel in that what I originated made not only a successful business for my wife and I, but also what this concept could do for mankind in general. That's a heady claim, so here is the story.

A regional president, Mel DeSouza, of one of the local divisions of IT situated in Riverside, California, asked me to come over one day. He had a performance problem with his project teams that he wanted me to help solve. Remember, my role in this company is to improve quality. In his opinion, his "project teams" did not fully understand their role as a team, nor did they fully understand their own individual jobs, in relation to others on the team, or for that matter their own work, fully enough. That was a lot to unpack, and a typical trainer would approach this with some kind of team building exercise or other intervention to get everyone on the same page. However, by now I had become not so conventional or single minded in my thinking, largely because I had often had to solve complex problems for companies and typically deployed more analytical, behaviorally based multi-intervention solutions, to such issues. My various mentors had taught me well. Besides, I had grown up in a junkyard with all its challenges and advantages: It was kind of simple for me to figure out the solution to this company's complex, multi-dimensional work issue.

During the first twenty years of my career I discovered that I had a way of looking for the obvious that others often overlook when it came to solving work-related issues, we are faced with solving for management. For me this meant that, instead of going immediately to solutions that don't necessarily work, I first look to what the underlying problem is and work to solve that; only after then devise solutions. This "needs assessment," as we call it in my profession, was especially true of the challenge Mel DeSouza had confronted me with to solve: his project teams needed total clarity of their work. Rather than throw training at this challenge, as most would have done in my profession, I instead first asked myself "What is work?" If workers and managers don't have a clear and operational understanding of their work, then interact with others who face the same lack of work clarity, the team finds it difficult to implement together and solve mutual problems. I was faced with a series of interrelated questions: "How can each worker clearly understand their own role and then, as they work together in partnership with others, know and act in common with the mission of the team's work? "Do they have a commonly understood way to view, talk and plan together, then implement, and continually improve work together?" Do they have a commonly understood Language of Work as I came to label it? I found they didn't and I set out to change this.

Believe me, even in the preponderance of business today, work clarity as I like to call it, is a very fundamental issue with literally everybody's job and how they implement work, and most companies and their management have still not really addressed it in meaningful, behavioral ways. For a guy with a chemistry background and lots of experience in behavioral science by this point in his career, "What is work?" became a key inquiry in need of an answer. The answer I formulated to this question would impact me professionally as a major contribution to my field of professional endeavor and especially all the companies I and my partner/wife would subsequently come to work with in our consulting practice. By analogy, when I ask what water is and you say H_2O, it's very clear between us that we are looking at it in the same way. If we could only do the same for our more complex individual and mutual work, how powerful might that be? Very powerful as it turns out.

I developed and validated (with many businesses, big and small, profit and non-profit), a work/business model that would be become known as, The Language of Work Model™." I am not going to try and teach you that model here and now, but you can Google Scholar me and find all kinds of resources that will do it for you—mostly for free, as of my retirement. This model is predicated on a formula for work, the Work Formula, which helps everyone in business understand his or her work as well as the work of others in such a way that everyone achieves clarity, and they then can suggest how to solve work problems or meet or formulate new work improvement. They also don't have to rely on me (or ignore me) or others like me to solve their work issues or needs. Rather, they figure it out themselves and as such are committed/empowered to the solution(s) they really know already but didn't have a way to articulate or be perhaps heard by management. For example, the formula has a way to reorganize a company or department that is so much more effective than the one-sided ideas of any executive or reorganization task force! We have also used the Model with companies to re-engineer processes and jobs, improve their work culture, merge with others, and start new businesses. As I have said to others, the marvelous thing about this model is that we go to companies big and small, profit/non-profit, introduce and facilitate the model, and they do the work and make the improvements. They send us money for helping them. What's not to like about that? Besides, they learn a skill they can do on their own without us the next time and save all kinds of money typically spent on consultants. What a lucky guy from Idaho to have innovated such a thing! My wife and I did that until we retired in our seventies and now, we travel the world. Here is one of my resources you can google to learn various aspects of my model for work: IS THERE A WORK FORMULA? – HPT Treasures – for Evidence Based Performance Improvement (wordpress.com)

Seminal Moment: The Language of Work Model™

This business model that I formulated, and we based a business on, made me realize that I had contributed something very significant to business in general and that will live on after me. Living life with joy and success is paramount: leaving something useful for others forever.

- *When implemented with our clients you saw how they lit up with satisfaction that their need was met.*
- *Clients gained a methodology they could deploy on their own in the future and thus committed to the solutions they generate themselves.*
- *Kathleen and I had a successful business because of it and that allowed us to do so many pleasurable and satisfying things with our lives together.*

A little more about our business from the personal side.

I have rarely found many couples who were in business who said they enjoyed the experience of working together. That was certainly not the case in working with Kathleen. I loved working with my partner in life and business. As I noted before when courting for only the second time in my life, I had learned enough to know what I wanted in a partner. Those reasons I've already noted, and it involves how one processes stuff. The short version of her life (in my opinion as an "army brat," as they are called) is that she, like me, had developed not only her own career similar to mine, but had developed herself in ways she can best explain. The short of it is that I found a perfect partner, different from me, but oh so skilled. This translated in practice to working with someone who could do what I could not, and I think the same was true for her. I used to watch and literally marvel at her during our facilitating sessions with a company we had never seen before as she used the model and was soon speaking their language with such insight that they were stunned at the level of her understanding. That spoke to me both about the power of this work model I had developed and equally to her great skill as a master facilitator. She is a pleasure to work with in business and life! I shall tell you a little bit more about our business to end the account of my professional career.

After two years with IT, I was again laid off by a company. Always assured that my being laid off was for financial reasons, which was certified by the fact that those companies, unlike the sabbatical fiasco, folded two years after I was let go! Interesting how that all worked out!

I had just published my seventh book, this one on the Language of Work Model™, titled, appropriately, "The New Language of Work." Kathleen and I decided to start our own business doing consulting in the things that we had done only for others as their employees. She would continue her existing business for a while as an independent training consultant for various companies in the LA area, and I would get our new business up and running. It took us a while, but soon we were making a comfortable living, all the while assuring (at Kathleen's insistence) that we always had six months of disposable income on hand. We did and went after fairly sizable projects, reorganizing business entities (like IT departments), defining jobs, improving business cultures and process improvements, and other such business improvement needs. We were aided in obtaining new clients, at times, by other people in our field who needed expertise like ours as a subcontractor to help them do their projects. It was great to go somewhere—anywhere—in the US and internationally, and spend three to six weeks doing the work, all expenses paid. We were meeting our personal business goals and desires along with my passion for travel. What a combination in life!

Work almost always called for us to use the Language of Work Model™, thereby causing us to hone how it would be facilitated, and we were developing tools that made it work more efficiently and effectively. We conducted workshops for others telling them how to use "our" model. We helped one very large company reorient its marketing effort, with another a complete reorganization of their entire IT effort, and yet another to improve the culture in various departments of governmental ministries. Our daughter, Kim, developed software that would make using the model more efficient. That software turned out to be a story in and of itself.

During the fourth year of our business, we had contracted a software developer recommended to us by a client for which we had done a project. He was charged to write more advanced software to collect and diagram "work models" for jobs, work groups, core processes, the business entity, and a display of their prevailing and desired cultural climate. Development of the software with him was going along fine and its potential for improving our overall consulting was very clear. I paid him for the work as it progressed. However, one day, I got a call from our bank wanting to know if I would authorize a $125,000 check they were holding. It seemed our software developer had stolen a blank check from my office during a project update meeting, written the check to himself, told his wife that all their financial woes were at an end (telling her he'd just been paid a 10% royalty). He was now at his bank wanting to deposit said check. We probably didn't have more than $1,000 in that particular checking account and so it wouldn't have cleared for that reason alone, but primarily because the check was a forgery. We lost not only the money we had already spent on software development (but not the $125,000), but also what was shaping up to be a nice piece of software. A hard business lesson was learned.

Beyond such grief our business was a real success. It was a success in my opinion because we were working together. We performed all the work as a team, individually got paid the same amount by clients, and supported each other's contributions. We often went from whatever location we were working to other places for pleasure as our vacations. For six years we went to London 3 times a year. We gave invited professional presentations in some foreign countries (China, South Africa, Germany, Kuwait) and then traveled elsewhere. We didn't always make it known that we were a married couple; Kathleen went by her professional name, Kathleen Whiteside. We must have presented ourselves pretty well as a team because this one time we had a client who (jokingly, I assume) told us to go to a hotel and "get it on" with one another, we looked that close, not knowing that we were indeed married. Another time we fired a client because he kept changing his mind every instance when we had given him what he had asked for. We wrote a three-book series that gives away all our intellectual knowledge for use by executives, managers, and workers. We looked back with great pleasure on our mutual careers and marched into retirement to do the other things we like to: volunteer, art, and, of course, travel, travel, travel. So let's go travel!

CHAPTER 9

Danny, the Travel Addict: Age 17 to the Present

I am a professed, dedicated, and persistent traveler for sure, considering I've been on four airplanes that have experienced mechanical or a bomb scares, landed in more than one unscheduled place, had vasovagal syncope (look it up if you dare) a half dozen times on international flights and experienced my share of odd travel screw ups. Still I continue and will never give up the wanderlust addiction I have for travel — just ask my wife who proudly tells others I am a Travel Addict. She says I'd rather recover from an operation on a remote island (and I have on the island of Crete) than at home. I carry catastrophic injury, illness, and death transportation insurance in case anything serious happens, but I am 86 and have only once submitted a medical travel insurance claim for a planned trip to Indonesia. Before describing how I became addicted to travel, here is a brief sample of near misses and adventures I've had while flying the friendly skies.

In the first incident, the plane I was on blew a tire on takeoff. I was making my way from Boise, Idaho, to Denver on business. You distinctly heard the popping sound the tire made at lift off and the pilot informed us of such and that we would continue our flight, landing in Denver with its better emergency facilities in case they were needed. Upon arrival in Denver we circled the airport to lose some fuel and then flew by the tower so they could visually inspect the tire. It's kind of spooky to fly by an airport tower so close and see everyone looking at you as you look at them! But we landed with numerous fire trucks lining the runway, flapped on our bad tire along the runway, came to a jerky stop because of the flat tire, parked, disembarked, and went our separate ways.

On a second occasion, Kathleen and I were taxiing down the runway in the Seychelle Islands (off Africa). We had been invited to give a workshop in Johannesburg, South Africa, and as usual added on a pleasure trip to somewhere else since we had traveled that far. As we taxied, I looked out from my window seat and saw a dangling hydraulic line leaking fluid. Fortunately, the pilot also got an instrument reading

Danny's various passports and required health vaccination records and health documentation history for international travel and living abroad

of the same, taxied back, and shut us down. We swapped into a different plane and were off again. By the way, I highly recommend a trip to the Seychelles for their pristine, white, sandy beaches and magnificent black rocks that protrude from the bluish-green ocean.

On a third occasion in LA there was a bomb scare just after we had completed boarding the plane and the doors had been shut. Everyone was instructed to get off so the airplane could be searched. After twenty minutes an announcement was made that eight passengers, whose names were called on the PA, should proceed to a designated area. Who among us was the suspect, I am sure all the other passengers thought. It turned out that we eight were frequent flyers and were being placed in a separate room for their comfort while we awaited an outcome on our airplane. Soon we were on our way, although I found it personally discomforting to know that we were on the same plane that they had just searched for a supposed bomb. It wasn't as comforting or enjoyable as you might imagine until the flight was finally over, parked, and we were on our way.

On a fourth occasion, I was flying on a small 18 passenger Bombardier turboprop. We were flying not very high, maybe 1500 feet, over the jungles of Columbia, from an interior coal mine to a coastal port on the Atlantic. The company I worked for (MK) was constructing a coal mine, and a railway to the port. Twenty minutes into the flight I looked out the window and I saw that one of the two propeller-driven airplane's props was not moving. I mean it was stuck straight up and down. You know what you do when you realize what you are seeing? In my case, I immediately looked to see if the other propeller was going around and around. It was and I glanced into the cockpit (which you could see into through the pulled curtain), and the pilot and copilot were busy in Spanish planning what to do next. One of my observations that I thought they might want to consider was a road I saw not a quarter mile away that they might think to fly over just in case it became handy as an emergency landing strip. The pilot was, of course, too busy to take my advice, and I didn't speak Spanish anyhow. Thirty anxious minutes later we were on approach to landing on a modest field and I saw a single fire truck there. We landed and all was safe, although I discovered that one in our party had no idea what had just transpired. I was sorry I ever looked out the window.

As I have noted, none of these four incidents dissuaded me from ever flying again. I went on another occasion, to ride in a hot-air balloon high over my farm in Idaho, becoming an official member of the Air-o-Nuts for doing so. There is the thrill of the balloon's carriage as it swoops towards a grounding you didn't select yourself and it lands with a thud, and you partially tip over. Another time I rode a glider in New Mexico. It's always a thrill when the glider lands, as it looks like your ass is going to hit the runway on the skids of that airship without a motor. Furthermore I can't say I like the way a glider swoops up and down so suddenly with the air current changes on which it (and you) depends. Now that I think about it there was a fifth airplane incident, but I won't go into that in much detail that might truly make you think twice about flying other than to say that it's difficult to land a plane that is on the leading path of a hurricane with cross-winds—think of the plane sliding sideways twelve feet or so as it is about to touchdown on the runway. Even the flight attendant, on this occasion, suggested we pray. It was one of the very few times we passengers were almost alone in baggage claim given that everyone else in the airport had long gone home to batten down the hatches! Come to think of it, it was the most frightening of any of the plane incidents I have ever encountered! But, as I'll describe, I didn't give up travelling.

Thus far I've only provided a glimpse into my passion for travel, including a study tour of Europe, the Peace Corps experience, and getting home again. This passion actually started earlier than college, and so I'll begin there, and only mention in passing what I've already described.

By the time of this writing I've been to 90 countries—so you've barely heard about 10% of my travel. You'll discover that I have not only a wide range of travel interests, but a focus on travel that gets more into culture and people, rather than tourist sites—although I do plenty of the latter as well. I have a view of travel that emphasizes self-realization and growth as a human being. I think I view travel as an opportunity for personal growth more than seeing the sites, experiencing a thrill, or trying to fill the limited time in a place—two or three weeks of vacation—with all the activity you can fill it with to exhaustion. Let's see how my view played out.

I can't possibly describe here all the travel and adventures I've had. Therefore, I'll give you my Cliff Notes version. Cliff Notes, in my college days, were the laminated cards you could buy that summarize a book, historical event, or anything about the world and what goes on within it. My Cliff Notes of travel will highlight those I am most fond of, learned lessons from, had real unusual adventures during, made some mistakes, and especially met interesting people, some of which remain in my life as longtime friends to this day. Grab your passport.

I began using my fledgling travel wings when I was 17 and old enough to drive. Since then, as I noted, I've been to 90 countries, and half of those three to four times. Kathleen and I have gone to our favorite island 17 times and have already signed up for our next six-week visit. I lived overseas for two years, spent a month in Germany on sabbatical, a month each in Peru, Ecuador, and Portugal, and lots of weeks in other countries working or just being. I'm not so much a tourist as one who would rather pick a spot, stay there for a month, and wander into local venues, visit unique sites, and especially commune with the locals. I like sitting in a sidewalk café, drinking a cappuccino, eating a delicious local pastry, and studying what's walking by. That way we live as if we were home, but now with different trees, sidewalks, venues, unique living accommodations, new people, different customs, and exploring their culture to understand them and improve our own. My travel philosophy is simple: avoid, generally, other Americans because I get plenty of them in America! Also, Americans (and several other "advanced" cultures) are a little too picky about living conditions in other lands, want to be entertained, come off as a little snooty, and rush from here to there and there. They also say they have been to a country, where in fact they got off a cruise ship and spend maybe four to seven hours there at most. I am primarily there (and others with me) to experience people, then see things. Sitting and talking to a local at the next table is perfect. Asking directions gets smiles and suggestions on other things to see, often not mentioned in the travel brochure. Seeing what I see there on the street is like a movie picture, except you are part of the scene. Then you can wander out into the countryside to see what magnificent things that country also has to offer, usually with greater insight since you have talked with their people. Take a local bus or ride the train. Here's a brief account of some of that travel—often paid for, by the way, by others. How lucky is that?

I began exploring from the base of my birthplace of Twin Falls, Idaho. My family started my lust for travel by their adventures, out of necessity, in living out of doors on the Little Wood River, trips to Yellowstone, and sponsoring my participation as a Boy Scout into many forests and then the National Boy Scout Jamboree at Irvine, California. All that was planned, paid for, and supported by my mother and father in his day. Since then journeys have been on our own, Kathleen and I, and often in conjunction with paid work, naturally by clients—a fact that I promoted in my business practice. Why not!

My intention is not to impress you with where I have been, although I have enough ego to support that. Rather my aim is to impart where I've been and why I went, and to encourage you, especially the young, to get out there now and don't wait until it's too late. We all benefit from the knowledge and experience of travel to be a better person who understands the world. "Get traveling!" is my message for you and start early in life before you (or your partner) may not be physically able.

I started to travel outside the geographical area where I grew up at age 17 because I earned my driver's license. I got into this habit of driving a path from Twin Falls to San Francisco, over the Oakland and Golden Gate Bridges, up the coast of California to Eureka, then Portland and Seattle, across the width of upper Washington to the panhandle of Idaho at Coeur d'Alene, then back south to Twin Falls. This annual drive took place for five years in my youth after summer work, which I've already told you about. I paid for the travel with money I had earned from various summer jobs. I benefited from the opportunity for work, and so why not the opportunity for travel, if one but chooses well?

Driving was a solo undertaking in my youth. I preferred it that way. I wasn't in a hurry, or into picking up hitchhikers (which was generally safe in those days), although I'd done that a couple of times. One was on a drive to Dorothy's ranch and the other on the way to the University of Missouri. Not sure what propelled me to pick them up, but there was something about each party I picked up that drew me in with caution. Could have been a big mistake, but I was lucky and nothing other than adventure came of either incident. I'll briefly describe them.

In the first case I was just north of Sun Valley, Idaho, on a back road that I knew as a shortcut to Challis and eventually my sister's ranch. Later in life I thought it would be an adventure to invite my wife, Kathleen, to experience this rough road with its corrugated gravel base. Over the course of an hour driving that road you could not hear yourself think given the way the car seemed to skip and constantly rattle from the sound of tires jumping across the corrugated gravel for miles. This time, with Kathleen at my side, as we approached the cutoff to that road or the alternate paved highway, I turned to her and said, "I just remembered that you're not my fishing buddy!" She laughed and caught the drift of my message. I didn't take her down that road. Let's get back to my brief stint at picking up hitchhikers.

I saw these two guys with their thumbs up at the edge of the dry, sagebrush lined road that ran up north. Honestly, they looked like two hit men from Chicago in their black suits and ties—one short, and the other a bit paunchy. They could have been a worse version of the Blues Brothers in their attire. I stopped, asked where they were headed, and gave them a ride to a point near Challis, not sure what was going to happen. Indeed we said very little to one another. In an hour they got out, stood again at the junction of two roads there in the desert, and I was on my way again. Never read a thing about them in the newspaper and fortunately nothing was printed about a kid in a car who picked up two strangers. I never did that again with older travelers, but once picked up a young guy my age outside of Denver.

I was driving to Columbia, Missouri, for my first and only year of graduate school. He was just standing there on the outskirts of Denver on the onramp, like any other person, with a sign that read St. Louis. It should have said, "East St. Louis," because that is where he was really going, as I ended up passing my destination, Columbia, Missouri, and taking him to his parents' home. St. Louis, by the way, is where that giant arch now marks sort of the East and West divide of the USA. He was not a college guy like me, but I judged rather a little more experienced in the ways of the world. We had a nice chat on the long drive. Later in my academic year he invited me to stay a weekend with him in East St. Louis, which by the way, is not in Missouri, but rather over the river in

Illinois. The difference, and the cities, were quite the experience for an unknowing lad of 21. After introducing me to his family and preparing a bed for me on a couch, he took me to one of the numerous dive bars in the city, leftovers of the real St. Louis across the river. There were lots of older women in the bar who tried to hang on and court your favor. Their rouge came off on your shoulder as they tried to get you to buy them expensive, watered-down drink after drink. I may be from Idaho, but I was becoming wise to such dubious efforts at trying to make a living. Remember the one-year membership I had in London, England where I could see a strip show performed to 45rpm records? I had learned at least something from that similar experience, although at least this time I had not paid good money for a membership and was taken there against my own free will. No worse for wear, I climbed out of that city the very next day and chalked my adventure with him up to an interesting sociological experience never to be repeated. Perhaps those experiences were why I preferred to travel by myself as a youth, but changed as I grew older to traveling with others who I trusted, like the person I was married to, or with fellow professional colleagues when we traveled to foreign lands to give presentations or workshops.

I really enjoyed driving from Twin Falls heading south through the boring desert of Nevada on a road you can see ten miles ahead of you to eventual civilization in Reno, Nevada. That's where I would spend my first night. At 17 I could not gamble, I'd mostly look around at the strange people pulling levers on machines they had fed with coins from their pockets or sat around tables with others who would spin a ball around a wheel or look sheepishly at cards dealt to them. It was, again, as my second wife came to accurately label for me, just an interesting sociological experience. For whatever curiosity it fed in me, I'd see it over and over again during each drive driving south at the end of five summers.

From Reno, I'd get up early and head to San Francisco. I think it fascinating, on reflection, that I didn't stop in San Francisco itself, but rather hurried to get across both bridges to the north side before the sunset. I was still cautious of big cities, having only been to Boise, Idaho (hardly big even in those days), and (the only slightly bigger) Salt Lake City. I had been to Irvine, California, but that was with scouting, living in a tent out in the desert. Driving myself for the first time over the Golden Gate bridge was nerve racking, but absolutely stunning! I wanted to do it again and again and so over the years I did. But now it was time to go to Portland, and of course I didn't spend time there, so I went to Seattle and repeated the same behavior. I mostly drove, stopping to see and get emotional over the giant redwoods or walk along the driftwood shores of the Pacific Ocean along the Oregon coast, and through majestic green forests. And to fill the car with gas. You can sense it might border on boring driving for most people, and to top it off I slept in cheap motels. But I was seeing my part of America, at least that part of the Pacific Northwest that I truly loved, and now reside in as my final home. Driving from San Francisco to Eureka, then to Portland, Seattle, and then to Coeur d'Alene was so breathtaking, not to mention driving the latter part of the journey back to Twin Falls down US 95—this latter piece that I would do so many times driving to and from during my college days attending the University of Idaho in Moscow.

One-time nearing Cheney, Washington, I was caught going too fast—the sheriff said 90 mph, but I knew it was a hundred mph, seemingly all alone out in the desert and farmlands—and upon stopping me, asked that I follow him to town where I would be required to post a $100 bond to assure, I would later appear in their court. Well I didn't have $100, so he kindly took me in his vehicle—in cuffs I might add—to the county office in Spokane where I could post only a $50 bond. Having paid said bond, he drove me back to my car, lecturing me again for whatever reason other than that is what he does, took the cuffs off, released me at my car, and I was on my journey again. I forfeited the bond three months later while attending the University of Idaho and only went through the outskirts of Cheney again several times at the speed limit. I had learned a lesson. But also, due to the lack of funds as a result of paying the bond, I slept in the car on the beautiful shore of Lake Coeur d'Alene. It was cold, but beautiful.

After college, my travels went ballistic in the way of my decision to join the Peace Corps. I've already recounted my travel to other parts of Africa as part of our honeymoon. I'll therefore pickup travel when we left Ethiopia. I should start by first describing the roundabout way we got to New York City from Ethiopia and believe me, it was roundabout, but full of marvelous adventures.

If one is halfway around the world in Ethiopia and you got there one way (east through Athens, Greece), why not keep going that direction to get home? Besides, it made more sense to land on the west coast of America where our families were, than to fly directly to New York where I would be attending graduate school. So we mapped out a rough plan and put all our belongings in two giant wooden crates the Peace Corps provided and would ship to our parents. We signed off Peace Corps duty in early July 1964 and said our goodbyes to mutual volunteer friends and our students and boarded an airplane to Aden.

Where is Aden you say? Aden is the capital of Yemen—a not so friendly country to travel to in today's world. I didn't exactly know myself, but I remembered seeing it on a world map when we were in Asmara, then the major hub of Eritrea, at that time still incorporated with Ethiopia. Aden is port city of Yemen and served as a two-day stopover through Djibouti on our way to Bombay, India.

In some ways, Bombay felt as if it would really be the start of our journey home in that it was a big city. We spent three days in Bombay, or Mumbai as they call it now, situated on the Arabian Sea. It seemed like utter poverty, combined with gorgeous temples and millions of people. Locals were very nice to a couple of Americans on a shoestring travel budget. After walking for hours around the city, we stayed the nights in a Salvation Army hotel. It truly did feel like a gateway—there is, in fact, a beautiful gateway on the shore of Bombay—to our getting home because we were out of Africa now and without the relative "comforts" we had come to know and accept as normal. Bombay was civilization, certainly one to two steps up from Ethiopia, but still second world as we knew the world then. We were glad to be there, but truly anxious being around so many, many people. We would have to get used again to masses of people scurrying between cars, bicycles, motorbikes, and buses that we had not generally experienced over the past two years. Believe me, that is quiet an adjustment; more so than going from a level of calm like Idaho to a quietness like Ethiopia.

We decided upon arrival in India to go across the entire breadth of India by train. I suppose only a couple of former Peace Corps Volunteers could think that they could ride the then-antiquated train system across India without any reservations or places to stay. We had not arranged any local transportation, nor could we have from Ethiopia, to see anywhere we chose to stop along the way. We didn't know any other languages other than our own, besides our few words of Amharic, useful nowhere outside Ethiopia, certainly no words that might help us talk to strangers in seeking guidance on where to go, where to stay, and even where and what to eat. We were, however, as previously noted about Peace Corps volunteers, able to take a shower with a glass of water only, so getting across a continent surely could not be that hard? We had successfully traveled around five countries of Africa on our own as newlyweds. Surely, we could cross India.

We had roughly mapped out an itinerary of three major cities we wanted to visit with an option for stopping in between at any place else that suited our interests once we learned what was available in front of us. Our main targets after Bombay were New Delhi (including Agra), Banaras, and Calcutta (now Kolkata). Two other Ethiopian Peace Corps volunteers, fortunately, were traveling a few days in front of us and prior discussions with them netted some useful travel intel. We would stop first at the ancient caves at Ellora and Ajanta on our way to Delhi. We bought third-class tickets, sat on wooden benches, and ventured forth on a train fed by coal burning engines. Along the way we met and tried to converse with several locals in their broken English and shared some food and drink (cautiously). I tried an orange looking soda that I thought was perhaps Hi-C, but I paid the price throwing up with an upset tummy. We also had a very fascinating, but sort of weird, conversation on the train with a group of young men our age. It was initiated in broken English when I happen to take out a string of toilet paper I had previously absconded with and blew my nose. They giggled with one another as if they were a set of teenagers, and when I inquired why they did so, they pointed to the wad of toilet paper. A conversation ensued for about 20 minutes centered on the relative merits—or not—of using toilet paper not as I had just used it, but rather that it existed at all for its actual use, in western nations, which was to clean one's behind. Not exactly a geopolitical topic that one might engage in, but since their society doesn't generally use either that product or our Western style toilet you sit on—preferring employing the way of water washing one's behind using what is sometimes known as a Turkish Toilet (look it up). The conversation made perfect sense. It was of course a ridiculous discussion, as if there were only one correct answer. I learned there were, in fact, two answers and both made sense within their individual culture. A subtle lesson in international diplomacy, I know, but eventful and a great story to tell others. I think they were taken with us, as we certainly were with them. These are the real adventures of real travel in the raw. And, by the way, I now have a bidet in my home. Those young men were much wiser than I am sure I gave them credit for at that time on that train. Again, lesson learned.

Hours later, we stepped off the train and who should appear before us but our fellow Peace Corps friends traveling ahead of us. One was my best man, Ray Capozzi from our wedding in Harar, and the other Paul Koprowski. We were so glad to see one another by chance as they boarded and we stepped off the train! We had just enough time to briefly exchange summaries of their experience at the caves and our soon-to-be experience. When I asked them, "How was your experience at the caves?" one of them replied, "You've seen one rock, you've seen 'em all!" I have since used that phrase hundreds of times in my life traveling various parts of the world to let others know how dumb that statement was, but that we found it so funny in the middle of India on our travels home.

The caves, two sets in two locations, are spectacular in that they are religious shrines (monasteries and worship halls) of India tradition hewn out of rock along the length of canyon walls. The Ajanta Caves have existed since 400 BC (or BCE). They display in intricate detail the centuries of wear making them ominous in the darkness of the caves, but absolutely breathtaking. They depict the past lives and rebirths of Buddha. The Ellora Caves are a combination of Hindu, Buddhist, and Jain temples dating from 600 AD (CE). There are in excess of 100 caves carved from basalt cliffs. They represent deities, mythologies, and monasteries of each religion. Our eyes couldn't possibly take it all in during the course of the two days we could afford to spend there. I'd like to go back for more, but there are simply too many places in the world and so little time but having gone to 90 countries I've been pretty lucky at that.

After two days we were back on the train to New Delhi, specifically Agra where the Tahj Mahal is located. What I thought was ancient in Europe was new compared to everything in India, including the Tahj Mahal. Again I could say many things, but beyond the pure beauty and symmetry of the Tahj Mahal and the structures that are around it, it is really the story of the love affair that sparked its creation that fascinated me the most. As you stood there (in those days with fewer tourists), you could look down at the long reflective pond and take in the jewel-like towers inlaid with dark granite and see for yourself the grandeur of its creation. I liked it a lot! It's a love story that you can read about or better yet go and see, on your own. Try to see it without a big crowd around you, as we were lucky to experience, but that may be impossible.

We took the train to the next stop on our grand adventure, Banaras (now Varanasi), the holiest city of Hinduism. There we saw, for the first time (and never to forget), a body being cremated along the Ganges River, and it seemed to me we were now discovering the more everyday India. Years later when Kathleen and I visited India, we saw another cremation by the river, this time that of a 12-year-old child. As the flames licked higher and higher you are reminded of your own existence and assess just how lucky you are.

By now we were traveling second class on the train, an upgrade that wasn't really worth the money, as the wooden benches of third class were much more comfortable and, if empty, you could lie down for a brief nap. Out the window through the smoke of coal from the engine, I saw young boys and girls on a makeshift teeter-totter having as much fun as I did on the river in Idaho, making our own entertainment among the willows that lined the creek bank. Other children simply bounced up and down on the limb of a fallen tree branch giggling with such delight at what they had found to do. There was plenty of poverty with what were many more millions of people than I had ever experienced. It seemed to me that many were living in worse hovel conditions than in Ethiopia, made that much worse because the number of souls were so many more and tightly packed in limited spaces. It made you sad, and you knew why beyond the sheer numbers. The caste system, while accepted there, made no sense to me but it was not mine to change, even as a Peace Corps volunteer—a former one at that! So we continued on, sleeping at times on the ever-jerking ancient train, other times laying on a sheet-only spring bed with a thin mattress at a stopping point for the night. It cost 50 cents for the overnight accommodation, so you knew we were not in the lap of luxury. For the final leg on the train, we treated ourselves to first class with dinner and a pull-down bed and made our final stop in Calcutta. For a few hours we were escaping the scene around us, but even that was temporary.

If I had thought I'd seen it all in our brief journey across India, I was not prepared in any way for Calcutta. I don't remember all that we did there, but I must have been in culture shock from our village-living in Ethiopia to see how the souls of Calcutta lived with little opulence in mass numbers. Just watching the women wash clothes in the river reminded me of my mother, in that hot warehouse, who had it so much better than they did. Often such stark comparisons get in your face as lessons not of judgment, but of the reality around us in a world that is so much different than any place in America. Travel and learn and you will be a different person when it comes to our country, to our planet.

To truly learn, you have to travel in ways that are not so comfortable, such as on a cruise ship. You have to get on a train in third class, ride a local bus with people and their bags of goods hanging on it, hire a local bush taxi with eight other locals, or stay long enough to walk the streets of cities or villages. Listen, talk to locals, and eat what they eat with the awareness and caution that you are not a local with their resistance to local microorganisms. I will summarize the rest of the journey as it too, provided us with so many experiences that it would turn into a travel log rather than an autobiography.

We had planned to stop in Indonesia on the way home, but we learned that there had been some political upheaval—street riots—in talking to others we met, so we decided to veer off instead to Cambodia, Vietnam, Thailand, then Hong Kong. Then home through Hawaii so we could touch America and release our energy and acclimate to America before landing on actual real estate we knew in California. I'm so glad we did, as these stops were, as with India in many different ways, real eye-openers, and would serve as an experience to be done again a few times later in life. From the huge numbers of people in India to the smaller Southeast Asia countries, it was a nice transition in both numbers and varying cultures. The topography of jungle-like conditions was the first thing that told us we had landed on a different continent. First, Cambodia.

I absolutely loved Cambodia. Then again, I seemed to like everywhere new I went. We flew into the capital, Phnom Penh, and looked around a bit, but we were anxious to make our way up north by a short airplane ride to the main attraction—Angkor Wat, the city of temples. We heard it was a massive temple site recently retrieved from the jungle after a hundred or so years of being lost to outsiders (but inhabited by monks). There were no organized tours in those days, so we hired a local driver and he first took us to several ancillary Buddhist and Hindu figures and temples scattered in the jungle, some of which had yet to be fully retrieved. I particularly remember a huge 20' Buddha figure made of sandstone intertwined on its face with the roots of a giant tree growing on top its head. It gave off a serene combination of the manmade with the artwork that only a tree's roots can create as it clings to the statues face, as if the two were designed by nature to be together. When I saw the scale of the main 12th century temple, Angkor Wat, I was simply awe struck. I could have spent days there because it would take days, if not weeks, to do it justice.

First, there was a long bridge to the main temple that passes over a moat that circumvents the entire main temple complex. The bridge was lined with some carvings, one after the other, which I understand have either been lost now or are being restored (the original bridge having itself been made of wood). I then come to the outer wall that encloses the main temples/galleries separated by paved walkways between. As I try to interpret what's the carvings on the walls mean, I feel that the moat keeps the enemy at bay. All the way around the inside is a continuous set of carved scenes of Hindu and Buddhist Devas (deities) appearing to be like some battle scene, but really a story of religious belief. There are also other scenes of the originator of the site, King Suryavarman, as he enters the "home of the gods" for the first time. These are in such detail that you need to spend a half hour on one small section of wall, but there are in excess of a mile of these scenes at least as they span the walls of the inside two temples that are yet to be explored. What does each individual carving depict and mean? I wonder but have to move on.

As I worked my way towards the middle of the complex I traversed different rectangular galleries, each raised above the next. I am steadily making my way to the center temple. You then come to this inner temple and climb a mountain of very steep steps revealing numerous towers. This is all designed to replicate and represent Mount Meru, the home of their gods. Its five towers are the five peaks of Mount Meru, while the walls and moat honor the surrounding mountain ranges and the sea. When we there you could go to the very top and get a view of the surrounding 400 acres with numerous smaller temples and statues scattered and partially or completely hidden in the jungle. I'd never seen anything like it and would again only decades later in Myanmar when we visited the 1000 pagodas of Bagan. No wonder Angkor Wat was later designated by the

Guinness World Records as the largest religious structure in the world. Nothing in America compares with its mind-blowing grandeur, except perhaps the (non-manmade) Grand Canyon. I had to go back someday and see it again with more time, so I did.

After three days we decided to take the bus from Siem Reap back to Phnom Penh instead of the quicker airplane ride we had come there on. What an unforeseen adventure we led ourselves into.

A bus ride in Cambodia is an entirely different experience than the metropolitan transit authority (MTA) bus in any US city, including my own Bellingham, Washington on the Blue Bus. Hold on to your seat, better yet buckle in, as I describe what happened.

We had had a marvelous time visiting the ruins of Angkor Wat and had to return to Phnom Penh to then resume our journey home. Rather than fly back the route we came, we decided to travel by bus back to the capital city, Phnom Penh. We bought our one-way tickets, and initially we were the only foreigners on the bus made up of primarily locals. At one stop along the way, a young German joined us who was mostly hitching his way on foot, sleeping in temples with bats and such. Speaking some English he turned out to be most of our conversation for the six-hour journey. At first the bus meandered, stopping frequently to pick up and unload local people with their goods in cloth bags or varied local produce in baskets, usually for short journeys to another village. The first thing we noticed was the manner of boarding and disembarking passengers. This was done with little—if any—entire stoppage of the bus itself. In slow motion, an attendant to the driver, riding frequently on top of the bus, would peek down and see who would be exiting. He inquired about how many and where their luggage (packages really in bundles) was on top of the bus. Then, as the bus slowed the passenger(s) would leap off, and his/her larger packages from atop the bus were thrown down to them by the attendant. Soon the repetitive manner of getting on and off the bus got swifter and much more intense. Why was this? That was because another bus with all its passengers joined us on our journey to the capital. The other bus, you might say, jockeyed with our bus for the few hours as the two buses raced one another to some finish line we had no idea of. The goal, apparently, was to see who would get to the capital first. Imagine if two buses in Bellingham, or in your town, did that!

All went well with some passenger encouragement through applause and cheering as one bus passed the other because of the need to often disembark its passengers (and their stuff) and let others on. The race was on! The need to cross a ferry over the Mekong River seemed likely to end this senseless racing, but the ferry accommodated both and the race continued on the other side. I am telling you that at times the two buses were side by side and you could literally reach out and touch the hands of the people on the other bus. This all occurred while careening down a dirt road hardly big enough to handle two buses side by side. People and carts pulled by animals had to scurry for their own safety and habitually seemed to know what was going on when they heard the thunder of the buses and the sound of horns blaring the eminent danger approaching. This went back and forth, and we were in the lead by two bus lengths as we neared the outskirts of the capital. This was when our driver, looking much like a kamikaze pilot with his gold front teeth and slightly hooked nose, made an abrupt right turn. The other bus continued straight, and we apparently lost one another. Not knowing where the finish line was, I assumed the race was over. After a kilometer, our bus turned left at an intersection, and we got up to top speed again. About two minutes into this last maneuver, I looked to my left from our front seat and noted in the distance what appeared to be the other bus in a cloud of dust. We were on a collision course at the forthcoming intersection. Due to speed and turn mechanics not worth making clear at this point in the story, the other bus entered the approaching intersection just before we did. It had to make a left turn to be on the same road as we were. If you are keeping up with me, you understand the speed we had entering the intersection, and we immediately passed the other bus on their left and into the lead we previously last had. Cheering broke loose in our bus with frantic waving to the other bus—goodbye! We stayed that way until both buses entered the town square, and all passengers silently slipped out into the town square and went on their individual ways. My best bus ride ever! It struck me I was a lucky survivor this time.

From Cambodia we flew to Saigon, Vietnam; it's now been renamed, Ho Chi Minh City. We designated this for only a two-day stop on our way to Bangkok, Thailand. This short stop was designated out of some necessity because we had heard Vietnam was perhaps not safe—some fighting was going on between factions of the South and North. The U.S. had not entered the fray (or so they said). That changed, as it turned out, the day we flew into Saigon. That was August 2, 1964, to be exact—the bombing of the Gulf of Tonkin. That became the US excuse to enter a war they should never have been in, but they were going to be so involved. The day before, in Cambodia I saw an American tank along a roadside and wondered why it was there. Today I had an answer to that tank being in Cambodia. This was the war I could have been drafted into had I not had an exemption to serve in the Peace Corps. As we were exiting service in the Peace Corps, I had gotten the news that married men would not be drafted. Then, a few months later by executive order, married men with children would not be drafted and we were expecting our first child in May. It was all due to the luck of the draw, without any plan or intention on my part, to avoid the draft. That was luck to its finest degree.

We stayed the two days in Vietnam feeling uncomfortable and anxious to continue our journey to Thailand for a week's stay. Before leaving the subject of travel in Vietnam I have a side story that needs to be told in the context of Vietnam and the war. Much later in life, in 2021, I returned to Vietnam with an American wartime Vietnam veteran buddy of mine. Those same Vietnamese could not be any more accepting and nicer to the two of us. What a change. Was that the power of Buddhism? I am inclined to think so. Through our guide on that trip, we met his parents in a small village. They had both been members of the North Vietnam regular army. In their hut on stilts hung a picture of the two of them, much younger, in their uniforms. It could easily remind you perhaps of a picture of other revolutionaries, such as 'Che' Guevara. They welcomed my friend Bob (a fellow warrior to them) and I into their home and made lunch for us. Our guests wife stepped into their garden area and killed and dressed a chicken right there, just as I had seen my sister Dorothy do at her ranch. We had a wonderful meal together there on a straw mat sitting on their floor, as is the tradition. As we left, the 80-year-old former North Vietnam soldier hugged and kissed this former 80-year-old former Peace Corps Volunteer on the neck as we embraced in a goodbye. It was a sign of new friendship—something I still get chills about to this day. We are all people under the skin you know! Again, these kinds of experiences are what travel should be mostly about in that they teach us not only tolerance but establish great friendships. I just learned recently that that dear Vietnamese friend recently passed.

By now we were kind of getting tired of the journey and anxious to get home. A week in Thailand saw us enjoying the temples, but mostly relaxing. We flew to Hong Kong which was really our first taste of a first world city in over two years. Imagine what it was like to then go from there to Hawaii for a few days' preparation for going home, speaking English to nearly everyone for the first time in two years. Once in Hawaii, we were kind of home, but had to cross the remaining segment of ocean to get there. Then life would begin for us as a typical married couple, anticipating our first child.

We first stayed with my wife's parents, then traveled up to my family in Idaho, and then finally on to New York to get settled into an America that was a stranger to us. Other than traversing a couple of times the width of the US to and from college days in New York, we didn't do much travel, besides small vacation family trips. We were beginning family life and had little money or time for travel. More extensive travel, mainly on the dime of someone else, would have to wait until being employed by several different companies later in life. That's a kind of travel in and of itself that I (and family) have been lucky to enjoy, not just because someone else is paying for it (although that's great), but the nature of such travel is as rewarding for the same reasons of being with others and seeing where they live and what they do. You'll learn that I often took full advantage of additional travel to places I wanted to see following paid travel by my several employers. Just one of the perks as I saw it. So while employed at the Job Corps, General Programmed Teaching, The American College, MK, and the IT Corporation, I had many opportunities to travel, sponsored by those enterprise's for meeting their needs and also feeding my own addiction for travel. Thus, at the Job Corps Center I visited other job training centers, did frequent business travel working for General Programmed Teaching, and at The American College I was allowed to take a six-month sabbatical leave in Germany (when we visited other countries) and included our driving around the US as part of the sabbatical through 25 states. The American College allowed me to go to England for professional conferences and of course I took the family beyond to Paris, Germany, Belgium, and other countries.

It was with MK, an international corporation with projects in various interesting countries throughout the world, that my travel stepped up a notch. I went to Columbia five times to do some training and nearly crashed in the jungle as I will account in my travel adventures. MK sent me to China to evaluate the training of a competitor and I was simply stunned at the China I first saw. Virtually no cars on the streets of Beijing, other than official ones. Thousands of people on bicycles, and hundreds of others being kept busy sweeping the street with handmade straw brooms. With such a large population that the country sought to keep busy, I saw a contrasting attempt to be modern, yet keep the citizenry busy. This was evidenced while I observed an eight-foot trench being dug by a huge excavator, while alongside it, a similar sized trench was being dug by hand by a hundred workers or so down in the trench, throwing out shovel after shovel of dirt. There were even a few rickshaws still employed as transport on the streets as if I were reading some good novel of intrigue. Due to government policy we had to travel the train by night so we Westerners could not see what we should not, apparently, and it was boring. However this was compensated for, in a way, by the inside of the passenger car with all of us crammed in and some were smoking real foul tobacco. It was choking, if not fascinating. Like something out of a movie.

After the train ride we went to our assignment to do our consulting work at what was to later become the largest coal mine in the world. At the mine site I climbed a flight of 25 steps to a truck cab. That huge truck could haul 50 tons of coal and would be a monster truck in any monster truck rally in the US. A long dragline scooped tons of coal from the earth's surface. In the vast open coal pit there were at least two dozen smaller trucks that could only haul 20 tons each. They were like ants on an anthill scurrying here and there. Then on the way back to our hotel we stopped to witness a dig site along the roadside. Locals were extracting ancient coins and artifacts more ancient than America. This boy from the junkyard was taking it all in. There were treasures in my boyhood jungle of iron, but nothing quite like what I was seeing by this roadside. Trying to dig that hole in my youth to China with neighbor kids was now being realized in much easier and realistic ways.

Most of my travel with International Technology was in conjunction with training requirements, mostly to their various regional offices; I also continued to attend professional conferences where I was active as an officer and presenter. But it was when Kathleen and I married that travel took on a whole new aspect of adventure combined with the pleasure of being with my partner in life and business. We had started our new business and it required, luckily, loads of travel. First, however, before getting to a description of business travel, there was our honeymoon travel.

When I married the second time, my wife and I naturally needed to decide where to go on our honeymoon. I'll never forget asking where Kathleen wanted to go, and her answer quite surprised me. I had suggested we get married on Mt. Kilimanjaro, but that idea was nixed by her girlfriends. Before the wedding, twelve of her closest friends had gathered for a girls-only celebration of our engagement at a swanky restaurant (Moonshadows in Malibu) on the Pacific Coast Highway. I tried to influence their support for marrying on Mt. Kilimanjaro by presenting, as a surprise, my wife to be with a beautiful, hand-crafted vase with two dozen red roses, and a white rose for each of her friends. My move backfired—there would be no destination wedding—as they concluded that such a man with such a woman should wed where they could all attend—thus we married in San Pedro with all of them in attendance. Back to my asking Kathleen where she would like to honeymoon: her answer, "an English-speaking country." Well, that narrows the list of available countries down a bit, and as I have noted elsewhere, I'm not generally drawn to countries that attract Americans (although there are a few exceptions). So we settled on Australia and New Zealand for our honeymoon, and I was all in for that. I threw in the mix the country of Fiji as well, not that she believed me, but at least it wasn't a predominately English-speaking country, although they do use English for tourist needs.

We first went to Australia, where her parents had been married (and she was conceived) during the Second World War. I thought that had a particularly nice touch to it when I learned that fact—very romantic, I thought. They had both been military personnel in the Army and met in Papa New Guinea where her mother was a nurse. Her father was all over the Pacific theater during the war under General MacArthur's command. We had a wonderful experience in Sydney, beyond the obvious. It was one of those travel adventures you can't find in any brochures or from travel agencies but are simply lucky to experience and cherish.

We located the hotel where her parents had been married on Whatson Bay in Sydney and decided to have a romantic dinner at the hotel restaurant that literally sat on the shoreline. Our table for two was as if out of a movie (like Shirley Valentine)—the two us at a small table, the sun setting, at the very end of a sandy point that protruded into the bay. We had a huge platter of shellfish as I recall, if anyone remembers something like that on their honeymoon. We finished our dinner and walked in to see the inside of the restaurant. The walls were decorated with huge sepia photos from the war period—just as it must have looked when her parents were there. The owners of the long-time, well-known restaurant (that often in that day appeared in American Express TV ads). were having their 60th wedding anniversary. During our dinner, Kathleen had asked questions of the waitress about the surroundings and spoke of her parents' wedding so many years ago. Soon after, at the urging of our waitress, a well-dressed, elderly eloquent lady (who happened to be one half of the couple who owned the restaurant), stepped from her anniversary celebration to talk with us. It was delightful as she reminisced of the bygone days when she and her husband were there, just as Kathleen's parents were there. As we departed, she turned to my new bride and said how delighted she was that we were there and so obviously in love. She concluded by noting, "Besides, isn't it better than being married to the same old bloke for 60 years?" The smile on her face was priceless, as was that experience as a newlywed couple! From there we went on to New Zealand, then concluded with travel to somewhere my new bride was sure we were really not going, but I kept assuring we were—and it was not an English-speaking country! That was a way of introducing her to all things possible in travel, even if you are not comfortable with another language. She has long gotten over that particular fear of travel and came to realize her Danny was, indeed, a travel addict—for which she is truly grateful.

As I noted, Kathleen didn't believe we were going to Fiji until we actually got on the airplane and landed. We returned there three more times thereafter in as many years during our early days as husband and wife. On one occasion we were witness to a lovely ceremony when a Fijian couple planted a baby coconut tree to celebrate the birth of their first child. Another time we went because I had received an advanced royalty on a new book, and where better to write than on an island. Later in life, as an extension of the two of us having been invited to speak in Kuwait at a conference on improving human resources, we were lucky enough to travel to another three places in Africa. She was simply in awe of what she experienced in such countries as Ethiopia, Kuwait, Israel, Kenya, Tanzania, and the many others that followed. She was learning how her Danny wanted her to see the world as much as he had already, but this time together with her.

In 1993 we started our own consulting business and it was then that we stepped up our travel together and had so much fun doing so. That is largely because we both love to work and travel together.

In running our business, someone else was now reimbursing our way to somewhere, picking up the tab on our hotel and food allowance. We typically took the opportunity to travel elsewhere in addition, on our own dimes, which we had earned from them. For example, early in our business venture we were discovered by a guy in London who contacted us about a business proposal he had. He was organizing and running workshops for other professionals like us (some we knew), in England. He wanted to represent us, and so we made a deal with him largely based on supporting our travel goals. We would like to be paid a fair fee for our services, but that wasn't the main driver in coming to London over the course of the five years that he represented us. Rather, if he could pay our expenses for flying, lodging, and eating, we would see that he got enough out of it to make it worth his while, and that we were paid at least modestly. We typically went three times a year over the course of those five years. That alone is obviously a great deal of travel. Imagine what you could do and where you could go given those circumstances; we did lots.

In London we were truly fortunate as we knew an absolutely marvelous couple (Jim and Brian) from our Santa Monica days. They lived in Kensington Square, of all the nice places, and together we had many good times. We even traveled together, meeting in the Philippines where Jim had numerous relatives. Jim and Brian were, respectively, law and data analytics professionals. Brian was also a great photographer on the side, and Jim the consummate concierge who knew London inside and out. And they had interesting friends who became our friends. In return, we organized their apartment, cooked an occasional dinner for them, did fascinating things together, and talked, talked, talked.

Usually in planning and executing travel I keep a careful written log of our business and personal travel—in those days there was no internet or electronic calendaring to take advantage of. I've always been one to make my own travel arrangements since my version of travel is a little different than most—almost exclusively void of tours—which means I can sometimes get things screwed up. When this happens, I am quick to find alternatives that have sometimes led to even more interesting travel experiences. Of course things can go awry, but I've learned such is part of the experience and one learns to quickly adjust. For example, during one of our travels scheduled from Heathrow Airport in London returning back home, we approached the United Airlines departure agent, as the frequent flyer program people we are, and he said, "I've got good news and bad news for you. The good news is that you have been upgraded to First Class. The bad news is that the plane took off two hours ago!" Seems I'd written the flight departure on the correct day, but the wrong time by two hours due to a faulty ink pen that didn't write the first number of the departure time: 12:00 noon instead appearing as 2:00 pm (the incorrect time). We lost both the upgrade and some of my pride. You win some, you lose some.

Beyond the regular workshops we conducted in London, our representative did manage to find us a couple of additional well-paying clients to work with, so the business arrangements for both parties were a win-win. For example, he got us some work in Ireland for a utility that proved very timely. Once there, having completed our work, I was invited by the professional association (ISPI) that I had long been associated with to be part of a three-person team that was being invited to go to Saudi Arabia to do some training in the principles and practice of our profession, Performance Technology, for a major oil company. I had become by then one of the leaders in this field through some of the instructional designs and the work model that I had originated. The Saudis at that time would not allow my wife, a woman, to accompany me, so she decided to go on her own to Israel and visit some other colleagues of ours. After completing the workshop, I would link up with her there. We had a great time and Kathleen has her own interesting stories on that account. Anyway, I arrived in Saudi Arabia and it is fascinating; unlike any other place I'd been in the world. One unusual thing happened that just goes to show you what travel can teach you about our world.

We were teaching in a hotel the oil company had arranged for in Riyadh when we learned that the "religious police" wanted to shut down our training because we had two local Saudi women in attendance at the workshop. As before when I had been confronted with racism such as that I experienced in college and on the boat from Europe, I was reminded that when you are confronted with ignorance regarding how to treat others (sexism in this case), you get a shock to your system of how others should be treated and what you will personally do about it. Fortunately, our sponsors were able to move the training to their protected oil facility, out of the jurisdiction of the religious police, and we went on to complete the training with everyone in attendance. I am just so lucky to see the world and learn from it in so many ways.

Kathleen and I were always on the hunt for anything that might fund our travels—usually in connection with work, but also other kinds of professional events. For example, we were invited to speak at international conferences in our field of work. We each presented at a conference on Human Resource development in Beijing, China, and another in Kuwait. Following the presentations in Beijing, we walked the Great Wall, toured the Forbidden City, and witnessed how the city, unlike my previous visit, was busy now with choking traffic. I wondered where all the rickshaws had gone from my previous visit years earlier. Once, a highly distraught woman approached us in Tiananmen Square, handed us a hurried note (she was obviously afraid of something), and vanished to a shadowy area. Having read only the first couple of lines that expressed her need for help in some way, we were afraid to read the rest of the note for fear of being arrested. We walked on and discarded the note. I have always wondered what further role she perhaps was requesting of us, but in a foreign land, especially China, one must be prudent in their travels!

While in China, we traveled on our own over to Xi'an to see the Qin Dynasty Chinese terracotta warriors. Now this is a tour I could sign up with others to get the full experience on the level with Angkor Wat in Cambodia. Years later while living in Santa Monica, a neighbor in our condo complex gave us a terracotta figure he had been given in China by a friend. "It would look better in our living room," he said.

While not likely one of the originals, it certainly reminds me of them as it currently stands on the display shelf in our living room area.

You might guess that my ideal method of travel is not a cruise ship, although I've been on a few: to Japan, around the Caribbean, Alaska, around Thailand to Phuket, in the Mediterranean to places like Santorini, Istanbul, Athens, Crete, and Ephesus. There's lots of food on a cruise ship and you can search for the few people of real interest to have good times. The problem is that you are not communing with the locals because there are no locals other than the cruise ship staff, who are from all over the world. Even these engagements are limited in scope as they are busy people taking care of your needs. That's nice, and I do try to chat them up, but you can't have coffee with them, walk around their towns with them, or eat in their home. Rather, I prefer to go somewhere, stay for an extended period of time, and create opportunities to commune and ask what sites to see. Or perhaps take the local bus, or hire a driver, or most often just wander around the city to a few select sites of interest. For example, we once went to Arequipa, Peru, for a month. We rented a flat with a nice view, including a rooftop space that we had full access to. We mainly cooked our own meals, mixed with dining out for local taste. We walked all around the city, stopping in shops to drink coffee in small cafes with great pastries. We watched local marching bands play and strut the street on festive occasions, saw locals in their traditional dress, and little kids being little kids with big smiles for tourists. It was New Years in Arequipa, and from the rooftop we saw the greatest display of fireworks we have ever seen. There were 360 degrees of rockets going off, brocades, crossette and Roman candles, I mean everywhere; and deep into the edges of the city! Seems everyone had a match for lighting up such a joyful time, and it went on well into the night hours until the last rocket went off around 3:00 a.m. We didn't sleep much, but that's what naps are for.

One afternoon while roaming the streets of Arequipa, we met a Peruvian couple with their soon to be American daughter-in-law and her parents as we all tried to cross one of the busy streets. Cars don't especially respect pedestrians there, so going en masse seemed to be the safer method of crossing, so we did; smiling at one another in the process. We started talking on the other side, and through some translation, discovered that the older gentleman—younger, however, than me—was the embassy representative of Brazil. Additionally, they owned a local hotel and two restaurants. The next thing we knew they invited us to their son's wedding. Sadly, we could not return in a month when it was to take place. We did go to their restaurant for an elegant reception held in celebration of the forthcoming marriage. Getting to know and participate in life with locals is what travel is about—at least 60% of travel in my opinion; with interesting sites filling in the balance—and maybe 15% on food and drink? So, I will go on a cruise, you just have to drag me onboard once every three to five years. On those rare occasions, I actually enjoy the cruise as long as it has a place to lounge in a spa whirlpool, and a hot tub or great massage.

I may have told a small white lie earlier in that there is a certain kind of cruising that I have liked and find worth recommending to others; that's river or clipper ship cruising. The smallness of the craft helps, as do the fewer passengers who are usually a mix of nationalities that this kind of cruising seems to attract. River cruises also generally allow you to disembark more often for onshore adventures, providing more respite from the ubiquitous boring (excuse me, sailors) ocean view. And you often get to interact with locals on shore—what's not to like about that. Some examples....

We have gone on three river cruises that were fascinating. I liked each for their differences. The first was the Nile River. The Nile sojourn went from Cairo up to the Aswan Dam. The ship was a large floating box so that every room had a balcony and view of the shoreline that was close for most of our journey. It was a tour reflecting ancient times to the max. It brought alive the hieroglyphics I had only seen in an encyclopedia as a kid. Real writing and symbols were common on numerous columns and temples, surrounded by the kind of people who created such history. This is the real thing at Luxor, and to go into the museum in Cairo is to see these artifacts in their natural setting; even with a little dust on them to boot. It's surreal right down to the local dress, language, and coffee. During my Peace Corps stint I had the opportunity to see the Abu Simbel before it was relocated due to the construction of the Aswan Dam. But we opted instead to travel on our honeymoon to other parts of Africa—a wise choice on our part, but that would have been something special to see before it was relocated.

In the same way, traversing the rivers, canals, and locks that take you through Russia, from St. Petersburg to Moscow, is quite fascinating. Combining that with the onboard entertainment of young Russians who had not lived the Cold War, is refreshing. Their honesty about their own country in private conversation we had with some of them sometimes made me wonder if they might not be arrested, but their expressions of their current thoughts seemed an accurate assessment of their hopes. Moscow is more than you see in the movies, on the news, or in magazines. It's very much an up to date, sophisticated city. By the way, we ran into, that same level of honesty about current government and political dynamics on another river ride when we sailed on a river cruise in Myanmar. For me it's these confrontations with the realities of life that make travel so fascinating, let alone practical learning experiences. I choose to experience them firsthand, rather than buying into the more conventional and sanitized version of vacationing which isolates me from the real-world.

After a sail on a clipper ship around Thailand, we caught a 30-passenger river boat in Myanmar (formerly Burma). It ran from Rangoon (Yangon now) and chugged its way up the Irrawaddy River to Mandalay. This was a fabulous journey because of a fabulous tour guide named Lennie. He was so honest about his country's challenging political climate, and so proud of his heritage. We got off the boat on shores without docks, rode on person powered carriages with side cars in a parade through a local village and visited the tour guide's family and saw how they lived and supped, and we talked with villagers through our guide's translation. This is real, personal travel, not by impersonal tour guides, but with the population as near to their life as you are going to get. As I often note, use your common sense, and enjoy the experience! Speaking of experiencing local customs, I, for some reason, really like massages and have had my share of them as practiced in different countries. One of these was in Myanmar, and the other during a travel adventure in Lithuania, which I shall later recount.

We were at the end of our journey in Mandalay and my wife and I each signed up for a massage. It was a beautiful setting replete with a lily pond; we walked across steppingstones to make our way to the massage center appointment. It had the usual meditation music, oriental grasses, and quiet, reflective feel with dim lighting. It's perfect feng shui! Our receptionist handed us each a robe and attire they preferred we wear for a full massage. My wife's attire looked standard with a body wrap, but mine consisted of a tiny nylon mesh piece. It was quite similar to a hairnet and about that size. At least it was my favorite color, black. Looking at it, I didn't know whether to put it on my head or wear it around my loins, but I assumed the latter. I didn't mind it so much, although a little embarrassed at how I looked as a 77-year-old guy donning such scant attire. Certainly, no pictures were taken for a later slideshow or posting on Instagram. Still, when in Rome or Mandalay, do as they do. By the way, it was a great massage. So I have come to really enjoy river cruises, and massages, in reverse order.

There is another kind of cruising that deserves some consideration for travel. This I have also come to like, but not as much as on the rivers of the world. That's clipper ship cruising out in open waters smaller in scope such as the Mediterranean Sea, Andaman Sea, and other seas of the world. At least you frequently get to see some shoreline from a distance. In this kind of travel much of the experience, for me at least, is the ambience.

Clipper ships, of course, use sails when the wind is available, combined with diesel engines to get around when the winds are not favorable. When in full sail they are worth the look and feel. You're not exactly a pirate, but then again you are not on the boat for that purpose. There is a kind of intimacy with your fellow passengers you don't get on larger cruise ships, as well as with the intimacy of a sea versus an ocean. Clipper ships are much better than on a huge cruise liner with everything that seems to want to be (and now is) Disneyland or some other onshore attraction—as if being on the ship wasn't enough. Can't imagine traveling with 5,000 other people on one of the behemoth ships available these days. Having said that, as I write, we have just scheduled ourselves on one such huge ship making it repositioning cruise from Barcelona to Ft. Lauderdale. See, I can experience to see what I might learn new about travel!

Our first clipper ship adventure was on the Mediterranean. This particular sea is as beautiful as the sights you see on its shores. As I noted, there is something special about a sailing ship with those giant sails unfurled, and remember, I am a guy who hates being on big bodies of water. Is there a difference when doing so on an unending ocean or the smaller sea? Perhaps there is. For one, as I previously noted, you occasionally get to see land, and sailing is usually much gentler on your tummy and your brain on a smaller body of water. Both are important to us landlubbers.

The second clipper experience was in the Indian Ocean sailing from Thailand to Vietnam, with a few stopovers along the way, disembarking at Phuket. On a relatively small vessel you can better get to know others, and as it happens, on one of those sailing was an equal number of tourists from Germany. It was sort of a culture exchange experience, but without the locals. To hear them sing an occasional German tune at dinner time was a delight. I might get a little seasick from just describing sailing, and so back to land as my most favorite surface to travel on.

This may come as a surprise, but I don't really have a most favored place I've been to. Since I've seen and experienced firsthand so many places, people often ask me what my favorite is. It, of course, depends on what you are looking for, how much you are willing to experience, how difficult it might be to find a bathroom, or how little or much you want to pay. I like to pay little and there are ways to do so and still get quality. But then again, my measure of a great trip is a broad experience with locals first and foremost, then the sites, activity, food, and general cost considerations. If forced to give an answer, I am in love with countries like Ireland, Portugal, Vietnam, and the entire surface of Africa. I think the most user-friendly country I've visited several times is New Zealand. This is first because of its very friendly people, but also the wide variety of things to see and explore in short distances of travel—and across two islands. Even the people at McDonalds are super friendly and the rules and regulations regarding driving—on the left side of the road—make sense and make driving much easier to navigate, even across one-way bridges, than in America. From fiords to deserts to lakes and jungles you can see it all. And for those who require it, they speak English, although you might wonder at times.

Now while I can't or won't give you a list of my favorite travel locations, I can tell you one of the oddest experiences we have had. This one is a doozy, in the realm of at least a half-dozen others that have been experienced, but none equals this one alone.

We were in Iceland for our second visit, this time concentrating on additional time at my most favorite hot springs in the world—the Blue Lagoon. I've been there four times so you know I must really, really like it. As a kid I loved the hot springs in Idaho, but nothing, not even Budapest's Szechenyi Baths, compares to Iceland. The Blue Lagoon is about 5 acres seated atop an active volcano. On a wintery night with huge snowflakes floating onto your nose from the sky, it's a breathtaking feeling as you sip on your favorite drink, sitting in heavenly warm water up to your armpits. However, I am not writing to extol the greatness of the Blue Lagoon.

The month before our third trip to Iceland, I am talking with one of the staff (Steve Meyers) at the local independent Pickford Film Center in Bellingham where I volunteered selling concessions and tickets. Informing him that we were returning to Iceland he told me of something I had not heard of but he thought we should see. Frankly I couldn't believe he is serious, let alone not telling me a joke. There is, he said, a penis museum in Reykjavik. Even the two words, penis and museum, didn't seem a good fit as the title to something, but especially where the second word is associated with seeing fine paintings, sculptures, and such which this museum does not have.

Not sure whether to have believed him or not, when we finally got to Reykjavik, we looked among the brochures to see if such a tourist attraction exists and indeed it does. So on a Tuesday morning we walked to the address, rounded a corner and there was a line-up of ten or so tourists waiting for the doors to open. From the exterior it wasn't even vaguely like any museum I've experienced before like the Louvre, Tate, Vatican, British, Egyptian, Guggenheim, or even the museums in Bellingham. Rather, it was on the order of a fish store filled with numerous water tanks at the mall. I don't mean to downgrade either its importance as a place to visit or its contents, but rather to at least note it's not on a grand scale as a physical structure. Its significance is in although its contents, where you are to consider and contemplate the collection of mammal penises that are to be found there. The only pathetic specimen, in my considered opinion, was that of the human species and I'll leave that to your imagination and your own visit. I must say, it's a must see when in Reykjavik, and will definitely give you bragging rights when in casual company at any event if you have the nerve to bring up in a casual conversation (which I definitely have).

Given how much travel I've done in my 86 years, it might appear we are rich, but we are not. It's just that we have learned how to travel and sacrifice what others won't. It's also a little of that Peace Corps mentality, combined with knowing everything won't be what you hope for, but you can go with the flow and still have a great, if not even greater, experience.

Probably all the wrong questions are asked about my favorite travel. My travel is more about how much you don't mind being inconvenienced, are willing to eat foods you don't normally eat, and to get over the idea that just because they speak another or multiple languages doesn't mean you can't get what you want or need—or don't really perhaps need. Hand gestures, facial expressions, sounds that depict what you are seeking, and pointing get you much further than you might imagine. It's not like charades, but it has some similarities in technique: always communicate with a smile—never reflecting annoyance. I've never been to any country in which I could not get done what I wanted to get done, seen, or do. Admit you can't speak the language, but if you are willing to learn just a little, they will respond to your effort to have at least tried. They will laugh and smile with you, not at you. My wife does that very thing with little French, German, Spanish, and some other languages and always gets smiles and gratitude for trying. My wife and I have taken just enough French and German, along with, in my case, Amharic, and her Spanish and Latin (being an English major), to be sufficient in piecing things together when speaking, scratching out on paper, or using translation software on our iPhones.

I do want to mention a few highly unusual travel experiences that I would only suggest to the sturdy—those who can tolerate differences that cultures have in their own ways of doing things, which may not necessarily be your way. These require patience and going with the flow. The first was in Guinea, West Africa, then Morocco, Lithuania, and finally Vanuatu—not exactly places you may have heard of or placed on your bucket list. But you should give them consideration. One tends to do these once you have plenty of experience in both the USA and other more user-friendly countries like Portugal, England, Ireland, New Zealand, and numerous others. But if you want exceptional adventure without frills, the following are full of adventures when willing to adjust while experiencing, and exceptional stories for others to hear upon your return.

We especially wanted to go see Kathleen's son in Guinea in part because he wanted me to see what it was like for him, now a fellow Peace Corps Volunteer, and how it might now differ from my experience of 35 years earlier when the Peace Corps first started. Getting there was one of the biggest, if not most difficult, experiences we have ever faced traveling. Guinea, as it turns out, is not a good place to start your wanderlust years in the world at large. Fortunately, I had loads of travel experience, and it all came in handy in facing what we did.

297

To even get to Guinea from America, you have to fly someplace close to West Africa, like Brussels. The night before our departure from home, at that time living in Santa Monica, California, Kathleen received a call that Nathan was being medevacked back to the USA for a medical need. At the tail end of their conversation, he mentioned he was flying back through Brussels. We already had our non-refundable tickets to go see him through Brussels, so we decided to try and meet in the airport during his six-hour, and our own, layover. The synchronized layovers worked perfectly. Seeing him in person and finding he was being well cared for by the Peace Corps, we decided we had come this far, so we might as well stay. On the spot we created a sidetrack vacation since there was no reason to go to Guinea, where he wasn't going to be for the foreseeable future. We rented a car and drove first to beautiful Bruges, Belgium, to be followed thereafter by some travel to the other Benelux countries. Bruges is a delightful major site to visit, and one particular adventure stood out.

Bruges is truly a city worth a visit. Old and charming, it's as fine an example of Europe as you want to experience. We arrived in our rented car late in the afternoon and as is sometimes our practice we decided to take a nap before venturing out. It had been a long day of travel from the airport and seeing Nathan. As is my practice, however, when reaching a new location and settling into our hotel room, I take a brief walk around the immediate area to get acquainted with where I am and what's available, like some store where I can buy something to drink and snack for the evening. I like to know my new terrain, you might say. I went out and soon discovered what had to be the biggest flea market I had ever seen. Wandering from table to table while hearing a brass band playing in the park, I immediately noted that what was on sale was mostly older than America itself. Fascinating brass ornaments, pots, chandeliers, trinkets, plates, and on and on. And not just small items, but more like body armor from a medieval knight. I had to tell Kathleen what we could see and went immediately back to our room. Still tired, she wasn't ready to tour as much as I was, so we took our nap.

After what seemed like an eternity, we awoke feeling we had slept the night away. The sun was shining, a pleasant change since we had arrived during a slight downpour. We concluded the morning had come and we arose for breakfast. It's was a quaint hotel so we went to the dining room and requested breakfast that came with the price of the room. The waiter looks a little puzzled but soon brought us ham and eggs with toast, with a side of beans and some cooked tomatoes. We soon became aware others were drinking wine and looking at us. What's up? This is breakfast time, isn't it? Not so, we learned as the waiter explained, but he had accommodated us, being the guests we were. It seemed we had not slept the night away; the change of weather had fooled us into thinking it was another day! Those Americans, you just never know. Great breakfast, although the brass band and flea market had long gone before we could truly experience it. So we went on to find other adventures.

A few months passed and we were finally on our rescheduled way to Guinea to see Nathan, for real this time. Back in-country Nathan met us in the capital, Conakry, since his assigned teaching location was way on the other side of the country. He would escort us to his physical location since getting there involved a great deal of planning and execution, as we would all too well soon learn. He was teaching, in French, mathematics to high school students in a small village named, S're'dou. They called him the "God of Math!" and naturally his mother was so honored as, "The Mother of the God of Math." Given that I wasn't his biological father, I was humorously dubbed, as his stepfather, the Faux Papa (there is no stepfather title in French), a title I think came too close to sounding, Fool Papa, but subsequently learned it means the "Queen's Consort,"—a title I definitely deserve and have held now for nigh on 33 years! Aside from that, the real challenge was to get us to his village, 775 kilometers (482 miles), not far from the Ivory Coast. That involved twenty hours of journeying in a series of taxicabs (and I use the term loosely) that he would negotiate from one village to the next, each typically for a stretch of maybe 40 miles at one time, after which they would go no further. Taxis, old rundown Toyotas with 500,000 miles on them, or similar vehicles were to be found in the town square and he negotiated a price per seat. These vehicles were typically without their original interior padding and often wired together in unique combinations whereby, for example, a screwdriver might be used to raise and lower the window. Oh yeah, and a five-passenger car would now be an eight-passenger mode of transportation, with perhaps two riding on the top. As much as we usually liked and preferred the local company, we opted to pay for the extra seats that were available, which would be occupied by our ghost passengers, with only the three of us. I do have my limits. Riding with five other sweaty bodies in a small taxi pushes the limit of comfort traversing in 30 to 40 miles segments one after the other to get where we were going. Of course, in addition to the three of us, there was a driver, and often his assistant. The assistant was kind enough to ride on top for his version of air conditioning. To make it all the more challenging, there were frequent stops at what are called, "Barrages." That's a kind of checkpoint established by a string of plastic shopping bags strung across the road by a couple of local, armed military/police. A few coins were given to the guards with rifles to allow us to pass, and we were on our way again until the next barrage. As I said, 20 hours and a couple of breakdowns later we were finally in his village. Next to the size of the village I had been stationed at in Ethiopia, his village barely qualified for a name on a map.

Nathan's assignment was so much different than mine and it was fun to share our mutual connection as Peace Corps Volunteers of different generations, but of the same continent—mine East and his West Africa. He was the only Peace Corps Volunteer in his village. By contrast I was with 30 Volunteers in mine. He had to go several kilometers to meet up with another volunteer, whereas I could go almost next door. Our experiences were mainly different in scope and the languages used for teaching—his in French, mine in English—but we shared a common bond of relating to students who appreciated our being there. We both came away better souls and wiser people about the world and our role in it, let alone, I am sure, as father and son. Imagine, a week later we had to repeat the several taxi rides getting back to the capital to make our way home. This had been a truly raw, but ever so pleasing adventure in Africa that we both cherish to this very day.

I wanted to include delightful Morocco in my autobiography, not only because it's one of the best travel destinations to experience, but mainly to illustrate an unusual occurrence that demonstrates who you might run into in the world. The world is, in fact, smaller than you think.

As a country and people, Morocco is one of the best examples of the Muslim world and has a special charm about it. During my many travels I've run into people in the world I know in some of the most surprising places that I ever imagined. For instance, there was a former college fraternity brother in London I met in an elevator. Kathleen and I came across a friend of hers while walking around in Santorini on a path overlooking the Mediterranean. There have been others in other corners of the world. None of these compared to what occurred in Morocco.

If you want to experience the Arab world in all its splendor (others would, of course, disagree with me), Morocco's food and charm abound, including a snake charmer or two. An Arab mecca, it has magnificent tile work, ornate wood carvings, the wonderful smell of varied spices, food, all amid winding streets and narrow alleys. We had just arrived in Marrakech and were seated at a sidewalk café, taking in the scenery in the largest public square. The café is on the edge of the gigantic public market area with colorful woven rugs, fresh spices, brass made items, and other such treasures. Long narrow alleys lined with rug or trinket shops enfold you, on both sides. You feel you might get lost, but you never do, and you can always ask for directions to the giant public square we were seated in. As I've noted more than once, I love watching people, like the snake charmer just across the way, while we are sipping Turkish coffee. At one point I turned to my wife, Kathleen, and said, "Now, just how many husbands from Bellingham, Washington, take their wives to Marrakech?" With that, I looked up and to my disbelieving eyes saw a colleague from the food bank where we both volunteer in Bellingham. There was Alan Rhodes, coming our way, so much the world traveler like me, who strode up with his wife. One other story about Marrakech before continuing your journey with me.

I've rarely been to a country where you don't run the risk of getting pickpocketed. I have my personal ways of mitigating such based on numerous travels. It must be an international way to make someone else's money! You quickly learn where to keep your wallet and passport to ensure they won't be lifted. The only place I can think of—besides my hometown—where pickpocketing isn't a concern is on the wonderful island, I've visited many times and shall describe shortly. I know my brother-in-law, John, had his wallet lifted in Rome, and I had someone try it on me in Venice with no success on their part. Well, there in Marrakesh someone tried that trick on Kathleen, and met his match. When he tried lifting some valuables that he thought were in her coat pocket, he only retrieved her reading glasses rather than any other valuables he was hoping to find. Feeling his lateral presence, she turned and scolded him, demanding the return of her spectacles. He was so stunned he immediately complied. I love travel but always be aware of your surroundings.

Half of my wife's heritage from her maternal lineage is Lithuanian, so we just had to go there. Vilnius, the capital of Lithuania, is a charming city with a river passing through and under a series of marvelous bridges you can walk over for the view. While traveling there we had an experience that has made us laugh many a time when recounted with good friends. We were a little tired, so we decided to request a couples massage through the hotel. Soon there was a knock at the door of our third-floor room. I opened it and there stood two beautiful women dressed in what looked like all white nurses' uniforms, down to the tiny, folded hats that completed the outfits. They also had red high heels on, which made me think of other professions closely akin to the strip joint in London and the seedy bar in East St. Louis I had experienced. One look at one another, my wife and I, say, "Why not?" We had lovely massages, and ever so much another quite innocent, sociological experience. Where else but in Lithuania? Well, probably a dozen other countries, I can imagine! If you ever go to Amsterdam, you'll know what I mean.

Finally, I come to a confession about my travel arranging expertise amidst the hundreds of trips that I have done. I am my own travel agent and perform such duties for any and all that go with me as well. I really like to research, plan, and complete arrangements for land, sea, and air. Cheap airline tickets (with upgrades as I have aged), charming three-star hotels and B&Bs, along with an infrequent occasional local tour, and we are all set. However, one time I met my match when booking to a country called Vanuatu. You should find it on the global map or internet just as I had to when I first heard of it and, naturally, had to go one day.

Vanuatu is a Pacific Island nation near Papua New Guinea composed of 83 islands. It was previously known in its colonial days as New Hebrides. I wanted to go there in search of a new island experience since I just love islands and will tell you shortly about my most favorite one. I had scheduled two separate stays at two different modest resorts since we knew virtually nothing about this country and thought that we would want an unusual upgrade while we got to know this second world country to perhaps earmark it for a return visit one day. As I had scheduled, we flew into the country's main airport landing at midnight, as airplanes, in that part of the world, take advantage of the cooler conditions of the night to fly in rather than the heat of the days. We landed and immediately searched for a taxi, told the driver the resort we needed to go to, and he looked at me with a stare that clearly suggested he didn't know what resort I was talking about. This was our first inkling that there might be a slight hiccup with our travel plans I had worked so hard to organize.

Our taxi driver asked a fellow driver a few questions. The other driver knew of the resort we were headed to but informed us that it was located on a different island, a half-hour flight away from where we found ourselves. There was no way we would get there that night. The realization of our situation slowly began to dawn on us: We did indeed have a reservation for the resort on the island where we now stood, but our reservation did not start for another five days. It appeared that I had gotten the locations of the resorts, as well as the dates of the reservations, mixed up. Whoops, what to do? Wait and go a day later? The thing is they only fly there twice a week and back. I conjure up my Peace Corps experience when confronted with such challenges. One needs an immediate action plan and bear in mind the success of solving previous travel problems. But, given the late hour, this is best done on a good nights' sleep.

By this time it was 1:00 a.m. and the taxi driver suggested that he take us to the resort we did have a reservation for during the second half of our journey. We agreed that, given our predicament, this was the best course of action. Get some sleep and then decide what next to do. He drove us there, woke up a security guard he knew—probably a relative—and that person ushered us into a vacant room at 2:00 a.m. to sleep the remnants of the short night away. We were instructed by security to check with the front desk in the morning, to pay for our unregistered night, and ask for their help on what to do next. I thought perhaps they could honor our soon-to-be reservation with them now, and then we would fly to the other island next week, after changing that reservation. But we had no such luck: all bookings were final and besides there was no room available anyhow for the days we needed. Pretty much exhausted by now, we decide to go to breakfast at the resort's restaurant and begin planning what to do next.

While sitting there eating our breakfast we began conversing with our waiter who commiserated with us concerning our situation. It turns out, he informed us, his grandmother owned two vacation housing units, and was building a third. Never mind it was on another island, just a half-hour journey by banana boat from the island we were on. And to make it a complete travel package, his cousin and his other cousin had, respectively, a transportation van and a banana boat. It looked like we suddenly had a complete tour package a' la a third world nation! We seized on the opportunity (noting it was the only one available at the moment) and the next thing you know we—along with all the luggage we were carrying—are seated on a van along with seven others packed with their goods, to go to that new island we had never known existed.

Imagine, if you will, there are 83 islands that comprise this nation! We couldn't wait to see them all! The banana boat was crammed full of supplies for the island people, including by the way, actual bananas.

Half an hour later, we pulled up on the small island shore—not a dock—jumped in the water and two guys acted like safari porters with our bags on their heads. We all trekked down the shore a hundred meters or so to what looked like two shacks. It seemed his grandma had had her husband build two corrugated-roofed, single room structures with stucco walls to give her two sons something to own and do in life and, and she would manage such accommodations until the boys found their way in life. There was no lighting other than a single bulb hanging from the ceiling, powered by a (short-lived) battery she provided us, no indoor plumbing, no heating needed in the tropics (could use some AC, but I am not about to complain about the lack of it), and an outhouse 30 feet down a path with a rain barrel where you scooped water to flush, as well as take a shower (pouring water over your head from a scoop) if you so needed. Three meals were prepared by Grandma who did not speak any English. There were no stores on the island of 300 or so inhabitants, no roads, no cars, and no medical facilities should you need them. We settled in for our five-day stay.

As you can guess the days were quiet, the ocean waves lapped at the shoreline, and occasionally you might see a local on the beach fishing. You had to be your own entertainment as there was no radio, TV, and very spotty internet service with no streaming. Since your iPhone would run down, you relied on Grandma to recharge its battery with her one and only solar panel. Two days into our stay, another outsider, a German, showed up. He was working in Australia in the Outback and came away from that for some sun and isolation. He got plenty of both and provided some conversation that was nice to have. Otherwise there wasn't much to do and we took full advantage of being truly away from civilization.

On the one Sunday we were there I observed a small group of women and children, well dressed in local attire, scurrying down a jungle covered path behind our "bungalow." Due to the curiosity I have for anything out of the ordinary, I followed them till they came to a clearing where a hundred or so people were seated on the ground near the shore. As it was Sunday, I decided that there was soon to be a church service. They were all seated on the ground with blankets to lie on, except for three chairs at the front with the ocean in the background. I hurried back to get Kathlen, we dressed appropriately (for foreigners), retraced the well-worn path, and sat on the perimeter of those gathered, not wanting to intrude too conspicuously. People smiled and nodded in welcome to us, even offering some fruit morsels to nosh on. The singing was outstanding in a chorus of anthem, back and forth, between women and men with deep bass voices. Then a tall young man, who we learned was leaving the island to go to seminary studies, was being honored with a sendoff. Everyone there came and hugged, kissed, and said goodbye to him one by one. What a perfect vacation experience. You could not have prearranged that adventure no matter who you booked with, including Trip Advisor. It was one of the best, if not the very most interesting sociological experiences we have ever had in all our travels, and we have had plenty. Most times, Danny knows how to get around for a boy from Idaho, but not absolutely every time! Still, he (and he's lucky to have a partner) goes with the flow to have memorable adventures.

I'll close my many travel experiences and their associated addictions with mention of what is my very favorite place in the world to be. When I say favorite, I don't mean as some kind of vacation, although it is certainly that, but a place to go and live and relax and just be. It's idyllic in every sense of Bali Hai without being Bali Hai. The thing is, I won't tell you the name of this place! It's not that I am mean, but I am trying to protect it more than save it just for us. Its long sandy shores and sunsets are breathtaking, its people so nice and willing to share with you, and it has very few Americans that know of or go to it. There are a couple of other usual nationalities that show up but revealing them might help you deduce the location to a part of the vast oceans that occupy 85% of the earth, which would leave only 15% of the remaining land area to guess and explore until you find it. Part of this is so that you will travel and find your own island or country through your own experiences, not mine. If I told you to go to Disneyland and you hated it, that would not be nice. If I told you my favorite place and you hated it, that would be my bad and perhaps unpleasant experience and waste of money. So I suggest you find your own. I have a couple of stories about this favorite place that I hope will encourage you to find your own stories (but not discover the coordinates to my island).

There is more than one island to this favorite place. We always stay on the largest island because it has wonderful beaches, a Saturday Market, and all the other things to make for a complete island experience. We have gone to two of its outer islands just to see what was up since they are so well spoken about. The first of these is the next largest of the island chain and has a magnificent lagoon to snorkel and to send pictures back home to make others envy where you are. There was an experience on this island that I have told many times and will always endear me to the people of my favorite place in the world to go.

I had never operated a scooter before, but we were staying in a small habitat, and they had scooters for rent and were willing to have me practice on one in a field until I mastered it, and then, I could get licensed. I went into the field, and just like riding a bicycle, but with much greater speed and potential harm to you, I got the hang of it.

One morning we wanted some local fruit for breakfast, and I head out on one of the very few roads on this small island, knowing that I couldn't possibly get lost. I initially discovered a small local combination gas station and grocery store, but there was no fruit to be had. I was directed to the one and only local dock, since practically all the fruit consumed on the island arrives there. Needed supplies usually originate from the main island by airplane (that we have just left and to which we will soon return) or a monthly cargo ship. I made my way to the dock, and again no fruit, so I am thinking there will be no fruit on this island during our stay. I decided while out there to take a longer shaky ride on the scooter that I had not quite mastered (still without a driver's license) to see what I could explore on this island. To make it even more daring, the roads on this island often have large land crabs regularly crossing the roads.

This island is fairly small, and I was nearly to the other end of it when I stopped at a roundabout. I was trying to decide which of the remaining two roads I might choose or if I should turn back from whence, I had come before I really did get lost. I was there literally by myself on that scooter, having seen no other traffic, when another scooter with a woman about my age showed up and stopped next to me. We smiled at each other! She said, in perfectly good English, "I've been looking for you!" "Really?" I said with some curiosity as to why that would be. "I've got this pineapple for you," she said. With that she got off her scooter, opened the seat cover, and handed over a perfectly shaped and ripe pineapple. She had pursued me for at least 4 kilometers and wanted me to have that piece of fruit, found no place else, apparently. It's representative of the kind of travel experiences I truly cherish. I'll describe just one other recent example of getting to truly experience a culture, then we will leave my favorite island for one final travel story and the profound effect it has had upon my very being as a human desirous to be in contact with others throughout the world.

We were recently on "our island" again for the 17th time, and especially glad to be there, since my 85th birthday would occur while there. Near where we always stay, we noted a relatively new marae, many of which dot the island in various neighborhoods. A marae is a kind of gathering spot for each neighborhood. It's a holdover from their more tribal days where villagers would gather for important events at the beckoning of the chief and elders. They serve today as a place where people gather socially, if not spiritually. They are places where the long traditions are emphasized and passed on through sharing of stories, craftmanship, and a significant space to embrace the elderly for their wisdom and need to be recognized as people still of value. Older "mommas," whose husbands have since passed to glory, come, and share their loneliness and pass on to their grandchildren, gathered there with them, their craftmanship and deep love of one another. It's something we in America should learn to emulate in our sterile "communities" where there is no passing on of culture, let alone valuing of the wisdom of elders.

This marae was having an exhibit of their beautiful cloth work and we stopped in to have a look. Mommas Jennifer and Vaine, as well as the younger Tumutoa and her young daughter that live in the neighborhood, greeted us and made us feel right at home. Over the next few days, Kathleen came back again and again to talk and share her own artwork and an immediate bond was established between the ladies. As it turned out, in a couple of days there would be a final gathering for the year, with a dinner of fine food prepared by the mommas, and they invited Kathleen to come and bring along her husband, who they had only seen once during the initial visit, so on the appointed day we went. We sat at the end of a lengthy line of 20 or so plastic chairs on which mostly elders (of our own age) sat facing where the meal would soon take place. But before the meal was begun several of the ladies stood and took the opportunity to express their appreciation of one another for their kindship and what having a marae means to each of them. It was very touching to get to know not only their lives at the same moment of my own dotage, but that we were sharing many similar feelings about our long lives lived. As is my custom when these kinds of gathering present themselves in any part of the world, I stood in turn to thank them for sharing with us and being allowed to say who we are as a couple. We obviously bonded with many smiles, laughter, and even the fact that it happened to be my 85th birthday, and they sang "Happy Birthday, Danny," as well as, "Long Live Danny," to the same tune. We supped together and the local food was quite good. As we left, many called me Papa—a sign that I was now considered one of them. I can't adequately tell you what it is like to connect with so many different cultures in my travels and realize how we are all fellow human beings seeking to find ourselves, express what we have done, and how we are so much alike with everyone else, but uniquely different. I've had these kinds of experiences happen on my favorite island at least four times in different ways and other places in the world in other ways. On our island we have made good friends, like Dora and Glynne, and now we go annually (minus COVID). We have Tuesday Taco Night once a week and that's been going on for 17 wonderful years. Do find your island no matter if it's in the next county, state, or country.

I'll close my travel adventures with one, surreal travel experience that reflects the glory of not only the continent of Africa, which has meant so much to me, but to the person who brought me into this world to experience it.

I wanted to take Kathleen back to that part of Africa (Kenya, Tanganyika, Uganda) where I had first seen all the various wild animals that call this land home. We would, of course, begin in Ethiopia, where I had lived for two years as a Peace Corps Volunteer. We went to Ethiopia as an extension of having been invited to speak in Kuwait at an HR conference. We first visited my old teaching school in Harar, but the school had unfortunately been shut down since the revolution of 1974. Still, the charm of Harar was present. We even saw a hyena one night from our hotel as we stayed for a few days and walked around. Its presence there in the still of the night, around 3:00 a.m., reminded me of those hyenas I visited under a streetlamp 32 years earlier. It was fun to revisit and remember the time in Harar, and noting that while Ethiopia was progressing, it still had room to go. Too soon, it was time to move on.

As we were making our way by air from Harar back to Addis Ababa to board an airplane to Kenya, we had one of those travel experiences that was totally unplanned for, but which we were blessed to have experienced. We were flying from Dire Dawa (near Harar) to the capital of Addis Ababa. It's typically an uneventful two-hour flight, yet within an hour of our flight we descended and landed on a dirt field that I had no idea we were scheduled for. It was on the edge of an area much like the Grand Canyon, but even more spectacular, if you can imagine. Seems this stop was not on the flight path I had reviewed and scheduled for us, but the airlines in third-world countries sometimes have their own schedule to meet local needs of life and necessity. So we landed in this field (think dirt and grass) lined with rocks that had been painted white to mark the two sides of the runway. We taxied and parked fifty yards from the massive canyon edge. We all got out and milled around the grassy area—certainly no security or TSA here! After ten minutes, from over a hill comes what looks like a parade of six people, well-dressed in local colorful attire, sporting a couple of very colorful umbrellas to shade themselves from the hot sun, and carrying satchels of clothing and other goods. There is, you can guess, no enclosed terminal, nor flight control personnel, no emergency equipment if needed, and no one else except us passengers and the crew and new passengers standing there in a field. We all get on the plane again with our new travel companions, take off over the Grand Canyon of Ethiopia and realize we have experienced an adventure not on any travel brochure that I am aware of. You further see, I hope, what I love about travel. It's sometimes the unexpected events (like the time I scheduled to the wrong island) and all that they provide to enhance your life experiences, and your storytelling. An overnight stay in Addis Ababa, and we are on our way to Kenya and Tanzania.

Unscheduled Stopover in dirt field between Dire Dawa and the capital, Addis Ababa, Ethiopia to let some locals board the plane

Just before we reached Mt. Kilimanjaro, during a stopover in Moshi, I learned my dear mother had died at age 85. Our first thought, of course, was canceling our journey and returning home immediately. However, after a phone call with my sister, Lucille, and her ever-present, head-on-his-shoulders husband, John, the conversation culminated in a plan that would delay our return home to a time after Christmas when all the family would gather to celebrate her life. So we continued our journey and eventually came upon the plains of the Serengeti. I'll never forget what happened there early one morning, so emblematic of life and death.

I was sitting in the back seat of a Land Rover, driven by our guide. I had my head down, and was in deep thought about my mother, when I looked up and there before me were hundreds, if not a thousand or more, animals. My quiet reflection about all that she had done for her son was startled by the sounds of numerous animals hooves, as if a herd of horses were in full gallop. I stood erect in the jeep with my head out the roof top and the sound grew louder, clouds of dust rising everywhere. All these animals were in migration, and they mixed together without fear of one another. They wove back and forth across the barely visible dirt roads and paths like a winding river. It had the same impact on me as the river of migrating fish, as far as the eye could see, that I saw many years later off the coast of my favorite island. You could even swim with the fish (they were Striped Bristletooth) as the swarm parted around your body. You just kind of hold your breath and take it in as best you can, for you know a moment like this will never be seen by you again. Who knows if you'll keep going places and be privy to unusual occurrences such as hundreds of fish or wild animals in migration or seeing a solitary mighty Rocky Mountain Bighorn sheep just standing alone on an Idaho hillside. It's not dissimilar to experiencing the Milky Way on a dark starry night without any man-made light to detract the view, or the northern lights when you see them for the first time in Iceland. As I stood erect in that land rover, I thanked my mother for her constant love and for being such an example to her son. Travel brings out the best in us if we but experience it and let it reveal what the world, or the universe, has to offer. At her passing, she had 22 grandchildren, 36 great-grandchildren, and 10 great-great-grandchildren. Nice legacy for a woman who had offered so much during her time with us! We were all her lucky children!

CHAPTER 10

Danny Setting His Compass

As I previously traced my journey in my youth from East to West, then South to North, it involved generally exploring and getting comfortable with my immediate environment, then expanding to the greater world. That was well and good in my youth, as I was finding my way mostly physically around the immediate community with others and getting some much-needed bearing for a growing kid, youth, and teen. What I want to address now is also a kind of different compass setting with a more granular view of what I felt I did to become a man, professional, easy and adventurous traveler, and human in relation to others into the world at large. That is, if it could be distilled so, to describe how I became a responsible person who is comfortable with himself—professionally and spiritually—and with society around the world.

As I am nearing the conclusion of my life and looking back, especially having done so in the writing of this autobiography, I consider myself to have been a particularly good human being who lived an active, creative, and productive life. This is largely confirmed for me by what others have said, the most important spokesperson being my partner in life and business, my wife, who considers me a good husband. I've been labeled by some, even strangers upon first meeting, as an "old soul," by professional colleagues concerning my model for business as a bit of a shaman, and in general by friends who have told me I am an all-around good guy and husband, as well as by my children who have told me what it was like for them to have me as their father.

Of course we all come with certain innate traits and emotional characteristics, shaped by the setting in which we were born and raised, as well as by those who were involved with our life experiences. I was lucky to have had a warm and loving family and a safe community in which to explore and grow, all while living in a rather unconventional environment—one that allowed for exploration by a very curious boy like me. Beyond all that, I have with forethought done certain things to set or guide a vision of life for myself and with the ones I cherish the most, as well as in relations with friends and total strangers, both here and abroad. So what did I do proactively to become a good and productive person? Much of this you have hopefully gleaned from the description given thus far of my life, but I'd like to focus here on a few of my self-development goals—what I am calling here the compass I set for myself. In this way these may become useful lessons learned and of some guidance for others. These are best understood in four developmental categories:

Personal

Social

Professional, and

Spiritual

To the extent I may seem to lecture in this section of my memoir, I apologize. But please know that I have good intentions rather than telling you how to do things, passing judgement, or seemingly bragging. Any good teacher wants to pass on their wisdom, and I have been a teacher, in one form or another, for nearly 65 of the 86 years of my life.

Personal Development

I Decided to Learn Who I Am and What I am Capable Of

I developed confidence from the activities I engaged in and was successful at, as well as what I wasn't so good at. And I tried lots of things.

314

Those I didn't do well, I did not let bother me as a FAILURE. Instead each became a lesson learned, or as my wife so eloquently remarks, "an interesting sociological experience." Perhaps the rattlesnakes of my life taught me what one must do in life to continue to grow: confront, go around, or learn to be more cautious the next time. Mostly I observed challenges in front of me to learn what each was about in their relationship to me. Only then did I act and learn what I was capable of for future action and reaction. The snakes of my world and I must live together, and that's true of virtually everything. I can't stand bats, but there they are, flying around my house during the nights I want to sleep on the deck and see the Big Dipper in the Milky Way, shooting stars, and satellites. Bats actually do good by eating mosquitoes and other bugs, so I must live with them around my house. Mosquitos like me and drive me nuts, but that's what anti-itch cream is for. I adjusted and even learned how to use a hair dryer, of all things, to ease the scratching. Lots of metaphors there, but you get the idea.

In addition to using an attuned self-awareness, there were available tools I made use of to learn who I am and how I could best respond to various things and negotiate or navigate generally with other people in life, especially my partner in life and business. Here are some of those tools I made use of, mostly discovered in my professional role as a trainer and researcher.

Right Brain/Left Brain Profile

During the early part of my professional career, I worked with a man who would become a dear friend and colleague. He, beyond his teaching skills, was a leading expert in Right/Left Brain Theory. This was a self-awareness framework espoused by Ned Herman in the 1980s. Gene Myers, whom I had the privilege of working with at two companies (I kept taking him with me), was one of the two leading experts in deploying a tool for measuring so-called "brain dominance." Gene conducted one of the early surveys on me and my staff at one of our first meetings. The results showed that I was far-left brain dominant, meaning highly analytical, which was not surprising since I am a logical, systems thinker and doer with a science background. However ten years later he retested me and I had had a major shift (enhancement, really) to the right which marked me as then a more holistic person of action. It was the biggest shift, according to Gene, that he and Ned had ever found in their careers. There were things that I had done that caused this kind of shift, and I'll get to these. The summary of my second brain profile reads as follows:

"Your profile, a 1-2-1-1, represents a person who is multi-dominant in the following ways: double dominant in the cerebral mode, both left and right, and also with a primary dominance in the right limbic mode. Individuals with this profile would have capabilities for very effective logical, analytic processing on the one hand, and integrative, synthesizing, holistic conceptualization on the other. Their processing would also be characterized by a preference and sensitivity for interpersonal relations and emotional activity."

If you ask my wife, that is me through and through. I wasn't always that way, as I noted in the mention of my shift/enhancement from left to right brain dominance. Initially I was a little too logical (and stuck) in my thinking, lack of sharing myself with others, and a bit of a bore, often with no smile on my face. I changed myself, through certain interventions that I'll shortly elaborate on, and I became more people-oriented and engaging. Knowledge of this became useful in my personal life, but especially in professional interactions with others, since I was a training manager who had to manage a staff and deal with our internal, and later in my own business with external, customers.

Enneagrams

On a second occasion, about the time of my divorce and move to California where I connected with the woman who became my second wife, Kathleen and I regularly attended a magnificent community-centered church. We built a strong group of friends, single and married, of both gay and straight persuasion. We often met at our condominium for church-related or pure social events, and we all became close friends. The church offered a different tool: the Enneagram, administered to me and others to build both understanding of one another and how better to relate in social and church sponsored activities. I was in my 50s. It, like the Brain Dominance Profile, did something similar towards helping me realize more of who I was and could be, and how to relate to others. From the Enneagram I learned that I was considered a 5, "The Investigator," while my wife was a 3, "The Achiever."

The 5 is known as an Investigator because, more than any other type, this person wants to find out why things are the way they are. They want to understand how the world works, whether it is the cosmos, the microscopic world, the animal, vegetable, or mineral kingdoms—or the inner world of their imaginations. They are always searching, asking questions, and delving into things in depth. They do not accept received opinions and doctrines, rather feeling a strong need to test the truth of most assumptions for themselves. My being a 5 is strongly confirmed by the many new learning methods I developed in my career, as well as the Work Formula that I originated and made a business of.

The 3 is The Achiever. When these types of individuals are healthy in their relationship with the world, they can and do achieve important things. They are "stars" of human nature, and people often look up to them because of their graciousness and personal accomplishments. They are usually well regarded and popular among their peers, the type of person who is frequently voted "class president" or "homecoming queen" because people feel they want to be associated with this kind of person. That's the kind of person Kathleen is.

According to the experts on the Enneagram here is a description of Threes and Fives that accurately reflects the relationship that Kathleen and I have as soul partners:

Threes and Fives are a combination that is frequent, but unexpected because they are so different, but can be so compatible in supporting each other's goals in life. The Fives often give Threes depth, new areas of expertise and credibility, while sparking creativity. Threes give Fives confidence, presentation skills, and awareness of the importance of communicating effectively with others. Both Threes and Fives are primarily focused on their work and on objective issues and concerns; especially in their professional areas where they support each other in outstanding ways. Although both have deep feelings, both tend not to focus on them for the sake of getting on with their work and relationship—with personal relationship superseding work. They tend to understand each other's need to balance closeness with their need for personal space.

I can say with certainty that all these qualities, and others, represent how Kathleen and I relate in life and business. It has been such a pleasure to work with her in both environments.

For additional information to determine and use your Enneagram, you may investigate your type on the Enneagram Institute website at: https://www.enneagraminstitute.com

Myers-Briggs

My wife and I are complete opposites in most personality tests we take. That's not bad, in any way, as it merely indicates our differences and similarities, so we know what strengths of each we have to build on, and how to deal with differences through our communication and actions.

In the Myers-Briggs personality indicator, I am an ISTP, while Kathleen is considered an ENFP.

A concise description from the Myers/Briggs Foundations website describes me and my wife as:

Danny: ISTP: Introverted, Sensing, Thinking, and Perceptive

ISTPs are realists who apply expediency and reasoning as they manage and adapt to situations. They are aware of what is going on in the environment and are able to respond quickly to the actual facts, making sure the odds of success are in their favor. They do not like

to be tied down and will feel hamstrung when they must operate within tight structures and schedules. They are able to anticipate immediate, practical needs in situations and to present a logical, straightforward plan for meeting those needs. They are at their best in situations that require immediate attention.

It turns out that less than 6 % of the US population has my type, so it is not surprising that not everyone has even met someone like me.

Kathleen*:* ENFP: Extroverted, Intuitive, Feeling and Perceptive.

ENFPs are initiators of change who are keenly perceptive of possibilities, and who energize and stimulate through their contagious enthusiasm. They prefer the start-up phase of a project or relationship and are tireless in the pursuit of new-found interests. They are able to anticipate the needs of others and to offer them needed help and appreciation. They bring zest, joy, liveliness, and fun to all aspects of their lives. They are at their best in situations that are fluid and changing, and that allow them to express their creativity and use their charisma.

As is to be noted, both of us share the Myers/Briggs "P," which can sometimes cause people to keep seeing options, rather than deciding to "get it done." Fortunately, we can be rather "J" for Judgment, and so life is good together. Which may explain why we get so much done together.

These three self-assessment instruments I and my wife (and often friends and colleagues we managed or work with) took advantage of to learn who we are and how we can better relate with others. They are ways of analyzing who we are, as well as understanding how others are different from us—not less than, nor better than, but different than! With this knowledge of myself, I became better at interacting with others at home, socially, and in the office. These assessments revealed or confirmed my strengths and weaknesses. I could choose to work on my strengths to get stronger in them, but also to know where I could improve on some of my weaker traits. I haven't felt the need to seek help from experts for help – yet. This knowledge of self allows me to let others (like my wife/business partner in my case) do what I cannot do. For example, I am lousy at editing and should not pretend I am otherwise. I am also not as good at summarizing findings or attending to client needs as well as Kathleen. But we also work well together because we have that knowledge of self, and we have lots of discussions about supporting each other's strengths and not focusing on our (inevitable) weaknesses.

We were clear about three elements with respect to understanding our personalities and their interactions:

1. If we were in conflict in a client engagement, we made the decision based on what supported the client's interests, rather than our own personal preferences.
2. We made sure our relationship between ourselves was more important than that of any client relationship. We never had to make that choice, but they assured us we work well together.
3. We respect the intellect that we each bring to our mutual professional efforts.

These realizations are part of the patchwork of figuring out who you and others are and how you will interface with the world to maximize performance and relationships. They are puzzle pieces for self-awareness and action.

I Fostered My Curiosity

We are all born with a natural curiosity about things. The thing is, like a flower, curiosity needs proper nutrients and water to flourish. Due to the circumstances I was born into—a playground of metal and other items—I was privy to an enormous number of stimuli that piqued and fostered my curiosity. What is that thing? How does it work? What was it composed of? In the junkyard and the playground in which I played, I saw and could take things apart or assemble them in new ways that were right there in front of me without fear of any kind of retribution. There were cars, motors, wires, parts I had no idea what they were, and gadgets of all sorts. These things I could mess with and then could always return afterwards as junk or assemble or reconfigure to new intended use.

My curiosity did find other outlets in my youth: in exploring the canyon near my neighborhood, then into my greater community, and then to the world at large where I have traveled and explored new adventures and interacted with foreigners as much as possible. As a result throughout my life I have been disassembling and assembling all kinds of ideas, be it a new instructional design for learning, a formula for work, or something around the home or farm. I credit my love of writing, education, creating, and my professional career, as well as my volunteering and commitment to leading a caring and quality life to my curiosity without retribution by others. And it all worked; even when I went to the wrong island. I think the freedom, safety and opportunities of my generation helped foster curiosity more than any internet game can do today or AI has the potential to do in the future.

I Made Up for My Lack of Book Reading

I have often joked with others that I have authored more books than I have read from cover to cover. If you include the 13 books I've written, as well as the chapters in a dozen others by various authors, and the 40-volume series I originated and edited, then the statement might be true. I am not necessarily proud of this, but it is what it is, and I've successfully compensated and feel very comfortable overall in my reading, writing, and comprehension skills. Why is that so and what did I do to make up for the lack of book reading?

I am a little envious when I learn about the reading habits of others, or when I'm not able to participate in a casual group setting when the latest books are being discussed. It's just that I have always gotten tired while trying to read novels and my attention span is relatively short. My wife, for example, is a voracious reader. She often tells me about the current stories she is reading, and I am relegated to listening more than participating, although I do ask pertinent questions to learn more.

321

It's pretty obvious where the source lies in my not really enjoying book reading: the first grade. Struggling with the introduction to reading by being introduced to two different methods of learning to read really had a profound effect that took a few years to learn how to cope with and work around. Fortunately, I compensated over the years and did get better at reading by using various sources other than books. I consciously use these other sources to this day on a continuing basis. Due to this intentional effort, by all measures I am a learned person. I hope how I did this is a lesson useful to those, like me, who struggle with becoming informed and knowledgeable. Here are the sources I use(d).

In my youth I found a source of reading that appealed to me, and I think it got me on the road to other subsequent sources of reading. It may not seem too relevant to the hardcore book reader, but I remember in my early grade school days I liked to read the then popular comic book series known as Classics Illustrated. This was a series of over one hundred "great novels" shortened into a comic book version with illustrations that told their tales. From such classics as *Gulliver's Travels* to *The Mutiny on the Bounty*, a subscription brought a monthly Classic comic book; I looked forward to the new read with great anticipation. I even constructed a latched bookcase where I kept them under lock and key. I also subscribed to another series titled, *Stories By Famous Authors Illustrated.* Well-worn, I still have both of these illustrated works. I keep them both as collectors' items and as a remembrance of what I learned. Not exactly the usual best seller list or book-of-the-month many read, but still to use as a kid—a step up from reading comic comics, such as *Superman*, that I rarely read.

Of course, I had to do assigned reading in school, but even that was a task I did more in a skimming fashion than by deep reading. Keeping my attention, getting tired, and I think a little of the lack of word meaning seem to get in my way of enjoying reading. So I have to find and read other sources of personal interest to me and I work at it. These include sources I have enumerated elsewhere such as extensive use of researching in the libraries in my youth and college days, consistently reading magazines and newsprint, today using the internet for facts, news, and research, and generally measured listening to experts (such as scientists) and learned people (Joseph Campbell would be a good example). I also simply love the stories from the American science documentary series, NOVA. There are other more contemporary sources such as audio books, and lately, in the writing of this book, I've used the READ ALOUD feature found on my laptop for various print resources. Even my iPhone has become a source of reading material for me.

Fortunately, I am a good listener as well and seem to readily pick up on the words and phrases used. Thus, I think you will by now agree, I am able to know, write, think, and talk about subjects with clarity, insight, style, and, of course, humor. I have an above average vocabulary and know how to express wit and wisdom. And I rely on editing by others certainly more skilled than I, such as my wife, friends, and paid editors (i.e., Roby and Bonnie) whom I've come to know quite well. This is all said not to brag, but to know there are other ways to be educated other than purely by reading alone—a lesson for those who are bored with traditional schooling. For those of us who struggled in school to learn to read, to then know and use the alternatives to learning and enjoyment is incredibly important. We can succeed given the encouragement of others (my mother, teachers, parents, friends, a spouse) through the use of unconventional means and resources.

I Kept Myself Informed

I have prided myself on keeping informed. I think that is why, from an early age, I liked listening to the news. As an old person I listen to the news a couple times a day.

Keeping accurately informed was easier in the good old days because our news sources were pretty dependable and not as self-serving as today. On the radio we listened to drama, game shows, mysteries, news summaries, documentaries, and lots of music. TV was introduced during my generation (in my case around 1953). The mild-mannered content, initially in black and white only, then in color, was done live, as were most of the commercials. There was little in it that was ever scary, sexual, or pushed boundaries by promoting falsehoods, no ridiculous reality shows (that are not really reality) or pundits pushing their narrative.

I found the news pretty dependable, with just 3 networks that were much the same in their straightforward presentation and content—not like today when some are very much one-sided, sometimes inaccurate, and others just lie; so, take your pick—carefully! And while commercialism with ads was present then, it wasn't as dominant as it is today, with far too many ads pushing what drugs you should consume, products you just really need, or drinks you should drink. Even the emphasis on news today is much too short of real content, vying instead for our attention by using short, snappy content and sensationalism that the media creators feel will gain our attention and pocketbook. And there are far too many ads with the news, because the news half-hour today must also carry its share of the advertising cost, whereas in my day it didn't because it was the news. Today it seems it would be more accurate to label the news "The Ads," rather than "The News."

Though the print medium of keeping informed seems to be going away because of electronic media, I still try to read print sources like *Time*, *Newsweek*, *The Week*, and I subscribe to *The Seattle Times*. These I can pour over and reread at my leisure and give careful thought to. I discern the truth: I evaluate between those obviously trying to dissuade me from truth or redefine what they then call the truth (which it isn't) and what I should really confirm as true myself, not by them. I read with a discerning view those whose articles and essays are telling me how I should think—especially evangelists of both news and religion. It isn't that hard to tell really; I have to watch that my bias doesn't get in the way of "truth." I do think that because I have extensively traveled the world, I often have perspectives that help get to truth. To that end I do listen to a little Al Jazeera, BBC, plenty of PBS, Japan News, and a smidgen of the crazies, just to know what they are crazy about.

I have found the internet challenging to use as a source when it comes to being informed. There is such a thing as being too informed—for example about nonsense. I do read the electronic media feed on my iPhone while ignoring much of the entertainment and buzz that is a time filler more than being meaningfully informative. The entertainment segments are mostly useless. I use the internet mostly for emails, staying in touch with family and friends, occasional texting, and some Zoom calls. You might call me a troglodyte, but I use modern media sparingly, so I don't get all overwhelmed or caught up in it as if it were an important part of living, which it truly isn't. I kind of feel a bit sorry for the youth of today with their eyes constantly on their screens rather than the world around them. They need their own version of a junkyard (whatever that might look like) to fashion their imagination and curiosity, like I had.

Finally, as far as being informed, it has always served me well to listen more than to talk. I guess I've concluded it's a good idea to back away from the internet more and listen to yourself and others in person. I want to see the truth, not make it up.

I Embraced Risk Taking and the Necessity for Change to Get Better

I was (and am) a risktaker and I was comfortable with doing all the youthful things I did and have continued to do as an adult. I believe there is an unavoidable link between risk-taking and proactively engaging to change if one is to improve oneself. In other words, I probably won't change without taking a risk to do so. Thus, measured risk-taking is a behavior to get comfortable with, as is change. It's a conundrum, I know. We can't learn nearly enough unless we are willing to change. For example, traveling to strange and seemingly uncomfortable places is a useful way to practice risk taking leading to getting used to foreigners—or one can stick to virtually negligible risk by exclusively traveling on a cruise ship. I found that travelling to seemingly uncomfortable places may not always get me exactly what I wanted or paid for (remember arriving on the wrong island) but I would learn to adjust. The adventure actually got better, or okay enough, in retrospect—much better than complaining and feeling sorry for myself. Getting the genuine experience—not the luxury—of travel, like riding third class on a train in India, is a vastly difference experience from the comfort of a tour group on a bus. These are examples of learning how to become comfortable with risk taking as an adult in order to realize the greater adventure (and growth in confidence in your abilities).

Much of my learning to take risks was experienced as a child growing up—consider that for your children and take them out into the world to practice and get used to things they might otherwise not be so comfortable with. For example, get them to volunteer to help others and see how they react to strangers in need. I know it helped me face life much better when my mother took me to see polio patients in our local hospital. As a result, I did my own thing with my scout troop to collect money and buy records that were much appreciated in the children's ward.

In the scrap iron heaps—junkyards—of my youth, I took all kinds of risks with sharp and rusty objects. In the canyons of my hometown I explored other risks. Hell, I would decide to walk up a mountain or run around a lake just to see if I could. I survived and learned, and other adventures just seemed easier to take on and learn new things because of it. Remember, I stuck my finger in a light socket when I was a teen because I was shown by a trusted adult that it's actually safe if you get your mind around it. That knowledge actually came in handy when I had an electric fence around the entire perimeter of my little six-acre farm. Knowing what electricity can and cannot do, I didn't have to race back to the power source to turn it off, then run back to the spot in the pasture where there was an issue to fix the electrical wire that had grounded or broken. I fixed it down in the pasture, where I first saw it was a problem, and knew what I could do about it. There are ways around electricity and the shock that it gives, as there are with so many other things we do in life. When my wife—also a risktaker—and I landed on the wrong island, we initiated a work around (a form of change). The vacation turned out even better for the opportunity to face up to my mistake and take the risk of going to another adventurous island.

To engage in virtually any of the risks I've already noted, I had to learn to embrace the notion that change is a necessity if I was ever to learn new ways. Charles Darwin, the imminent naturalist, is once quoted to have said "It is not the strongest of the species that survives, nor the most intelligent, but the one most responsive to change." Thus, it's accurate to say that risk taking and change go hand in hand. To say that we humans resist change is to put it mildly, so recognizing the need to get comfortable (or uncomfortable) with change is paramount to getting better. So I readily embraced both risk taking and change as things I had to concur with to get better as a human being.

I have always considered myself a work in progress. Of course, everyone is in their individual way, but in my case, it was a little more deliberate and planned. And I am, even if it takes a while to recognize, always open to change. I can resist it at times, but eventually if it proves needed, I go for it. My wife knows well that I may need encouragement to change more than once, but once I commit, I am all in. And it's a never-ending recognition of what I am and what needs to change. There was a particular place and time when I committed to change and presenting it here will demonstrate where a good education pays dividends.

When I was in graduate school, my graduate advisor, Dr. John Rufi, said during one of his lectures, "Change is needed and that's not all that bad!" I can't tell you exactly why I found that statement so profound, but I latched onto it. It was made even more relevant when I subsequently became a change agent in my professional life for 50 years. My work was mostly all about change. For example, I developed and implemented various kinds of new behaviors for individuals, groups, and whole businesses. This included training programs for changing people's jobs and core process improvements and the very culture of a company. I innovated methods of change, such as my Language of Work Model™. I also became an expert on numerous ways of change—interventions, as we in the profession call them—and compiled a book called, *The Interventions Resources Guide*. (It's available in Korean if you want to read in that language.) But I want to mainly describe what I did myself, on the personal level for me, as it was a conscientious effort to change my behaviors when and where I realized the need. For instance, when my brother's friends often noted, "Danny's awfully quiet," I realized I needed to do something about it. When others said at the office that I was too serious looking, I needed to learn to smile more. I wanted to be better, so I took the risk—yes, these are all kinds of risks—how to be better.

Here's one of the more dramatic examples of change on the personal level that I engaged. I decided to improve one particular aspect of my husbandly role. Credit for helping me recognize this particular need for change should be awarded to my wife, Kathleen. The change derived from times when we were discussing an issue or problem important to our relationship and how I was not really helping her in the way she asked. She has made me aware that my role is not to provide my answer to the problem she is addressing for herself. In fact, me providing an answer diminished her own feeling that she was capable of solving the problem herself! She made me realize she is fully capable of solving her own problems and what she needs is to be heard and affirmed, not provided with my solution to her need. Does not that seem familiar to us men who think we have all the answers? Her feedback to me, and my commitment to make myself better—to make a change—in our marriage helped me to improve myself and one aspect of our discussion of things. So I made changes in me, the person who could do it. After all, only you can change yourself.

I Proactively Take Care of Things

I believe in resolving—or solving— things before they either get out of hand or simply get in my way or the ways of others: if it isn't taking out the garbage on time, it's getting gas for the car before the indicator shows it's needed, or stocking the shelves or fridge with needed item, or helping my artistic wife with an art piece for display. In my marriage I call them, *My Connubials*, a designation I devised for these varied obligations as I see them. I think of these as an extension of my marriage vows, put into daily actions. I've written extensively about these in my book titled *The Good Husband: 50 Practices That Will Make You Nearly*

Perfect. The coined word connubials is silly, I know, but serious. If I see something that needs fixing, I fix it. If it needs doing, I do it. If it's out of place, I put it in place. A friend of me and my wife's, Kathleen Dowdy, a documentary film maker (think the John Lewis film, *Get In The Way: The Journey of John Lewis*), once advised my Kathleen, when she had lamented about my food buying habits:

> *"Listen, he doesn't drink, he doesn't chase other women, he doesn't smoke, and he takes you anyplace in the world. Let him do the grocery shopping if he wants to."*

Of course, I don't do any major buying without consulting my partner: it's just that I like things to be in order and fully stocked. I also take care of things in a timely manner as I am not one to put things off. Believe me, my wife does plenty of her own connubials.

My motivation for taking care of things, I am quite sure, emanates from two characteristics. First, I am by nature an organized person, both in personal habits and work. Having done my right/left brain profile, Myers/Briggs, and Enneagram, I know precisely where my strengths lie, so I make use of them. I am a systems guy, so that explains my organizational and execution skills. Second, I don't like a mess around me since that only gets in the way of getting things done. I distinctly remember the mess (of sorts) that was around me as a child: I lived in a junkyard environment and that is by its very nature a mess. Also, my mother had lots of things, including numerous collectibles, in the rather small house we lived in. I would, at times, organize her stuff so that I had some control over our shared living space. I know she appreciated my organizing things as it made her life easier. That's the least I could do for someone who really took care of me. The same applies to my wife now and has also extended throughout my life to me doing things for my children and for those with whom I worked and managed. I've done it without being obsessive about it; it's a win-win as far as I am concerned. It keeps my life—and others,' by extension—in order and easier to live within and operate. And, oh, let it be known that I am not a control freak or have-to-have-it my-way kind of person. I just believe in getting off my derriere when it comes to my living environment and being considerate of those whom I love. Life works better when I take the initiative.

I Tried Some Complex Things to Prove I Could Successfully Accomplish What I Never Dreamed I Could

There were various activities I engaged in over the years that really proved something to me about building confidence. I've often heard others say how they would not try this or that, but that wasn't me. Even in a failure there is a lesson learned. For example, I had had in my teens the experience of rebuilding an old Crosley car back into working order. I had never done such a complex thing before and I certainly approached it with a great deal of trepidation. I was not into cars, like so many boys my age were, a fact that I am sure made them a bit envious given the junkyard I had access to. It was immensely helpful that in approaching this particular truly complex task that I had the tutelage of an experienced man—in this case one of my mother's hired hands. We worked our way together through learning and achieving success in rebuilding the Crosley. It could hardly be considered a car given at the start, given that much of it was simply not present any longer, but with his help we got it working. Years later there was a similar major project I undertook that convinced me I could do most anything myself if I put my mind to it. This activity was performed solo and involved removing and repairing the engine of an antique car: a 1930 Dodge DC-8 Business Coupe. It was gutsy to take on such a task by myself with no assurance of success, but I had done something similar in getting the Crosley operational. Here's the story.

In my teens, as she had done for my brother, my mother (as you may recall from chapter 5) gave me a junk car when I was 17. I would like to delve a bit further into the history of my interactions with the Dodge as my time spent with it taught me especially useful lessons about life.

The Dodge had arrived in the scrap iron like any other item, but mother apparently realized that in giving it to me I would not only enjoy it for the kind of freedom it offers, but other important things about life as well. I had learned to drive at the coaching of sister Dorothy, and so it made sense to give me a used car—a very used one considering it was built in 1930. She was so right. My numerous and challenging adventures and lessons with it first occurred when driving it back from college. I experienced a major breakdown that rendered the car useless until the engine could be removed and fixed. However, I was soon to be off overseas in the Peace Corps.

After returning from Ethiopia, I towed the car from Idaho to California hitched to the back of my station wagon. Driving back from college I had thrown 3 bearings in the engine. No need to know what that means exactly, only that you can't drive said car in that condition without bigger, worse things resulting. The only way to fix it was to remove the engine entirely from the car and repair everything that needed fixing, and there were a lot of things that needed fixing to make it drivable . Newly married, I had no discretionary money for someone else to do the work for me, so I decided to fix it myself. It was a huge risk, as I could end up with nothing to show for my time and effort but a pile of unworkable parts. Imagine taking the engine out of your car: Are you up to the task? Do you even know what needs to be done? I didn't have much experience, besides my previous limited work on the Crosley. My choices were to either do the work myself, or give the car away, or keep towing it from city to city in its undrivable condition. I decided to take the risk and do the work needed.

I was living at the time in Pleasanton, California, and we had purchased our first house, complete with a two-car garage. After towing, with some challenges, the car from Idaho, it sat on blocks in one of the two garage spaces, gathering dust and some rust . I decided to change all that and restore the Dodge—if I could—to its original running order. I began by removing all the rust under the car using steel wool, then applying a caustic rust remover. I could not afford a real face mask, so I used cheesecloth tied around my nose and mouth. After a month's effort, the rust was gone and I spray painted the underside with a rubber waterproof compound, which didn't seem to harm my lungs any more than as a kid handling the mercury or the burning dirt. The car now had a beautiful underbelly that no one could see, but it was a step forward. The big task, with no experience, was to take the engine physically out of the car, disassemble it, have the bearings repoured, and complete several other mechanical and electrical needs—basically none of which I knew how to do, let alone how to remove 600 pounds of motor from its housing. The approach I decided upon would be to remove one bolt, valve, electrical wire, timing chain, spring, or anything else, one by one, until I had some 200 or so separate pieces of the motor scattered on the garage floor or my modest workbench. As I did, I wrote everything down in the sequence I had removed it. I disconnected the motor from the drive shaft, then unbolted and lifted the engine with an engine hoist I was told to use. I sorted out the parts that would need to be fixed by others as they were clearly beyond my skill level, and then I cleaned and replaced a number of parts that had worn (i.e., flywheel, rings, etc., all of which I was seeing and learning about for the first time). There was no YouTube or Google for me to consult. I sought out some needed parts generally no longer available, such as points for the distributor, in the recesses of old auto parts stores in the greater Bay Area of San Francisco. I especially had to have the giant radiator flushed and checked for leaks. I cleansed out the gas tank that had accumulated some particles of rust and such. Then, I worked in the reverse order of disassembly and put it all back together over a period of about 3 months. I added oil, hooked up the battery, and turned over the ignition. Within a few tries it started up with a backfire, and after I adjusted the carburetor, it was drivable, albeit with a front wheel (damaged while towing from Idaho) that wobbled slightly and awaited future work to correct. I had only three bolts left over, and I have no idea to this day where they belonged. I hoped they were left from something else in the garage, but I had no idea. The car ran for another 50 years until I had it repainted to its original color and enjoyed an occasional drive around town or to a car show. As I noted earlier, I gave it to America's Car Museum where it currently resides in

Tacoma, Washington if you ever find yourself there one day. Look for the beautiful yellow and black coupe there amongst the other antique cars in the basement level of the building.

I found that this experience, along with other major ones, advanced my confidence for other complex tasks I've since done solo over the years. This is to say that taking on tasks with uncertain outcomes, and ultimately succeeding, gives one confidence that such successes are possible. Among other things I have fixed or built: a broken washing machine, house vacuum system, a recreation room made from scrap pallets, converted a crawl space into a spa area, constructed elaborate outside decking, built three ponds, and remodeled our home. The same applied to solving complex business needs, if not more so. It's amazing what you can do even if you don't think you can. We have to take the risk to learn. And when we do, we learn not just whether we can make the car run, but things about our risk-taking propensity. It takes the same confidence and outlook to travel to unknown foreign countries. It's really about the image you have of yourself, isn't it? And if we are willing to try, we gain not only a sense of accomplishment, but to then do the next things that come along. My advice is to at least try learning new things, and to include some complex ones in the mix of life's trials.

Social Development

I Decided I Had to Become More Approachable

I hope you have gleaned from the story of my life that I like engaging with people, but—believe me—I had to learn how. For such a shy boy stretching to my college years, I had to change if I were to ever become approachable to and by others. For example, just this last weekend after a flight from Boise to visit my daughter, I engaged in a conversation with a young man on the Airporter shuttle bus from SeaTac to Bellingham. His name was Thyatira, a young Black person, and simply fascinating young man with an interesting occupation and family background. I invited him to sit next to me on the full bus and had I not done so it would have been just another dull, two-hour trip. Instead I approached him and had a wonderful journey talking on a variety of subjects, and we plan to stay in touch in the future. As a start, we shared a recent lunch with his charming wife and child. They are, by the way, the caretakers of an island in the San Juan island chain. What's not interesting about that? We must plan a visit there in the near future to reconnect. Without taking the risk to connect, I'd have never learned something new and met such fascinating people.

Being approachable is important to me on a personal level: with my wife in marriage, as a father to my children, and friends to remain friends, and with strangers to become more than strangers. Other than my wife, strangely, it wasn't so much through personal interactions that I learned to be more approachable. Rather, out of necessity I found more motivation in the business world when confronted with my various roles in helping others professionally as a teacher, consultant, partner, and colleague. To highlight how I did learn to be more approachable, I will address four things that I worked on that proved highly effective, and which now use on a continuous basis without much thought given to each, although I do have to remind myself now and then. These are smiling, eye contact, humor, and asking questions, pretty much in that sequence.

As I noted before, while I was growing up, others often told me that the look on my face made me seem so serious and a bit unapproachable. I didn't feel that way inside, but their comments and a mirror confirmed their assessments. Even so, I was not proactive in doing much about my lack of a smile as a teen and during college. However, once I got out into the wider world and started my professional career, smiling became a necessity. For example I could be a serious, successful teacher or trainer, but I found that a smile helped students in many ways better relate to me, so I started to smile more at my students. In the same way at professional conferences when my colleagues commented (usually to others who in turn informed me) that I was so serious that it warned off others from approaching me, I started to deliberately, with forethought, to smile more in face-to-face conversations, while lecturing from a podium, and when with clients. By the way, I often mix in my form of humor and that goes well with the smiling. Not surprisingly, people smiled back at me. That was a start.

Now that I had mastered a smile on my face, how to get people to engage me, or really me engage them? The next thing I realized is that I wasn't looking at people while they talked. I knew I was not engaging in eye contact because I was looking either at the ground or over someone's shoulders. It was hard to look into their eyes and maintain eye contact. I felt that that was very impersonal and made the other party feel that I wasn't particularly interested in them or what they had to say. I had to find a way to change, so I practiced, practiced, practiced, looking eyeball-to-eyeball. I soon got more comfortable with that and could move on to the next thing I needed to do to truly be engaged. That was carrying on a meaningful conversation.

The secret sauce to talking with strangers, and even those we know, is asking questions. Most people love to talk about themselves, so when you ask a question, they will at least say something. They either respond with a lot of words, or very few, acting as if they were answering yes or no on a questionnaire. When they stop talking, I comment on what they have said, then I ask another question and on and on. In this way, they may even ask me a question, but if not, we are not going to have much of a conversation, so I might as well move on to the next person. Most people do respond and slip in a few smiles, some laughter, and you now have a conversation going on.

Finally, the key to making the smile, eye contact, and asking questions work even better is the use of humor. Fortunately, among the four, humor comes rather naturally to me, so I didn't have to practice it as much as make sure it's appropriate. I use humor in two ways. One: humor as an icebreaker or mood setter to getting started or continuing in smiling, eye contact, and asking questions. The second is using humor to make a point or simply lighten up the conversation for mutual enjoyment. My wife sees me doing this constantly with strangers in the grocery store, on the streets of Bellingham, and on virtually every foreign shore with total strangers; often those I am trying to get help from. I like to think of my humor as a bit of both Wit and Wisdom.

Using my four-pronged approach to approachability—smile, eye contact, asking questions, and humor—took a few years to seed and grow; change doesn't always necessarily come suddenly. Now I can and do, talk to anyone; even movie stars I've met. I treat everyone for that matter like ordinary people. I am not star struck, except for perhaps the time I met President John Kennedy. I've met and talked to Martin Sheen, gave the kiss of peace to Nicole Kidman, shook the hand of Haile Selassie, and many other well-known people and celebrities. We get along fine, but we are not of course close friends.

Today, I am an old man; I use being approachable as a way to get younger people to engage with me, particularly since younger people generally ignore or dismiss older people or perhaps just don't know how to relate to them. So I get the young—and anyone else—to engage using the four pillars of engagement. I smile without any signs of devious intentions, engage with some light humor, keep eye contact as much as I can, and ask questions. To quote a friend who reviewed the first draft of this book, "You are a philosopher, and this makes you think about the implications and effects of greeting the world with a smile. It connotes your openness, warmth, and acceptance. You radiate those things from your core." (Thank you, Brenda)

I Established a Workable Reality to Family, Neighbors, and Friends

I think it's critically important to have a healthy reality to operate from when it comes to family, neighbors, and friends. That's to say that I don't tolerate bad behavior amongst any of these groups when it comes to their interactions with me or in relation to my loved ones. If this happens, I simply stop having a meaningful, ongoing relationship with them. First: family.

Fortunately, I love all my immediate family and most of my extended family, BUT I do not blindly support any of them when they behave

336

egregiously! Bad behavior can reach far in the family. In my case, it has included just a couple of members acting out poorly. The often-deployed notion that "blood is thicker than water" for me is not a workable credo for family relations. A fool is a fool is a fool. Fortunately, almost all my family members (and I include my spouse's family) have been good, with only a few exceptions. One is a drug user and criminal (multiple arrests and prison time). Another stole her cousin's husband—a big no-no in my book! I expect my family to behave with goodness as I do myself towards them. Bad behavior has nothing to do with the genes we happen to share, so acting poorly does not work for me.

In the category of people you don't get to choose, I think neighbors should be the next best people to associate with after family. They, after all, live next door or within walking distance. They are part of not only a community you sometimes need to interact with but also form a kind of safety network in what is otherwise a troubled society these days. Of course that doesn't work well for some neighbors, but we need to encourage neighborly relations as much as possible. In my neighborhood it works, and it's wonderful. We share one another's house keys and hold occasional block parties. I try my best to get along with and do things for my neighbors. That's because, no matter what else I may think of them (no criminals here), they are my neighbors. And they reciprocate by taking care of our mail, sharing their Dungeness crab haul, clearing the rare snowfall from this old man's driveway, quiet their dogs when needed, and do their part to get along. "Best neighbors ever," is a motto I try to support for all.

Between family, neighbors, and friends, friends are the group to promote the most since we can select the friends, and the kinds, we want. I can say that over the years my wife and I have done a pretty good job of selecting and associating with friends that shared our mutual interests, supported our children playing together, and also chose some from work to socialize with over dinner and other outings. As of retirement, I find that we must proactively find new friends because old, dear friends die or cannot wander the globe with you due to infirmities, and we keep these because they are so near and dear to us. I think I made a new friend on the bus, the other day, for example.

For old men like me, one source of such new friends might seem a bit odd, but it has worked pretty well for the period of life it has been available. Look for groups of men (Starbucks is a good place) that get together just to jaw about things. In my case I found a group that calls itself ROMEO: Retired Old Men Eating Out. We gathered biweekly for lunch, usually at one of the well-known craft breweries in our community. We drank, ate, retold old stories again, and just talked about anything that came to mind. Some, of course, talked more than others, but it made no difference because the conversation, as it turned out, was far less important than the camaraderie. Women, such as my wife, seem more apt to connect around mutual interests, projects or hobbies like quilting, art, playing cards, reading interesting books, and such. Informal friend exchanges, especially for the elderly, keep interests high and blood flowing. It's been really good for me, and I appreciate how my wife seeks out new friends who then also become my friends.

One other thing, especially about friends found abroad, is to be noted and which I highly recommend. It's something I personally promote whenever we make a journey anywhere in the world. Bringing friends of another culture home—not literally—to stay in touch with by Zoom or emails refreshes my belief in being a citizen of the world, let alone learning how their lives are different and fascinating. There are really interesting friends to be made in foreign lands (generally because we mutually like travel). It happens on some island as you walk the beach or go to the Saturday Market, or just crossing a street, sitting in a local coffee shop, or even on those ocean style cruises that I don't particularly like. I have friends who saved my life when I was almost taken out to sea by a riptide. I have friends on my favorite island. I do like people and these friends can be some of the best because they are a little or a lot like us. They are mainly adventurous. Staying up to date on life events over Zoom calls helps, but I do miss seeing them in person and sharing a meal. Still, I keep them in my memories.

Finally there are the friends from high school or college that you can enjoy meeting up with at reunions to recall the days of old. I have attended five of these reunions and it was always so nice to become reacquainted with old friends, and to meet new ones you might have been friends with, had you have known at the time, back then and taken the opportunity to engage with them. There are also the friends from my Peace Corps days so long ago that I email now and then. What good memories to share about the past.

I Volunteer to Help my Fellow Human Beings

This I obviously learned watching and participating with my mother, the consummate volunteer. Read the book I wrote about her, *My Mother Can Beat Up Your Father*, and you'll learn the whole story. As I previously noted, she sometimes used to take me along for her one-on-one volunteering outings. Buying groceries for a person in need around Thanksgiving, for example, was a common one, or visiting someone living alone she knew. Today it's easy to invite a child or a good friend to come for a ride-along as I deliver for the food bank. When I saw the pleasure my mother derived, and the way those she served responded, I got the idea immediately. Others we serve make them and us happy while solving needs, comforting, or making life a little easier. Become a Peace Corps volunteer, Vista volunteer, or part of some community outreach program, and you'll get smiles in bunches and see and experience interesting things you've never imagined.

I'll enumerate more of my particular brand of volunteering shortly when I describe my kind of retirement. For now, just know I do it and everyone should, if for no other reason than getting out of your own self and into the good feeling of what you can do for your brethren. And don't wait until retirement to do the volunteering. It builds character as a kid or youth. As an adult it sets a splendid example for your kids, and they learn from the experience of helping others. The time I led our patrol as a boy scout collecting coat hangers to buy a record player for the hospital was rewarded not only in time spent with my fellow scouts, but especially when we went to the hospital and saw firsthand what joy looks like on the face of little kids. Kids need to experience the joy on others' faces! It does wonderful things for self-esteem.

I Loved Traveling for How it Made Me Understand the World, Let Alone See Wonderful Things

By the time I was 40 I had been in every one of the 50 states of the USA. Following my initial study tour in Europe in my last year of college, I went to lots of other places around the globe and had numerous adventures. Travel, at first glance, may seem like it's about the places you see, and the activities or entertainment engaged in, and of course that is why most people travel. But for me it's more about the people in those places and what they teach us about ourselves or even your nation. That includes what's good and bad and needs changing or improvement or feeding or eradicating on our planet. Besides, when you talk to the people of another country or region you really learn so much about the things you came to see. They often redirect you to more interesting things that were not included in the tourist brochure or websites. That's because they live with the things you came to see and to experience. And then if you seek and are lucky you make friends with a few people across the oceans and, as in my case, they certainly improve your life and the lives of those traveling with you. For example, I took my children to Europe twice in their youth and they learned a great deal. Another time we took all our children and their children to our favorite island. We wanted them to experience what we had enjoyed so many, many times. We wanted them to broaden their perspective of the world and what it has to offer. They had great fun on the beach yes but also learned a little about another culture and how loving the people were that they interacted with on the beach and in the water. They learned even more about their grandparents. To this day they are still talking about what they learned.

I want to say one other important thing about travel and the relationship it has to where I ultimately chose to reside as my final residence—our home. We live in Bellingham, Washington, because it is a beautiful and

340

caring community with plenty of outreach opportunities that feed my desire to volunteer. The weather is a little lousy because of the on and off eight months of drizzly rain, but the other bennies are worth the rain that feeds the magnificent forest and lakes. Since I am addressing travel, I want to address what might be labeled our "souvenir strategy."

When we traveled to all those places we have gone to over the years, we usually brought back something special to remind us of those places. For example, there is a moving statue made of spring stone carved by a noted African sculptor with a wonderful first name. We learned that many locals in South Africa have such poetic first names. Gift Muchenje is a talented and internationally recognized South African sculpture artist. One morning we were walking in the Kirstenbosch National Botanical Garden in Cape Town when we happened upon Gift seated in the garden, developing one of his unique sculptures. He was forming beautiful smaller versions of an array of large statues that adorn the entrance of the gardens. We talked with him for a while and bought a small statue, titled the *Chorist*. It now resides in a special spot in our living room with many other items from other continents. Similarly, while in Budapest, we saw, in a Christmas kiosk in the town square, a single watercolor painting, along with the regular assortment of Christmas knick-knacks on sale. The painting was quite beautiful, as was Budapest. It turned out to be a work of Edward Belsky, a noted Ukrainian artist we later learned, and we purchased it. It now hangs on the wall in the dining room. Imagine, we bought it for $50. We also subsequently purchased another of his works online for much more, when we remodeled our living room, as well as one by a fellow Ukrainian artist, Mikhail Mikora. Still another time, while in Nepal, I briefly left our tour guide to go and buy a painting from an artist so obscure that he had not even signed it. I asked him to do so personally, and he did. He was quite taken by my asking as he put his right hand over his heart to express his gratitude. It's one of my most treasured items, and it hangs in our bedroom. What is this all about? It's not the cost of said items, which in our case, is usually fairly little, but what they remind us of regarding our experiences of travel, where and who was involved and under what circumstances. Our house is like a museum, with a silver-plated Coptic cross from my days in Ethiopia, a 3' x 4' painted cloth storybook depiction of the story of Solomon and Sheba from Ethiopia, an icon from Prague, various graphite sketches from Nepal, Laos, and Myanmar. There's an old pair of mother-of-pearl laden window shutters that once hung on a house in the Philippines. There is a three-foot high wooden manikin of the Virgin Mary. I am assured it was once adorned with silk cloth and religious symbols as it paraded down winding streets on the shoulders of revelers at a religious festival. I like to bring the outside world inside all my living spaces. These items of remembrance brighten my soul and make us feel richer for the little money wisely paid for each. They are certainly better than the touristry tee shirts which I also buy and wear. Better perhaps, as reminders than some trinkets most likely made in China of a country you visited. Visitors and friends who come to dine with us in our home always want to know where our artifacts come from and the stories behind them. What a way to relive a lifetime of wonderful worldly adventures with others.

Professional Development

I Didn't Let Money be the Primary Driving Force as the Measure of My Success

It's going to seem counterintuitive, but throughout my professional career, I never worried about what I was earning. Mainly, I took jobs because they were interesting and intellectually challenging, where I could be allowed to innovate and work with interesting people I could enjoy and manage well. I am not one to put up much with others' negative attitudes, playing mind or political games, or failing to do their share. I don't enjoy downers, complainers, or whiners! I also do not tolerate long meetings with excessive talking simply to hear oneself speak. My benchmarks for choosing a job were when I knew I'd learn intellectually interesting approaches or would be allowed to do things with ideas I had.

I think I felt if I did interesting work, innovated, and got paid reasonably well (and wasn't taken advantage of) that the financial rewards would ultimately follow. While that was generally true working for others, the financial reward finally came when working for myself, with my partner, based on all that prior experience where I was allowed to innovate and then subsequently use on our own, in our personal and business ways of doing things.

Financially, I started teaching after the Peace Corps at $4,400 a year, doubled that to $8,800 in my Job Corps assignment, and went up from there. One of my bosses at The American College said I was so below the average wage for my skill and experience, that he gave me a 25% raise one year. This didn't mean I ignored financial needs, and I certainly don't like debt—I've always paid off my credit cards on time! I knew I needed to support my family, so when a financial need arose not covered by my paycheck, I would organize my own workshop on the side. Or I consulted on projects with publishing houses, editing their publications—thus I'd learn, in the process, others' ideas and how these related to my approach to individual and business improvements. I'd have worked at 7-Eleven if that was needed, but why not do things on the side in my own field, by my own efforts, and learn in the process? How might doing independent work prepare me for eventually working for myself? As it turned out, that approach to professional life worked very well for me and I can honestly say I genuinely enjoyed the ride intellectually and as far as the work I did.

I Used What I Considered My Superpower by Solving the Obvious

I seem to be a guy who sees the obvious that others don't. This is confirmed in my Myers/Briggs profile as an ISTP, "I See The Problem." As the old saying goes, "Can't see the forest for the trees," I seemed to have the knack for clearly seeing the forest and not letting the details or worry—trees—get in the way. As such, for example, I designed a new learning approach because I saw a need to account for assigned student preparatory study—homework if you will—to a lecture and developed a teaching/learning methodology that benefited both students and teacher. This had been something that had perplexed me for years as a student myself: that teachers assign homework, especially in college, and then don't account for what students had learned on their own from such assigned reading—rather giving their lecture as if the reading assignment had never been made. Instead, why not account for student preparatory time and effort and devote most of the class time to what students still need to learn and not waste time on what students have learned on their own? Taking advantage of this insight, I devised a way to account for self-learning and have the teacher build a lesson plan at the outset of the lecture. This learning method (The Construct Lesson Plan) referred to as an instructional design in the business, worked like a charm for the continuing adult education programs that were offered by the college I worked for. I also developed a couple of other learning methods for practical self-learning needs. Based on these new methods of learning I authored several articles about my findings, and eventually had my first book published. A few years later I originated, developed, and edited a forty volumes series with several of my contemporaries. One other example, then I'll describe, in my opinion, the most significant professional contribution in my professional life.

During my early years as an instructional designer, I was managing the development of what was to become a series of ten audio-based instructional programs. Again, by viewing the challenge I was facing in simplistic terms, I got to thinking about the differences between the written (i.e. study guides), spoken (i.e. audiotapes), and visual (i.e. slideshows) modalities used for learning. For example, most everyone has been told at one time or another that "a picture is worth a thousand words." If that's true (and it is), why do we typically write a thousand words and then add the pictures? Isn't that the exact opposite of what should be done if we genuinely believe a picture is worth a thousand words? Would it not make sense to begin with pictures, then add the words? Similarly, if we are going to produce an audio-based recording, why do we write a thousand words—a script—then record that script? Why not start with an audio-based recording? It can and should be done!

With this premise in mind, in producing the audio programs we were given to create, I had my developers sit with a subject expert, turn on a recorder and have the expert speak to that content (rather than write it). In other words, the medium of creating (audio in this case in the form of the recorded interview) was the same as the desired medium (audio) of the end product. The developer was then instructed to test to see if the student had learned the audio content. If not, some additional recording was done or only then were written words added. We transcribed the recordings verbatim, with the aim of only editing for accuracy and flow. The results were not only much quicker production times, but most importantly, the learning outcomes were better. That is an example of taking the obvious—in this case the difference between written and spoken words—and creating a more successful product for learners. I did that repeatedly throughout my career with great success, and professional satisfaction.

Now for what I consider my most significant professional contribution. This one solved the problem of something everyone does but could do so much better if they thought of it in a new way: that is your and my way of approaching "work"! I will briefly explain what I mean and refer to you to other resources I've written where you can learn more, if you are so inclined.

I previously introduced to you my Language of Work Model™, which my wife and I built into a successful consulting business. I want you to see this model in light of what I call here, the obvious.

We all, generally, believe we know the requirements and expectations of our individual job (work), be that at home or in the office. We believe we are good at our jobs or could do better with some help. We might even have had thoughts on how to improve our work and could do so if "they" would but listen. Would you say the same about some other person's job—say people you work with? How well do you think they know their jobs or your work? It turns out, even when we know our own job well,

345

there is often no way to fix the job ourselves (it's not always the fault of management, by the way). As I began to see it, there was no way to get clarity of our work and others to the extent that we can mutually solve the problems we face ourselves, let alone with management. As a result, companies turn to experts, like me, in training and other services to fix things. What's the obvious issue here when it comes to improving our and others' work? It's simply this: we don't have a common way between us to define and communicate—other than generally complaints—our own or mutually shared work. What is the solution? There should be a paradigm—what I came to call a Work Formula—we share in common that tells us what our and others' work is, behaviorally (operationally). It would be something that acts like a figurative lightbulb over our heads, something that clearly shows the way my job works, how my fellow workers' jobs work, and how those interactions look between us when we are required to work in concert. I figured out we needed a work formula between us—that's the chemistry guy in me thinking that way about the obvious need. So I developed the formula for what work is. If you want to learn the formula, you can access my free YouTube link: https://www.youtube.com/watch?v=Nn7tLm4nRLU&t=52s

I am sure by now I've worn you out a bit with my somewhat technical and detailed explanation of the problem with "work" that I solved, but bear with me just a little more. It can be important to your work (and I am, as I said, always teaching). The net result of achieving work clarity is what it does for you and the business you work for. Work clarity empowers you to know your work better as well as the work of others (i.e., work as a team), and the whole of the enterprise you work for, thereby allowing everyone to solve and improve work needs together, especially alone on your own initiative. That is much better than paying people like me so much money to solve these problems for them—as much as I dearly love the income.

I have authored books, articles, and several free resources (see Appendix) concerning the "clarity of work" embedded in the Language of Work Model™. It may be useful to also Google me under Google Scholar.

I just happen to be the guy from Idaho who figured it out—with the help of so many colleagues in my field, and of course my dear wife and business partner. Enough of my teaching, so let us move on.

I Assured Equity

Assuring equity is a question of achieving human justice. That's particularly true on a personal level, and has been so easy to promote, when it comes to my business partner. I hopefully did this as well with the numerous professionals whom I managed over the years. It's probably obvious when and where and why I believe equity is important between women and men. My mother, after all, served both roles in the same body. That translated to a firm belief that my wife is equal to me, or even better yet, we are (or should) be equals in both life and business. For example, I have always treated her that way and insisted in our business dealings that she was paid what I was paid—we were, after all, doing the same work as a team. I was the modelmaker and she the master facilitator. She's the one who knew how to please clients, and I had ideas of how to improve the approach to work clarity. She got paid exactly what I did for equal effort. Easy, you may say, when it comes to work, but what about around the home? Same, same, same. The easiest way to assure equity at home is by being a good husband (see my book on that account). As examples we share the tasks of food preparation, laundry, making the bed, and other life necessities.

I Made Sure to Give Others Credit

One of the things I immediately noticed when working with other professional colleagues was that there was a propensity for taking all of the credit when others were due some (even if not much) of it. The first time this happened was in a project I worked on during my graduate studies at the University of Missouri. I was crunching data for a professor I had been assigned by my advisor, Dr. Rufi. This professor subsequently wrote an article in which my name appeared for the very first time, yet not only did I not receive the level of credit I should have received, but he also ended up spelling my name so completely wrong that no one would ever recognize it was me. Another time, one of my bosses took it upon himself to write about a concept that I had developed yet he did not credit me by name. Fortunately for him, he asked me to review a draft of his article and I had enough courage to point out that he had not credited me. We ended up co-authoring the article. Because of experiences like these I learned useful lessons. I was not about to treat others as I had been treated. I give people credit, even if that is some person in a call center who does their job well in responding to my needs.

As I innovated, produced, and wrote about new things, I always pointed out who had helped. That was particularly important when I first thought of and developed the Language of Work Model™. I had built on a lifetime of professional efforts by others (Tosti, Rummler, Deterline, Kaufman, et al), and I gave them credit in my books and articles. For example, my wife has done so much to make the work model much more effective with implementation tools that aid in its application in business. She appears in our co-authored books and articles, as she contributes her own ideas, and makes plenty of edits (that I so sorely need). It's a question of ethics and personal practices: it could be little things for a mutual meeting, a volunteer effort, or the high school dance decoration you helped prepare with others. "It's not all about me" is an attitude that will serve anyone well.

I Wrote to Freely Share My Ideas & Learn Why

Everybody has a book inside them. I learned, from one of the two writing courses I've ever taken, a wise adage that has motivated me to actually write and not procrastinate. Jean Horton Berg, the author herself of over forty children's books, said in class one evening, "The difference between those who publish and those who don't, are those who write." There is a lot to that simple statement, so I started to earnestly write. Some things got published and others did not, but I kept writing. I even delved into some poetry and have a couple of unpublished works that I think are rather good. I can't tell you how many people I've met, who, on commenting on what I've written, tell me they have a book to write, but never do. The sage words of my teacher were prophetic, and I latched on to them. Here's what I learned about writing, beyond the content of writing itself, that may be useful to you.

I have discovered through the experience of writing a half dozen of my own thirteen books, especially the one about my mother and the other about being a good husband, writing brings into focus, from the substance of a book's entirety, what was at play in the subject of the book. Thus, in writing about my mother in my book, *My Mother Can Beat Up Your Father*, I learned her drive to survive made her do the things she did. In writing the book, *The Good Husband*, I learned that it was profound love for my wife that makes me strive to be a good husband. For this autobiography you are now reading, it's the exploration of my life within an extraordinary environment, how a wonderful mother and her offspring set examples for me, and from there how it gave me the freedom to be myself and do what I am capable of with great confidence and drive. Writings such as these put into perspective things I would not have otherwise noted or paid much attention to as I lead my life, day after day. That is why I write, and why I suggest you write as well, if not that book inside you, then at least your own obituary or some form of journaling. An even simpler undertaking would be to create an audio recording you make yourself of your life experienced. This could be either a monologue or done in the form of an interview with someone else asking questions such as your son, daughter, or grandchild. Or, as my wife has done, by putting together and binding with a nice leather jacket, the pictorial history of her mother who served as a nurse in the Second World War in Papua New Guinea. Now there is a story worth knowing and passing on to family. The act of writing, or creating other media forms, will put a perspective on what you or others have done or may even still want to do. In authoring this book I have self-evaluated my journey, and it makes me feel very good and has helped prepare me to die. Oh, and if it should come to be that you do decide to write, if at all possible, get an advanced royalty and write on an island somewhere. I did a couple of times, and it was terrific!

Spiritual Development

I Constantly Sought Serenity

According to the dictionary, serenity is "the state of being calm, peaceful, and untroubled." There is a story my wife likes to tell about me and "serenity." It's as good a description of how serenity manifests itself as any could be, especially about my version of it.

We were doing some work for the U.S. Coast Guard at their training site near Petaluma, California, in the Sonoma Mountains. There was a B&B that we loved there that sat high in the forest, run by a very delightful gay guy. With a grand living room surrounded by a balcony that circled the entire second floor, you could look down and see comfortable leather easy chairs set amidst a giant rock fireplace, works of art, immense bouquets of flowers, and a grand dining table. Fresh berries with breakfast made it all marvelous, if not surreal. It had a "Crow's Nest" bedroom where the morning sun streamed in on you as you lay in a large clawfoot bathtub and looked at eye level out above a forest of trees and see an occasional eagle glide in the clear blue sky.

One morning we walked down a dirt road and soon found ourselves in the midst of several giant redwood trees. They were easily two to three hundred years old, if not more. My wife describes the look on my face and the way my body seemed to unfold from a tense state of seriousness (the state I was known for) to one of total relaxation and being one with nature. It was just like my days as a kid on the Little Wood River in Idaho. That look, that feeling, is one example of serenity. Of course, serenity comes in different forms and can be caused by a multitude of things. I don't know if it's my old soul in me, but I constantly crave it and do what I can to assure that it is present. That's because I want to enjoy my existence and want others to as well, since their very serenity (or not) affects my serenity (or not).

There are numerous things, both on the personal level as well as within my own living environment, that I deliberately plan to make sure I—and others—enjoy life. First, I have typically not let worry be on my face or within my body: life is too short for such and besides worry just makes me look old and cranky. That is also why I learned to smile more often and use lots of laughter. Next, I try to assure that my loved ones, friends, and colleagues are allowed to enjoy themselves, get things done, and receive recognition. For example, when I was a manager of lots of others, I hired and developed people for their capabilities and then let them do the work without undue supervision on my part. I assured them clear paths were set for what was to be accomplished but left it pretty much up to them as to how they got there. As such they were much more fulfilled, happy at work, treated others well, and, as an added bonus, made me look good through the quality work they produced. I created a serene environment for personal and collective growth. I found the same outlook applicable at home and with friends, but by utilizing different ways and means. My wife and I, for example, know how to process things together, prepare meals collectively, talk without being accusatory, help one another fulfill our interests (her art, my writing) and socialize and travel with others. As I am writing this autobiography, she helps me edit, and while she is preparing a new collage piece, as an artist, she asks for my assistance. We maintain serenity so that we can enjoy life both singularly, as well as side by side. With friends we do things we all will enjoy, have loads of laughs, and can be serious when needed during challenging times of health or sadness.

What I've described thus far to assure my (and others) serenity is on the personal level, but there is one other vastly important thing I've done, especially in approaching retirement, to assure serenity manifests from the environment in which I spend my final days: that is the residence we have come to occupy and the physical setting in which it sits. The latter harkens back, especially, to those redwood trees mentioned before.

In 2001, as we were approaching retirement, we decided to move from Santa Monica, California, to Bellingham, Washington, 21 miles south of the Canadian border. The move was precipitated by the recognition that we were never likely to pay off our mortgage living in Santa Monica. Also, the hustle and tussle of Los Angeles was getting to be too much for us. It was time to decide where we would spend the rest of our lives —especially in winding down our business and sliding into retirement.

A trip to pick up Kathleen's daughter and her then-boyfriend in Bellingham and bring them to California to continue their journey to Mexico resulted in discovering the charm of this Pacific Northwest town. He lived in Bellingham and she had spent the summer there with him. When we drove to pick them up for the first time, we immediately fell in love with the community and its surroundings in the forest and decided we could retire there. So we returned a month later and undertook a house-hunting search. Being as different as we are and comfortable with such, Kathleen wanted to live in the city, and I was more drawn to the countryside (after all I had had a gentlemen's farm, you will recall). We started with our rural option, as my wife described it at the time, "looking for six acres and a stream." She knows Danny well, yet at the same time I was not stuck on the need for such if something more ideal presented itself. No little farms were to be found during the initial hunt that suited our fancy, even though there were a few in the immediate countryside. For instance, there was one that came with two gigantic buffalo, but even that was too much for me. However, we found a home by chance, not in the countryside, but a compromise that suited both of us. Most importantly, it was a place with a lot of potential given the interior layout and the view it had—especially the view. The view, as is said about certain things, is to die for. The house is up in the forest on the side of a mountain. There is a ten-mile-long lake below with a view of the Canadian Cascades in the background. Yes, we can see Canada. And it's an easy drive into town; so we got both country and city to satisfy both of us.

From the moment I first gazed at the simple 1970s-style modest bungalow and its then inferior interior, I had visions of how it could be transformed: how we could further create serenity inside looking out over the magnificent view below. Don't know where my sense of interior design emanated from, but I had a vision; a feel for what this house could become with that view, but currently wasn't. The vision, not too surprising given my personality, was, as I was eventually to learn, minimalist. We had something along the same lines in our Santa Monica condo, but definitely without the view. We had earned a little money from the sale of our condo and so decided to renovate the interior of this new house to our tastes, as this would be our final home, and we could thereby incorporate and display all the numerous artifacts that we had gathered over the years in traveling the world.

Without a blueprint, I worked with the local ReStore (a non-profit recycling enterprise of house items) to remove dated kitchen cabinets, oak flooring, wooden banisters, a fake rock fireplace, and other items we didn't want to see again. I personally ripped much of the oak flooring out myself and laid it in two bedrooms in the downstairs' guest area; then remodeled the guest bath—it's a three-level house. Working with a dozen subcontractors, I served as their general contractor, a role I'd never performed before, but it wasn't much different than the managing of others I had experienced in my own field of expertise. Remember as well that I had learned to take on complex undertakings like extracting and repairing the motor from an antique car and fixing it to run again. Different I know, but still risky when you haven't totally remodeled a house before. The difference, outside of the obvious of one being a car and the other the interior of a house, is that you have to do a better job of working with people—contractors in this instance—as they are a breed of their own. For example, they rarely ever come to your particular job and stay the entire day until they are done (unless it's just a day's worth of work). Rather, they come in and out over several days, juggling several jobs in the neighborhood. You have to know this and cooperate, because the alternative of their getting mad at you, or you at them, won't favor you. I was attuned to this knowing that it takes a lot to manage a junkyard, as my mother had. Combining that with some design savvy I apparently possess, the result is a beautiful interior that others have simply delighted in—often expressing surprise as to why it's not featured in some interior design magazine. I learned I might have made a pretty decent interior designer. While it's true I might have liked that profession, I really liked what I innovated for others, wrote about, and got paid well for.

What's this got to do with serenity? Well it was loads of fun to remodel and make the home our version of serenity. For instance, the bathroom downstairs has a clawfoot tub, bought from an elderly retired lady in Bellingham, and installed by me. She informed us she had used it for 80 years. The bathroom also has one of those old, two-part English style toilets I bought for $50 from that same ReStore in town. With a chain you pull to flush, the water comes rushing down from a tank above your head. The pipe the water flows down, about two inches in diameter, bent beyond use when I was installing the toilet system. So I went down to an automotive store that specializes in antique automobiles—this is where the experience of taking apart that old Dodge comes in—and bought an exhaust pipe. It worked perfectly, with just a little bending of the tail pipe required to account for fitting from the water closet tank to the toilet. I have subsequently wondered what it would be like to have included the muffler with that original exhaust pipe, but even I won't go that far (yet)! Through all this, I learned that I really loved doing interior design. Just one little thing more about our house.

We really love the house, mostly because it sits in a forest with the view I previously described. The interior and the surroundings, as you look out from a vaulted ceiling with huge windows, exude serenity in the quiet forest. There are migratory birds that fly in and chirp in the surrounding pines, cedar, and deciduous trees, and I've made use of several iPhone apps that can identify birds and plants. There are numerous deer, racoons, squirrels, bald eagles, and other creatures who stroll freely by and sometimes sit in your yard, as if it were theirs to begin with, and of course, it is. I have a vegetable garden (not 10,000 sq. feet like in Star, Idaho) in the community garden area so we enjoy all that that provides, including interaction with fellow gardeners. In a while when I address my version of retirement, I'll describe other things that were planned and incorporated into the layout of the house as a reflection of our life. To transition over 60-plus-years from growing up in a junkyard to now living in a forest is transformative. It's about coming from numerous and exciting life adventures to a state of needed serenity in one's final years. I have and am thoroughly enjoying both. I am still that guy who liked laying in the field when I had the farm in Star, or sitting in my rowboat, who now likes his serenity viewing stars at night, and snow in the winter. I could do with a little less rain, but then again, you take what is best of what exists and what's needed to produce all that greenery. I have created our serenity in house and view, among other things, so that our golden years are truly golden.

I Established a Personal Faith/Spirituality Foundation to Compass My Life

In my quest to be my version of a well-rounded human being, I strove to have a functional (as opposed to dogmatic) spirituality as a moral compass to guide my being—my life—especially in relationships with others. The opposite was to be self-centered and narcissistic, which I despise. I had experienced a narcissist for a long year as my immediate supervisor at MK and I knew that wasn't the way I wanted to be with others. I had had the role model of my mother and siblings as people of faith who treated others well, so that is what I decided to be.

While growing up we attended what I consider a middle-of-the-road Christian faith—neither strict, nor dogmatic. We attended semi-regularly and learned how a personal relationship with God manifests itself. My experiences included some Sunday School, how to evaluate boring sermons, operational guidance of what the scripture calls for in the way of action, and volunteering to serve others, mostly outside of church. We were guided to be respectful of people of different faiths with the belief that there are different paths to salvation. Our belief system was centered, I would say, on mutual respect.

I found my journey in faith to be a slow steady growing process. I read the Bible in my early days, trying to understand what it was saying rather than focusing on specific passages as rules by which to judge others, but rather to guide myself. I had no need or right to dictate those "rules" to others. Over the years I was ecumenical in that I attended various church denominations with my family. I attended those that provided community and were led by reasonable shepherds who taught but did not dictate belief and actions. There are after all, multiple roads to faith, and in general each needs to be respected as we are all human beings trying to find our way.

For all the faith work I subjected myself to, I ended up with a very personal kind of relationship to the divine. It's very much the same as the personal relationship which I witnessed my mother live by her action in dealing with others, but also how she viewed herself with kindness. I believe it's what the various spiritual prophets (i.e. Jesus, Mohammed, God, etc.) or philosophers (i.e. Buddha) would expect of us and act accordingly. If they said, "understand and help the poor," you do. If they said, "treat your neighbor as well as you treat yourself," you do. But it's not what the self-appointed spiritual leaders here on earth often espouse that promotes exclusivity and vitriol against any others faith. It's pretty simple and straightforward. You are not to be a zealot who thinks yours is the only way. Be human, be nice, be respectful, and enjoy what little time each of us is given on earth.

I began the development of my faith in attending the First Baptist Church of Twin Falls, Idaho. I have always said to those who have asked, that I am a "Western" Baptist so as to distinguish from any other sect that might be stricter and more repressive of its flock. I even taught some Sunday School, was an elder in a Presbyterian church, attended for a couple of years a weekly bible study at 6 in the morning with 600 other men, attended a Quaker church for a few years, and while not a practicing Catholic in the capital "C" sense, I am a small "c" catholic. I attended Catholic services because both of my wives were Catholic. In essence, I respected and supported their faith. I have to admit I didn't let the Catholic Church dogma dictate my actions because it can be a little overboard about faith like most churches. For example, you are supposed to be Catholic to receive communion, a rule with which I don't agree. Instead I took communion even though I was not supposed to according to their rules, but I figured that was a decision between me and God, not the church. Shortly, I'll explain how that worked out in sort of a comical, but functional way.

Every time we moved because of my work, I sought out a church to find community with. First on my list of considerations were ministers/shepherds who would guide people in their faith—something hard to find anywhere—rather than be so preachy. I needed (for myself as well as my family members, although they did individually get to decide their own paths), a place that would provide some faith guidance—shepherding—and especially some community with others, and the more diverse the flock of believers the better. I loved every other faith for the most part unless it was a cult of blind obedience; that makes no sense to me. I think I do really know a fool of a leader when I hear one, and there are loads of them on TV. They seem to want your money as much as your obedience—even selling prayers for it. Something's wrong there.

So, that's my faith base in a nutshell. I'd like to close the topic with the description of a couple of things that happened along my faith journey that were just odd, but in their own special way instructive and useful to my overall journey. With my sense of humor that I hope you have appreciated, if not at least tolerated, these two odd experiences helped keep my faith on the light side, where it most desperately needs to be. That way I remain practical and don't act so holy around others. Besides, given the way humanity is working out, I think Got has a profound sense of humor.

I was, as noted earlier, an elder in a Presbyterian church for a while. I was designated as such because the church needed an audiovisual guy and all my previous experience in running the film projector in junior high finally led me to this esteemed position. This also meant that I would occasionally serve communion when asked. One time during a quarterly meeting of the elders I was informed that one of the older parishioners objected to my wearing a leisure suit while serving communion of wine (grape juice actually) and bread. It was suggested that I wear other, "more appropriate" attire. Being a smartass when the occasion calls for lightening up things, I said to the other assembled elders "I don't recall ever seeing a picture of Jesus wearing a suit and tie." Nothing more was said about the leisure suit issue, and so, out of respect for the sensitivities of others, I stopped wearing leisure suits to church. Actually, leisure suits were so ridiculous looking that they soon went out of style, and I stopped wearing one to work—verified in that you don't see them today anywhere!

My other faith story is a classic, even for me. As I already noted, I had attended Catholic churches for many years because my first wife was Catholic, and she felt, compelled as Catholics are taught to do, attend weekly Mass, and wanted me to attend with her. That was easy at the time to do as we were living in Ethiopia and the local Catholic Church was interesting because it was naturally predominately filled with Ethiopians. Later, my second wife was a fallen-away Catholic, and if you can believe it, I was the one who brought her back to her childhood faith. I have concluded that I seem to have a specialty in bringing fallen-away Irish Catholic girls back to their faith base. Surely that must say something about me and my brand of faith that qualifies me for a place in heaven!

During our days in Santa Monica, Kathleen and I were attending what turned out to be the most marvelous, spiritually centered church I have ever attended, and probably ever will. It was a real community of varied ethnicity and the full spectrum of ages led by four priests who knew how to relate to and guide their flock. With a following of about 10,000 people it was simply amazing. St. Monica Catholic Church had the most inspiring music (prayer like) I have ever heard (although I do love good old gospel), and everyone was singing exuberantly as we stood there near the front of the church. The congregation especially had the widest possible range of different ministries for everyone, including the gay community, of which there were about 300 parishioners. Young and old were always acting out their faith with and for others as I so believe in doing myself. It was what I think Jesus had in mind all along, but somehow has gotten lost by the larger flock of believers. This is all a prelude to a story I want to tell that I think is so revealing about me and my approach to spirituality.

As previously noted, (please excuse the repeat, but I need to set the context for the story that follows), I grew up a Baptist, and attended the Catholic Church on and off with two different wives—that alone disqualified me to be a Catholic—over a period of about 50 years. In between we attended some other churches, but these were brief, two-to-seven-year time frames. Spirituality, in my view, is not to be exclusively found in one faith or location. Understanding I was never officially a member of the Catholic Church over a period of approximately 36 years up and until that time, I took, you might say, my own path. It was, for example, my personal belief that I could receive communion without being a confirmed member—essentially a no-no in the Catholic Church's belief/rules. Indeed. I was also, for a while, the head of Eucharistic ministers without being a confirmed member. I was not a registered one of the flock. All this is okay with me as I have a personal relationship with Christ and my faith in him/her, not with the church, big or little "c." The thing was, I suspected our priest in Boise knew my little secret. One day I considered becoming a registered Catholic. I called our local priest, Dr. John Ruffle, and asked him to lunch at our company's cafeteria. I had some questions that I wanted him to answer, so that I might perhaps become a member in good standing. After our lunch, I got around to asking my questions.

Here's how our conversation went:

Question 1: "Having grown up in the Baptist church, we believed that the wine is taken in remembrance of Jesus, not the actual consecrated blood? We also believe the bread is not the actual body, but also in remembrance." He, the priest, responds, "Well we don't actually know, and you may be right" That answer was acceptable to me.

Question 2: "I am not certain Mary should be given as much significance by the Catholic church that she is. She was obviously important, but to elevate her to the position the Catholics do seems a little bit over the top, doesn't it?" He says, "Again we don't know, but you might have a point." All's going well from the answers to my first two questions. Here comes the big one!

(Please note this is all true and pretty much verbatim, as I can best recall)

Finally, Question 3: "I don't think I believe in the infallibility of the Pope." I thought that might really get to him, although the previous two questions should have. But, he says, "That may well be, but we don't know." I said, I'll sign up.

It was actually sealed when he said to me, and this is the truth, "Given what I know about you, you may well be a more informed and enlightened Catholic than many of the Catholics I know." Following our conversation, I did not have to sign on a dotted line, and he accepted my baptism in the Baptist Church (March 25, 1951) as proof enough that I was sincere in my faith. Now I could serve communion for real, as if that somehow made a difference to me. By the way, with my second wife (imagine the church's view on a second wife), we were allowed—due to the generosity of another fantastic priest in Bellingham—to serve communion to one another as a couple. Imagine that! Again, it's something you just apparently can't do, but we did, and it was a sign to other married couples that we liked one another, so some started doing it as well. Of course, other parishioners objected to our serving communion to one another as a couple, but we had our pastor's (Ft. Scott) approval. I mean, just think of it. A husband sharing his deep faith and love of God with the wife he loves madly, truly! And she does the same to him, recommitting their vows and love to each other every week! I have never been one to follow seemingly arbitrary, unnecessary rules—that's so old testament—and I'm not fond of ritual for ritual's sake. Love is what God is really about, and so we should be able to show that love openly and regularly. Let's face it, I am really a small "c" catholic of many faiths, but also a person who has acted upon his spirituality/faith!

Finally, I simply must relate one final story of faith outside the church that is a doozy! All my stories, including especially this one, help one learn what I am all about, and also make some important points about life's journey. This is the whole point of an autobiography, I think.

There is a wonderful play you can see that is likely to remain here on earth until doomsday! My wife and I had heard wonderful reviews of the play and decided to take the opportunity while we were living in Santa Monica, California. It's called, "Midnight Catechism!" The play is a satirical comedy. It is a monologue, acted out by a pretend nun, who humorously recounts events of what it's like growing up Catholic at school and in life in general. Members of the audience are make-believe participants in her class—even if virtually everyone in the audience was, in fact, a practicing Catholic. There are loads of laughs as she recounts what it's like to be a Catholic, most of which the predominately Catholic audience can personally relate to. At the end she asks the audience for any questions they might have, and naturally I couldn't resist. So I stand up and the following exchange ensued:

I said: "My second wife and I were recently informed by The Church that we have a choice when it comes to communion. Since we are Catholics that were married outside of the church, we can either have communion or sex, but not both! What do you, sister, recommend we do?"

Her response: "Well, given your situation, it makes no difference as you are obviously going to hell anyway!" (Audience laughs). And I said in return, "It seems clear enough to me what to do: I'll just have sex one week then take communion the next!" The audience roared! I feel—I hope—God has a sense of humor like me, and I kind of think s/he does!

I think my faith comes from my realization that I am merely a small part of a great, expansive universe. When I look at the sky on a clear night or watch a NOVA TV program on the subject of the universe, I know there is a grander universe than I can imagine. This is one of the many things you realize from travelling to certain parts of the world. For example, go to Iceland or to some island where it gets totally dark, or perhaps there is some place really not far from where you live where you can experience this. I have, many times, and the universe outside of us is both massive and breathtaking. It's especially there, in total darkness, that I realize again and again I am simply a bit player, as are we all, and we should be kind to one another. We are born from that universe, and we will return to it. Having a working, solid understanding of faith simply makes life easier to live with others!

CHAPTER 11

The Old Danny:
Age 70 to the Present

Deciding to embrace old age rather than deny it is the practical side of me that really realizes that I am mortal and could die any second. I haven't, obviously, though I have come close over the years, so why not face it? I am an old soul as it is anyhow, so why not enjoy it all as long as it lasts?

Being the methodical guy that I am (5 on the Enneagram remember), it's only natural to assume that I would be systematic in how I approached being a ROG (Retired Old Guy). I'll describe my five-part plan for retirement, followed by a personal take on how I view being old and what I do in the hope that it perhaps helps others carefully plan their retirement. The five parts are: Financial, Home, Community, Keeping Active, and (naturally) Travel.

Financial Stability for Retirement

In reflecting, I had had a very successful career(s) by most any measure that included 25 years in business with my partner, Kathleen. I did the traditional thing, "kind of" retiring at age 65, in the days when Social Security allowed full benefits at that age. It might be more accurate to say that I slid into retirement, in that while taking the Social Security benefits I had earned (and two other small pension retirement benefits) we actually worked part-time for an additional five years. That was only because a local major Fortune 100 company had learned of our Language of Work Model™ and wanted their internal HR staff to become proficient in the use of the model. We conducted a series of workshops, at the end of which they received certification in our approach to work clarity. The nice thing for us is that it provided additional income we had not counted on, thereby financing nearly ten additional years of mostly travel that we are still enjoying.

Kathleen, being seven years younger than I, took her Social Security benefits early; we devoted her income for a number of years to paying down our mortgage, so it is so small currently that it is not a financial burden. She also has a modest pension with monthly payments. As planned, we approached retirement with no other long-term debt and had always paid in full our credit cards at the end of each month. With debt for the average couple being so high in today's world, we were fortunate to have been part of the lucky generation that did not generally experience having large amounts of debt to adversely impact daily living and retirement. Given all this, I can say that the smartest thing in preparing for retirement, however, was marrying Kathleen, and that was beyond the benefits she brought in the way of Social Security, her annuity, and some inheritance. It's important and I'll tell you how.

As I noted already, in our business practice, we were equals getting equal pay. It's something I am proud to say I insisted on with all clients who never challenged the notion otherwise. Whenever we consulted with companies like Hewlett Packard, Microsoft, Boeing, Northrop Grumman, Connecticut Power and Light, the California Department of Water Resources, and others as well as some non-profits, we each were paid the same daily rate and slept in the same hotel room. We did well, although the work was constantly challenging in that you were waiting and hoping for the next paid work, over the course of 25 years. Due to the ebb and flow of our employment status, one of Kathleen's rules was that we had to always make sure we had at least six months of spendable income to cover daily expense needs in our checking account, while savings were kept and maintained separate for other uses such as travel, eventual retirement, and special needs that would surely arise (i.e. a new roof). We stuck to that rule pretty well. But there were other rules that we agreed on, too.

For one, always take the maximum you can when filing your business taxes when it comes to the retirement option known as SEP (Simplified Employee Pension). It's a little complicated and you can consult a tax person, but for people who have their own business and not a personal retirement program as they might have with a company they work for, this tax feature allows you to take a certain percentage of your business income and sock it away, thereby delaying tax on it until you retire with a lower tax rate. That's more than you need to know for now, but believe me from experience, putting that money away consistently year after year makes a huge difference when you retire—which you will certainly have to do, self-employed or not. For those without this benefit of a SEP, getting into the habit of putting a portion of your income away really, really makes a difference in retirement. Smart Kathleen: she made certain that we did our SEP year after year.

One needs to be proactive in your working years, self-employed or not, in preparing for retirement. That means relying on the use of someone other than yourself to do the financial planning, as few of us are that good at planning—let alone following through—on financial considerations for retirement. This requires, by the way, that I get over the notion that I am paying for someone else to do this planning for me. I found we earned more money with their guidance than we spent on fees they charge, so I learned to make my peace with it. Get used to paying for financial guidance. We found a financial planning company that fit our goals for retirement and how we would successfully reach those goals, i.e., steady income, comfort, travel, philanthropic ends, and meeting unexpected needs that might arise .

Financial planning resources are numerous: some good and some bad. For example, prior to engaging with a formal financial planner, we had used stock and mutual fund enterprises and experienced very mixed results. It was our impression that these advisors seemed to be looking out for themselves, in the way of commissions, more than us. Fortunately for me, I had had experience working for The American College that prepared professionals for financial planning, so I knew a little more than the average person, and perhaps just enough to be dangerous to myself, without Kathleen. A little more about Kathleen since she had the kind of experience that I didn't, and I learned that I had better pay attention to her.

Kathleen's father had done an excellent job preparing for his own death and financial stability for his wife, Kathleen's mother, and thus Kathleen had borne witness to it when her mother went into assisted living. Through spending time with her mother during her retirement I could tell that she was being well taken care of. She never wanted for things to make her senior years comfortable within the retirement community she resided in, so her husband had planned well. So when our own real financial planning arose for retirement, at the suggestion of a friend we went to a financial planning company called, Thrivent for Lutherans, now simply Thrivent.

Now we are not Lutherans by faith, but it makes no difference as they are quite ecumenical when it comes to financial matters. We could not have been any more fortunate. We came under the guidance of complete competency with a woman who became not just our financial advisor, but a close friend. It so happened that this particular person and I were at the time in a spiritual discussion group known as JustFaith. Thus we initially knew one another personally before employing her services as a financial advisor. That, I believe, let us know more than one would typically know about this particular financial advisor in that she had a form of integrity we could count on. I fear that the questionable integrity of some FAs may not be discovered until it's too late, so we were very fortunate. I am not here to sell you on that financial planning organization, or her (as she is herself now retired), or exactly how they do it, but unlike many others, this is a non-profit that turns back part of their earnings into philanthropic community efforts, the food bank for example. If they do that for others, imagine what their attitude is when suggesting what to do with your own money? It's certainly wouldn't be giving to themselves excessively or unwisely investing what's yours to begin with. The advice that their agent, Holly was her name, in our community provided was noteworthy in the way our capital grew and allowed us to do what we like, even far beyond our initial ten-year plan for retirement—with much travel. It's comforting, beyond what words might convey, to know that every month money appears in our banking account for everyday needs as well as travel; you go on with life the way you want day after day, with virtually no worry. Again, thanks to Kathleen and Holly for guiding us (given the challenge I can be) in the best direction. Let's move on so that Kathleen doesn't get too big a head.

Seminal Moment: Holly and Thrivent
The financial planning that occurred through Thrivent, represented by their agent Holly (our friend), was monumental in that it established and nourished a plan for our retirement that works to this day:

- *It provided a feeling of economic comfort we realized nearing the end of all that planning and execution that we would never have to worry about our future and could live comfortably for all the years of our life that remain.*
- *Our surviving partner would be taken care of*
- *We would be able to continue to travel.*

Retirement Home – The Location Is Important

I've already enumerated on my goal of assuring serenity and how our retirement home is situated in a forest, has a wonderful view to wake up to each day, and how we designed the interior to reflect our travel and support what we like to do individually to keep active in our retirement. All of this, while describing what was done physically to achieve those ends, doesn't quite capture the feeling that it gives us in our retirement; perhaps more difficult to express than any other thing I've described thus far. I'll try on a very personal level to capture what I mean so that hopefully you get an idea of how important an ideal home environment is to me in retirement.

When I first wake up each morning I kind of lay there in our bed and look around. I see what the room has in it in the way of artifacts, mostly from our travels, which sets the ambience, and it feels very warm and pleasant. Then you'll have to read in my book on *The Good Husband* how my wife and I always spend the first moments of our typical morning in our retirement: it's 10 to 20 minutes lying there in bed talking, before meeting the day. It's serenity at its finest as we begin the day. Then we get up, open the two sliding shades in an alcove area that is an extension of the bedroom, and there is the forest at eye level. There are typically a few birds drinking water from the rain gutter above, while others are chirping melodious songs in the numerous trees. As I walk out of the bedroom and look left past the banister to the downstairs, I see through several large, two-story windows a grander view of not only the trees, but a full bright sky of clouds and sun, and below is the ten-mile-long lake. In the early light the water of the lake is calm, and the surrounding mountains and trees reflect in the water, and the Canadian Cascades are in the far background with some remaining snow on the peaks. The general scene makes one calm and I feel awfully lucky to be experiencing where I am and what I am seeing in my retirement.

I step over to the kitchen and prepare my breakfast and, if the morning is warm enough, I sit out on the deck to eat and soak in the warmth of the sun that I can't seem to get enough of in our often rain prone setting. Perhaps an eagle flies by and I observe it floating there, so easily, in the sky and wish I could fly. It's quiet except for an occasional car on the road that is distant enough not to disturb the feelings I am having. I'll then go inside, sit at the round dining room table with my laptop, and write for a while. Writing is generally my morning ritual, during which I'll take a break and have a cappuccino on the front deck when the sun is up enough. There I'll sit for a while and perhaps see a deer pass by and look at me as if I were the stranger—which, of course, I am, but so appreciative that it lets me see and be there with it. I spend the rest of the day doing all the kinds of things I enjoy in my retirement: writing, gardening, repairing this or that, volunteering, walking on the nearby roads with virtually no cars, seeing and chatting with a neighbor, napping, and finally sleeping again, with the windows open and a light breeze and perhaps the hoot of an owl in the night. And I do it again and again, except when winter arrives and I want to get to my favorite island for some sun, friends, and hopefully strangers from some other country. That's my personal version of retirement with my wife who experiences her own version of serenity with friends, conversation, book reading and study, her art, some volunteering, and her time in retirement with Danny. Planning your home for retirement is very important from the vantage point of how it makes you feel day after day. I'll just note as well one other important feature that is so critical.

Because as we get older and perhaps a little or lot feebler, we have to ensure that we can physically access our home, otherwise we may have to abandon it and live elsewhere, such as in a retirement home. That may be necessary, of course, but I do all I can to mitigate having to live any place else. I, like most anyone, enjoy my freedom and the physical environment we have created in our retirement. I have nothing against retirement homes but prefer, as most would, not to live in one but rather to live independently. This means that the layout of the home must be as accessible as possible for us to get around should it physically prove harder to do so in the future. In our case, we bought the home because, in large part, the basic living quarters for the two of us are on the first floor—this includes bedroom, bathroom, kitchen, dining room, living room, utility room, and access to the outside decks (front and back). These are the essentials for physical living in our residence. All other spaces in the downstairs (which we may not so easily access at some future time) are secondary and delegated as places for storage, parttime activity, housing visiting guests, a library, and the only one other item to be missed: in the way of health equipment (massage and heated beds), which could be moved upstairs when and if we decided. This is all to say, we can live in this house well into our time of retirement with a plan for an active life, and with accommodation for outside help when needed. By the way, we have adequate insurance to cover both medical needs and long-term care. We are very fortunate in that regard.

The Kind of Community for Retirement & Community of Friends Are Important

As our retirement was approaching, we were still living in Santa Monica, California, which did not exactly exude the serenity of a forest, unless your idea of a forest is concrete and glass with about 11 million people in the greater LA area. Don't get me wrong as I loved Santa Monica, which was surprising for a boy from Idaho, and could have considered retiring there. I liked it mainly for its diversity of population. I had learned there were 90 or so different nationalities in the city (sometimes referred to as the Republic) of Santa Monica alone, and I think over nine years I saw and talked to many of them. That included lots of Ethiopians, for example, that I could greet in their native language and see their wonderment at how this white guy knew not just their language, but that they were Ethiopian in the first place rather than generic African. I also greeted some movie stars as well while walking the streets of Santa Monica or sitting in a local coffee shop. At the International Café I was studying a guy a few tables away who stared for the longest time at me as if he knew me, but he didn't. It was Al Pachino. Some of my nieces and nephews used to say I looked like Michael Caine, but I am not convinced. I just think in the Hollywood area everyone is on the lookout for the next person or thing they think they want to be a part of. Once I even showed up to play an extra for a movie and saw myself (barely for 2 seconds) in, *The Dorothy Day Story*, along with my—hardly so—costars Martin Sheen, Moria Kelly, Heather Graham, Lenny Von Dohlen, and others. They cut my hair in the '20s era style, and I had to look like that for a month before I returned to myself. My hair stylist was not exactly happy with my decision to be a movie star, but she got over it, as did I. I also worked on the production staff of a documentary that a friend of ours wrote and produced, *The Story of John Lewis*, the noted civil rights leader and congressman. The film has appeared on PBS and in several other venues over the years. I even experienced a magnitude 7.1 earthquake, and witnessed a river of wine over the sidewalk from all the bottles that broke in the liquor store just down the block. Finally, there was the time we were filmed as a couple in the background scene of a guy trying to eat fire that appeared as the lead to the opening of the nightly Jay Leno Show. We were temporary celebrities in LA in our own right for a good 18 months every night his show aired. It was a great place to experience, but not, in our collective thought, a place to retire.

For community and faith needs we attended an outstanding church of our liking, St. Monicas, that had 10,000 parishioners. We met lots of people and became very close friends with a couple dozen who enjoyed each other's company. We were the older couple amongst lots of single women, gay and lesbian friends and couples, and a couple of couples like us. When we went away on vacation, we could count on them having organized a party on our return at our condo! There was also a larger gay community associated with that church and we were honored to count a dozen or so as friends; we occasionally conducted sessions for them on couples relationships. I remember one day going down into the basement where a large supply room was organized with caged areas to house the needs of various church ministries. There I see signage designating each. There was one labeled "Gay and Lesbian Supplies." Now that is a church! I have a gay daughter and support that branch of human beings. I've even written a chapter in a friend's book on my experience learning that I had a gay child. *A Friends and Family Guide to Sexual Orientation*, was a best seller in Portugal from what I am told.

At our church, we especially loved the fantastic singing by everyone, the communion, the washing of one another's feet at Easter, the after-mass conversations, and donuts, but mainly it was the people that we so loved. It was a church that had excellent priests who knew not to act so holier than thou! Anytime we subsequently pass through Los Angeles on our way to somewhere, we stopped for a few days to see old friends over dinner and remember those who have passed.

As much as we loved Santa Monica, we made a conscious decision that we could not retire there. In addition, we recognized that our life would have to dial down from the hustle and bustle of what was a very active life working and living in an environment such as in the greater LA area. Then there were the very practical financial considerations. These included the knowledge that we would have likely never been able to pay off the loan on our condo, let alone stand the traffic that was becoming a nightmare—just try to drive on Lincoln Blvd these days! So the question began to rise to the surface: Where might we want to go to retire?

As it so happened, Kathleen's daughter was annually hitch hiking her way from Bellingham to Mexico over a few summers, so one fall, around my 62nd birthday, we drove to pick her and her boyfriend up in Bellingham with the intent of driving them to the border of Mexico. However, they decided not to go that summer to Mexico, and we looked into the idea of moving to Bellingham since we really enjoyed what we had seen during our brief stay. We went back to Santa Monica, and two months later made Bellingham our permanent and hopefully last residence.

We especially liked the fact that we are nearly Canadian and can easily get to big cities like Vancouver or Victoria or drive south to Seattle or Portland whenever we want. During COVID I was hoping the Canadians would annex us, even if just temporarily, but they never did. Of course, I love having another country so close to me as I enjoy being a citizen of the world, perhaps even more than being just a citizen of one country.

Speaking of being a citizen, when it comes to community, Bellingham is very much about caring for others. We wanted to be in our retirement living in a community that would support our versions of being in commune with others—not anywhere near like in Santa Monica (been there and done that), but more on a person-to-person level that suits retirees—there is a difference. For one thing, in Bellingham there are lots of young people—a university of 10,000—to be around, and old people (like us) need young people! "Hamsters"—a local portmanteau of the words Bellingham and Hamster—as the young people sometimes refer to themselves, are mostly from the local university and many find it hard to leave Bellingham after graduation, given all that it has to offer. They often end up living five to a house just to stay and pretend they can make a living. That's okay because it keeps the community young and for old people like us that's good to be a part of. Volunteering at the food bank, for example, I've gotten to know a number of giving young people (David and Nate) and enjoy the exchanges we had. I think it keeps my perspective young and in tune with what's going on, even if I won't get (yet) a tattoo or dye my hair green.

Bellingham is, thankfully, a relatively small community on a beautiful bay and the hiking and biking trails help keep one fit. It's richly inhabited by numerous kinds of wild creatures who, after all, own the environment we share with them. The community has numerous programs that well serve the needs of its residents and those who are less fortunate. With so many homeless people these days, it's great to live in a community that cares for all its citizens. For example, there is a place called Base Camp, where the homeless can find services, day and night for shelter, meals, and various forms of support to help with their special needs. And as older retired people, there are numerous ways for volunteering that you can engage in which is so important to maintain vitality in retirement. Bellingham provides those opportunities and I'll address more of that in the next and final chapter.

Of course there is the physical community you select for retirement, such as we did in selecting Bellingham, but then there is also the community of people one needs to foster for a healthy, active retirement with others of your age and interests. We obviously gave up a wonderful community of people when we left Santa Monica. We'd have to foster the same in our new community, and while it took some time, on a much smaller scale, we have. Again, we found much of that by being involved in a local church that was shepherded by a wonderful priest. He has since left on another assignment, as was required, but the friendships he helped foster for us have endured for the most part. Unfortunately, death takes some of these away, but we have cherished them and others. So creating and maintaining a community with people requires constant attention to foster new friends and Kathleen is the leading force in doing so. We do have wonderful friends in our neighborhood: Bob, Clarine, Jerry, Matt, Clair, Sara Jane, Kelly, Sean, Ian, Jay and Jen, Jessica, Phillip, and Steve and Doug and their twins (who sadly had to recently move). We also have friends in town or elsewhere like Karen, Jess, Mary, Nick, Kari, Jennifer, Maureen, David, Tom, and others like Thyatira on Vendovi Island. Some have been our travel companions to foreign lands or to a baseball game, sailing, and on plenty of walks or to the local breweries. Kathleen has fostered friendships with fellow artists, while I am pretty much a loner, with some exception, who mooches off Kathleen's friends. Must admit that I do generally enjoy the company of women over men, which isn't to say I don't have male friends, both here and abroad. This is all to say, in retiring, we picked well both our physical location and community of friends.

Keeping Active

Starting retirement is easy; keeping it active in meaningful ways takes planning and effort. If I don't proactively keep active, I might sit—as many do—in an easy chair watching TV and watch my life passing me by. Can't imagine doing that.

As I previously noted, we kept working a little at the beginning of our retirement because of workshops we conducted for a locally based company. This, as it turned out, mitigated that feeling that many have experienced on their sudden retirement of feeling that they don't know what to do with their free time and so miss the hustle and bustle of their working days. This was a concern for us, especially as the busy couple we had been. So working a little longer, although officially retired, was useful financially, but also psychologically. Also as it turned out there was a related project we undertook, prompted at the suggestion of a professional colleague. He encouraged us to write a monthly blog so that we could share with others our years of work experience, knowledge, and successes. All of this was helpful in the transition from a very busy work schedule to a more relaxed retirement state of being.

Presently at the time of this writing, now that I am in "real" retirement, I find that my writing keeps the wheels of my brain greased and rotating, so I know it's good for me. I don't mind doing things for free as long as they help me learn new things and keep me intellectually and/or physically involved. Kathleen sits on the advisory board for a university and another community initiative on racial equality, while I occasionally hear from someone who is using my model for work; it's fun to learn what they are doing with it and how I might provide some further insights for their use. But mostly these days, delivering food door to door for the food bank is exactly the kind of thing I like to do, and I meet so many interesting clients of the food bank in the process. We even now know one another on a first name basis—including Evelyn, Henry, Paul, Lindsay, and Rodney.

Kathleen, for her part, has developed an interest—and quite the skill—of a collage artist. She, like my previous spouse, has the bent for art, as the Irish seem to, and she is very good at it. I love to be asked to help her frame her work for shows, and when she wants to know what I think of a particular piece of her art. She is an avid developer of relationships with others, especially women, many of whom she has mentored in business, as well as personal life. People consider her "practical" when in the throes of emotional issues.

I, for my part, keep active in retirement. That manifests itself in several different ways. First, I like to volunteer! My main volunteer activity, as I have noted, has been the local food bank. Bellingham might well have the finest food bank in the entire US and the director , Mike Cohen, I've known for years has much to do with its success. But he knows (and I know) that it's about volunteers and as I said, volunteering in Bellingham exists as a culture of service to others. It's an extension of the community that is so involved with helping people, especially those in need, of which there are so many in today's society. I like it because I like serving and it provides something meaningful to do every week. Initially I sorted and cleaned vegetables collected or gleaned from the local stores and farms and did distribution during the bi-weekly sessions. Soon, however, I needed more action and started driving the truck to pick up produce and other food items from the local grocery stores, coffee houses, and even a bagel store. I initially drove with old guys like me for a couple of years, but soon it was gradually younger guys and gals, and they were a hoot for me, as the older person, to be with. A few were gay or trans and we had wonderful times talking about their brief experiences in life compared to this old guy. I did that for ten years and got to know and counsel many a receiving clerk in the half-dozen stores we stopped at to recover food from each day. Trader Joe's definitely donates the best quality food and regularly contributes 1500 to 2000 pounds per day. Costco was right behind them. Haggen, a local food store chain, did well, but it was a major food retailer that could have done so much more yet didn't. Doing this kind of volunteering shows you what Americans consume compared to other countries, such as what I learned from my experience living in Ethiopia, where food and water is at a premium and of a limited kind. Just saying, it teaches you things and you try to be a little better from what you learn about it.

The food bank eventually got a little more professional and were able to hire full-time staff (Roland, Matt, Melanie). Therefore the volunteers were no longer driving the food truck, for reasons that made legal and liability sense. I switched over to riding shotgun with various drivers and got to know one, Bill Piersall, rather well. We had lots of laughs and enjoyed exchanges between this old man and that younger man on his journey to getting older (and wiser). I finally morphed into directly delivering boxes of food to the homes and apartments of those in need during the COVID pandemic and just finally retired recently. Occasionally I got to talk to some of my clients at their door and they are were so thankful for the delivery. I am equally thankful to them for the opportunity, remembering well when I went with my mother for such volunteer work.

Seminal Moment: The Bellingham Food Bank

This volunteer effort on my part represents my contribution to society beyond just living, work that I did as a professional, and the business we had. It gave me a continuous opportunity to give back as much as it gave me something meaningful to do in my retirement years.

- *I met so many wonderful people such as fellow volunteers, clients, and store personnel where I picked food up.*
- *I learned much more about the kindness and generosity of the community in which I live.*
- *It was a kind of travel in my own backyard.*

Beyond the food bank, I took on a couple of other volunteer efforts because they matched up to my kind of volunteering. I became actively involved on the board of a non-profit. I just completed three years of service. The Bellingham Community Meal program serves a monthly, usually hot, meal where 200 to 300 homeless people and others can come to eat, commune, and perhaps obtain needed items, like socks for example. Before COVID, I especially liked washing the dishes because it's a fast-paced operation that uses my organizational skills. Having an occasional patron hand me their dirty dishes, a smile, and his or her gratitude is all that I need, as if I needed that, considering the life I've lived. When COVID came on and we were relegated to providing only takeaway meals, I took on the assignment of purchasing around $1500 of ingredients needed by the chef who prepares the monthly meal. I can't seem to get over having been tasked with buying 150 lbs. of meat for example, compared to what I buy when I shop for Kathleen and me.

Finally, on the volunteer side of things I like, I occasionally sign up to gather bagels from the local shop, The Bagelry; they smell so fresh. I deliver these to two or three centers that serve the needy as well as to a teen center for troubled youth. Again, you get that thank you in recognition that you have made someone's day.

Retirement for me on the "keeping active" side has also included committing to paper and electronic means that which I have cherished as work, my rich family history, and sharing with others my thoughts on how to be a good husband. I have already told you about the book I wrote on being *The Good Husband*, but I also wrote a memoirbiography, as I labeled it. It recounts my impressions of what my mother did for her children, others, and of course her life's story. I titled it, *My Mother Can Beat Up Your Father*, and I meant the title not so much literally (which she never did), but rather to convey the extraordinary person that she was. Hopefully, in these pages, the reader gleans the account of the son who learned so much from his mother, and also how he went out into life to live it just as she would have liked to do (and indeed prayed for), had she had the time and opportunity to do so herself, if not for the fact that she was tending to her children and business. We were the lucky ones for all her efforts and love.

Aside from what I just described about my active retirement—sort of program wise—I want to address what I consider miscellaneous activities I engage in regularly to keep active and to help ensure I will live long enough to enjoy the travel and volunteering I crave in retirement. These may be of some benefit to consider doing yourself when approaching retirement.

First, I believed in (and still practice) getting around quickly. No, I don't mean running a marathon, hiking, going to the gym every day, playing golf, or similar activities. Neither am I opposed to these for others, except to the extent when they excessively wear on your body or consume some of that time better helping others. Each to their own, and here is my own.

When I say get around quickly, that means I walk with an uptick to my gait. It's not running and it's not a fast walk as if in an Olympic event. Rather, it's getting from here to there at a steady pace. Inside or outside the house, I find that helps keep my limbs limber and my heart rate at a comfortable rate above a normal walking pace—a Fitbit can easily help one figure out what that gait should be. Call me crazy, but it works, and my overall health is excellent compared to the average 70- or 80-year-old. Now 86 I get around better than most of my contemporaries.

I know it works since people often compliment me for being so young and spry. Just watch me!

Second, I am going to take a break in the writing of my autobiography to do something that I do nearly daily. It illustrates an activity that I suggest doing in retirement. Like the active gait I just described, and essential to your long-term wellbeing and health if not survival, is taking a break to reflect on things. It's another version of napping except in this case you are awake, but relaxed. My usual version of this, especially after writing at the computer for an hour, is to prepare a small cappuccino, get two chocolate chip cookies I made the day before, and step out my front door and sit for 15 minutes with nature. It's a moment in which to listen and contemplate things. It's a daily ritual for me, except when it's extremely cold and I am even known to challenge that on occasion and walk briefly somewhere in the neighborhood. As an alternative, I've created two other such break areas around the outside of the house for different views, one of which has a large previously used bathroom mirror to reflect the forest, no matter where I sit.

As a part of my daily break, I recently downloaded an app (Merlin) for identifying birds. I've learned that there were four different birds making melodious sounds just outside my front door: a Red-breasted Nuthatch, American Robin, Spotted Towhee, and a Violet-green Swallow. Now, I am not—nor ever will be—a birder but sitting and hearing their sounds really relaxes me. I've never been one to readily identify the names of various kinds of trees, cars, bushes, flowers, or much of anything else, let alone birds, but that has not kept me recently from trying. I am proud to note that I can finally identify the beautiful shrill of the Spotted Towhee. Most important is how relaxing it is to sit—sometimes, especially with my wife, for a while in director chairs I bought from the local Salvation Army store for $4.00—and contemplate life, let alone have a nice conversation or hear the other sounds found in our particular forest. That's my version of easy chairs without the TV. I highly recommend you find yours and do it at least 3 times a week in your dotage. (Excuse me for fifteen minutes while I prepare a cappuccino, get my cookies, and sit outside; then I'll be back to continue writing one of the more important things I insist upon in my retirement that is fully my responsibility to constantly monitor.)

The third thing I do with regularity is monitor my health. Part of this is just my curiosity (my science background) to know what's going on both within and outside my body, but mostly it's preventative maintenance. You'll recall my describing the full body scan I had in my middle age just to see what my insides look like. I have both curiosity about my well-being as well the knowledge that I should be proactive in monitoring my health, lest something adverse develop to my overall wellbeing, especially in retirement. Being in good health is key to my favorite activity: travel. So I schedule an annual physical. Then about every three to five years, I make appointments to have my heart, gut, and colon monitored, as well as to check on the three aneurysms that were identified years ago. I have learned the latter have not grown, so I am a happy camper about that. Years ago, when my vascular surgeon, the delightful Dr. Michell Sohn, told me that when an aneurysm breaks it's a catastrophic event that you are unlikely to recover from, I got the point. So we check the aneurysms out now and then, and I have been told to not come back for another five years, and that five years is coming up, and so I will go again. I've also had an artery in my neck checked and repaired with some kind of artificial material. Oh, the doctor who did that operation was new in town when he performed his repair of my artery, and a year later he was gone. It makes you wonder if they found out he was actually a board-certified plumber rather than a surgeon! I'll never know, but I have done fine for the seventeen years since the operation. Best to keep checking it now and then, I think. I also utilize a wonderful chiropractor (Dr. Keller) who adjusts what needs adjusting based on an analytical, scientific approach to his practice that is especially noteworthy, and much appreciated, by this analytical guy. This is all to say that I have appreciated all that my medical community over the past decades has done for me to live a healthy life. I've always mentioned to them all that, if I can someday afford it, I'll take them to my favorite island. So, many thanks to Drs. McClusky, Hopper, McAllister, Fisher, Sohn, Venose, Dickey (a fellow travel addict), Levinson, Van Dusen, Santoro, and Moreno.

The fourth thing I do is take a walk almost every day. I have one of those Fitbits and look at it to measure how many steps I have taken (about 6000 daily) and my heart rate. Just another thing so easy to do that monitors you in your latter days.

As a kind of semi-scientist (i.e., chemistry teacher, remember), I also believe in science. To my way of thinking and acting, it means there are drugs and vaccines that work. If you want to ignore science you take the risk that you know better than science, or your doctor, or both (or some damn conspiracy going around). I believe in science and making it work for me. I know I have settled in my retirement on the right combination of both prescriptions I put into my body to mitigate certain issues (i.e., cholesterol, blood pressure, gastric juices, arterial disease), and also choose to be aided by the taking of certain homeopathic ingredients that work in concert with prescriptions. I utilize the services of a delightful homeopathic, natural path doctor, Dr. Van Dusen, that I literally trust with my life. This combination of prescriptions and natural things really seems to work for me, and I am religious about taking my pills, morning and evening, every day.

The fifth thing I do—and suggest to other husbands—may come as a surprise to men and even some dread to wives, but it is, for me, marvelous in my retirement: I suggest men regularly prepare dinner with their spouse.

When I was a kid of about twelve, I started cooking a little. First, I learn how to make a pie (I guess because I liked pie). It turned out to be interesting to try to do in that it's not as easy as it looks. There is an art to using two tableware knives to mix flour and butter to make a flaky pie crust from scratch—yes, I know there are more modern means, but sometimes the old ways are just more fun. With a little practice I got the hang of it and was soon on to making some different kinds of pastries filled with jams, apples, berries, and other fruits. It was encouraging to get raves from my sisters and brothers. When I was in graduate school, I often cooked my own meals—they were pretty rudimentary but I preferred them to eating out, and fast foods were not so prevalent in those days (thank god). Fast forward to being married: I could often be counted on to strike up the barbie for family dinners. But I really came into my culinary skills—if they can be labeled as such—during retirement.

I don't subscribe to the traditional role for women of being the chief cook and bottle washer, likely since my mother was a working woman and father rolled in one. My wife is an excellent cook whose claim to fame, she says, is that she can prepare any meal in five minutes if needed. The point I want to get to here is that in our retirement we cook dinner together, using virtually no processed ingredients, and it is with great joy that we both participate in doing so. Watching us dance around one another in the kitchen area is a work of art I might say as we each smoothly (if not in one another's way on occasion) decide who will do what. A healthy gourmet level meal often results from recipes we have in our repertoire, housed in a binder, or harvested from the internet, or occasionally experiment with or the several prepared meals we have put together for those times we don't feel like cooking. There is something about cooking together that brings a couple joy in ways that nothing else can and, of course, good conversation void of processed ingredients is a bonus to health. Then there is putting the dishes in the dishwasher that I can't say either of us truly enjoys, but we do it together, with myself I as the chief organizer of how best to arrange them in the washer (which my partner is only too happy to relinquish the right to do so to me).

Finally, I am going to suggest one other activity. You may think that perhaps going a bit too far this time, but I think singing really is important to one's health in retirement. If you can't sing, then find something else that rocks your boat, like listening to recorded music, perhaps while dancing or a nice drive in the countryside. I started learning the guitar at the time I went overseas in the Peace Corps and felt the need for some form of personal entertainment that would otherwise not be available, let alone for others to enjoy. I wasn't very good at it initially—it was somewhat embarrassing participating in a talent show we teachers put on for our Ethiopian students—but I kept at it. When the internet came to be, I found that I could look up the chords to all the songs I like and with more practice I got better and better. I am still not really good, but I've got a little Willy Nelson or Buddy Holly in me, so it's okay with me and others. I've put together a song book of around 120 hymns, folk songs, country and western tunes, and even a couple of rock and roll oldies but goodies. I get the guitar out now and then and let it rip. After building up my confidence that I was a decent vocalist (like my dad and brother Buzz), I started singing for others beyond my personal concerts for my wife, who readily reinforces my behavior with her request for her favorite tunes. I've gone to a couple of retirement homes to entertain a crowd that really responds to music even if they may not know what's going on around them. This one time, for example, I was playing for my wife's mother who was in one such retirement home. We were all alone together in a large sitting room, except for another resident who had Alzheimers and was seated in the far corner. The woman was there in absolute silence and rocking a bit back and forth. When I begin playing and singing "When the Saints Go Marching In" she stood up and started marching around the perimeter of the room to every lyric. Soon she came over to Kathleen and laid her head on her shoulder, mouthing the words coming to her from a deep recess of her life's experiences. You don't think singing is good for you and your health? See what it does for others—the elderly especially—and, in turn, to you. With that said, I shall conclude my description of my version of retirement by recommending a mechanical device that I have found to be a godsend in my retirement years, as well as in many years leading up to it, while I was still actively working. No, this is not an advertisement, and I will not be receiving any professional fees.

One day Kathleen told me about something she experienced while out with friends strolling and shopping on the Third Street Promenade in Santa Monica. Seen through the window of a storefront was a kind of massaging bed. They walked in and learned that, after a short 10-minute video you had to watch, you could lie on and get a 40-minute mechanically provided back massage for free. You could come back as many times for the free massage as you liked, but you had to watch the video every time—quite the sales job, I thought. It took lots of encouragement from her (I am sometimes known to resist new things), but I finally went in for a try. I'd say I probably went three times before I was sold on the benefits of this particular device.

Fast forward a few years, when we moved to Bellingham, we bought (at a discount I might add) one of the massaging beds from a dealer that was moving elsewhere. Lying flat on your back, the device in question has a set of heated jade rollers that go all along your entire spine from your tailbone to the occipital bone on the back of your skull. The device can be programmed to perform a couple different patterns where it stops at certain key pressure-points, as it rises up or down to massage the full length of your spine. What it does to relieve aches and pains is remarkable. (What a sales job on my part, and without any commission!) The name of the device (and again I am not a salesman on commission), is Ceragem, but I just call it, my girlfriend, Sara!

Now since I do lots of writing, seated for hours at a computer, often well beyond what I should, (let alone the arthritis that comes to every elderly person), this device is simple nirvana. Including it as part of my daily routine of walking, needed prescriptions and supplements, attitude of being relaxed and not worrying, some bird watching, and contemplating our forest, and getting around at a steady pace, I do pretty good in my retirement. Sara is my other lady love, but I unfortunately, can't take her on vacation with us. Wish I could! Once while traveling in Cambodia, we were walking down a side street of simple shops when I saw in this dusty store an older version of Sara, and I was stunned that they had discovered it too, so far from its origin. I signed up for a treatment far from my home and was so relieved by the benefits it gave me from all that walking and touring.

Travel Is My Elixir in Retirement, As It Was Throughout All My Life

It only seems right and just that I end my description of retirement on the topic of travel. You have read a great deal about where I've been all over the world, lived for a while in Africa and a sabbatical in Germany, and started my journeys in my own backyard—the Pacific Northwest—starting in my late teens. Travel throughout my life is abundant, to say the least , but its importance in retirement is especially so for me. To believe that I can still, and do, travel in my eighties and is significant both to my personal well-being and with what I've done in life as it is to my optimism that I yet have things to see and enjoy. I will not focus here again on where I've gone and what I've seen and experienced as I have already done so in other pages. Rather, I'd like to describe what travel has done to make me very satisfied during my youth, middle aged, old person, and a citizen of the world. I am a US citizen, but I think and act like a citizen of the world and the significance of this cannot be lost in its importance as manifested in the ways in which I treat people.

I am a very satisfied old person. Lots of experiences in life have led to such, but the biggest reason for this, aside from a wonderful marriage, children, professional life, and my growing up years with a fabulous family, has been my travel. When I crossed that train bridge as a youth, I learned something about the other side of the tracks, and the journey getting there and coming back. I've since obviously taken that to the extreme in traveling to numerous places in the world, and several of these again and again. So other than seeing lots of great things, experiencing numerous adventures, and meeting and interacting with some fascinating and interesting people, what has all that travel done for my retirement and final days?

I have found travel continues to enhance my understanding of humanity in terms of how we should treat one another. It's truly a never-ending thing as society is not as fixed in its ways, means, and behavior as it might seem, but rather circumstances change and people are impacted often by things they have absolutely no control over (floods, famine, economics and political conditions, and so on). To function within this, we have to know, appreciate, and understand one another as best we can; act accordingly for the betterment of mankind. It's too simple, for example, to just ignore a war, famine, or such. For example I don't believe in borders, although I do understand the need to control entry for economic and political reasons. Still, there is a need for some form of openness because of economic factors (e.g., agricultural needs) and to escape political repression. Traveling has made me realize that we are all—except indigenous people—immigrants on some level and must respect those who seek to immigrate just as our own relatives did at some distant time, for reasons not so dissimilar. Reseaching your family genealogy, as I have my own, will reveal this fact for you. Recognizing this helps to strengthen a nation and its economy much more than hurts it, let alone what they add to the mix of people that make up our country.

The second lesson I have learned from travel relates to learning our differences and similarities as humans simply eking out a living and attempting to provide for our offspring and get along with fellow human beings. When I lived in Ethiopia, I saw the huge difference between how they and I lived in general. No matter the poverty one sees amidst diseases, lack of water and such, I realized people are people and must be respected, and that I should be not just sympathetic, but willing to help in whatever big or small ways I can. I can't get that kind of gut-level check of the human condition (and my responsibility to do something about it), by cruising on a cruise ship. I must go amongst the people on foreign soil to see and get to know what they are like, talk to them, and what might be done to help (let alone what we share in common).

There is so much more to note about what travel teaches us, but I shall close with the friends and strangers I have met along the way and how I so love each for the memories they have provided me with in my older days. There were, of course, the long-term friends that were established and we went back again and again to see and have good times with. There were the transitional friends we met only while on some island or crossing a street and started talking, or sitting at a coffee bar and conversing, or on a train or public bus ride from here to there. And there were so many, many others we exchanged a simple smile with to acknowledge one another of different cultures, ethnicity, economic strife, or treated with respect as they serviced us on some ship, island, or hotel we stayed at or ride we shared in their taxi to the airport. There was especially the Austrian couple (Mo and Gunther) I met on my favorite island. They saved my life when they rescued me from a riptide that was taking me out to sea. I was only saved when one of them—the smart one of us—was in a kayak and she stewarded it so I could hold on, and her husband –the other smart one—had flippers that I—the only dumb one—didn't—and they pulled and pushed me to safety together. With my snorkel mask still on in the midst of this panic (and it was all of that), I'll never forget seeing a river of sand rapidly slough off the sandy bar as fast as any river rapids I'd seen in the world or walked in with my fishing waders in my youth. Just moments before we had all been walking on that very narrow sandbar to get to where danger was lurking. Who knew what danger lay ahead in what seemed like peaceful waters? Isn't that the way life is at times we don't expect? Upon return to our Bach (a beach house we were staying in), Mo, our new Austrian friend said to my wife "I bet you won't let Danny come out and play with us anymore?" She did, and I am still here and still traveling.

When we truly know people of the world, we treat one another with respect, genuine interest, a bit of curiosity, and, in my case, with shared humor and lots of smiles. We have to leave one another, of course, but we had a brief encounter and good times. It's an understatement to say that I learned and benefited from travel.

Now to the final topic nearing the end of retirement that nobody seems to want to talk about, but I will, as it doesn't really scare me (much).

CHAPTER 12

Danny's Approach to Finality

The guy approaching his mortality is not the same as the kid who started his journey being born in The Warehouse and exploring the various junkyards during his youth. All of us change in our own way; and the change is more fulfilling for some due to a myriad of factors. In my life I made conscientious decisions about certain things I deemed needed improving and others that were just there and beyond my influence. As I now approach finality/death, I have made plans that most simply ignore and leave to others. I have done this with the belief that my wife, in particular whom I deeply love, and the family in general, would appreciate it if I did certain things in advance that they would otherwise be compelled to do in more emotional times. It's important in that it makes me feel good to have done so.

I've taken care of the more usual things that they say you should do in preparation for death. I have a will in place, power of attorney, designated who gets what and have updated it over the years as things have changed. I have, as part of that, an Advanced Directive and decided to be an organ donor, which is noted on my driver's license. This pre-planning, as it might be thought of, is driven by my own varied experiences with the deaths of my loved ones, too numerous by far. That, naturally, includes my own parents, most of my brothers and sisters, and several good friends and professional colleagues. It's especially driven by the too-early in life death of my own daughter,

Lisa, at the age of 48. I've also held a dying 16-year-old boy in my arms as I witnessed an auto accident right in front of my car and came to his aid holding him in his last breath as his father was buckled in the seat next to him. I've given comfort to two different neighbor friends as I administered CPR (unsuccessfully) from heart attacks. So I know death. All of that has been enough for me to realize my time is coming and so I had better prepare with grace and a plan, and a good attitude towards the inevitable. Thus my preparation for finality, some of which I've already mentioned, has taken on several different forms. Some you'll find a bit unconventional, but they really work for me.

First, I've written my own obituary. A little unconventional I know, but I am very comfortable with having done so. I have often read, as most elderly people seem to do, others' obituaries in the newspaper and have wanted, on occasion, more details and a personal touch than generally provided. With the ever-decreasing reading of newsprint, I am afraid this practice is fading and that is, in my opinion, truly a shame, as one can learn lessons of life from the departed. One learns a great deal about others' lives from reading obituaries, not to mention it reminds the living that they had better get on with productive things during their own time on earth, and the days they are using up. You read about people your own age, some that have passed long before you, fewer of those older of course, and even the young who got cheated out of even a reasonable period of time. The thing for me is that these obits often seem so impersonal, written to a script (I am sure) provided by the mortuary or the newspaper itself. They don't typically give you the essence of that person and what they valued about life, not really containing enough detail of what they personal thought, from their own point of view, or treasured. Instead, much of the latter often comes, if at all, during a vigil, if they or their loved ones, have chosen to have one for their passing and usually takes the form of a slideshow and/or testimonials of friends and family telling what they think needs telling or showing. That being said, I understand the practicality of the average obituary needing to be short due to costs (which itself seems ironic), and the struggle of a family or friend, or even the need of the obit writer at the newspaper in writing an interesting account. Still, the obit should truly reflect who the person really was, or at least who he or she thought they were. Everyone is important in their own way. Why not get a more truthful, complete sense of that from your own point of view? Therefore, I recommend writing your own.

I have written, and continue to edit occasionally, my own obit. It has the usual information about when and where I was born, my parents, brothers and sisters living and those that died, and when and where I went to school. I had to restrict the listing of numerous places I've traveled, but the reader will get the idea I've been to lots of places and had unusual adventures. These things are all important, but I also wanted to reflect how I felt about life, what I valued, and what I believe I contributed. And, of course, my sense of humor towards life.

Like writing a book (such as this one), the obit has provided a kind of reflection on the whole of my life, that I was a good person. I have jokingly said to others, after telling them that I have written my obit "Just don't let my wife edit it, as she has fortunately done for all my other writing." Of course I jest, but reflected in my final writing should be me, even perhaps with my sentence structure issues, use of too many words, and the spelling errors from failing and having to retake the first grade again. That was—and is—Danny. It's not in my obit, but I've even apologized to my wife for my passing (even though I haven't yet), just so she knows how much I loved her, and how she will miss me, but her life must go on. On that note, I have always remembered the words that an elderly woman spoke, nearing the time of her own passing, to her grandchild, when that child remarked "I will miss you," and her grandmother responded, "I know you will." There is a special kind of sincerity and honesty in that response that tells a great deal about the grandmother's sense of her life and death. I hope I have that same calmness and celebration of my life reflected in my obituary.

In preparation for writing my obit—and this very book—I did

something which was additionally insightful to my life and finality. I had plenty of laughs doing so and wonderful memory recalls. This particular activity I highly recommend even if you don't end up writing your own obit. It's kind of like running the movie of your life backwards.

A year ago I gathered up, went through, and organized the artifacts of my life that had accumulated by me, as well as other items handed down from my mother, and some from my siblings. Not just photos in my case, but lots of other things like articles I'd written, old badges to conferences I had attended, slips of paper jotted with ideas of things I wanted to pursue or write, old passports, travel knickknacks, boy scout badges, and on and on. As they came into my life over the years, I had placed these into four hanging file folders for safekeeping within our personal and business file drawer. There were my original social security and draft cards, drafts of ideas I had written but never published, things the kids drew and gave to me—especially a poem by Lisa, written at age 7. She noted that our dog, named Sweetwater, seemed to like Dad the most, as well as dedicated the poem about spring, summer, fall, and winter to her dad. How that poem touches me so to this very day.

I also had lots of articles I had written, awards received, ideas I had but didn't get to, all my grade school report cards, you get the idea. Recently I went through these and sorted out what's keepable, and what has meaning probably only to me. I partly did this so that others wouldn't have to do it without even really knowing what some things were. But mainly I did it for myself: to be reminded, be thankful, and say "Did I really do that, and now I remember?" For me, it helped determine what to include in my autobiography with a greater degree of accuracy and specificity. It helped me piece my life together with details I had forgotten. It was fun, I cried a little, and I used the collection to write my obit, this autobiography, and to tell stories as I do with friends, and of course, my darling wife. Here's a preprint version of my obit, and with it, I'll move on to what else I've done to prepare myself (others, really) for death.

Obituary: Danny G Langdon

I can honestly say that I had a great life. I was part of a wonderful family of nine children: five of my mother, Marian Orena Smith Langdon and father, Lambert (Bert) Lucius Langdon. I was born (in a warehouse) November 16, 1938, and I didn't really know my father since he died when I was but seven. Never mind since my mother was simply the best. She ran her own scrap metal business for 40 years and was every bit a lady and man rolled into one. Mother Of The Year in Idaho and runner up in the nation, she was a generous person to everyone. I wrote a book about her titled, "My Mother Can Beat-up Your Father," and while I suspect she could, she never had a mean bone in her body. My brothers and sisters, six of whom (Marian, Lynn, Archie, Dorothy, Buzz, Bertine, and Lucille) predeceased me, were all very talented and wonders in their individual ways. Only one sister, Lorraine managed to outlive me and, even though older, I congratulate her for that accomplishment and look forward to camping out with all in due time.

I was born in Twin Falls, Idaho, had a wonderful childhood of exploring, playing (loved Anti-Anti-I-Over), and laughing with neighborhood kids. We listened to the radio, used our imagination, and played various outdoor games. I was part of what I called the Lucky Generation. I was an Eagle Scout, as well Order of the Arrow. High school was fun, and I participated in many activities and held some leadership roles, graduating in 1957. I attended the University of Idaho for a B.S. (Chemistry Education), a master's degree from the University of Missouri (M. Ed.), and numerous graduate courses at New York University, University of Pennsylvania, and Catholic University. I joined the Peace Corps (met John Kennedy at the White House) when it first started in 1962 and served two years in Ethiopia at the Harar Teacher Training School; at the time I was the only fulltime high school chemistry teacher in Ethiopia. I was privileged when Haile Selassie, the emperor, and King of Kings of Ethiopia, entered my classroom one day. My career as a training manager, instructional designer and adult learning researcher spanned 26 years before I became a recognized international consultant in business modeling with my wife and partner in life and business, Kathleen Swanick Whiteside Langdon in our company, Performance International. I was the innovator of the Language of Work Model™ that is used in many businesses and was recognized by my professional colleagues as an Honorary Life Member of the International Society for Performance Improvement (ISPI). I was the association's international president in 1989-90 and received three awards of excellence. I wrote thirteen books, was the series editor of a 40-volume series that captured the prevailing training and education methods, wrote chapters in at least a dozen other books, and authored many articles and a blog. My book, "The Good Husband: 50 Practices That Will Make You Nearly Perfect," was a joy to write since it spoke to the love story, I had with my wife Kathleen. She taught me so many things. I loved singing and playing the guitar, especially Kathleen who loved each and every country and western, rock and roll, folk song, or hymn. My love song to her was, "Loving Her Was Easier Than Anything I'll Ever Do Again."

More than work, I liked to travel. My wife often referred to me as a "travel junky" and it was true. I lived, worked, spoke at international conferences, or just traveled for pleasure to at least 90+ countries (many repeatedly). I really liked people of all cultures, finding them generally more fascinating than most Americans, and often commented that travel is half about seeing things and half about meeting and getting to know and understand other cultures and being appreciative of our differences. I especially want to thank the lovely people of Ethiopia and the Cook Islands (especially Glynn and Dora). Also, our close friends in Bellingham, including our wonderful neighbors and our special travel friends, Bob, and Clarine. I was a friend to the gay community where I often found many more interesting people than in the straight population. I so enjoyed for over 16 years volunteering at the Bellingham Food Bank; driving the truck and interacting with many at the various stores in our town from whom we collected food. I had great conversations with my fellow volunteers, receiving clerks, and the

Food Bank staff. I also volunteered at the Pickford Film Center, the Food Recovery Program, and served on the Board of the Bellingham Community Meal.

I had two wonderful children, Kimberly, and Lisa (who preceded me, sadly, in death). My grandchildren were a wonder to be with, including Brittney, Justin, Trevor, Ryan, Annika, Miles, and Ethan. It was a special blessing to have at least one great-grandchild, Zoey. I thank my first wife Patricia for two wonderful children and for years of good family times. I especially thank my second wife, Kathleen, who is the love of my life—a true partner that shared life to the fullest and I loved so deep in my soul I could not help but constantly express it. Collaborating with her in business was the best part of working; being in her presence was such a joy and pleasure to emulate for others. Her gift to me of her two own children, whom I always thought of as my children as well, were icing on the cake of life. Johnilee (my spare daughter as she so warmly liked to refer to herself) was such a joy, as is her daughter, Ethan. Nathan was and is the unusual child that makes life so interesting and the closest I came to having a son.

In closing, I'd like to leave some advice. As I think I demonstrated throughout life, it is helpful to not worry about things on a daily basis. If you do worry, it shows up on your face for everyone to see and makes you far older than you should really look or act at any given age. I loved life, smiling at things seemingly minor and making sure to make others smile and be happy. I remembered well the lessons my mother taught me by example that I, in turn, hopefully passed on to others in family, friends, or just strangers with whom I came into contact in this wonderful, fascinating world. Hope to see many of you in that other place that I am sure must exist given the vastness of this tiny spot we lived on in the endless universe. I came to realize, in my own words, that:

I am in the universe, the universe is in me, and there I will always be.

Most of what else I've done in preparation for my finality are practical things when you closely digest them. For one, I've written a User Manual (in the safe deposit box) for my wife to help her with the things that I normally did when we were together. That's the systems person within me, who trained so many others in the business world, and developed a Work Formula for workers, managers, and executives. The manual is sixteen pages long and has reminders or instructions of what's needs to be done to run the house, pay the bills, and regular maintenance like winterizing. I was surprised, as was Kathleen, that there are so many things involved in running our lives these days both with and for your spouse. Add on all the numerous things she does and the number of pages grows longer. I didn't want her to wonder where the insurance policies are or what the password to our checking account is or how to generally manage the house, which she will have to abandon one day. We talked over this User Guide, added some things, and she is confident that she will be able to carry on without her Danny Boy, who would have loved to stay and be doing it all again with her. This guide should help out, if not remind. It's a loving thing to do, and very practical, if not very cheerful.

I've also planned where, with Kathleen's concurrence, we will be laid to rest. In my case that was pretty much preordained. As it happens—you know my mother by now—our mother had a half dozen burial plots leftover at the local cemetery in Twin Falls. This cemetery is where many of the Langdons have been laid to rest. Why, you say, would a woman have a bunch of extra burial plots? Well, my mother was an extraordinary woman who planned not only for herself, but for others. If it wasn't the hired hand who worked all those years for her, a dear friend, or just a poor person whom she knew and heard had died and didn't have a place of final rest, she offered up one of the extra plots she had bought, just in case it was needed. I never asked how she came to obtain them, but (like her salt and pepper shakers collected in the hundreds), she had several, probably numbering 15 plots in total. As I and my remaining siblings approach our own need for a final resting spot, we had to decide what to do with the six spots that remained. My wife and I have chosen one for our mutual use, rather than waste space separately for two. Besides it's kind of romantic—and our style—to be close even in death. That left five plots, so I asked all the relatives and offered one for anyone who might choose, but they have their own thoughts and locations they are planning to utilize, or else just haven't, as most people are apt, taken the time at present to plan for, as if it will never happen. So an arrangement has been made with the Twin Falls cemetery manager (Rodney), to designate these to be given to persons in need, just as our dear mother would have wanted. As a matter of fact, at the time of my writing this autobiography, one burial spot was just given to a homeless vet. A nice legacy, I think, for the person who started all this from the time she arrived on the train siding in Hailey, Idaho at age 4 and began what has become. My wife and I have selected our own marker for the head of our burial spot and inscription thereon as well, and yes, it has a forest scene of serenity, just as we have had in life. Related to this we have done something that is a beautiful addition to our particular mutual finality that has given us great joy while we are still alive and together.

One day while in downtown Bellingham in the old Fairhaven district, in an artisan pottery shop my wife saw a kind of vessel that looks like a prayer wheel mounted on a carrousel so that it could be turned 360 degrees. We had seen similar prayer wheels of all sizes when we traveled to the temples of Nepal and elsewhere in Asia. As is the tradition, on or sometimes within a prayer wheel, there is written an identified mantra, or prayer, if you will. Thus spinning the wheel has a meritorious effect similar to reciting prayers. While prayer wheels have primarily a faith or life-based use, they can have, in concurrent form, a practical use. Designed in such a way, this object can additionally function as an urn for one's ashes. That is what we decided we wanted for us. Therefore we commissioned a local artist, Chris Moench, of some renown to prepare an urn. We requested be placed on its surface various symbols we have chosen to represent our life together—love, work, holding hands, travel, service to others, community, and faith. It was completed at the time of this writing, and it is truly a work of art, but also a vessel of our final existence as a couple. It resides for the present in our living room in a display area amongst travel objects we have collected from throughout the world. There's an eventual final resting place for the urn in our burial plot in a beautiful cemetery in Twin Falls, Idaho, near a small stream and pond with swans. There, one day, it will be amongst my brothers and sisters, my mother and father, and souls that could not afford their own final resting spot.

Some years ago, just as I was retiring but still highly involved with my professional association that I had been a member of for 50+ years, I decided to do something that I felt I needed to do in gratitude to so many fellow colleagues. It became another part of my preparation for finality. I started thanking in person my colleagues for sharing their ideas and concepts so freely over the years. I also did this with friends for their friendships. When I did, some were fearful that I was about to die or had an illness to announce, but I assured them neither was the case. I just valued their being and generosity and wanted them to know how much it meant to me. So, one by one, I started thanking them (with the inclusion of not-dying proviso). It's been an interesting experience to have given their varied reactions, but really all positive. On a recent Zoom call with other former presidents of my professional association, ISPI, I thanked those who I knew for their years of comradeship and support. All these people know the kind of person I am: caring, a sometimes smart ass, very serious, and full time going with the flow. So "Thanks to those who I have not yet thanked! Yours Truly, Danny."

It might come as somewhat of a surprise, but writing this very book was part of my plan for preparing for dying. I learned early in my writing career, such as with the book about my mother's life and the other titled, *The Good Husband*, and even the 3-book series on the Language of Work Model™, that writing brings forth a sense of "why" that you don't intend to write about, but it emerges as a bonus. For example, it wasn't until I completed the writing of *My Mother Can Beat Up Your Father* that I learned what truly drove my mother to be the person she was and of the life she had dedicated to her children. It was a case of her sense of survival that got her through the challenges of her childhood, the death of her wonderful grandmother, and to then deciding to marry a man 29 years her senior to having a successful business and family. It was in writing the various books on the Language of Work Model™—such a technical subject really—that revealed to me, and as such to workers and managers, the power of work clarity. In the same way, it is in the writing of this autobiography, for all the stories and anecdotes, which brings into focus what motivated me, how I got to where I got to and how blessed I was to have been Danny. I am, after all is said and done, an innovator and solver of problems and needs for others, let alone in my own development. And I sought to be a good person by caring for others. Take the time to at least jot down a few lines about yourself if you can't or don't choose to write an autobiography or obit. You'll discover lots of things about the why and what of life. Done early enough, there remain opportunities to change or just to feel extra good. And if put in the form of your obit, it will be revealing what you have to say to others about yourself in the final hours, and forever!

I have specified what kind of service I want at my passing. While I am a person of faith, I don't feel the need for a formal church service. I have always had, all along, a personal relationship with my divine. However I believe in a celebration of life, as it is more commonly referred to. My wife and I have visited a couple of venues in our community and picked one that suits the celebration needs as I see them and reflects the beautiful environment in which we lived, and in which others would feel comfortable. It's a quiet retreat near the bay with a large room in which 50 or so people could gather. I've specified that four tables be arranged around the room and on them placed the artifacts that I mentioned earlier that I had gathered over the years. I want my friends and their company, some who may never have met me, to see and pick up and come to further understand who this man was and how he just simply enjoyed life and achieved so much. I want a string quartet playing in the background: some light classical music for ambience (love ambience) and a couple of songs played in remembrance for my wife. If this book is in print, they can take a copy home to read or perhaps share with others. I want each person to come away with a smile.

Finally, in the way of preparing for my finality, I've already mentioned that we will be using a specially prepared urn/prayer wheel for our final "resting" place. To get to that point I am a believer in planning how my ashes will be prepared. I know people don't like to plan for such and prefer it be left to others to take care of, but I am just not one to shift the burden on others. Thus, I've contracted with those who typically prepare remains in a form that I want. I've chosen a fairly new process known as "recomposing." It's a natural process that prepares one's remains in the form of soil to be returned to the earth. This appeals to me because I have a profound sense of being tied to the soil and to the universe as a whole. Thus, part of me will be in the urn with my partner in life, and the preponderance of what is left spread in a designated forest area—with perhaps a little scattered elsewhere at other locations I loved such as my favorite island, a stream or two I once fished or stayed the summer at with family of origin, or over a bridge I crossed. I loved having been born in a warehouse, thriving in a various junkyards, creating and innovating things, doing gardening, traveling to foreign lands, meeting interesting people of the world, standing in awe in the forest, having a farm, being a kid in the dirt digging a tunnel to China. I kind of feel like I need to return to all of that because I came from it. My epitaph, in my own words, will read:

"I am in the universe, the universe is in ME,
and there I will always be."

Epilogue

I have always found the hardest part of writing a book is not the writing itself but giving it up. I've typically spent days at the computer, given lots of thought to organization, content and emotions, written and rewritten, and withstood reviewer comments and edits. It's a lot of work, writing is. It's kind of analogous in its way to life in that both have to end and that's what makes it hard. It's kind of like when your children are going off on their own, after all that work you put into raising them to get them to that point. Still, the nice thing is that you are left with memories, and of course they come to visit— like rereading—a favorite book and that's nice. So, in the final analysis, writing is much like life itself because you have to let the writing stop, but reading is just beginning. And, as I already noted, writing brings clarity and focus to whatever you are writing about and that's very pleasing—especially to focus on your life story for its meaning. So I am willing to give up this writing about me, knowing that I have written about the lucky life I was blessed to have. I now turn over my writing to your reading, which gives me great joy.

Danny

Memoir Sources

Books

Ethnicity and Family Therapy, Monica McGoldrick, Joe Giordano, and Nydia Garcia-Preto, The Guilford Press, 3rd Edition, 2005. Chapter 37, "American Families with English, Ancestors from the Colonial Era."

Shirley Langdon Wilcox, genealogical information concerning the Langdons.

Life Types, Hirsh, Sandra and Jean Kummerow. Warner Books, Inc.,1989.

My Mother Can Beat Up Your Father, Danny G. Langdon, Publish America, 2006

The Good Husband, Danny G. Langdon (Inspired by Kathleen Langdon), Performance International, 2021.

Twin Falls Centurybook: 1904 – 2004, Mary J. Inman, Hosteler Press, Twin Falls, Idaho, 2003.

Articles

The Oregonian Magazine, March 12, 1939, pp. 1-8.

Times News, Twin Falls, Idaho: Issues printed: March, 1952, May 2, 1952, May 11, 1952, May 15, 1952, June 15, 1952, August 9, 1952; April 1960, May 1971, Oct. 25,1963, 1956, 1966, Aug.,1993.

Article in the *Jamestown Post*, Jamestown, NY: May 1952

Friends

Fellow Peace Corps Volunteers:
　　Eldon and Adriene Katter
　　Ray Capozzi:
　　Kent and Carol Richert
High School Classmates:
　　Mac Soden
　　Annita Turner Philbrick
　　Warren Wubker

Websites

Enneagram Institute website: https://www.enneagraminstitute.com

Myers-Briggs website: www.myersbriggs.org

StoryCorps: https://archive.storycorps.org/interviews/mby010998/

The Work Trilogy (Language of Work Model™): www. Performanceinternational.com

Other Books by the Author

Educational Technology Publications, Englewood Cliffs, NJ, 1978
Interactive Instructional Designs for Individualized Learning
The Adjunct Study Guide
The Construct Lesson Plan
The Audio-Workbook
The Instructional Designs Library: Series Editor,
40 volumes by various authors

HRD Press, Amherst, Massachusetts, 1995
The New Language of Work

Jossey-Bass/Pfeiffer, 1999
Interventions Resource Guide

PublishAmerica, Baltimore, 2006
My Mother Can Beat Up Your Father

Smashwords, (free online download) **2014**
Righting The Enterprise:
A Primer for Organizing or Reorganizing the Right Way

Performance International, Bellingham, WA 2021
The Work Trilogy: (available Amazon)
The Worker Model
The Managing Model
The Business Model
The Good Husband: 50 Practices That Will Make You Nearly Perfect

www.ingramcontent.com/pod-product-compliance
Lightning Source LLC
Chambersburg PA
CBHW060853120626
46553CB00001B/62